Camb 80/-

the
spiritual
conquest
of
mexico

the spiritual conquest of mexico

*An Essay on the Apostolate
and the Evangelizing Methods
of the Mendicant Orders
in New Spain: 1523-1572*

by ROBERT RICARD

*Professor at the University of
Paris (Sorbonne)*

Translated by Lesley Byrd Simpson

*University of California Press
Berkeley & Los Angeles 1966*

University of California Press
Berkeley and Los Angeles, California

Cambridge University Press
London, England

Library of Congress Catalog Card Number: 66–16286

Original title: *Conquête Spirituelle du Mexique,*
published as Volume XX of *Travaux et Mémoires de
l'Institut d'Ethnologie by the* University of
Paris, 1933

Published with the assistance of a grant
from the Rockefeller Foundation

Printed in the United States of America

A la mémoire de Joaquín García Icazbalceta

Translator's Preface

ROBERT RICARD'S renowned *Conquête Spirituelle du Mexique,*
here offered in English, was a timely book when it first appeared,
in 1933, for Mexico had just been through the frightful religious uprising known as the Cristero Rebellion, and feeling on both sides was
still running high. Ricard was certainly innocent of thinking to intervene
in it (he began his study in 1922), but he did perform the notable service
of reminding the country of the colossal debt it owed the Catholic Church
by bringing into focus the profound revolution in Mexican life brought
about by the Mendicant friars of the Orders of St. Francis, St. Dominic,
and St. Augustine in the all-important sixteenth century. Indeed, in the
words of the author: "In the religious domain, as in the others, the
sixteenth century . . . was the period in which Mexico was created, and
of which the rest of her history has been the almost inevitable development."

Here, then, told with the utmost fairness, is the story of that revolution,
in which heroism and cowardice, greatness and weakness, triumph and
failure, are explored calmly and in detail. All resources of modern
scholarship are brought to bear upon it. Ricard's frank admiration of the
first missionaries (which the reader will certainly share) is not allowed
to becloud his judgment. Many of the early churchmen are revealed as

vii

all too human, and bickering, jealousy, confusion, and pride at times come close to wrecking the mighty enterprise. And yet, in spite of heart-breaks and disappointments, death and unimaginable hardships, the Mendicants did suceed in establishing, however haltingly, the Mexican Church, and monuments to their success are visible on every hand. To translate this moving story, without sacrificing its flavor, has been a challenging and invigorating experience, and its numerous difficulties have been greatly lessened by the author's generous and unfailing co-operation. Some editing has been necessary to economize on space and to clarify a few passages. Otherwise I have left the text intact, but have had regretfully to trim some illuminating commentary from the Notes, which in general have here been limited to bibliographical references.

Such a book, appearing in such a heated atmosphere, could hardly fail to stir up criticism, most of it, to be sure, discreetly mild. In the Preface to the Spanish edition of 1947 (see below, Appendix I), Ricard meets his most formidable critics, Left and Right, on their own ground, but does not yield an inch. To answer them in full would have entailed a complete rewriting of the book, which in my opinion would have been a profitless task, for, despite the abundant literature on the subject produced during these past thirty-three years, Ricard's original thesis has never been seriously challenged, and it retains its place today as the most authoritative account of the heroic period of the Mexican Church. Besides, as he himself says: "We cannot spend our lives redoing our work in a chimerical and sterile quest for perfection."

The Institut d'Ethnologie of the University of Paris generously gave permission to publish this translation.

LESLEY BYRD SIMPSON

University of California, Berkeley
1966

Contents

ix

Chronology

xi

1546–1558: *Fray Martín de Hojacastro, O. F. M.*
1563–1570: *Fernando de Villagómez [secular].*

BISHOPS OF OAXACA (ANTEQUERA)
1535–1555: *Juan López de Zárate [secular].*
1559–1579: *Fray Bernardino de Alburquerque, O. P.*

BISHOPS OF NEW GALICIA (GUADALAJARA)
1548–1552: *Pedro Gómez Maraver [secular].*
1559–1569: *Fray Pedro de Ayala, O. F. M.*
1571–1576: *Francisco de Mendiola [secular].*

Introduction

FOR easily understood reasons of clarity and simplicity I have entitled this book *The Spiritual Conquest of Mexico*. The subtitle, I hope, will remove any notion that I may have been too vague and too ambitious. In particular, it explains the geographic and chronological limits within which I have tried to keep myself. I have used the term "New Spain," not in its administrative sense, but in the meaning commonly given to it in the sixteenth century. The jurisdiction of the Audiencia of Mexico did not embrace all New Spain, for New Galicia, which has always been considered an integral part of it, had its own special and autonomous audiencia. Also, the province of Yucatan, with its dependency of Tabasco, although administratively a part of New Spain, in practice was treated as a distinct region and was willingly transferred to the Audiencia of Guatemala. In fact, it has always had its own history and personality; it has frequently rebelled against the governments of Mexico, and even today the states that make up the ancient Province of Yucatan (Yucatan proper, Campeche, and Tabasco) have their own way of life, very different from that of the rest of the country, their interests being directed principally toward the United States and Central America. The state of Chiapas has a similar history. Attached at times to the Audiencia of Mexico, at others to the Audiencia of Guatemala, it was never really

1

regarded as a part of New Spain, and in the nineteenth century was brought into the Mexican Republic only after a good deal of shifting back and forth. Like its neighboring states, Chiapas has always had a separate and very personal life.[1]

It is to be borne in mind, therefore, that the territory commonly designated as New Spain in the sixteenth century does not correspond exactly either to the jurisdiction of the Audiencia of Mexico or to the territory of the present Mexican Republic. In the period with which I am concerned, it is to be understood as including the whole of the archdiocese of Mexico and the dioceses of Tlaxcala-Puebla, Michoacán, New Galicia, and Antequera (Oaxaca)—roughly present-day Mexico, except the outlying states of the south (Chiapas, Tabasco, Campeche, and Yucatan), which form a special group in their geography and history, and so have been deliberately excluded from this study. Such considerations, moreover, seemed to me to impose easy and natural limits upon a work which for many reasons I have had to keep within a precise framework, that is, the country lying between the present northern frontier of Mexico and the Isthmus of Tehuantepec, which is where Central America really begins and is the gateway to a different world.

Its chronological limits have been fixed in a similar way by the nature of the facts. I have taken as my starting point the year 1523–1524. Hence, the work done since the landing of Cortés on the Mexican coast [in 1519] appears only as a prelude, subject to the hazards of the first military operations and unable to undertake the evangelization of the whole country. Although 1524 is the year of the arrival of the first mission of the Friars Minor, "the Twelve," the beginning of the Franciscan evangelization may be properly dated from 1523, when the famous Pedro de Gante, with two other religious, who died almost immediately, established himself in New Spain. The year 1523, therefore, marks the beginning of the period in the history of the Mexican Church traditionally known as "primitive," which ended in 1572 with the arrival of the first religious of the Company of Jesus. It rarely happens in history that one finds a chronological sequence so clearly and naturally delimited. During this period the conversion of Mexico was almost exclusively entrusted to the three so-called Mendicant Orders: the Franciscans (from 1523–1524), the Dominicans (from 1526), and the Augustinians (from 1533). This one circumstance is enough to give the years 1523–1573 a unique character. The Jesuits brought a spirit of their own and their own preoccupations. The Company did not neglect the indigenous population, but it was to devote itself in New Spain especially to the education and spiritual strengthening of Creole society, which the Mendicants had somewhat neglected, and to the improvement of the secular clergy, whose level was very mediocre. In this sense the activity of the sons of St. Ignatius was to contribute to the progressive secularization of the Indian parishes, and consequently to the elimination of the primitive Orders, which were obliged to abandon their ministry and retire to their convents, or to undertake the conversion of remote pagan regions. It is therefore not arbitrary (insofar as divisions of this kind can be *not* arbitrary), to hold that the establishment of the Jesuits in 1572 brings one period to a close and opens another. It is interesting, moreover, to note that during this period the diocese of Mexico was governed by two Mendicant prelates: the Franciscan Fray Juan de Zumárraga (1528–1548), and the Dominican Fray Alonso de Montúfar (1553/4–1572). The year 1572 marked a further retreat for the Mendicant Orders, when a secular archbishop, Dr. Pedro Moya de Contreras, occupied the metropolitan see.

The reasons why I have selected this period of 1523–1572 in the religious history of Mexico, in preference to all others, are so easy to understand or to assume, even if one knows the history of the country only superficially, that it seems needless to elaborate upon them. In the first place, the sixteenth century is the fundamental period for the history and formation of post-Conquest Mexico. It is the period in which the clash of civilizations (which ethnographers love to talk about) occurred in the sharpest form, a period in which native American elements and imported Spanish traits are sometimes fused and sometimes juxtaposed, together giving Mexico its present personality. The sixteenth century contained in embryo the subsequent evolution of the country; it was to leave its strong imprint upon the following centuries, which in many respects were only the development, rarely corrected or impeded by the unpredictable reactions of men, of this epoch so extraordinarily pregnant with the future. In the second place, it is by long odds the most interesting period in which to

3

study missionary methodology. A great deal has been written about the California missions, possibly because their ruins are to be seen in the United States. They have become virtually a stereotype, probably owing to the tendency to give more importance to the romantic aspect of their abandonment than to their establishment and organization. In my opinion, indeed, the California mission is much less instructive than the Mexican mission of the sixteenth century, because the foundation and organization of a Church, which is the primordial aim of every mission, did not occur in California. California remained in the preparatory stage, whereas in New Spain one can follow almost the complete evolution. I say *almost* complete, because the evolution was interrupted before its indicated outcome, that is, the methodical training of a native clergy, the breeding ground of a native episcopacy. It is true, nevertheless, that during the years 1523–1572 the Mexican Church was founded and organized, and this in turn emphasizes the unity of the period I have selected. Then it was that the "spiritual conquest" of New Spain took place.

Who were the architects of this conquest? Who the founders and organizers of this Church? This conquest, this foundation, this organization, were essentially the work of the Mendicant Orders, and, if I may be permitted to insist upon it, the Mendicant Orders *as* Orders. It is a singular and most remarkable fact that the churches of Spanish America were founded by the Mendicant Orders independently of the episcopacy, whose authority broke against the pontifical privileges granted to the regular clergy.[2] Besides, the mediocrity of the secular clergy, in number and quality, deprived the bishops of the opportunity of engaging in apostolic activity distinct from that of the Mendicant Orders. Thus the role of the seculars in the work of conversion may be considered negligible, and the bishops, at least in their relations with the Indians, are in second place. There are, to be sure, illustrious exceptions, such as Vasco de Quiroga, who left an imperishable memory in Michoacán, and López de Zárate, who in his diocese of Oaxaca worked closely with the Dominicans. But the influence of a prelate like Zumárraga upon the evangelization of the country owes less to his rank and title than to his personality and to the excellent relations he always maintained with his

4

Order. Likewise, the difficulties that his successor, the Dominican Montúfar, was to experience with the regular clergy would doubtless have been more severe if the archbishop himself had not been a religious. I find nothing comparable to the organization of present-day missions, in which the bishops and their collaborators belong in general to a single institute, where, in spite of the inevitable internal tensions and jurisdictional conflicts that arise between the Ordinary and his regular superiors, there is a much closer identification between the activity of the apostolic vicar and that of the missionaries.

For all these reasons I have limited myself exclusively to the accomplishments of the Mendicant Orders, and especially to the methods they employed to found and organize a new Church. I have touched only in a subsidiary way the internal history of the three Orders and that of the secular clergy and the episcopacy, and then only so far as these questions concern the Christianization of the country and the methods used by the Mendicants, and serve to clarify and make them comprehensible. To put the matter briefly—what we are studying here is the methods of the three primitive Orders in the conversion of the natives and the foundation of the Mexican Church.

This book, therefore, does not claim to be a history of the Mexican Church in the sixteenth century. It will be useless to seek in it episodes such as the introduction of the printing press by Zumárraga and the founding of the University of Mexico, which are justly considered, especially the latter, as important facts in religious history, but which do not seem connected closely enough with the activity of the regular clergy and the evangelization of the Indians to be included here. Besides, that history has been written too recently by Father Mariano Cuevas [3] to allow one to think of rewriting it. Nevertheless, for the understanding of the present work, I think it will not be out of place to call to the reader's attention, briefly, the pattern within which the apostolic task of the Mendicant Orders was accomplished.

The arrival of the first [company of] Franciscans in 1524 occurred shortly before the establishment of the Mendicant hierarchy in Mexico. The diocese of Tlaxcala (Puebla) was founded in 1526, and at the end of the following year the Franciscan Fray Juan de Zumárraga was nominated for the episcopal see of Mexico, although, to be sure, it was not formally constituted until 1530, and did not become metropolitan until 1548, just before the death of Zumárraga. The episcopal foundations speedily followed: the diocese of Antequera (Oaxaca), in 1534; the diocese of Michoacán, in 1536; the diocese of New Galicia, in 1548. Before 1572 the sees had only a small number of incumbents, who were often men of worth. I have already mentioned the two archbishops of Mexico. The diocese of Tlaxcala suffered the most vicissitudes. Its first bishop, the Dominican Fray Julián Garcés, who died in 1542, was not replaced by the Franciscan Fray Martín de Hojacastro until 1546. When the latter died, in 1558, his successor, the secular Fernando de Villagómez, was not appointed until 1563, and he died toward the end of 1570, leaving the see vacant until 1572. The dioceses of Oaxaca and Michoacán, like that of Mexico, had only two incumbents during the period with which I am concerned: for Oaxaca, Juan López de Zárate (1535–1555), and the Dominican Fray Bernardo de Alburquerque (1559–1579); for Michoacán, the famous Vasco de Quiroga (1537/8–1565), and Antonio Ruiz Morales (1567–1572), the latter then taking over the see of Tlaxcala. The bishops of New Galicia were, successively, Pedro Gómez Maraver, who died in 1552, the Franciscan Fray Pedro de Ayala (1559–1569), and Francisco Mendiola (1571–1576).

Parallel to the organization of the secular dioceses, the regular clergy was being organized. In 1525 the Franciscan establishment was a small custody attached to the Spanish Provincia de San Gabriel de Extremadura. In 1535 it was made an autonomous province, the Provincia del Santo Evangelio, and in 1565 the custody of Michoacán-Jalisco was separated from it and set up as the Provincia de S. Pedro y S. Pablo. The Dominican establishment, which at first was subordinate to the superior general of the Order, was later attached to the Provincia de la Santa Cruz of Santo Domingo, and in 1532 was elevated into the independent Provincia de Santiago. In the same fashion the Augustinian establishment, which at first was subordinate to the Provincia de Castilla, in 1545 became the autonomous Provincia del Santo Nombre de Jesús.

The double task implied in these various administrative arrangements was completed by ecclesiastical conferences and synods, to whose decisions I shall frequently have occasion to refer. The first *junta eclesiástica,* sometimes called the first Mexican synod, was assembled in 1524. It included several secular priests and the Franciscans, who by this time were in Mexico. It limited itself to a few decisions concerning the administration of the sacraments, specifically baptism and penitence. The second *junta,* called in 1532, had a more general character and a wider field. It included the Franciscan and Dominican delegates, Bishop Zumárraga, and members of the Audiencia, and sent the Crown a number of suggestions about the political and social organization of New Spain. In 1537 there was a meeting of the bishops alone. Zumárraga, who had just consecrated Francisco Marroquín as bishop of Guatemala and Juan López de Zárate as bishop of Oaxaca, took advantage of their presence in Mexico to discuss with them various problems touching upon the evangelization of the country. The outcome of their meeting was a long letter to Charles V, in which they reviewed these problems, particularly the question of [organizing] Indian villages, the question of the secular clergy, the question of the position of the friars, and the persistence of paganism.

Two years later, in 1539, a general assembly included the bishops of Mexico, Oaxaca, and Michoacán, and a numerous representation from the three Orders. It was concerned above all with as definite a regulation as possible of the administration of baptism and marriage, which had given rise to difficulties and disagreements. Two more *juntas eclesiásticas* were called during the tenure of Zumárraga. That of 1544, ordered by the visitor Tello de Sandoval, had as its purpose the examination of the New Laws [of 1542] passed by the Crown following the agitation of Las Casas. That of 1546 is known only in a fragmentary way. Zumárraga's successor, Fray Alonso de Montúfar, convoked the first two Mexican synods, in 1555 and 1565. That of 1555 put under the presidency of the Metropolitan all bishops of New Spain (except New Galicia—its see was vacant), the Audiencia and the high [civil] officers of Mexico, the delegates of the diocesan chapters, and, in a general way, all ecclesiastics and religious who held offices or dignities. Their decisions fill ninety-three chapters and cover the whole life and organization of the Mexican Church. The synod of 1565, conceived in the same fashion, proposed essentially to study the application in New Spain of the reform measures promulgated by the Council of Trent. Both set the pattern for the third synod, the date of which (1585) puts it outside the scope of this study. It was held during the episcopacy of Moya de Contreras and had an importance even greater than that of the first two.

I am not unaware of the inadequacies of the study I am offering the public. I believe, nevertheless, that I have some claim to the indulgence of the reader, if he will take into account the "deplorable conditions" (to adopt the unexaggerated words of Marcel Bataillon [4]) in which Hispanists and, I may add, Americanists work. In American studies one is perpetually frustrated by the extreme dispersion of the materials and publications, which frequently prevents the historians of one continent from knowing and using the researches undertaken in the other. In France the scarcity of works dedicated to the colonial history of Spanish America is perhaps attributable to such difficulties. With the exception of the now outdated thesis of Jules Humbert on *Les origines vénézuéliennes,* I have not seen any work of the order here offered.

French scholars, who have played such an important, one might say glorious, part in the study of indigenous civilizations, have almost completely neglected the history of Mexico during the Spanish domination. The three chapters that Father M. A. Roze, O. P., devotes to Mexico in his little book, *Les Dominicains en Amérique,* are less than mediocre. And it would be better to pass over in silence the lines in which a historian of the [Franciscan] Order has attempted to describe its apostolate in New Spain.[5] On the other hand, the account of the evangelization of Mexico, in *Les Dossiers de l'Action Missionaire,* by Father Pierre Charles, S. J., is remarkable, coming from the pen of a writer who is not, and does not claim to be, a specialist, and is, moreover, a Belgian; but it is only an extremely brief summary, in broad strokes and essential facts. In the United States, the active interest in the history of Spanish America that has been evident for some time, has produced no publication of real value in the religious history of Mexico in the sixteenth century. For reasons that I have stated elsewhere,[6] Charles Braden's

Religious Aspects of the Conquest of Mexico is not in my opinion of such stature as to exempt me from publishing this essay of mine. The contributions of German scholars are more numerous. It would be unjust not to mention the work (necessarily obsolete, but, despite several omissions, very conscientious) of Friedrich Weber, in *Beiträge zur Charakteristik der älteren Geschichtsschreiber über Spanisch-America.*[7] The *Katholische Missionsgeschichte* of Abbé Joseph Schmidlin contains a good chapter on the Mexican mission. Some errors, to be sure, have crept in owing to insufficient documentation, but these weaknesses were inevitable in a manual dealing with such a vast subject.[8] Father Leonhard Lemmens' account, in his recent history of the Franciscan missions, is equally worthy of keeping,[9] for it happily completes the résumé, exact but somewhat outdated and much too brief, of Holzapfel's classic manual.[10] I should add that all these works, however worthy, are dominated by the monumental *Bibliotheca Missionum* of the late and lamented Father Robert Streit, O. M. I., the fruit of a life of toil, which I shall frequently cite.

With the exception of Father Streit's bibliography, it is only natural that the most important works are those of Spanish and Mexican scholars. Vicente Riva Palacio's paper, *Establecimiento y propagación del cristianismo en Nueva España,* doubtless deserves the oblivion into which it has fallen, and the thin brochure of Father Ramón García Muiños, *Primicias religiosas de América,* seems superficial and inadequate. Vicente de P. Andrade's amateurish *El Primer Estudio sobre los Conquistadores espirituales de la Nueva España, 1519–1531,* is based upon sources, but turns out to be hardly more than a catalogue. Finally, Father Pérez Arrilucea's articles on the Augustinians of Mexico merely summarize too frequently the chronicles of that Order.[11] I have already emphasized the importance of Father Cuevas' *Historia de la Iglesia en México,* an attempt at a sysnthesis, the faults of which should not be allowed to obscure its true usefulness. To it should be added the biography of Zumárraga by the great Mexican scholar Joaquín García Icazbalceta, which is still a fundamental study of the religious beginnings of New Spain. Finally, the bibliographical researches on the Franciscans of Mexico by the eminent director of the Archivo Ibero-Americano of Madrid, Father Atanasio

9

López, O. F. M., belong equally among the essential works that one must digest and consult. Specific references to them will occur later on in this book.

My debt is not only to books, or, more exactly, to their authors, but also to the men whose aid and encouragement have been singularly precious to me, given the disorganized state of Spanish American studies. First, I wish to express my gratitude to those who have gone from among us: the learned Augustinian bibliographer Father Gregorio de Santiago Vela, to whom I am indebted for many useful pieces of information; Luis Rubio y Moreno, who, while subdirector of the Archivo General de Indias at Seville, guided and counseled me with tireless devotion; especially the director of the École des Hautes Études Hispaniques, Pierre Paris, whose fruitful work it is not for me to praise, but whose friendly and paternal reception of me in Madrid made it possible for me to spend a number of unforgettable years in Spain in the company of Hispanists like my very dear friend Maurice Legendre. Also in Madrid I shall never forget what I owe to the suggestive observations of Carlos Pereyra, and to the learned conversation of Father Atanasio López, who knows everything there is to know about the history of the Franciscan Order. In Seville the friendly help of Cristóbal Bermúdez Plata, director of the Archives of the Indies and successor to Torres Lanzas, has been of the greatest value. And what can I say of my reception in the various Dominican and Augustinian houses in Madrid, the Escorial, Salamanca, and Almagro?

My welcome in Mexico was no less cordial, nor was the help I was given there less valuable. I find it impossible to mention here all those who outdid themselves to make my stay there so long ago agreeable and fruitful; but I should like to name, nevertheless, the revered secretary general of the Antonio Alzate Academy, Rafael Aguilar y Santillán; Ignacio del Villar Villamil, the most Parisian of Mexicans; my eminent colleagues of the University of Mexico, Ezequiel A. Chávez, Joaquín Ramírez Cabañas, and Pablo Martínez del Río; Dr. Ignacio Alcocer, my learned guide to Texcoco and Huejotla; Jean Balme and Albert Misrachi; Father Roustan, curé of the French parish of Mexico [City]; Bernard Vincent, director of the *Journal Français du Mexique;* and Gustave

Bellon, whose charming hospitality in Oaxaca I shall not forget. Most of the illustrations in this volume I owe to the generosity of José Benítez, acting director of the National Museum of Mexico, and his associate, Jorge Enciso, director of the Servicio de Monumentos Históricos. Luis González Obregón and Federico Gómez de Orozco, with unfailing kindness, gave me the run of their magnificent personal libraries and the benefit of their incomparable knowledge of Mexican colonial history. To all of them my profound gratitude.

Once again let me express my respectful thanks to Jean Gotteland, director general of Public Instruction, Beaux-Arts, and Antiquities of Morocco, for his promptness in granting me leave for my work in Mexico; to Jean Périer, French Minister to Mexico, and to his assistants, whose simple and cordial reception touched me deeply; to Henri Hauser, professor at the Sorbonne, who spared neither time nor trouble to help me; and to Marcel Mauss, to whom no discipline is foreign, and who kindly suggested useful corrections. Paul Rivet, not content with placing at my disposal all the resources of the Société des Americanistes in Paris, with opening wide the pages of the *Journal* for my earlier publications, with supporting and guiding me with his advice for many years, gave me the opportunity for my long residence in Mexico, indispensable for the writing of my book. He even altered his itinerary for a mission to Central America in order to present me to Mexican scientific circles, with the authority of his personality and works. I take this occasion to express my deep gratitude to him.

In Spain and Mexico I was given the freedom of various public libraries. The [faulty] organization of the book division of the National Library of Madrid, at the time I was using it (1922–1927), made it difficult for me to work there methodically.[12] On the other hand, the manuscript division, the division of rare books, and the overseas division (Biblioteca de Ultramar), were under a more flexible management and more favorable to scientific research. For their competent and courteous personnel I have nothing but praise. I may say the same of the library of the Centro de Estudios Históricos and the Academy of History in Madrid, and of the library of the Antonio Alzate Academy and the Geographical Society in Mexico. The rich library of the National

Museum of Archaeology, History, and Ethnography of Mexico was opened for me with a generosity and trust for which I am extremely grateful. There also I found the staff most competent, devoted, and unfailingly obliging. To all these collaborators, some of them humble and often unknown, my most sincere thanks. Finally, I am grateful to the Institute of Ethnology of the University of Paris, which saw fit to accept and publish my book.

ROBERT RICARD

June, 1932

I: THE FOUNDING OF THE CHURCH

1 First Contacts between Paganism and Christianity

ALTHOUGH the methodical conversion of New Spain did not begin until after the arrival of the first Franciscan mission in 1524, it is known that before that date several isolated friars preached the good word to the pagans of Mexico. A glance at the work of these precursors will be of profit.

One cannot study the history of the evangelization of Mexico without giving emphasis to the religious preoccupations of the Conqueror Cortés. He was greedy, debauched, a politician without scruples, but he had his quixotic moments, for, despite his weaknesses, of which he later humbly repented, he had deep Christian convictions. He always carried on his person an image of the Virgin Mary, to whom he was strongly devoted; he prayed and heard Mass daily; and his standard bore these words: *Amici, sequamur crucem, et si nos fidem habemus, vere in hoc signo vincemus.*[1] He had another standard, on one side of which were the arms of Castile and León, on the other an image of the Holy Virgin.[2] His main ambition seems to have been to carve out a kind of autonomous fief for himself, theoretically subject to the King of Spain, but he could not admit the thought of ruling over pagans, and he always strove to pursue the religious conquest at the same time he pursued the political and military

15

conquest.[3] This is probably the only one of Velázquez' instructions that he obeyed. "You must," they ran,

"bear in mind from the beginning that the first aim of your expedition is to serve God and spread the Christian Faith. You must not, therefore, permit any blasphemy or lewdness of any kind, and all who violate this injunction should be publicly admonished and punished. It has been said that crosses have been found in that country. Their significance must be ascertained. The religion of the natives, if they have one, must again be studied and a detailed account of it made. Finally, you must neglect no opportunity to spread the knowledge of the True Faith and the Church of God among those people who dwell in darkness." [4]

The instructions of Velázquez are only an expression of the desire manifested by the Pope [5] and the Spanish monarchs.[6] Cortés followed them virtually to the letter. No one was against blasphemers more than he, and he made it clear in his ordinances that the aim of the expedition was the uprooting of idolatry and the conversion of the natives to Christianity. If, he added, the war should be waged for any other purpose it would be an unjust war. This, assuredly, was not the feeling of many of his lieutenants and soldiers, whose habits were anything but exemplary, and by whom he was frequently overborne. But, if his orders were not always respected, it should not be forgotten that later on many of his companions entered religious orders. Among such were the hermit Gaspar Díez, whom Bishop Zumárraga had to admonish to lead a less austere life; Alonso Aguilar, who became a Dominican; Sindos de Portillo, who was "almost a saint"; Medina, Quintero, Burguillos, Escalante, and Lintorno, all of whom became Franciscans. Even so, this list made by Bernal Díaz may not be complete.[7]

If one can reproach Cortés, it is not for his laxness in the conversion of the natives, but, on the contrary, for having undertaken it hastily, without method, and for having forged ahead without pause. Following his landing at Ulúa, he had to be told at every step, by the Mercedarian Fray Bartolomé de Olmedo, an excellent theologian and "a man of good sense," as Cervantes de Salazar rightly describes him,[8] to moderate his zeal and use more order and prudence. Father Cuevas, in his *History of the*

Church in Mexico,[9] stresses this contrast and, despite his admiration for Father Olmedo, is inclined to think that Cortés was right. The Conqueror, he says, was better acquainted with the temperament of the Indians, and was better able to handle them. Besides [he continues], the result proved the excellence of his procedure, because the natives committed few sacrileges and profanations. It must be noted, on the other hand, that we do not know what would have happened in many places where Father Olmedo dampened the inconsiderate ardor of Cortés. At the same time, I think Cortés expected too much of natives who were still idolators. One cannot demand of a pagan that "he renounce all at once all his chains, and to practice the Christian virtues, before receiving the means to do so." [10] However that may be, one may ask whether, in the cause of the [spiritual] conquest, the indirect approach, that is to say, the example provided by the Spaniards, the masses, ceremonies, and prayers in the presence of the Indians, would not have been more efficacious than fiery sermons, forced baptisms, and the violent destruction of temples and idols.[11]

Cortés and his companions arrived at Ulúa on Holy Thursday, April 21, 1519, and landed on Good Friday. A solemn Mass was celebrated on Easter Sunday. The Spaniards told their beads kneeling before a cross they had erected. Every day, at the sound of a bell, they recited the *Angelus* at the foot of the cross. The natives looked on in astonishment; some of them asked why the Spaniards humbled themselves before those two pieces of wood. Then, at the invitation of Cortés, Fray Bartolomé de Olmedo explained the Christian doctrine to them, and his exposition seemed so detailed, even to the excellent Bernal Díaz, whose knowledge of doctrine was probably not precise, that he wrote that a good theologian could not have done better. [Father Olmedo] explained to them that they should not worship their wicked idols, and at the same time he explained the meaning of the cross: how Our Lord Jesus Christ, Lord and Creator of all men, had died on such a cross, how He had risen from the dead after three days, how He had then ascended into Heaven, and how He would call all men to judgment. He strove equally hard to show them the horror of human sacrifices and to persuade them to give them up.[12] That was all, but it sufficed, nevertheless, to establish contact. Fray Bartolomé

17

did not have to intervene with Cortés, for the Conqueror was still uneasy in that strange land. But after Cempoala his action was more direct. In spite of Father Olmedo's appeal for moderation, he cast down idols; [13] as at Ulúa, he erected an altar, with a cross and an image of the Virgin Mary; a sermon was preached to the Indians; a Mass was said; the eight women given to the Spaniards were baptized; [14] and, before leaving, Cortés advised the lord of Cempoala, *el cacique gordo,* to look after the altar and the cross. Four pagan priests were forced to cut their long hair and remove their sacerdotal vestments, and Cortés charged them with the care of the Virgin's image. It should be added that he left an old soldier named Juan de Torres at Cempoala to be "a hermit there" and keep an eye on them. In another place Fray Bartolomé de Olmedo obliged the Conqueror to act with more prudence; he preached sermons against sodomy and human sacrifices, but he would not allow a cross to be raised. "It seems to me," he said, ". . . that in this village it is not yet time to let them have a cross, for they are bold and fearless, and, since they are vassals of Moctezuma, it is to be feared that they will burn it or commit some sacrilege. What they have been told will do them until they have a better knowledge of our Holy Faith." [15]

In Tlaxcala Cortés wanted the natives to renounce their idols and embrace the Christian religion out of hand. The Tlaxcalans firmly refused, and the affair might have ended badly except for the intervention of the Mercedarian, who advised Cortés to leave them alone until they were more seriously grounded in Christian doctrine. "It is not just," he said, "for us to convert them by force, and it would be useless for us to repeat what we did at Cempoala. Our warnings are enough." His advice was supported, moreover, by Pedro de Alvarado, Juan Velázquez de León, and Francisco de Lugo. Cortés yielded. Fray Bartolomé said Mass, preached a sermon, and the Indian women who had been given to the Spaniards were baptized according to custom. In Cholula also, Father Olmedo would not allow the removal of the idols. [16] It was over his objections and those of Juan Díaz, a secular priest who also accompanied the expedition, that crosses were erected at Cholula and Tlaxcala—such, at least, is the fanciful claim of Father [Diego Luis de] Motezuma, who may be accepted on this point. [17] But, wherever they passed, Fray

Bartolomé de Olmedo preached against sodomy and human sacrifices, and explained Christian doctrine to the natives, as, for example, at Jalacingo (in Vera Cruz, just below Tlaxcala), Chalco, Ixtapalapa, and Coyoacán.[18]

Even in Tenochtitlán itself, where the Spaniards arrived on November 7, 1519, one of the great preoccupations of Cortés was to convert Moctezuma—possibly so that he might be able to handle him more easily —and to institute public worship. Beginning with the first day, he summarized Christian doctrine to the "emperor," pronounced against human sacrifices, and told him of the coming of the missionaries. Moctezuma firmly refused to accept [any of this], resisted all his arguments, all the sermons of the Mercedarian, and the prattling of the page boy Orteguilla, for whom he had taken a liking.[19] He did not cease going to the temples and making human sacrifices in them,[20] and it seems very unlikely that he was ever baptized, even at the moment of his death.[21] Father Olmedo also opposed the construction of a church at Tenochtitlán, for Moctezuma did not yet seem disposed to allow it.[22] In fact, when Cortés asked for authorization to erect a cross on top of the temple and place an image of the Virgin in the sanctuary, to put the devil to flight, Moctezuma, deeply offended in his faith, refused point blank.[23] The Spaniards at least installed a chapel in their quarters and erected a cross outside. They heard Mass daily, up to the time the wine gave out.[24] Thereafter they had to content themselves with coming to pray before the altars and image. They did so, said Bernal Díaz, first because it was their duty, and also to give an example to Moctezuma and the other Indians. Moctezuma had, in fact, yielded: he allowed Cortés to place an altar, a cross, and an image of Our Lady in the great temple, apart from the idols. Father Olmedo chanted Mass, which was attended by Licenciado Juan Díaz and a large number of soldiers. Cortés ordered one of his men to keep watch over the altar and prevent the Indians from profaning it. Not satisfied with that, he finally took complete possession of the temple.[25] Later he had to leave to oppose Narváez, and the Aztecs during his absence attempted to remove the cross and the images. They were unsuccessful and were badly mauled.[26] Then followed the evacuation of Mexico City by the Spaniards (*la Noche Triste*), the retreat to Tlaxcala,

19

where the wounded were attended to and the army reorganized, and the slow and methodical reconquest of the capital undertaken. In spite of all these grave worries, the ardor of proselytizing was not extinguished, and Fray Bartolomé de Olmedo baptized the old cacique of Tlaxcala and the young lord of Texcoco.[27]

Thus, although he may not have been perhaps the first Catholic priest to see the country of Mexico,[28] the great precursor [of the Church] was Fray Bartolomé de Olmedo, to whom one may give without reservation the name of the first apostle of New Spain. When he died, toward the end of 1524, mourning was universal. He was a holy man, as Cortés wrote to Licenciado [Alonso de] Zuazo, and the whole city wept for him; the Indians owed him their knowledge of the true God and their eternal salvation.[29] Licenciado Juan Díaz, the secular priest who participated in the whole expedition, played only a modest part. The Mercedarian Fray Juan de las Varillas,[30] the Franciscans Fray Pedro Melgarejo and Fray Diego Altamirano, who came to Mexico shortly after them, but before the end of the Conquest, did little, although they were unquestionably men of good will.[31] In 1523 they were followed by three other religious of the Franciscan Order, Flemings, two of whom were Johann van den Auwera and Johann Dekkers (known in the Spanish documents as Fray Juan de Aora and Fray Juan de Tecto), and a lay brother, Fray Pedro de Gante. The first two, shortly after their arrival, accompanied Cortés on the Honduras expedition and died during it.[32] Pedro de Gante spent the rest of his long life in Mexico. His work was very beautiful, but, working alone, it is probable that despite his apostolic ardor he was forced to operate without a definite plan, just as Father Olmedo could only sow a few grains here and there, without order or method. It was necessary, therefore, to organize the Christianization of the country.

Cortés soon recognized it. In his Fourth Letter to Charles V, dated at Mexico, October 15, 1524, he reminded the Emperor that he had emphasized the necessity of providing for the eternal health of the natives. "Every time I have written Your Majesty," he said in substance, "I have brought to your attention the attraction that Christianity seems to have for some of the natives of this land, and have begged you to send here some religious of good life and example; but, up to the present, only a few

20

have come, or none, so to speak, and, since their coming would be of very great usefulness, I beg Your Majesty to send them with as little delay as possible." Cortés insisted upon the need in New Spain for missionaries to convert the Indians. It would be necessary to found monasteries, which would be supported by a share of the tithes, the rest of which would be used for the maintenance of churches and their priests. The tithes would be collected by the fiscal and distributed by him to those interested. Cortés had once asked for bishops, but he had changed his mind. Only friars were needed; bishops and canons would cost too much, and they often set an unfortunate example, which would be fatal for the conversion of the Indians. Consequently, the King should ask the Pope to give the religious of St. Francis and St. Dominic the widest powers, so that they could administer the sacraments of ordination and confirmation.[33]

Meanwhile at the moment when Cortés was thus expressing himself, the famous mission of the Twelve had arrived, some months before, landing at San Juan de Ulúa on May 13 or 14, 1524. He evidently thought that twelve religious were hardly enough. The event was, nevertheless, of capital importance. Even leaving out of consideration the exceptional worth of the friars of this mission, the arrival of the Twelve meant the beginning of methodical evangelization. Hence, although I am interested in the collective work, rather than in the action of individuals, I shall list below the "Twelve Apostles," as tradition has named them, who arrived at Mexico [City] on June 17 or 18, 1524, and who belonged to the Order of the Friars Minor of the Observance: Fray Martín de Valencia, Fray Francisco de Soto, Fray Martín de Jesús (or de la Coruña), Fray Juan Suárez (or rather Juárez), Fray Antonio de Ciudad-Rodrigo, Fray Toribio de Benavente (Motolinía), Fray García de Cisneros, Fray Luis de Fuensalida, Fray Juan de Ribas, Fray Francisco Jiménez, Fray Andrés de Córdoba, and Fray Juan de Palos.[34] Martín de Valencia was their superior; Fray Francisco Jiménez was ordained shortly after his arrival in New Spain; Fray Andrés de Córdoba and Fray Juan de Palos remained lay brothers.

For the rest, the arrival of the Twelve was the result of proceedings and negotiations that had been going on for a long time. Even before the final occupation of Tenochtitlán, two Franciscan friars (the Fleming Juan

Glapión and the Spaniard Fray Juan de los Angeles, whose family name was Quiñones) had offered themselves to work among the new subjects of the Crown of Castile. Pope Leo X, in his bull *Alias felicis,* of April 25, 1521, had authorized them to go to America. The year following, Adrian VI completed the dispositions of his predecessor in his bull *Exponi nobis feciste,* addressed to Charles V. In it he sent to the Franciscan religious and to those of the other Mendicant Orders his apostolic authority to do everything they might think necessary for the conversion of the Indians, wherever there were no bishops, or wherever the bishops should be two days' journey distant, except for those acts that required episcopal consecration. During these preliminaries, however, Father Glapión died,[35] and, in the general chapter meeting at Burgos in 1523, Father Francisco de los Angeles was elected general of his Order. It was no longer possible for him to think of going [on the mission], but he always held the evangelization of Mexico dear to his heart. He it was who organized the mission of the Twelve and selected Martín de Valencia to head it.[36]

The Dominicans arrived in Mexico probably on July 2, 1536.[37] They also numbered twelve. Eight of them came from Spain: the superior or *vicario*[38] Fray Tomás Ortiz, Fray Vicente de Santa Ana, Fray Diego de Sotomayor, Fray Pedro de Santa María, Fray Justo de Santo Domingo, Fray Pedro Zambrano, Fray Gonzalo Lucero (who at the time was a simple deacon), and the lay brother Fray Bartolomé de la Calzadilla. Fray Domingo de Betanzos, Fray Diego Ramírez, Fray Alonso de las Vírgenes, and the novice Fray Vicente de las Casas came from Española.[39] Their beginnings were unfortunate. Five religious, Fray Pedro de Santa María, Fray Justo de Santo Domingo, Fray Vicente de Santa Ana, Fray Diego de Sotomayor, and Fray Bartolomé de la Calzadilla, their health impaired by the voyage and the climate, died within the year; Fray Tomás Ortiz, Fray Pedro Zembrano, Fray Diego Ramírez, and Fray Alonso de las Vírgenes, in bad health, returned to Spain at the end of 1526.[40] Fray Domingo de Betanzos alone remained, with Fray Gonzalo Lucero and Fray Vicente de las Casas, both of whom had by this time professed, and so he thus deserves the title of founder of the Dominican province of Mexico, at the expense of Fray Tomás Ortiz. Besides, the departure of Fray Tomás Ortiz does not seem to have been a great loss. Judging by what we know of his

22

quarrels with Cortés,[41] this unquiet intriguer could only have set his religious upon a bad path.[42] In 1528, Fray Vicente de Santa María arrived with six companions, and from that time on the province had a normal development.[43]

The Augustinians, who were the last to arrive, landed at Vera Cruz on May 22, 1533, left for Mexico on the 27th, and arrived there on June 7. They numbered seven: Fray Francisco de la Cruz, Father Venerable, Fray Agustín de Gormaz (or de Coruña),[44] Fray Jerónimo Jiménez (or de San Esteban), Fray Juan de San Román, Fray Juan de Oseguera, Fray Alonso de Borja, and Fray Jorge de Avila. Father Venerable was the superior of the mission, which was to have included Fray Juan Bautista de Moya, unexpectedly detained in Spain.[45]

These beginnings were modest enough. There were too few workers for such an abundant harvest; but the number of missionaries, although too small for the population, increased rapidly: every year the vacancies caused by death and by returns to Spain were filled by a fresh contingent. As time went on, the missionaries were able partly to recruit their numbers in the field. Creole religious began to appear. In all Mexico, in 1559, the Franciscans had only eighty convents and 380 religious; the Dominicans, forty convents and 210 religious; the Augustinians, also forty convents and 212 religious.[46]

There was nothing in that country, however, except love of souls and, possibly, of adventure, to attract [missionaries]. Leaving to one side the long, painful, and dangerous voyage from Spain, from the moment of their landing at Vera Cruz, the newcomers were immersed by the warm and heavy humidity in a tepid bath; they were assailed by unknown terrors; if they climbed higher, they found, to be sure, a purer sky and a more caressing light, and an apparently more healthful environment, but one which, with its sudden and unsupportable cold spells, perfidious changes in temperature, and rarefied air, tired badly frayed nerves, and in the long run made every sustained effort arduous and brutally aggravated the mildest sicknesses. It should be borne in mind that the Valley of Puebla is 2,000 meters above the sea, that of Mexico, more than 2,200, and that of Toluca, more than 2,500. And the friars generally traveled on foot, panting up over the rough mountain trails on the flanks of volcanoes. The innumerable streams (Motolinía counted twenty-five in ten kilometers), far from easing communications, were nothing but obstacles, for almost always the way was blocked by torrents, which at times forced the travelers to make interminable detours. If the missionary avoided this rough country, he only fell into the tropical forests or frightful deserts, where he ran the risk of dying of thirst. There were other enemies besides: insects, snakes, and ferocious beasts, not to mention the dangers of the road, where certain ill-subjected Indians could attack almost with impunity. For the population no longer seemed to encourage the religious and offer them the hope of an abundant harvest. The following is a summary glance at the nature of that population and the impression it made on the first apostles.

The Aztec empire, toward which the principal effort of the conquest was directed, and which occupied the essential part of what was later to become New Spain, extended from 15° to 20° N. Lat. Its northern limit was the [territory occupied by] the nomad Indians, grouped in the Spanish documents under the generic name of Chichimecas. To the northwest it reached the vicinity of Lake Chapala; to the west it touched the kingdom of Michoacán; to the southwest and south it extended to the Pacific, surrounding Michoacán; to the northeast and east it extended to the Gulf of Mexico, from the Pánuco River to the Alvarado, not including Cholula, Huejotzingo, and the republic of Tlaxcala, which were always at war with Tenochtitlán. These frontiers, however, were anything but fixed and precise, so it will perhaps be clearer and more realistic to say that the Aztec empire occupied, roughly speaking, the whole region between the Isthmus of Tehuantepec in the south and a line running from the Coajuayana River [in Colima] to the Pánuco River in the north. But within this region Michoacán, the Huasteca, and a part of the Mixtec-Zapotec country [of Oaxaca] remained independent,[47] as well as Tlaxcala. Its organization was complex and very flexible. Along with regions conquered long ago and incorporated in properly Mexican territory, and governed by a lord named by Tenochtitlán, certain groups kept their political autonomy. The former were forced to receive the Aztec officers who had the duty of collecting taxes; the latter were obliged to pay only

24

an annual tribute.[48] This organization, which was precarious at best, did not survive the conquest, and affected the work of conversion only in so far as it contributed to spread the knowledge of the language of the empire, Nahuatl, throughout New Spain.

Linguistic varieties continued, however, to be very many, and we know how extremely important languages are in the evangelization of a country. I do not propose here to make a catalogue of the languages and dialects of New Spain, but only to sketch their essential traits. Nahuatl, the official language of the empire, extended far beyond the plateau of Anahuac, for it was spoken not only in the allied or subjugated states, but in Tlaxcala and in a part of the modern states of Jalisco, Colima, Nayarit, Aguascalientes, Zacatecas, and Sinaloa.[49] Other languages were still very much alive: Huastec and Totonac on the shores of the Gulf of Mexico; in the west, Tarascan (in Michoacán, part of Guanajuato, Guerrero, and San Luis Potosí); the languages of independent territories (besides the Huasteca) were even more flourishing. The charms of Tarascan are frequently boasted of. These were the principal languages,[50] but there were many others, spoken by small numbers of people, such as Pirinda or Matlaltzinca, in the Valley of Toluca and at Charo (Michoacán);[51] Popoloca, spoken by some natives of the present states of Puebla, Guerrero, and Oaxaca.[52] I shall mention a few others when I discuss the linguistic works of the missionaries.[53] Here I shall only remark that this linguistic multiplicity was a grave obstacle to preaching, and that it was fortunately lessened by the spread of Nahuatl as a second language. But the obstacle was still very great, because it was necessary to know at least five or six languages, not, of course, for every missionary, but for the Order in general, and because all these languages were extremely difficult.

At the time the Spaniards arrived in Mexico, Atzec society was divided into phratries,[54] which in turn were subdivided into twenty secondary local clans called *calpullis,* which had their private domains and governed themselves freely. They were the ordinary units of this society. All these groups were fused into a single one, the tribe of Mexico, to which the territory and the city belonged. Within the tribe, legislative and judicial functions were entrusted to a tribal council of twenty members represent-

25

ing the twenty clans. When all the members of the council were unable to reach an agreement, their difference was resolved by the great council, composed of all the chiefs of the city, which met every twenty-four days. The executive power was distributed among a large number of functionaries, the most important of whom were the *cihuacoatl* and the *tlacatecuhtli*. The former presided over the tribal council and was charged with carrying out its decisions; he was the head of the civil service and the police; he supervised the collection of taxes and tributes, and parceled out the land. At the same time he was the priest of the goddess Cihuacoatl, mother of Huitizlopochtli. This fact should be emphasized, for it shows how much the Mexican organization was penetrated by religion. The functions of the latter [the *tlacatecuhtli*], whom the Spaniards called the emperor or king, were first of all military; but little by little they had become more general, at least at the time of the Spanish conquest, when he appears as a kind of supreme head of the Aztec state. He it was who named the *cihuacoatl,* who was subordinate to him.

The command of the army devolved upon officers elected by the clan or tribe, since the clan was the basis of the military organiaztion. While the clan was the military and judicial unit, it was at the same time the territorial unit, or, possibly, the landholding unit. The tribal territory was divided into twenty clan territories, and into wards and neutral or common plots, such as the market, the temple, etc. In turn the tribal territory was divided into parcels, each of which was assigned to a married member of a clan, who was obliged to cultivate it or have it cultivated. If he died, or if the land was left fallow for two years, the parcel reverted to the clan. It goes without saying that there were exceptions to this rule. The functionaries who lacked the time to look after their parcels were supported by the public lands, which were tilled by what the people called *tlamaitl.*

The Mexican confederation, that is, the alliance composed of Tenochtitlán-Mexico, Tlacopan (Tacuba), and Texcoco, was therefore, writes Beuchat, "a military democracy, the organization of which depended upon clan rule, with land held in common," and at first the citizens formed a single class. But things turned out differently. Those who refused to marry or to cultivate the land were expelled from the clan and

26

deprived of their citizenship. They were reduced to working for wages. The Spaniards took them to be slaves, but they might enter the clan again, to which their children, if they had any, legally belonged. Craftsmen and merchants were also considered apart. But craftsmen did not constitute closed castes; they did not live in special districts, and their trades, at least in theory, were not hereditary. Merchants served also as explorers and spies; they made long journeys, sometimes dangerous ones, to barter their merchandise in distant regions, from which they brought back all kinds of information. Merchants and craftsmen did not cultivate their lands, but had to have them cultivated. Spanish writers also speak of a kind of aristocracy; but in reality there were no nobles, strictly speaking, among the Mexicans, other than the officers elected for life, and the citizens who by their excellence in war had won honorific titles. The error [of the Spanish writers] is, however, easily explained, for certain Mexicans, upon attaining puberty, submitted to an initiation that included very severe penances and thus won the title of *tecuhtin,* which was not a title of nobility, nor did it imply political power; but sons often followed in the steps of their fathers, and, besides, the chiefs and higher officers were almost always chosen from among the *tecuhtin,* or from among the warriors who had won honorific titles. In short, this was a kind of general staff, rather than a nobility.

It is noteworthy that Mexico, at the time of the Spanish conquest, was probably undergoing a social transformation. The great expeditions that had preceded [the Spanish conquest] had brought about an extraordinary prosperity. Besides, by this time the inheritance no longer reverted to the clan, but went directly to the children. Many families had thus become rich, while the functionaries for their part enriched themselves with the tributes of subjugated peoples. Thus family or private fortunes were created, along with the landed property of the clan.

Mexican laws were extremely severe. Homicide and adultery were punished by death; other crimes also, such as sacrilege, treason, theft of gold or silver, and rebellions against certain decisions of the clan. Drunkenness was tolerated during public festivals and among men of more than seventy. Otherwise, it was punished with great rigor. The Mexicans had an extraordinarily complicated calendar, but their system of

27

writing was still rudimentary. In the manuscripts dating from before and after the conquest, two elements must be distinguished: some of them are true illustrations, while others were written in glyphs. Their writing as a whole was ideographic, but the Aztecs had taken a step toward phonetic representation. "In order to render the syllables of the names of places or people," writes Beuchat, "they made use of images and objects having a similar name or sound, without attaching any value to the meaning of the sign chosen." The system corresponds exactly to our rebus writing. The Aztecs were not the only ones acquainted with writing, for there are Mixtec and Zapotec manuscripts dating from before the Spanish conquest.

Despite their development of urban industries, of which I shall speak more later on, the Aztecs were an agricultural people. They had four principal crops, which are still the basis of the Mexican diet: maize, from which they make *tortillas* and a kind of gruel called *atole;* beans (the inevitable *frijoles*); peppers (the classical *chili*); and the agave or *maguey,* which was used, as it is still used, to make the beverage called *octli,* or, more commonly, *pulque.* They were also great gardeners, in spite of which their technique of cultivation was not advanced. The Aztecs had no domestic animal capable of drawing a plow. They knew, therefore, only hoe agriculture, and their implements were very rudimentary: curved sticks for tracing furrows, wooden spades for turning the soil, and a kind of copper sickle for pruning trees. Fortunately, the soil was rich. They had only to let a piece of land lie fallow for a little while to restore its original fertility. The Mexicans also practiced irrigation. And alongside their cultivated fields they had gardens where they grew flowers and medicinal plants.[55]

Aztec civilization is, however, known to us mostly in its urban aspect. This is not the place to describe in detail the city of Tenochtitlán at the beginning of the Spanish occupation. The only thing I shall mention is that the Aztecs had two types of construction which survived the conquest: a house of cut stone, of a single rectangular room, its floor of *terre pisée,* the walls whitewashed; and a smaller house of adobes or rough stone cemented with clay. The temples were built upon quadrangular pyramids, oriented toward the four cardinal points. At one side of the pyramid a stairway gave access to several terraces. Just as Spanish cities were built around a *plaza mayor*,[56] so the Mexican villages had a large square in the center about which were disposed the municipal buildings and the main temple. When the Spanish missionaries founded villages, they readily accepted this tradition, which was so like their own. Clothing was simple: for the men, a loincloth, and a blanket over the shoulders reaching to the knees, the ancestor of the modern *sarape;* for the women, a kind of long gown of coarse material, and a skirt. Warriors wore distinctive costumes, and civil chiefs had the right to wear special insignia. Ornamentation was more varied, for the Aztecs were skilled workers in feathers, gold, silver, copper, tin, and hard stones. During festivals they wore their best. Their basic diet was maize and beans; but they also consumed a great deal of cacao, which they brought from the hot country, and they ate meat. They drank fermented beverages, the best known of which is *pulque,* and they used tobacco. Their industrial arts were highly developed: fabrics of cotton, maguey and palmetto fiber, and of rabbit or hare fur; dyes extremely varied, their colors justly celebrated; stuffs, embroideries, and feather mosaics. Their ceramics had the same diversity; three types may be distinguished: vessels of light-colored clay, of a reddish yellow, mounted on legs; objects of unpolished baked clay, with ornament in relief; and vessels of different shapes representing human or animal figures. The decoration was at times in relief, at times painted. The painted design was at times geometric, at times of animal or human figures.[57] The stone sculptures, in the round or in relief, had attained a certain beauty by the time the Spaniards arrived.

Their religion was an extraordinarily rich polytheism, owing to the Aztecs' custom of adopting the divinities of conquered tribes. Along with their belief in the great gods, who controlled the principal forces of nature and the various forms of human activity—the listing of whom would have no interest [here]—it is apparent that in Mexico there was a survival of totemism, of the kind called *nagualism,* an individual totemism that allowed a man to believe himself in rapport with an animal or a natural object revealed to him in a dream. On the other hand, the distribution of deities according to districts is likely a survival of the clan religion. All acts in life were more or less religious, so that the Mexicans performed innumerable ceremonies during their lifetime. Besides, their rites were often sanguinary, and certain gods, such as Huitzolopochtli, required the sacrifice of human victims. There was a numerous body of priests. Parallel to, or mingled with, the official cult, magic rites were extremely widespread.[58]

For fear of making these preliminaries too burdensome, I shall say only a few words about the non-Aztec populations. Among most of them one finds human sacrifice and ritual cannibalism. On the other hand, some of them, like the Totonacs,[59] and especially the Tarascans (one of the most interesting native groups of Mexico),[60] had reached an appreciable degree of civilization. The Zapotecs of the state of Oaxaca, whose civilization is akin to that of the Maya of Yucatan, can bear comparison with the inhabitants of the Central Plateau. They possessed a brilliant art, hieroglyphic writing, and a calendar, all of a rather individual character. The ruins at Monte Albán and Mitla, in their territory, are especially celebrated. Perhaps unique in America, they seem to have used the arch (at Monte Albán). The Zapotecs practiced cremation, and many of their funeral urns have been preserved. Cruciform tombs have also been discovered, and some fragments of pottery. In a general way, their religion seems to have been slightly different from that of the Aztecs. Their sacerdotal hierarchy was very simple: high priests, called "prophets" or "seers," and ordinary priests, [called] "the guardians of the gods" and "sacrificers." The clergy was recruited from among the sons of chieftains, who were given the appropriate training in a special college. The Zapotecs also were polytheists; they honored their gods by burning incense, sacrificing birds and animals, and by drawing blood from their tongues and ears. They practiced human sacrifice on certain occasions, but much more moderately than the Aztecs.[61]

Within this complex assemblage were there elements that might be used by the missionary without too much danger, either as a promise or as a lure for conversion? It is difficult to describe what the character of the natives was before the arrival of the Spaniards. Moreover, it must have varied from region to region, and we know how frail and teeming with errors these speculations about ethnic psychology are. The missionaries themselves sometimes made sweeping judgments, which were mistaken in all directions. At times they erred from an excess of optimism; at others, with exaggeratedly somber colors. Besides, they disentangled only a few and very indistinct traits. Many of them reproached the Indians for their propensity to steal and lie (which arose from their timidity), and for letting themselves drift weakly into laziness, drunkenness, and even the most shameful passions of the flesh. They praised the Indians' docility, gentleness, courtesy, simplicity, patience, and skill in handicrafts.[62] But it seemed certain [to them] that the character of the natives of Mexico did not equal their intelligence. Their religion, indeed, appeared to be only a lot of rites and beliefs, unconnected with morality; and the rites themselves (human sacrifice, drunkenness, and ritual cannibalism) were too often sanguinary and immoral.

The Aztecs, nevertheless, did believe in eternal life.[63] To them the soul was immortal and, once having departed this world, continued to live, in heaven or in hell. But this eternal life was not a sanction: heaven was not a reward, nor hell a punishment. It mattered little how a man had lived on earth; what mattered was the circumstances of his death.[64] Could the preacher use other elements better than this belief? Evidently one must not attach any Christian meaning to rites and beliefs whose similarity to some Catholic rites or beliefs forcibly struck certain spirits.[65] The Aztecs were acquainted with the sign of the cross, which was a symbol of the four cardinal points and an attribute of the deities of rain and wind.[66] They believed, moreover, that their great god Huitzilopochtli had been born of a virgin, the goddess Teteo-inan.[67] Mendieta affirmed that they had a vague notion of the true God, for whom they had a special name. Indeed, they worshiped a kind of supreme deity, Ometeuctli, or Omeyotl.[68] Mexicanists, however, rarely agree on this point, and the principal result of their discussions is that at the present time it is impossible to form a precise idea of the Aztecs' concept of divinity.[69] Moreover, the Aztecs practiced communion under various guises, by one of which, the absorption of the heart of the victim which thus became one with the substance of the god,[70] it formed a part of ritualistic cannibalism. But it did have less sanguinary aspects. [For example], twice a year the Mexicans ate pastry images representing the god Huitzilopochtli.[71] It is

31

not clear, however, whether these images were mere symbols of the god, or became the god himself. Finally, the Aztecs practiced a kind of baptism and a kind of confession. These last two rites are most interesting.

It seems likely that this kind of baptism implied a more or less confused notion of original sin. When water (and *pulque,* adds Mendieta) was poured over the head of the newborn, the midwife said, among other things: "Whoever thou art, thou who art a harmful thing, leave him and go thy way; get thee far from him, for at this moment he begins a new life; he is reborn; he is purified again; our mother the water gives him form and engenders him anew." [72]

The matter of confession deserves a somewhat closer scrutiny, for it reveals, not only the essential differences between Mexican rites and Christian sacraments, which were apparently similar, but also the very peculiar notion that the Aztecs had of sin. [73] The Mexican confession seems to have had a moral significance, up to a point. Absolute candor was required in the avowal as well as in repentance. There must be no fear of telling the confessor everything, or of trusting to the mercy of the divinity he represented, according to Sahagún, who may have unconsciously Christianized this rite. Lying and willful omission were very grave errors. The confessor, moreover, was held to the most rigorous secrecy. It should be noted, however, that the Mexican confession formed part of temporal justice. For example, drunkenness was punished by death [in civil law], but the drunkard who confessed escaped the penalty and was subjected only to a religious penance. The same was true of adultery, which was considered to be a sin and a crime at the same time. If, on the other hand, it is inexact to say that one could confess only once in one's lifetime, it is true that temporal punishment was remitted only once. It was useless for the drunkard who succumbed again to his vice, to confess again, for he could not hope to escape the legal sanction. For faults that did not carry the death penalty, in practice it was to one's interest to confess as late as possible, which one could generally do only once. Besides, confession applied only to two kinds of sins: drunkenness and sexual irregularities, such as adultery and fornication. The confessor had, therefore, only to pardon sins of a physiological kind, those having to do with needs and functions of the body. This concept of confession resulted in a purely material notion of sin. Sin was not a spiritual blemish that stained the soul, but was simply a kind of poison that had invaded the body through the exercise of a physiological function, and one eliminated it by the confession and by undergoing the imposed penance, which generally involved the letting of blood. For the rest, confession was known to others than the Aztecs: the Zapotecs and Totonacs practiced it also, as did the inhabitants of the Mistequilla, south of Vera Cruz. Among these last, confession does not seem to have concerned only the errors of the flesh.

The missionaries, nevertheless, seem to have neglected entirely to use the minute particle of truth which in their eyes the Aztecs might have held. Doubtless, that is to be regretted, but their attitude is easily explained. For one thing, the civilization they found in Mexico seemed inferior to them. Many Indians had not advanced to the same degree of civilization as the Aztecs; and about the Aztec civilization itself, which has been frequently described with overly brilliant colors, one must not nurse illusions. In the judgment of an objective specialist like Beuchat, although it represents one of the superior forms of American civilization, one should not exaggerate its value and interest. The religious, therefore, were not dazzled by the so-called marvels of Tenochtitlán. The spectacle seemed to them mediocre, often puerile, often cruel, and almost always sacrilegious. This baptism they found, this confession, this communion, far from seeming to them survivals or institutions heavy with hope and promise, gave them the impression of demoniacal parodies, from which they recoiled in horror.[74] In general, native civilization seemed too remote from truth for them to attempt to make use of the odds and ends [of agreement] that might be present in it. It should be added that the Aztecs were surrounded by scattered tribes that did not have the same religion at all. An adaptation of a dogmatic kind (not, of course, an adaptation of dogma, but an adaptation in its representation), would have run into some very serious practical difficulties. An extraordinarily numerous personnel would have been necessary for the training of strictly specialized missionaries. Now, it would have been impossible to push specialization indefinitely. It would have been necessary, for the needs of evangelization, for each religious to be capable of working effectively, if

33

not over the whole of Mexico, at least over its greater part. Their training, however serious it might be, could only be general. It will be seen that these considerations led the religious, while pushing their linguistic adaptation very far, to extend the use of the Nahuatl tongue, which was already the second language [of the country] before the conquest.

It may be objected that, along with a general adaptation, there might have been room for an adaptation of a dogmatic kind in the field itself. The missionary [in that event] would have received a general training in the study centers, so conceived as to permit him to proceed with this adaptation, once he was installed with his flock. But I believe that in such conditions adaptation would have been very dangerous and would have risked jeopardizing very vexatiously the unity of method, for the difficulty in such matters is precisely to reconcile diversity and flexibility with the necessary unity. Moreover, from the time the missionary took his post, he saw that almost all his time was taken up by his apostolic labors, and that he had hardly any leisure for a task that would demand patient observation and lengthy reflection. Nothing was more useful, nothing at times more indispensable, than that the missionary should adopt the language, the dress, and, so far as they were not contrary to Christianity, the customs of his neophytes. But adaptation of a dogmatic kind is a singularly more delicate instrument to manipulate. The discussions raised by the Malabar and Chinese rites demonstrate the prudence with which it must be approached. The missionaries of Mexico were aware that they could be led into dangerous compromises, especially at the beginning, when their knowledge of the country and its religion was still scanty; that they might breed confusions and erroneous notions in the spirits of the natives. In practice, certain religious, otherwise zealous and righteous, might be tempted more or less consciously to sacrifice the integrity of the dogma to their desire to swell the number of their neophytes. In their mind superficial resemblances were obstacles, rather than favorable elements.[75]

In this, perhaps, there was an excess of timidity, but it should be borne in mind that in the early days they were beginning the grand work of evangelization, one of the glories of the sixteenth century. In 1524 missionary work was still new; methods had not been fixed by experience; the missions of the beginning of Christianity and the late Middle Ages had been somewhat forgotten. So it is understandable that a solution was adopted which was doubtless too abrupt, which had the disadvantage of ignoring precious elements [in the native religion], but which did have the advantage of being simple and clear, and very likely avoided a great deal of groping. In time, assuredly, methods were perfected; but the missionaries would be caught up in their initial decision and carried along by the current. By 1570, the ditch that had been dug in the first years could no longer be filled.[76] It is worthy of note, as I shall have occasion to repeat, that there were always two clearly marked tendencies among the missionaries of New Spain, one favorable, the other hostile, to the natives, and that about 1570 a violent antinative reaction may be observed among the Franciscans. Today, after four centuries of missionary experience, we can be bolder,[77] but it would be wrong to reproach the evangelizers of the sixteenth century with having been less bold. The missionaries, the reader is reminded, came from a country that had always been particularly touchy about orthodoxy, one that had shown a profound horror of heresy,[78] one in which the Inquisition had gone farther than elsewhere, one in which a king, Philip II, who came to the throne during the spiritual conquest of New Spain, wished to be the champion of the true faith in the world. Finally, the period with which we are concerned coincided with the Counter Reformation in Europe; the Twelve Apostles landed in Mexico [only] four years before the condemnation and revolt of Luther; and the Council of Trent was sitting from 1545 to 1563. It is easy to see why the phobia about heresy that raged in Spain was exaggerated in America among the religious who were perpetually in contact with a pagan civilization. It was to have consequences of extreme gravity, for this state of the spirit was to be one of the causes of the failure of the Indian College of Tlatelolco, and eventually was to weigh heavily upon the history of the Church in Mexico.

All these reasons make it comprehensible why the missionaries insisted on presenting Christianity, not as a perfecting or a fulfilling of native religions, but as something entirely new, which meant an absolute and complete rupture with the whole past. Nevertheless, in whatever did not impinge upon the domain of religion, either closely or remotely, they tried to continue the past; they respected [native] languages; they respected all the usages of current life which struck them as having no bearing [on religion]; they adapted their teaching to the temperament and aptitudes of the Indians; and they even went to the extreme of establishing sanctuaries upon the sites of pagan temples. Such were the convents of Huejotzingo and Huejotla,[79] and the sanctuary of Chalmita, near Ocuila [Mexico], the miraculous grotto of which is still today the object of a great pilgrimage. Further than this they did not venture, but deliberately avoided any accommodation, in ritual or dogma, and they stubbornly destroyed even certain usages that had little bearing on religion.[80] If they curtailed some baptismal ceremonies, they did so to gain time, because they were too few to baptize immense crowds. They did not do so for the same reason they had in the East Indies, where saliva and breath were regarded as excrement and aroused the utmost horror among the natives. The Aztecs had constantly engaged in religious ceremonies. The missionaries multiplied the ceremonies and instituted edifying plays; but, by so doing, they replaced—they did not continue, they did not develop [native ceremonies].

This is where one should seek the cause of their fury against certain native practices, against temples and idols, and against all manifestations of paganism—which many have failed to understand.[81] In particular, a large number of historians have sharply criticized the religious in general, and especially the first bishop of Mexico, Fray Juan de Zumárraga, for having destroyed Mexican antiquities. But the religious, as we have seen, truly believed that the Mexican Church could not be erected upon the ruins of the native religions.[82] They were few, and the pagans innumerable; they could not permit pagan ceremonies to be practiced beside the places where Christianity was being preached; they were forced to destroy the temples and expel the priests. In this they did no more than put into effect the instructions of the Crown, which prescribed most emphatically the extirpation of every manifestation of idolatry.[83] The destruction of idols was even more necessary, for they could be concealed, while a temple could not. With respect to saving a few temples and idols as souvenirs, as Cortés wished, that would have been next to madness, and to establish a museum would have been still more extravagant, for at that time an act of this kind would have been considered a mark of respect and could only have fortified the Indians in their attachment to their old religion. Besides, to judge the question from within, it seems strange that a Catholic missionary should be attacked for preferring the establishment of the Church and the saving of souls, of which a single one would be infinitely precious to him, to the conservation of manuscripts and native sculptures.[84] Such an attitude is only a proof of logic and conscience. As Icazbalceta has justly remarked, a missionary is not an antiquarian. It is interesting that the missionaries are not reproached with having been mistaken in the method of evangelization they were obliged to adopt, but with their lack of respect for the rights of art and science. But, from the missionary's viewpoint, the primacy of spiritual things must be asserted, not merely for their bearing on policy; the rights of art and science must themselves yield before the soul's right to eternal life and the Church's right to a visible establishment. To put it more exactly, arts and science have [in the missionary's viewpoint] rights only so far as they do not endanger souls or compromise the foundation of the Church. It seems to me that the question has almost always been badly put, because those who ask it have not been sufficiently careful to phrase it as would the missionaries themselves. Meanwhile, it will perhaps be of use to bring things into their proper focus.

There is no doubt that the missionaries caused the disappearance of a great number of native antiquities.[85] In 1525 Fray Martín de la Coruña destroyed all temples and all idols of Tzintzuntzan, the holy city of Michoacán.[86] Pedro de Gante, in his letter of June 27, 1529, stated that one of the great preoccupations of his pupils was to cast down idols and destroy temples under his direction. He wrote again, on October 31, 1532, that for the past six years he had been busy, among other things, in destroying idols. Zumárraga, in his famous letter of June 12, 1531, wrote that he had destroyed more than five hundred temples and twenty thousand idols. Similar claims are made by Martín de Valencia and other religious, in a letter addressed to Charles V, of November 17, 1532. All this testimony is corroborated and completed—to mention only a few names—by the unquestioned texts of Motolinía, Sahagún, Durán, Mendieta, Dávila Padilla, and Burgoa,[87] who also wrote of the destruction of manuscripts. It is incontestable, therefore, that the religious destroyed a large number of monuments and sculptures. In any case, however, the temples were doomed to certain destruction, for they also served as fortresses, and it would not have been wise to spare them in a country held by a handful of men. The Aztecs themselves, when they subjugated a tribe, were in the habit of burning their principal temples. These buildings, moreover, because of their plans, could not have been used for any other purpose, and uselessly occupied immense spaces, such as the great *teocalli* of Mexico, which had to be demolished to make way for the new city. Their destruction, besides, was neither as rapid nor as thoughtless as has been said. According to Motolinía, it began on January 1, 1525, and on November 30, 1537, the Mexican episcopate wrote to Charles V that the temples were not all destroyed, and it asked for permission to demolish those that remained, this for the purpose of extirpating idolatry once and for all. The Emperor replied that they should be demolished, but quietly, and that the stones should be used for building churches.[88]

Zumárraga has been accused of destroying in a gigantic bonfire the archives of Texcoco; but the archives of Texcoco had been destroyed in 1520, when the Tlaxcalans entered Texcoco with Cortés and burned the principal palaces.[89] For the rest, although the missionaries were implacable against temples and idols, they did not bother with manuscripts, at least in the beginning. Many of them had disappeared even before the arrival of the Spaniards; others were hidden or buried by their owners, who did not want to see them fall into the hands of the Europeans; that is to say, they were practically lost. Finally, at the time of the siege of Mexico, Cortés had to destroy almost the whole city, and many manuscripts disappeared at that time. This is not to say that the missionaries did not destroy manuscripts, but they did not do so either in quantity or systematically. Luckily, besides, they realized the interest that these documents might have. It has even happened that manuscripts, whose destruction had been charged to them, have later been recovered. Also, the *tonalamatl*, the 260-day calendar, which Sahagún wished to destroy, was preserved in the convent of San Francisco [of Mexico City].[90] All this should be borne in mind if one wishes to be just to the missionaries and to judge their intentions and acts sanely.

2 Ethnographic and Linguistic Training of the Missionaries

WHATEVER the newly arrived missionaries thought of native civilization, they were faced with the first necessity of a fruitful apostolate, that is, at least a summary knowledge of that civilization and of the languages that were the expression of it. Father Acosta wrote: "It is not only useful, but entirely necessary for Christians and teachers of the Law of Christ to know the errors and superstitions of the older people, in order to learn whether the Indians still practice them today, openly or secretly." [1] This necessity is behind the considerable and almost unique work of one of the great Franciscans of Mexico, Fray Bernardino de Sahagún.

Bernardino de Ribeira,[2] whose name suggests a Galician or Portuguese origin, was born in the rugged Tierra de Campos (León) in the village of Sahagún (once celebrated for its Benedictine abbey, but now dismal and almost abandoned) in the last years of the fifteenth century or the first of the sixteenth. He began his studies at the University of Salamanca and took the Franciscan habit in the convent of that city. Following the common usage of his Order at that time, he adopted the name of his birthplace, of which he, with San Juan [de Sahagún], is one of the true glories. He went to Mexico in 1529 with nineteen other Franciscans, under the direction of Fray Antonio de Ciudad Rodrigo, one of the Twelve. He died there in 1590, never having left the country. During his long life as a missionary he devoted himself, outside the ordinary duties of his ministry, especially to the study, in the most methodical and detailed way, of the history, traditions, customs, and language of the natives. His works are, or rather were, for many have been lost, innumerable.[3] But one of them overshadows all the rest, his monumental *Historia general de las cosas de Nueva España,* in which he attempted to condense all his learning and all his experience.[4]

Sahagún explains in detail his purpose in writing this kind of encyclopedia of Mexican civilization. "The physician," he writes in the opening pages of his book,

would be unable to treat his patient properly unless he knew from the beginning the humor and causes of the disease. And just as it is necessary for the physician to have a perfect knowledge of remedies and maladies in order to apply to each of the latter that which tends to counteract it, in like manner it is necessary for preachers and confessors, who are the true physicians of souls in spiritual sicknesses, to gain a knowledge of spiritual maladies and the medicines they require. The preacher must know the vices of the country to exercise his zeal there, and the confessor must be no less conversant with those vices, to the end that he may make them the basis of his questions and understand what his penitents are accusing themselves of in their confessions. Ministers engaged in conversion should not limit themselves to saying that the Indians have no sins other than drunkenness, thievery, and carnal excesses, for there are grave faults among them which insistently call for remedy. The sins of idolatry, the rites of a paganism, the auguries and superstitions connected with it, have not completely disappeared. In order to preach against such practices and learn whether they still exist, one must know how the natives used them in the time of their idolatry, for unless we have acquired knowledge [of these practices], we allow them to commit many idolatrous acts in our presence without our being aware of them, and a few of us try to excuse them by saying that these are only childish, foolish, and nonsensical things. In fact, they are ignorant of the true source of such acts, and, whether it is a matter of idolatry or not, the confessors never call their penitents to account. They know nothing of the language necessary for an investigation, and besides they would not understand the explanations.

It would not do, he concludes, for the missionaries coming later to reproach their predecessors with having failed to enlighten them.[5]

The *Historia* of Sahagún is divided into twelve books. The first book treats of the gods and goddesses worshiped by the Indians; the second, the feasts celebrated in their honor; the third, the immortality of the soul and their funeral rites; the fourth, judicial astrology; the fifth, auguries. These five books may be considered a first part, devoted to the religion and superstitions of the Mexicans. The sixth and seventh books treat of their intellectual life: rhetoric, moral and natural philosophy. The author then takes up their social and political life in the eighth book, in which he speaks of great personages and their methods of government; in the ninth, merchants, artisans, and their customs; finally, in two books that Jourdanet and Siméon happily describe as a "dictionary in action," Sahagún attempts to assemble all terms of the Nahuatl language, taken from the habits and way of life of the Mexicans.[6] The tenth book treats of the vices, virtues, and customs of the Indians; the eleventh, of the animals, plants, and metals of the country;[7] the twelfth, which is brief and poor, summarizes the conquest of Mexico.

Sahagún was at the convent of Tepeapulco (Hidalgo) when he began his work, and was later posted to the Franciscan convent of Texcoco. He tells us that he called together the principal people of the village, those of the entourage of the *cacique,* Don Diego de Mendoza,[8] and asked them to provide him with assistants for his work. The next day they appointed ten or twelve old men. "There were also," adds Sahagún, "four men whom I myself had taught Latin grammar several years before, in the College of Santa Cruz de Tlatelolco." For two years Sahagún had these four and the old men instruct him, all the work of collaboration being carried on in the Nahuatl language. At the end of these two years Sahagún was transferred to Santiago Tlatelolco, where he continued his work using the same methods. He brought together eight or ten Indians especially instructed in their language, added to them four or five students "who spoke three languages," and spent more than a year at the college closeted with them, to review what he had done at Tepeapulco. His principal collaborator was Martín Jacobita, who at the time was rector of the college and who lived in the Santa Ana district of Tlatelolco. Sahagún was then sent to San Francisco de México, where he spent three years arranging and completing his book, of which he had made a clean copy in Nahuatl [in 1569]. "To sum up," he wrote, the first sifting of my book was done at Tepeapulco; the second, at Tlatelolco; that of Mexico was the third. In all of them my collaborators were collegians expert in grammar. The principal and most learned of them was Antonio Valeriano, of Atzacapotzalco, and Alonso Vegerano, of Cuauhtitlán; another was Martín Jacobita, whom I have already mentioned. I should add Pedro de San Buenaventura. All three were expert in three languages: Latin, Spanish, and Indian [Nahuatl]. The copyists who made the clean copy in their good hand were Diego Degrado, of the district of San Martín, and Mateo Severino, of Xochimilco near Ulliac.[9]

In another passage Sahagún tells us that the medical section of his book was compiled from data supplied by some old physicians of Tlatelolco.[10]

One gathers from these statements of Sahagún that the work was done in three stages, at Tepeapulco, Tlatelolco, and Mexico, and that it went through three phases: a first manuscript was finished at Tlatelolco in 1560; a second version has been established [as completed] toward 1562, following the Tlatelolco revision; and finally the definitive text was ready in 1566, following the long scrutiny made in Mexico. This last edition was in turn copied with some corrections in the three years from 1566 to 1569.[11] Always and in every respect the work was done in close collaboration with native specialists and under their supervision—a scrupulous and rigorous method, singularly fruitful in the hands of one who was capable of using it with the necessary discrimination. It was also a singularly original method, which Sahagún seems to have brought to perfection.

The *Historia general de las cosas de Nueva España* was the great joy but the great torment of Sahagún's life. He tells us that when he began to work at Tepeapulco he did so by order of his provincial, Fray Francisco de Toral (later, bishop of Yucatan), who told him to write in the Mexican language "whatever he thought would be most useful to the dogma, practice, and continuance of Christianity among the natives of New Spain, and at the same time would be most useful as an aid to the ministers and their helpers charged with teaching them." Now, it was not until 1557, almost thirty years after Sahagún's arrival, that Father Toral took over the direction of the Provincia del Santo Evangelio [the Franciscan province of New Spain].[12] It seems certain, however, that the

42

Father Provincial did no more than beg Sahagún to undertake the methodical arrangement of the works that Sahagún had begun several years before. Fray Bernardino, in fact, writes at the end of his sixth book that he himself had translated it into Spanish in 1577, thirty years after having written it in the Nahuatl language.[13] The Nahuatl version would therefore date back to 1547. Without going so far as to think, with Alfonso Toro, that the first six books were completed by 1547 (even with the testimony of the author regarding only the sixth book, which could well have been written before the others), it is not reckless to conjecture, with Chavero, that Sahagún had devoted himself to the study of Mexican civilization as early as 1540, at least. One must bear in mind his habit of scrupulous documentation and the care with which he prepared his manuscripts. For the rest, it is evident that during the first years (less, to be sure, in the matter of natives usages and tradition), he must have worked still more slowly than during the period of his complete mastery [of the subject]. By 1569, therefore, when the second Nahuatl copy of the book was finished, Father Sahagún had been working on it for about thirty years. But his trials and troubles had not ceased at all. Father Toral, who had encouraged and protected him, resigned as provincial, and Fray Miguel Navarro, who had been provincial since 1567,[14] and who had favored him equally, saw the end of his term as provincial approaching. Now, the work had been composed solely and entirely in Nahuatl, and the enormous bulk had still to be translated into Castilian. The provincial chapter of 1570 showed itself hostile to Sahagún. Among the religious, some manifested great esteem for and interest in his work, but the others, either from jealousy or narrow-mindedness, declared that it was contrary to the spirit of poverty to spend money on such things. This last opinion enraged him.[15]

The chapter was somewhat agitated because Father Miguel Navarro, the retiring provincial, was at odds with the commissary general, Fray Francisco de Ribera, and because the Franciscans were split into two parties [about Sahagún].[16] The chapter took another decision that was fatal for Sahagún: It elected as provincial Fray Alonso de Escalona, who belonged to the party opposed to Father Navarro and, hence, to Father Sahagún, who was deprived of his copyists and condemned to finish the crushing work alone, in his trembling hand. But he did not despair. Fray Miguel Navarro kept his influence and his partisans, and, to judge by his letters and actions, was not apparently an easy man to beat down. When he left for Spain in 1570, after the meeting of the chapter, accompanied by his friend Fray Gerónimo de Mendieta (who for his part was of too open and curious a mind not to interest himself in the works of Sahagún), he took along a Spanish summary of the *Historia general,* written by Sahagún himself, and presented it to Don Juan de Ovando, President of the Council of the Indies, who liked it. But Father Escalona, learning of what he considered a grave breach of discipline on Sahagún's part, thought it his duty to impose severe sanctions, confiscating all Sahagún's papers and distributing them among the various convents of the province. Everything changed, however, in 1573. Fray Alonso de Escalona was replaced as provincial by Fray Antonio Roldán, and, most important, Fray Miguel Navarro was named Commissary General [of the Order], which gave him authority over all Franciscans in New Spain. He had the scattered papers assembled and returned to Sahagún, who applied himself to their translation, one part of which he finished in 1577, a year which saw a further change [in his fortunes]. In a *cédula,* dated April 22, Philip II ordered Viceroy Martín Enríquez to confiscate Sahagún's work and leave no original or copy behind, and to send it to the Council of the Indies for examination. No one, added the *cédula,* was to be allowed to describe the superstitions and customs of the Indians.[17] The order was repeated the following year, which seems to indicate that it had not been immediately obeyed, and Sahagún was able to work a while longer. He never learned positively, it seems, why all his papers had been sent to Spain, and died without knowing the fate of the work that had been the great purpose of his life, possibly convinced that his efforts had been wasted. In fact, the *Historia general* never had among the missionaries of New Spain the circulation for which he had so stubbornly fought. It was not until two centuries had passed that [Juan Bautista] Muñoz, who had been appointed historian of the Indies in 1779, succeeded in rediscovering the manuscript in the Franciscan convent of Tolosa.[18]

I have given all this space to Sahagún because his work was certainly the most methodical and substantial attempt to give the missionaries of

New Spain a training in ethnography. His effort, however, was not isolated. As an example of the same type of studies may be mentioned the *Relación de las ceremonias y ritos, población y gobierno de los indios de la provincia de Michoacán*, which the old men of Tzintzuntzan had dictated in Tarascan to a Franciscan friar, possibly Fray Martín de Jesús de la Coruña.[19] This account is evidently older than Sahagún's *Historia*, for it is dedicated to Viceroy Antonio de Mendoza, who left New Spain in 1551. The work of Fray Toribio de Benavente (Motolinía), which appeared in two different stages, the first in his *Memoriales*, the second in his *Historia de los indios de la Nueva España* may also be cited.[20] The *Memoriales*, in fact, seem to be a first draft of the *Historia*;[21] but the latter, although it is concerned especially with the history of the introduction of Christianity, yields a mass of information on native life before the Spanish conquest. The vicissitudes of this book are almost as many as those of Sahagún's *Historia*, and its fate was also unhappy. Motolinía never saw his book in print; nor did Fray Martín de Jesús ever see his *Relación de Michoacán* published. None of these three books was printed until our day. This was not merely accidental. I shall indicate below the common causes of what was neither negligence, forgetfulness, nor mischance.[22]

We have seen that the tenth and eleventh books of Sahagún's *Historia* were a kind of "dictionary in action." Sahagún, indeed, was not only an ethnographer; he was also a linguist. His profound knowledge of the Nahuatl tongue is attested by his own work and by many witnesses.[23] The two disciplines, as always happens, are not easily separated. Nevertheless, for practical reasons (more exactly, because the knowledge of languages was more immediately useful and evident in the minds of superficial spirits), the linguistic training of missionaries was more emphasized, linguistic studies were more general and numerous, and the Franciscans had no monopoly of them. The Dominicans and Augustinians did not produce so many works (besides, they had fewer people), but they did make an important contribution.

Before taking up the linguistic problem in the Mexican mission, it would be superfluous to look for precedents and points of comparison, or to remind oneself of the fundamental principles of the missionary's task. The study and practice of native languages, however strange and difficult they may be, have always been one [such principle], and I believe it would be impossible to name a mission, in any time or country whatever, in which this principle has not been applied, at least in part. The friars of Mexico, from the moment of their arrival, recognized that the knowledge of Indian languages was the essential prerequisite of serious evangelization. For one thing, it was the best means of penetrating the spirit of the pagans and conquering their hearts.[24] And then, if they were ignorant of languages they could not well administer the sacraments other than baptism and marriage.[25] Besides, it was at times imprudent to baptize adults who had been insufficiently instructed, for instruction carried on by signs or with the help of an interpreter could only be very imperfect. At the beginning, doubtless, preaching was done by signs. Muñoz Camargo tells how the religious could only indicate the existence of heaven and hell. To suggest hell they pointed to the earth, fire, toads, and snakes; then they raised their eyes, pointed to heaven, and spoke of a single God. The Indians barely understood.[26] The Dominican Fray Domingo de la Anunciación employed a somewhat less rudimentary device: He wrote a short sermon in Spanish, had it translated into a native tongue by an interpreter, learned it by heart, and recited it to the Indians, although he knew nothing about it but its general sense. He gave this up and set about learning Nahuatl.[27] Moreover, since it was necessary to administer the sacrament of penitence, it was easy to see how odious and imprudent it would be to hear confessions through an interpreter. This was one of the arguments advanced against the [employment of] secular priests, many of whom were unable to administer the sacrament in any other way,[28] for which reason a certain number of religious applied themselves to the study of the native languages.

Since that study was determined by the geographical distribution of the missions, it varied slightly from one mission to the next. It goes without saying that the missionaries learned only the tongue of the Indians they had to evangelize. Thus, the Dominicans, having no missions in Michoacán, never learned Tarascan, while the Franciscans never learned Zapotec. [The missionaries] learned all the languages, together with their dialects, within the limits of their territories. They gave preference to Nahuatl, but did not on that account neglect the less widespread tongues. We know, for example, that among the Dominicans Fray Domingo de Santa María and Fray Benito Fernández knew Mixtec,[29] Zapotec, and Chontal, in addition to Nahuatl.[30] Moreover, the simultaneous study of Nahuatl, Mixtec, and Zapotec (the Indians whom the [Dominican] Order was to evangelize belonged almost exclusively to these three groups), seems to have been almost the rule among the Dominicans of New Spain,[31] and they were especially encouraged in it by Pope Pius V.[32]

The first Augustinians, from the moment of their arrival, applied themselves to the study of Nahuatl. In their missions the study of languages soon became obligatory, and was much more extensive than among the Dominicans, not because of their superior apostolic zeal or scientific curiosity, but because the linguistic variation in the territories assigned to them was very much greater. While at Atotonilco [Hidalgo] Fray Alonso de Borja was learning Otomí, one of the most difficult languages of Mexico, and Fray Pedro de San Jerónimo and Fray Francisco de Acosta were studying the extremely complicated Pirinda language spoken by the natives of Charo [Michoacán].[33] Altogether there were ten Indian languages spoken in the missions: Nahuatl, Otomí, Tarascan, Huaxtec, Pirinda (or Matlalzinca), Totonac, Chichimec, Tlapanec, and Ocuiltec. Only the Augustinians knew the last two.[34] Nevertheless, there were not many polyglots among them. In 1571, the prior of [the covent of] Pahuatlán, Fray Pedro Serrano, was preaching and hearing confessions in Nahuatl, Otomí, and Totonac.[35] As for the Franciscans, they were considerably more numerous and their territories were more extensive and more varied. These two reasons explain why they developed a particularly large and remarkable group of linguists. Suffice it to mention the names of Mexicanists like Fray Luis de Fuensalida,[36] Fray Francisco Jiménez, Fray Juan Focher,[37] Fray Alonso de Molina, and Fray Bernardino de Sahagún; masters of Tarascan like Fray Pedro de Garrovillas, Fray Juan de San Miguel,[38] and especially Fray Maturino Gilberti; a specialist in Matlalzinca like Fray Andrés de Castro;[39] and polyglots such as Fray Miguel de Bolonia[40] and Fray Andrés de Olmos. Mendieta was doubtless thinking of Father Olmos when he spoke of a religious who wrote catechisms and preached the Christian doctrine in more than ten different languages.[41] This is evidently an exceptional case, but we do know that certain of the Friars Minor reached the point of preaching in three languages,[42] and that for twelve years Fray Francisco de Toral preached in two languages every Sunday and feast day.[43]

It is apparent that the religious who thus dedicated themselves to the study of native languages were not thinking merely of their personal ministry; they had to guide and help the missionaries who lacked their talents or their leisure. From the moment it was established that they were not seeking to Hispanicize the Indians and that the task of civilizing them was to be done completely and solely in the native languages, books had to be put into the hands of all the religious, to allow them to study the language of their congregation or to perfect themselves in it, to help them to teach the Christian doctrine, make known the Holy Scriptures, and administer the sacraments, particularly the sacrament of penitence. Hence [there were] two distinct categories of books: on the one hand the *artes,* or grammars, and the *vocabularios,* which were the tools of work and study; on the other, the *doctrinas,* or catechisms, the *confesionarios,* translations of the Gospel, the Epistles, lives of the saints, etc., manuals for every day services. These books today are extremely valuable for linguists. But the religious hardly thought of the future; they were not at all interested in collecting and saving these entirely practical writings, which were reprinted only in cases of absolute need. Thus many have been lost. Besides, many of them were never published, but kept in manuscript, sometimes in many copies, which the religious lent to each other, as students exchange notes. Others were not printed because the Holy Office was opposed, and some of them already in print were destroyed at its command. This is a matter which I shall return to.

It would be tedious to list here all the works of this kind written by the religious. I have attempted to make a list of them, which specialists will find in the Appendix. Here I shall only say that in the single period of 1524–1572, limiting myself to New Spain and to the books having to do with the task of evangelization, I find a minimum of 109, eighty of them written by Franciscans, sixteen by Dominicans, eight by Augustinians, and five anonymous. By languages they are distributed as follows: books in Nahuatl, or concerning Nahuatl, sixty-six; Tarascan, thirteen; Otomí, six; Pirinda, five; Mixtec, five; Zapotec, five; Huaxtec, four; Totonac, two; Zoque, one; in the dialect of Chilapa, one.[44] The preponderance of Franciscans, the cause of which I have mentioned, is striking. The works they published concern six of the ten languages: Nahuatl, Tarascan, Otomí, Piranda, Huaxtec, and Totonac. The Dominicans, in addition to Nahuatl, limited themselves to Mixtec, Zapotec, and Zoque, this last hardly represented. The Augustinians, also in addition to Nahuatl, naturally [limited themselves] to Huaxtec, Otomí, and the dialect of Chilapa. This distribution was, of course, the result of geographical distribution of the missions. It should be borne in mind, however, that in the present state of our knowledge the absence of known publications does not absolutely prove the lack of knowledge of a language. There is, for example, no known Augustinian publication on Tarascan and Ocuiltec, but we do know, from different and trustworthy sources,[45] that these two languages were assiduously cultivated by the Augustinians. My inventory, I insist, is therefore a minimum list. The preponderance of Nahuatl is equally striking, explainable by particular reasons—a subject to which I shall also return. All these works were compiled with the greatest care and with the manifest aim of reaching the greatest possible number of natives. One example: The *Doctrina Mixteca,* by the Dominican Fray Benito Fernández,[46] of which I possess two editions, was published November 22, 1567, and January 24, 1568. It is hard to explain why, within the space of two months, it was necessary to get out two editions of the same work. But the Mixtec language had a large number of dialects: the first edition was written in the dialect of Tlaxiaco and Achiutla; the second in that of Teposcolula, the most widespread.[47]

Despite their conscientious effort, the missionaries, faced with such a linguistic mosaic, realized the need of an auxiliary language. Such a language, luckily, they discovered upon arrival: Nahuatl, which was accepted by them without hesitation, for it was the language of the Aztec empire. Michoacán (Tarascan), Huaxteca, Mixteca,[48] Zapotecas, and the regions of the north had kept their linguistic independence as well as their political. But the Indians under Aztec domination, who were in the majority, spoke Nahuatl, or were bilingual, such as the Totonacs, who spoke their own language as well as Nahuatl, which served as the official language. So it was easy to teach these bilingual Indians directly in Nahuatl, or to procure through them the necessary instruction in their own language. The Franciscan Fray Rodrigo de la Cruz, writing to Charles V on May 4, 1550, explained the matter:

> It seems to me that Your Majesty should order that all the Indians learn the Mexican language, for in every village today there are many Indians who know it and learn it easily, and a very great number who confess in that language. It is an extremely elegant language, as elegant as any in the world. A grammar and dictionary of it have been written, and many parts of the Holy Scriptures have been translated into it; many collections of sermons have been made, and some religious have mastered it completely.[49]

This quotation reveals the thinking of the religious, and it also bears witness to the enormous effort they had already made to spread the knowledge of Nahuatl. Eight years later, Viceroy Luis de Velasco sent a similar request to Philip II. The Franciscan provincial, he wrote, had just returned from an inspection tour of New Galicia, where the religious had pointed out to him the obstacle to the preaching of Christianity in that region offered by the diversity of languages. To meet this difficulty he thought it would be necessary to set up a college in Guadalajara where the youths of the various regions should be gathered and taught Nahuatl before sending them home.[50] This solution does not seem to have been adopted, but we do know that the Franciscans of New Galicia, to remedy the diversity of languages, taught Nahuatl to all their Indians.[51] The Augustinians made a similar effort to achieve unity. In the beginning they preached in all languages of their territory, and their churches were so arranged that several sermons could be preached at the same time during one Mass. Soon, however, they attempted to induce the Indians to speak a single language, the dominant one, and sermons were preached in it. Only confessions were heard in the different languages or dialects of the region.[52] Nahuatl, as has been explained, was the dominant language of most regions, and the religious worked so zealously at its diffusion that by 1584, from Zacatecas to Nicaragua, there were Indians everywhere who knew it.[53] Because of its extension before the Conquest, as well as the importance given it by the missionaries, it doubly deserved the title of "the universal language of the Indians" given it by Philip II in his *cédula* of September 19, 1580.[54]

In it he emphasized the necessity of having the priests and religious of New Spain learn Nahuatl, and in another *cédula* of the same date he prohibited the bishops to ordain candidates for the priesthood who were ignorant of it.[55] More than forty years earlier, in the instructions issued by the Queen, in the name of Charles V, to Viceroy Antonio de Mendoza, she recommended that he encourage the study of native languages among the priests, religious, and children, since some of the last-named might be called to the priesthood some day.[56] The Crown was not at all hostile to the study and teaching of native languages, but it believed that none of them was sufficiently rich and supple to allow it to be used for explaining the mysteries of the Christian faith. It also dreaded the obstacle presented by the multiplicity of native languages. Hence, it never ceased to insist at the same time that all Indians be taught Spanish. The Dominicans and Augustinians received the formal order [to do so], as is proved by a letter addressed to their provincials, of June 7, 1550.[57] The Franciscans were begged to do the same, for the letter of Fray Rodrigo de la Cruz, just cited, is manifestly a firm, strong, and at the same time deferential, answer to the royal injunction, which became a dead letter. Catechisms, sermons, confessions, all were conducted, and continued to be conducted, in the native languages.[58] I have even seen examples of parochial registers written in Nahuatl.[59] The Crown insisted [in its stand] to the end of the [sixteenth] century, but without result.[60]

The religious did not lack reasons for their resistance. They held from the beginning that Spanish, in its structure and character, was too different from the native languages and almost completely inassimilable for the greater number of Indians, especially adults. This was affirmed by Fray Rodrigo de la Cruz particularly. In 1599, Viceroy the Conde de Monterrey, replying to Philip III, who had begged him to overcome this difficulty, said that it was not [exactly] a difficulty, but virtually an impossibility.[61]

Besides, the missionaries complained that they were too few for the task with which they were charged. How could a friar, already crushed

51

beneath his burden, be asked to take one or two hours a day from his ministry to teach Spanish? Or how could he be asked, when he was hardly able to support the fatigue of heavy daily tasks, to undertake several hours of supplementary work? Also, how could a certain number of religious be taken away from their ministry, as suggested in the royal letter of 1550, and be assigned to teaching? All these things were practically impossible. The teaching of Spanish, therefore, seemed to the friars only a useless added duty, and even a harmful one—harmful, indeed, because it would be the first step toward the Hispanization of the Indians. There was a disturbing clause in the letter of 1550: "that the Indians be instructed in our Castilian speech and accept our social organization and good customs." Now, as will be brought out in a later chapter, the religious had been very insistent upon allowing the Indians to live according to their native customs, so long as these did not have a religious character, and especially to protect them from contact with rapacious, greedy, and debauched Europeans, with their bad examples and evil counsels. The difference in languages seemed [to the friars] a salutary barrier, which they were not at all disposed to break down.[62]

It should be added that they considered their Indians to be a little like children, to be kept in tutelage and led by the hand. Knowledge of Castilian would have been the first step toward a dangerous freedom. To this may perhaps be added, at least among several, a secret and at times unconscious will to dominate. So long as the linguistic barrier remained standing, they were the indispensable intermediaries between the Indians and the civil officers, between their Orders and episcopal authority; they were the lords and masters of their parishioners, who were already accustomed to docile obedience in their long pre-Conquest servitude. They did not relish the prospect of giving it all up. On this delicate point one can speak only with a good deal of prudence and reserve, but many documents seem to prove that this feeling, although not general, was not entirely unknown.[63]

All this vast, persevering, and methodical work was, nevertheless, as certain examples and documents lead one to believe, insufficient. There is no reason to stress the fact that some religious, who in other respects were illustrious, certainly knew no native language. Martín de Valencia was fifty when he arrived in Mexico. He was in charge of the Franciscan mission from its very beginning and was twice custodian, in 1524 and 1530. All these tasks deprived him of the leisure for long and difficult studies.[64] A somewhat analogous case is that of Fray Jacobo de Testera, who taught by means of pictures because he was ignorant of the language. He was probably in his fifties when he landed in Mexico, for we are told that he had been preaching in Spain for twenty years and had led a busy administrative life. He arrived in 1529, was custodian from 1533 to 1536, and commissary general from 1541 to 1543. He died in 1544.[65] The same may be said of Fray Domingo de Betanzos, who, according to Mendieta, did not know any [native] language and had little to do with the Indians.[66] He was over forty-five when he arrived in Mexico, and was almost immediately absorbed in administrative duties.

Viceroy Luis de Velasco, who favored the religious, pointed out the insufficient number of interpreters; however, his testimony does not apply to the whole country or especially to the three Orders. He spoke of the religion of Tehuantepec when he stated that there were few priests and religious there who understood the Indians. This region, however, lies somewhat outside the limits [of this study], and, besides, the viceroy was writing at the beginning of the evangelization of that territory, when the Dominicans had just established themselves and could hardly have mastered the language by that time. In the same report the viceroy complained that there too few interpreters among the Dominicans of the archdiocese of Mexico and the diocese of Oaxaca. But from the letter itself one gathers that there were not enough religious either. In all they numbered 180, half of whom were novices—which brings the figure down to ninety, from which the lay brothers should be deducted, as well as the sick and aged who were unable to practice their ministry, and especially the administrative and teaching personnel needed for the government of the province and the training of novices. It is not astonishing [therefore] that the number of religious capable of attending to the Indians was so small. Besides, the death rate among them was very high, and many had died at the very moment they were beginning to learn the language and know the people.[67]

To sum up: At the time Mendieta arrived in Mexico, that is, in 1554, there were not yet enough interpreters among the religious, and the hearing of confessions through [native] interpreters was still being practiced at the time of the visit of Commissary General Fray Alonso Ponce in 1584. But we should not grant these two witnesses an authority that they do not have. Mendieta preached in Nahuatl and was himself aided by an interpreter "for a certain barbarous tongue." I do not believe that I am questioning his statements by thinking that when he wrote "that there were not yet enough religious capable of preaching in the Indian languages," he meant that the Franciscans knew only certain of them. His very words "not yet" imply that the number of interpreters among the religious had increased. Ponce's testimony is important for its lateness, and has to do only with the diocese of Jalisco in New Galicia, and proves that the religious did know Nahuatl, but were ignorant of the very numerous languages peculiar to the region. They preached and heard confessions in Nahuatl, and only the Indians who did not speak it were obliged to have recourse to interpreters.[68] All this, in short, is a question of individual ineptitudes and local inadequacies, and does not diminish the value or merit of the whole. Likewise, [these faults] were unavoidable, for the task was so vast and so far beyond human strength that it was fated in advance to be imperfectly accomplished.

A sane judgment, indeed, cannot be formed of it until the results have been assessed and the difficulties appreciated. These were many and great, at times rendered harder by neglect, for the missionary had to struggle against his own indolence, or the hostility or indifference of the Indians. The immediate difficulties had to do with the languages themselves and are so evident that I shall not labor the point. These strange idioms, so different in structure from the Latin languages, with such complicated and confusing sounds, as compared with the simplicity and phonetic clarity of Castilian, completely baffled the religious, for, as we have seen, there was an infinite variety of them, and each in turn was divided into a very great number of dialects or patois. Otomí had a multitude of dialects; two different Huaxtec dialects were recognized; [69] four Totonac; at least four Zapotec, and as many as eleven Mixtec.[70] Luckily, from the beginning the religious had teachers among the children they had gathered into their convents, whom they taught Spanish and Latin. The Franciscans also found a precious helper in the person of a little Spaniard, Alonso de Molina, who was later to become one of them [and the author of the great *Vocabulario Nahuatl*]. He was only a child when he arrived in Mexico and, as was natural at his age, assimilated Nahuatl quickly and easily, and became the teacher of his future brothers.[71]

Once the native language was mastered, a singularly delicate problem came up: how to explain the dogma in it. The question was to translate into the native languages notions that had never been expressed in them, notions for which they had no words, such as Trinity, Holy Ghost, Redemption, and so on. The problem arose everywhere. The missionaries adopted two contrary solutions: one group introducing into the language of the country all the European words they thought necessary; the other always translating and thus avoiding paraphrasing.

The first method was a better protection against heterodoxy, for under it all misunderstanding and confusion in the minds of the neophytes could be averted. It would have been vain to try to Christianize a word which had thus far been used only by the pagans, for it would have run the risk of retaining a part of its meaning and of being associated with ideas that were not at all Christian. Even so, it was not always possible to avoid such confusions. In Japan, for example, St. Francis Xavier used only the Portuguese word *Deos,* precisely to avoid equivocal expressions in use among the Japanese sects. Now, said the Saint, the Buddhist priests, "interpreting the name of God as they understood it, said that *Dieu* and *Dajuzo* were the same; [but] *Dajuzo* in Japanese means 'a great lie,' so it is necessary to be alert to protect our God." [72] But that was only an accident arising from the bad faith of the enemy. The procedure presented a much graver and almost fundamental difficulty, to wit, that Christian ideas, presented in foreign dress, ran the risk of remaining perpetually foreign to the native mind. "It is necessary," said Raoul Allier, "to give our ideas a native look, or they will always remain at the surface, and one will achieve only a veneer of civilization." [73] Not only will the ideas be badly assimilated, or not at all, but Christianity will appear as the religion of foreigners, the Universal Church as an institution peculiar to one nation or race, and the convert as a traitor to his country. The history of missions proves beyond question that there is no more fatal mistake.

With the second method this danger is averted; but another appears, for the instrument is a very ticklish one to handle and requires a thorough knowledge of native language and civilization. In his *La Réligion des Tupinambas,* Métraux gives a typical example of the errors that missionaries are exposed to. When they tried to find in the Tupinamba language a word to convey the idea of God, they chose, *faute de mieux,* the word *Tupan,* which means thunder. But this Tupan, in the mythology of the Tupinambas, was only a secondary spirit. Fortunately, the Indians were aware of the confusion and realized very well the difference between Tupan and the Christian God.[74] Similar confusions occurred in Mexico. The preachers, for example, gave the Holy Virgin the name of the goddess Tonantzin, whose shrine formerly stood on the site of the church of Our Lady of Guadalupe, at Tepeyac. Sahagún protested that "the true name of Our Lady, the Mother of God, was not Tonantzin, but rather *Dios etnantzin.* This looks like an invention of Satan for the purpose of concealing idolatry under the cloak of ambiguity, in the word Tonantzin." [75]

Meanwhile, the two methods, however different they might seem, could be fused.[76] The missionaries of New Spain generally preferred the former. In their minds orthodoxy was more important than anything else, and the Crown felt the same. At the end of a *cédula* dated at Valladolid September 22, 1538, ordering an ecclesiastical tribunal to examine a Tarascan catechism, appear these words: "And take particular heed that examiners determine whether these terms present any difficulties for the teaching and practice of the Christian religion, because of the meaning the Indians give them in their language." [77] This scruple was pushed to the extreme of never using the Nahuatl word *teotl* to designate God, but [instead] the Spanish *Dios,* to emphasize the difference between the pagan divinities and the single God of the Christians.[78] And even when Spanish words were thus used, they were hedged about with great precautions. To avoid confusion between the native priests called *papas* [and the Christian pope], Zumárraga ordered that the Latin word [*papa*] should never be used, but *pontifex* or *pontifice.*[79] His worry was unnecessary, because the Indians never called their priests *papas,*[80] but it is not the less revealing on that account. The principal result of this [second] method was that the texts written by the religious in the native languages were sprinkled with Latin and Spanish words, disguised or not in the dress of the country. One example out of a great number is Sahagún's *Evangelarium, Epistolarium et Lectionarium aztecum*,[81] in which, besides the word *Dios*, one finds the following: *sanctome, angelome, principatus, virtudes, apostolome, Spiritu Santo, gratia, evangelistame*—all this within twenty-three verses.[82] These are concerned, to be sure, with fragments of the Epistles of St. Paul, in which there is an abundance of ideas difficult to render in Nahuatl. Latin or Castilian words are less numerous in the Gospels, but there are still some. The case is all the more arresting since Sahagún was perhaps the missionary who best knew Nahuatl and who would be least embarrassed by the difficulties of translation. Some borrowing from Castilian can doubtless be explained by differences in culture. Thus, in the parable of the foolish virgins and the wise virgins, Sahagún was obliged to introduce the Spanish words *lámpara y azeite*,[83] but most of the borrowings are concerned with dogma or the history of Christianity.[84]

These notes may suffice to show how complicated was the task of the linguists and ethnographers among the religious. Different circumstances complicated it still further. Their obsession with idolatry and heresy came to dominate certain missionaries so profoundly that everything connected in one way or another with pagan civilization, without exception, ended by being suspect: studies of beliefs, customs, social and political organization, and the intellectual life and languages of the Indians. Thus, little by little, there sprang up a group in all three Orders, which was all the stronger for being encouraged by the ecclesiastical and civil authorities of the metropolis, and because the second archbishop of Mexico, Montúfar, shared their obsession and anxiety. In 1555, possibly owing to his influence, the first Mexican synod ordered all collections of sermons in the native languages to be seized, until [the Indians] should be given others within their comprehension—this because of errors of translation and confusion, committed by the Indians themselves. Besides [it was ordered that] no priest might deliver one of these volumes to an Indian without signing it.[85] The provisional synod of 1565, in its turn, prohibited the texts of the Holy Scriptures to fall into the hands of Indians, and, in general, everything but the catechism translated by religious specialists and approved by the prelates.[86] Even though this was not the only cause, the movement led, in 1569, to the formal establishment of the Holy Office in New Spain.[87] In the chapter of 1570 Sahagún was the victim of this spirit. The assembly marked a victory for the party I am calling, for the sake of simplicity, antiscientific and antinative. Its very date explains a number of things. Some of the first great missionaries, who had dedicated themselves to the study of the Indians, without self-delusion but with an ardent apostolic zeal and profound sympathy, were dying off, men such as Fray Juan de Goana (died 1560), Fray Juan de Rivas (1562), Fray Martín de Jesús, the supposed author of the *Relación de Michoacán* (1568), and Motolinía, the last of the Twelve (1569), not to mention Fray Francisco Jiménez and Fray Luis de Fuensalida, who had died long before (in 1537 and 1545). The rest were in their declining years, without strength and perhaps without influence. Olmos and Toral died in 1571; Pedro de Gante, a simple lay brother moreover and exposed to the hostility of Archbishop Montúfar, in 1572;[88] Focher in 1573. In a sense it was a new generation, or rather a new team, that was coming to the direction of affairs. The early enthusiasm and curiosity had died out long since;[89] the mission tended to become a town; [the missionaries] forgot they were not in Spain and wished to act as if they were in Europe; they were less interested in new things; and they were very desirous of starting a movement counter to that of the "old school."

Sahagún made the mistake of reminding them that they should not act as if they were still in Spain.[90] His *Historia general de las cosas de Nueva España* was therefore considered a useless work, devoid of interest and even dangerous. The Holy Office and the Crown, pursuing their policy of Hispanization [of the Indians], acted in the same way. In 1577, as has been noted, Philip II prohibited writing of the customs of the Indians. As a consequence of this order, doubtless, the *Coloquios* of the Twelve collected by Sahagún were not published, and the greater part of the work disappeared.[91] The Holy Office forbade the translation of sacred texts into common speech, which caused the disappearance of perhaps three copies of the *Psalmodia* of Sahagún,[92] a collection of the Psalms translated into Nahuatl, and stopped the printing of the *Evangelios y epístolas de las misas de todo el año,* by Fray Arnaldo de Basaccio.[93] And Fray Alonso de Molina was reduced to requesting that at least the translations of the Holy Scriptures, with commentaries, be left in the hands of the Indians, "because it seems to me," he said, "that they would profit by them as no other Christians do." [94]

He had, besides, some personal difficulties with the Holy Office, although the charges against him seem to have been frivolous. He was asked to correct a passage in his *Vocabulario en lengua castellana y mexicana,* a second edition of which he had published in an enlarged edition in 1571. Apparently, it was only a question of a simple typographical error, and therefore Father Molina was not molested further.[95] The same cannot be said of his fellow religious, Maturino Gilberti, who was obliged to submit to a 17 years' trial (1559–1576).[96] Thanks to the valuable publication of Inquisition papers entitled *Libros y libreros en el siglo XVI,* this long trial is sufficiently well known. I shall only summarize it here to end this chapter, for it seems to me characteristic of the difficulties attending the labor of beginning the linguistic work in New Spain.

The occasion of the suit was Gilberti's publication, in 1559, of his *Diálogos de doctrina cristiana,* in Tarascan. Bishop Vasco de Quiroga of Michoacán [97] had entrusted its examination to two secular priests of his diocese, Diego Pérez Gordillo Negrón and Francisco de la Cerda, who were interpreters of Tarascan. Pressed by time, they were able to read only the first dialogue, which they judged to be very defective in its language, and to contain several "evil-sounding and scandalous propositions." They stated further that there was no agreement between the Tarascan text and the Castilian translation that Fray Maturino had made of it, and that it gave the impression of two distinct works. Besides, they showed two passages of questionable translations to the Franciscan provincial and to Father Gilberti, which the latter admitted would have to be corrected. As a consequence, Archbishop Montúfar,[98] who was charged with the duties of Inquisitor before the formal establishment of the Holy Office, prohibited the sale of the work and ordered the volumes already sold to be seized. This did not prevent Fray Maturino (I am following the fragmentary records of the suit) from telling his Indians that the provincials of the three Orders had approved his book and that he would secretly restore to them the copies that had been confiscated. At the same time he warned them to beware of the priests coming from Spain (perhaps he had in mind the Jesuits as well as the seculars), and he beseeched them to trust only the religious of St. Francis, St. Dominic, and St. Augustine. He was brought to Mexico City to face the vicar general, who, in his manifest obsession with Protestantism, asked him to explain several passages in his book concerning the Trinity, the cult of images, the faith, the good works of sinners, the words of the *Pater Noster* "et dimitte nobis, etc.," and baptism. The result of this interrogation was a confirmation of the original sentence, that is, the prohibition and confiscation of the *Diálogos.*

But the affair rebounded, because the Franciscans paid no attention to the order and continued to make use of the book, and Quiroga's successor, Antonio Ruiz Morales, was unable to stop them. Toward the end of 1571, when the Inquisition had just been formally established, he again brought the matter to the attention of the Holy Office, accusing Gilberti, besides, of having translated a book, the author of which affirmed that faith without works sufficed for salvation (always the implication of Protestantism),[99] and of pursuing his campaign against the secular clergy. The *Diálogos* were subjected to a new examination, but this time very little was excised—only one proposition that was called erroneous and scandalous. The final decision is missing—perhaps there was none, because, although the attitude of Father Gilberti was open to criticism, his accusers were not altogether impartial.[100]

His trial appears, indeed, as an episode in the struggle between the regular clergy and the secular clergy, to which his principal adversaries belonged, and his case is evidently exceptional. But, as in Sahagún's troubles, [his case] illustrated the persecutions suffered by the religious who devoted themselves to linguistic and ethnographic researches for the purpose of training their colleagues and teaching the Indians. Similar conditions of work make their accomplishment even more meritorious. All these books represent not only arduous days of patient and meticulous labor, but also at times long hours of doubt, sadness, bitterness, and persecution.[101]

3 Geographic Distribution of Missions and Monasteries

a MISSIONARY, to begin his service, could not wait until he had profound knowledge of the country and its languages and civilization. He had to carry on simultaneously—and this was not one of the smallest difficulties of his task—a scientific study and a spiritual ground-breaking. We shall follow him in his work. We have seen his attitude toward native paganism; we have seen how his ethnographic and linguistic training was conceived and organized, and the discussions that it provoked. From this chapter forward we shall witness the actual founding of the Church; that is to say: the occupation of territory, preaching, and the administration of the sacraments, of which the first, baptism, marked the gathering of the neophytes into the Christian community, while the others held them together or renewed among them the grace that made them members of the soul and body of the Church.

It has been very difficult to fix the chronology of the apostolic diaspora and the monastic foundations of New Spain. The documents—correspondence, memoirs, semi-official chronicles, or administrative papers—are niggardly in precise information. At times they ignore chronology entirely; at others they give only round and very approximate figures.[1] Even the most painstaking writers are sometimes deceptive. They

Topia (F)

Peñol Blanco (F)

●DURANGO (F)

●Nombre de Dios (F)

●Sombrerete (F)

●ZACATECAS (F)

M   E   X   I

●Sentispac (F)

●Juchipila (F)

●Jalisco (F)

Ahuacatlán (F) ●

San Miguel el Grande (F) ●

●Etzatlán (F)

GUADALAJARA (F) ●   ●Tonalá (F)   Queré

Tlajomulco (F) ●   Poncitlán (F) ●   Ap

Cocula (F) ●   Chapala (F)   Ocotlán (F)

Axixic (F) ●

Zacoalco (F) ●   Yuriria (A) ●   Acá

Amacueca (F)   Cuitzeo (A)

Atoyac (F)   Jacona (A) ●   Huango (A) ●   Zinapécuaro (F) ●   Je

●Autlán (F)   Zapotlán (F) ●   Zacapú (F) ●

Zapotlán (F) ●   Tarécuato (F)   Santa Fe (F) ●   Cucupao (F) ●Charo (A)

Zapotitlán (F) ●   Erongarícuaro (F) ●   Tajimaro

Tuxpan (F)   VALLADOLID

Pátzcuaro (F) ●   ●Tiripitío (A)

Uruapan (F) ●   Tzintzuntzan (F)

Colima (F)

Tacámbaro (A)

Cupándaro (A) ●

(A). Augustinian
(F) Franciscan
(D) Dominican

Sketch Map of the
MENDICANT ESTABLISHMENTS
about 1570

TAMPICO (F)

Xilitla(A)

Tantoyuca (A)

Chapulhuacán(A)
Huejutla(A)
Pahuatlán(A)

Culhuacán(A)

Molango(A)

Metztitlán(A)

Ixmiquilpan(A)
Tututepec(A)

ongo(A)
Actopan(A)
Atotonilco(A)
Huauchinango (A)

Acatlán(A)
Tula(F)
Tulancingo(F)
c(F)
Tezontepec(A)
Epazoyuca(A)
Zempoala(F)

Otumba(F)
Tepeapulco(F)
Acolman(A)
Apan(F)
Cuautitlán(F)
Teotihuacán(F)
Ecatepec(D)
Tepetlaoztoc(D)
apotzalco(D)
Huexotla(F)
n(D)
MEXICO
Tetzcoco(F)
Chalco(F)
Chimalhuacán(D)
TLAXCALA(F)
Xochimilco(F)
Coatepec Chalco(F)
cuila(A)
Tlalmanalco(F)
Huejotzingo(F)
Mixquic(A)
Tenango(D)
co(A)
Totolapan(A)
Amecameca(F,D)
tlán(D)
Cholula(F)
PUEBLA(F,D)
Quecholac(F)
rnavaca(F)
Tetela(D)
Atlixco(F)
Acatzingo(F)
ayacapan(A)
Cuautinchan(F)
Tepeaca(F)
Yautepec(D)
Hueyapan(D)
Tecamachalco(F)
Yecapixtla(A)
Jantetelco(A)
Tecali(F)
Ocuituco(A)
Oaxtepec(D)
Atlatlahuca(A)
Zacualpan(A)
Izúcar(Iztucan)(D)
Tehuacán(F)
Chietla(A)
Tepeji(D)
Chiautla(A)
Zapotitlán(F)

Teutila(D)

Tonalá(D)
Coixtlahuaca(D)
Tlapa(A)
Tamazulapan(D)
Tanetze(D)
Teposcocula(D)
Yanhuitlán(D)
Villa Alta (D)
Tecomaxtlahuaca(D)
Achlutla(D)
Ixtepexi(D)
Totontepec(D)
Tlaxiaco(D)
Etla(D)
OAXACA(D)
Cuilapan(D)
Ocotlán(D)
Nejapa(D)
Jalapa(D)
Coatlán(D)
Tehuantepec(D)
Huaxolotitlán
Huamelula(D)

contradict one another in their dates, or fail to agree, as in the case of Arlegui's book, however precious it may [otherwise] be. The confusion is increased frequently by our inability to make out precisely to what the date they give us refers, for it is not always clear that it refers to the first installation of the missionaries at a given point, or to the beginning of the construction of a house—which could be either a sumptuous monastery or a very humble residence—or even the canonical founding of a convent.[2] Fortunately, among the documents there are several healthy exceptions: Mendieta, Tello, and Beaumont, among the Franciscans; Grijalva and Sicardo, among the Augustinians; and, to some extent, Padilla, Burgoa, and Méndez, among the Dominicans. These documents do not amount to much, but they do give us a base. The data they supply, collated with the vaguer information from other sources, allow one to outline the history of the progressive expansion of the three Mendicant Orders across New Spain between 1524 and 1572.

In 1524 the Friars Minor founded convents in two territories that were to become the principal fields of their apostolic activity: the Valley of Mexico and the region of Puebla. In each they installed two houses, selecting for this purpose large native centers of exceptional political and religious importance: Tlaxcala and Huejotzingo, in the Puebla region; Texcoco and Churubusco, in the Valley of Mexico, where the temples of Huitzilopochtli had stood, from which they were soon to remove to the City of Mexico itself.[3] The first villages that the Fathers catechized, [operating] from Mexico, were Cuauhtitlán and Tepotzotlán.[4] Besides these, in the very early days the valley of Toluca, Michoacán, the region of Jilotepec (Mexico), and Tula (Hidalgo) were attached to the convent of Mexico City. Texcoco had jurisdiction over Otumba, Tepeapulco, Tulancingo (these last two in the present state of Hidalgo), as well as all the country to the north between these towns and the [Gulf] coast. Tlaxcala had jurisdiction over Zacatlán and its mountains, as well as the region of Jalapa and Vera Cruz. Finally, Huejotzingo was given [jurisdiction over] Cholula, Tepeaca, Tecamachalco, Tehuacán, Huaquechula, Chietla, and all the Mixteca.[5] This was an entirely provisional organization of short duration, for the very multiplicity of the Franciscan foundations, and the arrival and expansion of the other Orders, made it ephemeral.

The period of 1525–1531 is the principal one in the development of the Franciscan apostolate in New Spain, a period of consolidation of the Order's positions in the Puebla region: the founding of the convent of Tepeaca by Fray Juan de Rivas; in the region of Mexico City, the founding of Cuauhtitlán, Tlamanalco, Coatepec-Chalco, Toluca,[6] and the construction of San Francisco de México.[7] It is marked by a thrust toward the region of Tampico (the mission of Pánuco having been founded about 1530 by Fray Andrés de Olmos).[8] It is also marked by the penetration of the region included today in the state of Morelos and the southern part of the state of Mexico. The convent of Cuernavaca was founded in 1525, and from it the Fathers visited Ocuila and Malinalco.[9] It is marked above all by their penetration into Michoacán and New Galicia. In 1525 Caltzontzin, the king of Michoacán, begged Martín de Valencia to send him some friars,[10] and in 1526 the Franciscans came to Tzintzuntzan, the heart and holy city of the Tarascan community, where Fray Martín de Jesús founded a convent.[11] In the following years, and in spite of vicissitudes, the Franciscans successively founded Pátzcuaro, Acámbaro, Zinapécuaro, Uruapan, and Tarécuato.[12] Then followed a certain number of other residences, of which I shall mention only the most important: Erongarícuaro, Guayangareo (Valladolid, now Morelia), and Zacapu.[13] But one should not give this imposing list too much weight, for some of the convents were certainly only modest houses, flanked by small chapels, with no resident priest, served from the principal convents. Such, for example, was the first status of Pátzcuaro and Erongarícuaro, which were visited from Tzintzuntzan.[14] Elsewhere, the first foundations of New Galicia were made in 1531: Tetlán (soon to be replaced by Guadalajara), Colima, and Axixic, [this last] on the shore of Lake Chapala.[15] After 1531, therefore, the main directions of the Franciscan apostolate are apparent: the immediate environs of the capital; those relatively distant (Morelos, Hidalgo); the regions of Puebla, Michoacán, and New Galicia. The northward drive toward the mines in the Chichimeca (Zacatecas, Durango), and the apostolic explorations, such as that of Sinaloa by Fray Juan de Tapia, appear only as the inevitable extension of the spiritual occupation of New Galicia.

It would be tedious to insert here a table of the Franciscan foundations from 1531 to 1572. I shall mention only the principal stages. In the regions of Mexico City and Puebla, after the kind of fever of all the first years, the founding activity died down. The country was occupied, and the task was now to stabilize it. The chroniclers, however, were more interested in supplying dates for the origins of missions than in their development. This lack of dates gives the impression of a collapse after the fever. Thus many convents were founded around Mexico City, in Hidalgo, and in the state of Puebla certainly before 1572, perhaps a great while before. The dates of the founding of Tlalnepantla, Xochimilco, Huexotla, Otumba, Tula, Zempoala (which had been given up by the Augustinians), Cholula, Atlixco, and Tehuacán cannot be safely determined. A few dates, some more or less certain, the others only approximate, float to the surface like flotsam about 1540 in the Puebla region: Tecamachalco, Quecholac, and Tecali.[16] The founding of Tecamachalco was perhaps the beginning of the evangelization of the Popoloca, which had been delayed by the difficulty of the language.[17] The evangelization of the Matlalzinca was begun in 1543 by Fray Andrés de Castro, in the valley of Toluca. It had been neglected up to that time, for it seems that no one knew their complicated language.[18] In 1548 the construction of the convent of Calpan, near Huejotla, was begun;[19] in 1555–1557, during the tenure of the provincial Fray Francisco de Bustamante, the convent of Cuautinchán (Puebla), a village already occupied by the Franciscans, but abandoned for lack of personnel;[20] toward 1558, Acatizingo, not far from Tepeaca;[21] in 1559, the convent of San Juan Teotihuacán, after the return of the Franciscans who had already evangelized that village;[22] toward 1570, San Martín Zapotitlán, among the Popoloca of the state of Puebla;[23] toward 1571, Tepetitlán, near Tula;[24] and, toward 1572, the beginning of the construction of the convent of Apam (Hidalgo).[25] The Mexican mission was at first (1525) attached to the province of San Gabriel de Extremadura as a simple custody, but in 1535 was made an autonomous province, La Provincia del Santo Evangelio.

The [Franciscan] missions of Michoacán, and especially those of New Galicia, developed at the same time, and the thrust toward the uncivilized territories of the north was sketched out and then made precise and firm. In 1533 Fray Juan de Padilla founded a small convent at Zapotlán, the future Ciudad Guzmán [Jalisco],[26] and in 1535 Fray Francisco Lorenzo founded Etzatlán, near Lake Magdalena, the first point of entry into Nayarit, Durango, and Zacatecas.[27] In that same year the Michoacán-Jalisco mission was raised to the rank of a custody of the Provincia del Santo Evangelio, with the name of San Pedro y San Pablo.[28] Three years later the great apostolic explorations in the north began: in 1538, indeed, by order of the provincial Fray Antonio de Ciudad-Rodrigo, Fray Juan de la Asunción and another religious, unidentified, had explored Sinaloa.[29] A little later, at the end of that year, Fray Marcos de Niza, accompanied by the convert Fray Honorato, left Tonalá (Jalisco) for Culiacán, and set out for the north on March 7. He traversed Sinaloa and Sonora, where he left Fray Honorato, who was ill, and later discovered the fantastic "Seven Cities."[30]

I shall not dilate upon the participation of the Franciscans in the expeditions over all the northwest of Mexico, in which the friars served especially as chaplains to the military and at the same time as explorers. Moreover, these excursions left few lasting results. The foundations were precarious, and evangelization was difficult and superficial. Their dates, moreover, are full of uncertainties. On the other hand, toward 1542, Fray Miguel de Bolonia established himself at Juchipila, from which he later explored all territory to the south of Zacatecas.[31] In 1546, Fray Jerónimo de Mendieta and other Friars Minor appeared at the site of the [future] city of Zacatecas.[32] Then, beginning in 1553,[33] the same religious made the great apostolic expeditions into Nueva Vizcaya, that is, the region of the present states of Durango and Zacatecas.[34] Finally, in 1556, Fray Juan de Tapia made his long journey across Durango and Sinaloa.[35]

While a few pioneers were thus scouting in these vast and mysterious stretches, in their rear the main body of the army was consolidating its positions. In 1540, [the convent of] Jalisco was founded, in Nayarit;[36] in 1542, Autlán[37] and Guadalajara (which replaced Tetlán), and Tonalá, close by;[38] in 1547, Amacueca, southwest of Lake Chapala;[39] in 1548, Chapala;[40] in 1549, San Miguel el Grande (now San Miguel de Allende, Guanajuato);[41] in 1550, Zacoalco, in Jalisco, and Ahuacatlán, in Nayarit;[42] finally, in 1551, Tlajomulco, not far from Guadalajara.[43] Even so, this chronological summary does not exhaust the list of convents founded in Jalisco before 1572. To it should be added, among others, the houses at

Ocotlán, Atoyac, Cocula, and Zapotitlán.[44] After that, when the preliminary exploration seemed to be sufficiently advanced and the moment at hand to take possession of the country, the foundations to the north, in Durango and Zacatecas, multiplied. In 1558, Nombre de Dios and Durango [were founded]; [45] in 1559, Topia, much farther to the northwest; [46] in 1560, San Bartolomé, the boldest far-northern point; [47] in 1561, Peñol Blanco, later removed to San Juan del Río.[48] But this consolidation was not easily effected. In 1564, the convent of Santa María de las Charcas, a distant post in Sinaloa, was destroyed by unsubjugated Indians and was not rebuilt until 1583.[49] Nevertheless, during the two following years, the development of the custody of Michoacán and New Galicia, with all its annexes and northern extensions, brought about a new canonical organization. In 1565, the custody was elevated to the rank of an independent province, San Pedro y San Pablo,[50] and, at the end of 1566, the custody of Zacatecas, with the five convents listed above, was created and attached to the Provincia del Santo Evangelio.[51] Almost immediately two [more] canonical establishments were founded: the convent of San Mateo de Sombrerete,[52] and that of San Francisco de Zacatecas,[53] completed in 1569, to serve the missions of the [west] coast, through the convent of Sentispac, Nayarit, southwest of Tuxpan.[54]

What characterizes the Franciscan expansion in New Spain is the freedom with which the Friars Minor were able to operate—not absolute freedom, of course, for they had to take into account a multitude of circumstances: climate, personnel, financial resources, the attitude of the natives, and the instructions of the bishops. But in its essential directions this expansion is noteworthy because it was not disturbed by any previous occupation. The Franciscans had a completely vacant territory at their disposal. Their two years' start over the Dominicans allowed them to install themselves in the center (Mexico-Puebla), and then to overflow into Michoacán and New Galicia, from which they pushed on to their northern missions. The expansion of the Dominicans was limited and conditioned by that of the Franciscans. The situation of the Augustinians was most delicate, for their predecessors had taken possession of all New Spain, strongly in some places, more weakly in others. They had to squeeze their missions into the gaps left by the

68

Franciscans and Dominicans, which is the reason why the geographical limits of their apostolate were much less sharply defined.

The expansion of the Order of Preaching Friars in New Spain may be described more briefly than that of the Franciscans. For one thing, it occurred in territories much less vast in extent; for another, the documents are less abundant and less precise. Fortunately the Dominican mission appears in a relatively simple way, in two groups of unequal importance, a dispersed activity (rather, insufficiently organized, it would seem, because they were annoyed by the presence of the Friars Minor) in the center of the country: the region of Puebla, the Valley of Mexico, Morelos, and a methodical and progressive apostolate in the whole region known as the Mixteca and Zapotecas, with the city of Oaxaca as its center.

When the Dominicans arrived in Mexico, in July, 1526, they were housed in a modest and temporary installation, and in 1529 removed to the convent that they had had especially built for them.[55] Beginning with 1528 they administered at least three native parishes: the village of Oaxtepec in the present state of Morelos, where their convent and hospital can still be seen, now occupied by a rural normal school; the villages of Chimalhuacán-Chalco and Coyoacán, very near the capital.[56] According to Mendieta, the convent of Izúcar (de Matamoros) was founded at about the same time.[57] This first installation was doubtless pointed toward the Mixteca, penetrated by Fray Francisco Marín and Fray Pedro Fernández, in 1538, by way of Acatlán. The house at Tepetlaoxtoc, between Texcoco and Otumba, was very probably founded in the first years of the mission, by Fray Domingo de Betanzos.[58] In any event, these convents appear in the list made by Méndez in 1538, all but Izúcar, that is, which had been only recently raised to the rank of a *vicaría*.[59] The convent of Puebla should also be assigned to this first period, for it was already in existence in 1535,[60] and was apparently made a *vicaría* by the chapter of 1540.[61] [But] there is no firm date before the year 1550, when the acts of the chapter mention the *vicaría* of Tepapayecan, in the diocese of Tlaxcala-Puebla,[62] and in the chapter held at the beginning of 1552 the house at Yautepec, near the stream of the same name in the present state of Morelos, is mentioned.[63] In 1554, the parish of Amecameca, at the foot of the Franciscan sanctuary of Sacromonte, was founded, and, before 1556, the parish of Tepoztlán, in the mission of Morelos.[64]

I do not wish to prolong this dry enumeration, but shall only mention that the Dominicans had, in 1572, besides the houses already listed, the following residences: Atzcapotzalco, in the valley of Mexico, completed in 1565 but founded earlier;[65] Coatepec-Chalco and Cuitlahuac, former Franciscan convents;[66] Chimalhuacán-Atenco;[67] Tenango [del Aire];[68] perhaps Ecatepec,[69] in the present state of Morelos; Tetela del Volcán and Hueyapan, both in the state of Puebla;[70] and, finally, in the diocese of Puebla, in addition to a number of secondary residences listed in López de Velasco,[71] the convent of Tepeji [de la Seda], which, like Izúcar, served as a liaison between the central mission and that of Oaxaca, just as Tetela and Hueyapan were the link between the valleys of Mexico and Puebla.

The central mission, in fact, despite its scattered appearance, was not entirely planless. The map shows that the Preaching Friars held all the southeast part of the present state of Mexico, and that, with Chalco, Tenango, Amecameca, Tetela-Hueyapan, Puebla, Izúcar, and Tepeji, their convents formed a more or less continuous line from Mexico City to the Mixteca. Their convents at Chila and Tonalá, more to the south, in the diocese of Tlaxcala-Puebla,[72] were in the Mixteca. It is noteworthy that the Dominicans strengthened their position in the Valley of Mexico by obtaining from the Franciscans the cession of Coatepec, and it was not their fault, as will be brought out below, that they failed to install themselves at Tehuacán, one of the keys to the Mixteca. The cession of Coatepec, nevertheless, and the incidents at Tehuacán, where the hostility of the natives prevented their equaling the success of the Franciscans, prove that they were troubled by the presence of their predecessors. Fortunately, the latter had soon pushed on to the west and north, and, possibly repelled by the aridity of the Mixteca and the difficulties of communication with the Zapotecas, completely neglected the south. Here the Dominicans found an immense and virgin domain, where they could have elbow room, where their activity could flourish unopposed, and where their effort would have the help of the episcopate. The first bishop of Oaxaca, Juan López de Zárate (1535–1555), short of personnel among the secular clergy, appealed for Dominicans.[73] Up to 1542 [fortunately] it was one of their own, Fray Julián Garcés, bishop of Tlaxcala, who had charge of the Upper Mixteca.[74] The Dominicans poured out over the Mixtec-Zapotec region with joyful ardor, and, by their zeal and success, made it so nearly an absolute monopoly that no one seems to have dreamed of contesting it.

In 1529, Fray Domingo de Betanzos sent Fray Gonzalo Lucero and Fray Bernardino de Minaya to Antequera, the latter as a simple deacon. Fray Gonzalo Lucero at once set about founding a monastery. Burgoa has preserved for us the deed for the land donated by the *cabildo* of Antequera, dated July 24, 1529.[75] At the same time [Lucero] visited the Mixtec and Zapotec villages of the vicinity, preached, and studied their languages, while Fray Bernardino built humble chapels.[76] This was a kind of prologue. By the connection it established between Oaxaca and Mexico City, it gave the Dominicans the opportunity to make contact with the tribes of the Upper Mixteca and to preach the Christian faith in Nahuatl. In 1538, when Fray Pedro Delgado was elected provincial, at the suggestion of [Bishop] Garcés he sent two religious there, Fathers Francisco Marín and Pedro Fernández, who entered the country at Acatlán, went on to Chila, and then descended to evangelize the valleys of Teposcolula and Yanhuitlán,[77] where convents were soon founded. Unfortunately, it is impossible to fix the precise date of the foundations in the Mixteca and Zapotecas, [which occurred] between 1538 and 1572. The Dominican documents tell us nothing about them.[78] So it is not possible, therefore, to establish in detail the progressive expansion of the Order there. In the Mixteca, it seems, at the request of [Bishop] López de Zárate, in 1548, it first spread out from Teposcolula and Yanhuitlán to the neighboring villages of Tlaxiaco and Achiutla.[79] The house at Coixtlahuaca, showing a slightly northward thrust, was already in existence in 1552.[80] To the northwest, Tonalá and Tamazulapan were established, the first before 1556, the latter before 1558.[81] The Teposcolula-Yanhuitlán group thus appears to have been the center of the dispersion of the Mixtec mission. Finally, in 1562, the existence of Tecomaxtlahuaca bears witness to a thrust to the southwest, and Teutila, near the present Jalapa de Díaz, to a sharp turn to the northwest, well beyond Coixtlahuaca.[82] The convents in Zapotecas are much less scattered, but are squeezed together in the region of Oaxaca City. Leaving out of the reckoning Antequera, which I have already mentioned, Etla and Cuilapan were both [established] before 1550; [83] Ixtepeji, before 1556; [84] Ocatlán, before 1562. [85]

The missionary expeditions from Antequera, however, hardly did more than mark out [the territory], leaving monasteries at great distances from one another. Indeed, they skirted or traversed the country of the fierce Mixe Indians, where penetration was very difficult. Beyond Ixtepeji, the eastern group included only Villa Alta de San Ildefonso, to which may possibly be added, between 1562 and 1591, Tanetze and Totontepec. To the southeast, on the route to Tehuantepec, where the Preaching Friars had established themselves before 1556, there were only two convents beyond Ocotlán in 1562, Nexapa and Jalapa [del Marqués]. Even the house at Tehuantepec was flanked only by that of Huamelula, that is, if I have correctly identified the Santa Catarina and Guametula spoken of by Méndez. [86] The southern group consisted only of Huaxolotitlán, a *doctrina* that the Dominicans had received from López de Zárate in 1554, [87] and Coatlán, a region marked for evangelization by the chapter of 1558. [88] The Dominican mission of Mixteca-Zapotecas appears therefore as a fairly dense network in the Mixteca, with its center at Teposcolula-Yanhuitlán, the territory in the vicinity of the city of Oaxaca, and a tentative installation in the Mixe country or on its border.

In its beginning the Mexican [Dominican] mission was directly under the superior general of the Order and was governed by a vicar-general. Later, it was attached to the Provincia de la Santa Cruz of Española, and, finally, by a bull of Pope Clement VII, of July 11, 1532, it was elevated to the rank of the autonomous Provincia de Santiago. At that date it included all houses in New Spain. In 1551, the general chapter of Santiago detached the dioceses of Chiapas and Yucatan, and the province of Coatzacoalcos-Tehuantepec, [all of] which, together with the dioceses of Guatemala, Nicaragua, and Honduras, formed the new Provincia de San Vicente de Chiapas. Coatzacoalcos and Tehuantepec, however, were soon restored to the province of Santiago. [89]

The Augustinians did not arrive in New Spain until 1533. By that time the Franciscans had founded many convents around Mexico City and in the Puebla region, were installed at Toluca, Cuernavaca, and in Michoacán, and had undertaken the evangelization of New Galicia. The Dominicans also had founded various houses in the vicinity of Mexico, and were established at Oaxtepec (Morelos) and Oaxaca. The great roads to evangelization were no longer open. Nevertheless, the mission network often lacked density. Enormous zones were untouched, and the Augustinians slipped into them—hence the capricious and at times confused design of their mission, which was obliged to mold itself into the inevitable lacunae of the Franciscan and Dominican apostolate.[90] Thus three essential directions can be distinguished in the activity of the Augustinians, outside the environs of Mexico. In chronological order, these are:

1) A southward thrust, toward the eastern border of the state of Guerrero, the foundations of which were soon attached to Mexico City along with those of eastern Morelos and the southwest part of the state of Puebla. This group was inserted between the Dominican mission of Morelos to the east and, toward the west, at first the Franciscan-Dominican group of Puebla, and later the Dominican houses of the Mixteca.

2) A northward thrust, among the Otomí of the state of Hidalgo, extended by the foundations in the Huaxteca to the borders of the states of Hidalgo, San Luis Potosí, and Vera Cruz. The Augustinian houses were at first wedged between the two Franciscan groups of Hidalgo (Tula-Tepetitlán and Zempoala-Tepeapulco), but when they reached the Huaxteca they found open air and spread out.

3) A westward thrust, toward Michoacán, with a string of houses at Tiripitío, Charo, and Yuriria, which were also wedged between two Franciscan groups. They were connected with Mexico City by way of the houses of the Toluca region.

Just as had happened with the missions of the Friars Minor and the Preaching Friars, these three directions were apparent from the first years. Like their predecessors, the Augustinians tended to take immediate possession of the field of their apostolate, to avoid all question of priority and all conflict of jurisdiction. The southern missions were founded as early as 1533. The provincial vicar, Fray Francisco de la Cruz, known as the Venerable Father, ordered Fray Jerónimo de San Esteban and Fray Jorge de Avila to evangelize the region of Tlapa and Chilapa, in the eastern part of the present state of Guerrero, by way of Ocuituco. These two religious, after stopping at Mixquic (Federal District), and especially at Totolapan, took possession of the latter village, where they decided to found a convent. Fray Jorge de Avila remained at Ocuituco, where he was soon joined by Fray Juan de San Román, while Fray Jerónimo de San Esteban, with a new companion, Fray Agustín de la Coruña, went on to Chilapa at the beginning of October [1533].[91] In 1534, houses were established at Totolapan, Ocuituco, and Chilapa, and, in 1535, at Yecapixtla, Zacualpan (both in Morelos), and Tlapa. To the south the Augustinians had no foundations beyond Tlapa and Chilapa; but between these two points and Mexico City they established several: Mixquic, perhaps in 1536; Chiautla, which had been decided upon by the chapter of 1550; Tlayacapan, by the chapter of 1554; Jumiltepec (?); Jonacatepec, by the chapter of 1566; and Atlatlahuaca (1570).[92]

The evangelization of the Otomí country and the Sierra Alta, toward the Huaxteca, was decided upon by the chapter of 1536, which ordered Fray Alonso de Borja, with two other religious, to found the convent of Atotonilco among the Otomí, and Fray Juan de Sevilla and Fray Antonio de Roa to found another in the Sierra Alta. These last two established themselves at Molango, although they had a good deal of trouble with the Indians. Father Borja undertook the construction of a vast church at Atotonilco.[93] From that time onward the foundations followed each other at fairly regular intervals: Epazoyuca (chapter of 1540); Actopan and Ixmiquilpan (1550); Tezontepec (1554); Acatlán (?) (1557); Chiapantongo (1566); Axacopan in the Otomí country (1569); Meztitlán, the establishment of which was decided in 1539, did not occur until 1543; Huejutla (1540–1545); Huachinango (1543); Jilitla (1550); Pahuatlán (1552); Culhuacán and Tantoyuca (1557), this last being in the northern part of the present state of Vera Cruz.

The founding of the western missions took place only a year after that of the eastern. It was, in fact, the chapter of 1537 that decided to send Fray Juan de San Román and Fray Diego de Alvarado (who was known as Chaves) to Tiripitío, and to found [a house at] Ocuila in the Toluca region on the road to Michoacán. The establishment of the Augustinians at Tiripitío was immediately followed, in that same year, by their descent into the hot country [of Michoacán], where they built a chapel at Tacámbaro.[94] The foundation at Ocuila was buttressed, in the chapter of 1540, by that of Malinalco, and, to a certain extent, in the chapter of 1550, by one at Cupándaro, in the hot country, about half way between Ocuila and Tacámbaro. In Michoacán, the favorite land of the early apostolate, the Augustinian foundations multiplied almost as fast as the Franciscan. Within a few years, from the chapter of 1550 to that of 1554, there were no fewer than seven, not counting Cupándaro: Cuitzeo, Yuriria (now in the state of Guanajuato), Guayangareo (Valladolid, now Morelia), Huango, Charo, Ucareo, and Jacona. The Franciscan houses were grouped around Lake Pátzcuaro, which the Friars Minor had justly recognized as the heart of Tarascan civilization; the Augustinian houses had as their main axis the line of Tiripitío-Guayangareo-Charo, and spilled over into the hot country, which the Franciscans had hardly touched, leaving that field entirely open.

Up to 1545 the Augustinian mission was attached to the province of Castile. In that year it was made the autonomous Provincia del Santo Nombre de Jesús.

I have attempted to present as clearly as possible the picture of the missionary expansion of the three primitive Orders across the immensity of New Spain. The map will allow the reader to see the respective positions of the three Orders in 1570, toward the end of the pioneering period, a geographical view that will sharpen the historical account I have presented. Besides, it will enable me to bring out several characteristic traits in the development of the Mexican mission.

The reader will see at once that the heart of the country, that is, the valley of Mexico and its surrounding regions, has a very peculiar look. With hardly an exception, no methodical distribution was made there among the three Orders, and the various convents are mixed up in an almost inextricable fashion. The Augustinian Acolman is next door to the Dominican Tepetlaoxtoc and the Franciscan Texcoco, Teotihuacán and Otumba. The present state of Morelos, to be sure, was systematically divided: the Augustinians taking the eastern part, with Ocuituco, Yecapixtla, Totolapan, and so on; the Dominicans, the center, with Tepoztlán, Oaxtepec, and so on; the Franciscans, the west, with Cuernavaca.[95] But this is a very small region, and the convents were not greatly distant from one another. Yecapixtla, Yautepec, and Cuernavaca were very close together; Oaxtepec was only two steps from Tlayacapan. Moreover, proceeding to the west and northwest, one finds the same confusion in the region between Cuernavaca and Toluca as in the Valley of Mexico. Leaving to one side, therefore, this central region, the missionary expansion, about the year 1570, may be sketched as follows:

The Franciscans.—The apostolic thrust of the Franciscans, as shown on the map, was in two main directions: one, to the southeast of Mexico City; the other, to the west and northwest. The first direction is represented by what may be called the Puebla-Tlaxcala group, with its great convents at Puebla, Cholula, Huejotzingo, Tepeaca, Atlixco, and the two foundations of Tehuacán and Zapotitlán in the south of the state, toward the Oaxaca region. The second direction is more complex and must be considered in its several parts:

a) The Hidalgo-Querétaro group, with the convents of Tula and Jilotepec to the east; those of San Miguel el Grande, Apaseo, and Acámbaro (already attached to the Michoacán mission) to the west. This latter group was in contact with the Augustinian houses of Michoacán and, through these, with the Augustinian houses in the Otomí country.

b) The Michoacán group, centered on Lake Pátzcuaro, with convents at Tzintzuntzan, Pátzcuaro, Quiroga (Cucupao), Erongarícuaro, Uruapan, and so on. This group was connected with the preceding by the houses at Valladolid (Morelia) and Zinapécuaro.

c) The Jalisco group, centered on Guadalajara, with convents on Lake Chapala (Axixic, Chapala, Ocotlán), and two other points: to the south, the Guadalajara-Colima line, with foundations at Zacualco, Amacueca, Zapotlán, and Zapotitlán; to the northwest, the Guadalajara-Jalisco line, with [convents at] Etzatlán and Ahuacatlán, which marked a transition toward the Zacatecas-Durango group.

d) The Zacatecas-Durango group, which had not been entirely stabilized by 1570, a territory for conquest rather than a systematic apostolate, with houses at Zacatecas, Nombre de Dios, Sombrerete, Durango, and so on.

The Dominicans.—Geographically, the apostolate of the Dominicans appears to be the simplest, for, outside the central region, their activity occured almost entirely within a single zone, in which they enjoyed an almost absolute monopoly, that is, the Mixteca and Zapotecas, with two principal centers of expansion, Teposcolula-Yanhuitlán and Antequera de Oaxaca. Their mission was connected with Mexico City by their line of convents in Puebla and the southeast part of the Valley of Mexico.

The Augustinians.—The map clearly shows the three main directions of the Augustian apostolate:

a) The southern thrust, toward Tlapa and Chilapa, marked by the line [of convents] at Mixquic, Ocuituco, Jantetelco, Chietla, and Chiautla.

b) The northern thrust, in what is now the state of Hidalgo, and in the north of the states of Puebla and Vera Cruz (Otomí and Huaxteca country), with convents in the Pachuca region (at Epazoyuca, Atotonilco, Actopan, and so on), and the Meztitlán-Molango group with its dependencies.

c) The westward thrust, marked by the Michoacán mission and the houses that connected it with Mexico City. In Michoacán the Augustinian foundations were wedged in between group *a* and group *b* of the Franciscan foundations. In this region, however, the Augustinians pushed farther to the south than the Friars Minor and descended into the hot country.

An examination of the distribution of convents of the three Orders allows one to distinguish, without too much strain, I believe, three types of missions: the mission of occupation, the mission of penetration, and the mission of liaison.

I am calling "missions of occupation" those sectors in which the convents occur in a relatively dense network, within a reasonable distance of one another, and in which they may be grouped about a center. Outside the Valley of Mexico, this type included the Franciscan missions in the

Puebla region, the Franciscan and Augustinian missions of Michoacán, the Dominican missions in the Mixteca, and the Franciscan missions in the Guadalajara region.

Each Order furnishes an example of the second type, the mission of penetration, represented by the precarious establishment of sporadic houses in zones of difficult relief, unpleasant climate, not yet pacified, or on the border of unsubjugated territories: the Friars Minor, with their foundations at Guanajuato; the Preaching Friars, with their mission among the Mixe (Oaxaca); the Augustinians, with their mission in Guerrero. These missions accompanied or preceded the military conquest, while [the missions of occupation] followed it and, by force of circumstances, consolidated it.

Finally, I consider as "missions of liaison" the strings of convents which, instead of appearing in groups like the first kind, appear in a more or less straight line, connecting any group whatever with the City of Mexico. The Dominican establishment of Puebla, which included the Mixtec mission and that of the Valley of Mexico, seems to me the most characteristic example. In the same category may be placed the Augustinian mission in Morelos, the link between the house in Mexico City and those of Guerrero; also, the Augustinian mission in the Toluca region, which served as the link between the house of Mexico and those of Michoacán. It was very important to the progress of the apostolate that the religious might move from one mission to the next without going outside the jurisdiction of the Order. They would thus be more certain of a proper resting place and a cordial welcome, and the docility and respect of the natives; they would avoid friction with other Orders and unpleasantness with Indians under different rule; finally, they would be less exposed [to the necessity of] living outside their accustomed atmosphere, and could more easily observe their rules—these hospitable relations contributed to hold together and strengthen ties between religious of the same Order, and to assure unity of method and action.

The development of the Mexican mission, which may be likened to a military conquest and occupation, is also like it in the care with which the religious destroyed all strongholds of native paganism and installed themselves in them afterward. Many foundations, especially in the course of the first years, were established in pre-Hispanic religious centers. I have already mentioned this in the case of Churubusco, Texcoco, Tlaxcala, and Huejotzingo, to which could be added Cholula, Tula, Huexotla (in the state of Mexico), Teotihuacán, Cuernavaca, Tepoztlán, Yecapixtla, Tzintzuntzan, Charo, Zapotlán, Achiutla, and many others. This is a characteristic that we shall rediscover when we examine the influence of missionary conditions upon conventual architecture.

Certain other factors affected the distribution of mission sites. The principal ones also had to do with the two interlocutors (if I may be permitted the expression) of the apostolic dialogue: the Indian community and the friars. It is evident that the missionaries, when they established themselves at a given spot, had to anticipate the reaction of the natives, whose disposition was not always favorable. For example, the hostility of the Tarascans according to Zumárraga, twice forced the Franciscans to abandon Michoacán at the very beginning of their mission.[96] I have already mentioned how the convent at Santa María de las Charcas was destroyed by unsubjugated Indians. The same thing happened to the convents at Topia and San Bartolomé.[97] In like fashion the Augustinian convent at Jilitla was attacked several times by the Chichimecas, who partly burned it in 1587.[98] The Christian Indians, even those who had been seriously converted, also played their part. In general they were deeply attached to their first missionaries, who had initiated them into the new faith,[99] and their influence certainly restricted the exchanges [of missions] that occurred at times between the Orders, as I have already indicated. When the Dominicans undertook to establish themselves at Cuauhtinchán, by agreement with the superiors of the Franciscans, who had withdrawn their friars and reduced the village to a simple *vista* of Tepeaca, the natives stripped the church of its ornaments, refused to supply the friars with food, and went off to attend services at the Franciscan houses of Tepeaca and Tecali. By this action they achieved the return of their former pastors and the construction of a Franciscan convent.[100] At Teotihuacán and Tehuacán similar incidents had the same origin and the same outcome.[101]

In the last mentioned case, and probably in the other two also, the Franciscans had to withdraw for lack of personnel. The total number of active missionaries in New Spain in the middle year of 1559 could be impressive (380 Franciscans, 210 Dominicans, and 212 Augustinians, or 802 altogether), especially if they are compared with the sometimes skeletal personnel of present-day missions,[102] but it should not delude us. One must subtract from this number, as I have already had occasion to remark, a large number of religious who could not actively take part in the ministry: the lay brothers, the novices, the students, the aged and the infirm, and, up to a point, the whole headquarters staff of provincials, guardians, priors, and deputies [of chapters], all of whom were prevented by their administrative duties from dedicating themselves entirely to the direct apostolate among the natives. This shortage of personnel was most keenly felt, naturally, during the first years. The early foundations in Michoacán were limited by the small number of religious, five or six.[103] The same circumstance forced the Augustinians, in 1536, to cede Santa Fe, near Mexico City, to the secular clergy,[104] and [obliged] the Franciscans, in 1538, to consider relinquishing Cuauhtitlán, Xochimilco, and Cholula, although the resistance of the Indians prevented their doing so.[105] Nevertheless, at a late date, 1568, the Franciscan provincial, Fray Miguel Navarro, decided to give up seven or eight convents for lack of personnel—Tehuacán is an example.[106] The number of active missionaires had increased, but the needs were greater and the task required more workers. On the other hand, although the problem of recruiting was never acute, mortality among the missionaries was very heavy, for they were frequently badly or insufficiently fed, and were prematurely worn out by excessive toil in an unhealthy climate.[107]

The shortage of personnel was aggravated by bad distribution. The Orders at times solicited or accepted charge of immense territories, the evangelization of which was beyond their strength, but in which they would not admit other religious or secular priests.[108] Besides, convents frequently multiplied and religious thronged in certain regions where life was easy, abundant, and agreeable,[109] while personnel could not be found to undertake the evangelization of distant, poor, and desolate lands with a harsh or pernicious climate. The Crown was obliged to remind them, in a *cédula* dated at Madrid, March 17, 1553, that the monastic foundations had the duty of looking after the spiritual needs of the country, not "the consolation and pleasure" of the religious called to live in the new convents.[110] Four years later it repeated the charge,[111] and in a *cédula* dated at Aranjuez, March 4, 1561, Philip II ordered that the monasteries must be built at least six leagues apart. "We have been informed," said he, "that monasteries are built very close together, because the religious prefer to establish themselves in the rich green lands near the city of Mexico, leaving stretches of twenty to thirty leagues untended, because the religious avoid the rough, poor, and hot regions." [112]

The high plateaus of the north and of New Galicia were particularly neglected, as Fray Angel de Valencia and his deputies had foreseen in 1552,[113] and the greater number of religious would not go there. In 1561, the second bishop of New Galicia, Fray Pedro de Ayala, begged Philip II to send him some Franciscans for his poor diocese, because the religious at his disposal were aged and worn out, and the new ones preferred to remain in easier and more agreeable dioceses, such as Mexico and Michoacán.[114] His testimony is confirmed by the Licenciado Oseguera, who wrote in 1563 that Franciscans could not be found for New Galicia because of the sterility of the country and the barbarism of the natives.[115] Two days later, the bishop in his turn emphasized the matter.[116] The problem was not soon solved, for two years later he was still complaining of the trouble he was having in recruiting personnel for his diocese. The priests, secular or regular, he said, who arrived from Spain preferred to install themselves in the dioceses of Tlaxcala, Mexico, and Michoacán, where everything attracted them, and would not come as far as New Galicia, which had been described to them as an exceedingly hot country, without resources, scantily populated, speaking various languages, and abounding in poisonous snakes, where one ran the risk of being murdered or flayed by some band of Chichimecas.[117] These justified complaints [of the bishop] had little effect, to judge by a letter of Philip II, dated at Madrid, January 27, 1572, in which he begged the general of the Franciscan Order to authorize the dispatch of twelve Friars Minor to New Galicia, which, he said, was badly in need of religious for the apostolate of the Indians.[118]

This insistence on the part of Fray Pedro de Ayala shows us that elements other than the actions of the Indians and of the friars themselves were at work, although much less deeply. I shall take up elsewhere the relations of the regular clergy with the episcopate and the secular clergy, also with the temporal power, although they are of interest here only so far as they were affected by the geographic directions of the evangelization and the distribution of the missions. The hostility or the favor of the Ordinary was one of the circumstances that the religious had to bear in mind before establishing themselves in a region. We have seen the part played by [Julián] Garcés and López de Zárate in the beginning of the Dominican mission of Mixteca-Zapotecas. If we may believe Burgoa, it was persecutions by the secular clergy that forced the Dominicans to abandon Villa Alta and its region for a while, and it was the combined action of the Crown, the viceroy, and the Audiencia that persuaded them later to reverse their decision.[119] Although it goes without saying that the religious penetrated no region without the consent of the temporal authorities, these [authorities] did intervene in the most decided fashion. Every apostolic exploration in the north was made by the Franciscans in close collaboration with Viceroy Mendoza, Coronado, and Ibarra. It was also at the demand of Vasco de Quiroga, at the time merely a member of the Audiencia, that Fray Alonso de Borja founded the Augustinian convent of Santa Fe, near the capital.[120] This positive action of the episcopate and certain functionaries did not, however, amount to much. In the spiritual penetration, the choice of routes and the founding of monasteries, the initiative and the zeal of the Mendicants hold the first rank by long odds. There, as elsewhere, regardless of the merits of the great bishops, they were the kingpins of the young Mexican Church.

4 *Prebaptismal Instruction and the Administration of Baptism*

IF o n e limits the scope of the word "church" to the existence of a certain number of Christians in the charge of a few priests, the Mexican Church was created very quickly, for baptism was administered to the Indians from the beginning and without delay. Admission to the Church was not preceded by any proper catechumenate, a relatively recent institution which had not been really active since the fourth and fifth centuries, and which was not reestablished until the nineteenth, and then only in mission countries.[1] It was virtually unknown in the missions of the sixteenth century.[2] In the [East] Indies, for example, at the time St. Francis Xavier arrived there, the custom was to baptize in great numbers, without previous instruction. "Conversion," says Father Brou, "took place, so to speak, in three stages: acceptance in principle of the more important dogmas, briefly explained, baptism, and catechism."[3] The Saint himself baptized his pagans before completing their instruction.

The same routine was followed in Mexico, where, as in the East Indies, haste was at times excessive. The synod of 1555 forbade the baptism of adults who were insufficiently instructed and not legally married ("natural marriage" is to be understood here), and who had not completely and definitely abandoned idolatry, or made restitution of what they may have unjustly kept.[4] Nevertheless, it should not be believed that the missionaries of New Spain had fallen into the excesses, with respect to the Indians, which were to be severely reprimanded in the seventeenth century, in the *Instructions* for foreign missions; that is, haste in listing the names of the baptized, excessive credulity in the admission of candidates, and exaggerated alacrity in the administration of baptism.[5] Pagans were [indeed] accepted for baptism with great facility, and were not obliged to suffer a long delay; but none was admitted to the Church without a preliminary training, as is attested by many documents and cases. This is why, at the beginning of their apostolate, the Augustinians baptized few Indians, because they thought there were not enough priests to prepare them properly for the sacrament.[6] Mendieta earnestly says that candidates were instructed before baptism,[7] and we know that Fray Francisco Lorenzo did not baptize a single adult without previous instruction.[8] We also know that Pedro de Gante used his young pupils to prepare the pagans for baptism,[9] and that if Ixlilxochitl, the lord of Texcoco, and his vassals were baptized by Martín de Valencia upon the latter's arrival in 1524, it was because they had already been instructed by Fray Pedro de Gante, who had arrived the year before.[10]

Even so, Pedro de Gante had had time to instruct his disciples carefully. Most frequently he satisfied himself with giving them a brief training only in the essentials, that is: a single omnipotent God, eternal, all-good and all-knowing, Creator of everything; the Holy Virgin; the immortality of the soul; and demons and their perfidies. Such, according to Motolinía, were the dogmas to which [the missionaries] limited themselves when they prepared the Indians for baptism.[11] This, more or less, was what was proposed to the Indians of New Galicia in 1541: They were asked to believe in a single God, Creator of heaven and earth, and Creator of man, soul and body; original sin; the divinity of Jesus Christ; heaven and hell; good and bad angels; and the recognition of themselves as subjects of the Pope and the Emperor.[12] The Augustinians admitted the pagans to Mass before baptism. After [the reading of] the Gospel, a preacher explained the meaning of the ceremonies, and, to emphasize the difference [between them and] pre-Hispanic rites, pointed out the nonsanguinary nature of the [Christian] sacrifice. "God," he said, "does not demand, as your idols do, the lives and hearts of men. It is He Himself who descends to the altar to pour out His graces upon His servants." Thereupon he gave them a brief lesson in the catechism. The Indians were not admitted to baptism until they had learned the *Pater Noster,* the *Credo,* the *Commandments* of God and the Church, and not until they had formed an adequate notion of the nature of the sacraments.[13]

We should not look too severely upon this preliminary examination, for these people, as Motolinía tells us, with their fearful and timid character, were easily troubled, and some of them were so moved that they could not repeat a word of the prayers that they knew perfectly. Could the gates of the Kingdom of God be closed to these simple souls, full of good will?[14] They may have lacked the "knowledge of the mind," but they did have the "knowledge of the soul."[15] Much less was required of the sick, who were asked only sincerely to repent of their sins and to believe truly in the efficacy of the sacrament.[16]

The administration of baptism, therefore, was always preceded by a more or less summary, more or less hasty, instruction, depending upon the case and the circumstances. Unfortunately we are much less informed about this preliminary instruction than about the catechism that followed baptism, which will be taken up in the next chapter. To my knowledge, details and precise information are supplied only by a single document, the *Pláticas* of Fray Bernardino de Sahagún, which were discovered by Father Pascual Saura and published in 1924 by Father Pou y Marti.[17]

These *Pláticas* are nothing else than the first sermons preached by the Twelve to the chiefs and pagan priests of Mexico, collected in Spanish by Sahagún and translated into Nahuatl at his direction. We have the original and the translation, but neither is complete. The *Pláticas* were to have filled two books. In Spanish we have only the first thirteen chapters of Book 1, and the beginning of the fourteenth, and in Nahuatl the first fourteen chapters complete.[18] Sahagún tells us of these two books: "The first includes thirty chapters containing all conversations, discourses, and sermons that occurred between the twelve religious and the chiefs, lords, and satraps of the idols, up to the moment they accepted the faith of Jesus Christ and very insistently demanded baptism. The second book treats of

85

the catechism, that is to say, of the Christian doctrine. It has twenty-one chapters containing the catechism and the Christain doctrine, and all adults who wish to be baptized should first of all be instructed in them." [19] The essential part, consequently, is missing, that is, the catechism proper; but the preliminary discourses of the Twelve, nevertheless, are extremely interesting.

"Do not believe," said the missionaries to the lords of Mexico,

that we are gods. Fear not, we are men as you are. We are only messengers sent to you by a great lord called the Holy Father, who is the spiritual head of the world, and who is filled with pain and sadness by the state of your souls. These are the souls he has charged us to search out and save. We desire nothing better, and for that reason we bring you the book of the Holy Scriptures, which contains the words of the only true God, Lord of heaven and earth, whom you have never known. This is why we have come. We do not seek gold, silver, or precious stones; we seek only your health.

The missionaries then explain who the Pope is and what the Scriptures are. But who is this God, whose representative on earth is the Pope, and whose revelation is contained in the Scriptures?

You have a god, you say, whose worship has been taught to you by your ancestors and your kings. Not so! You have a multitude of gods, each with his function. And you yourselves recognize that they deceive you; you insult them when you are unhappy, calling them *putos y bellacos*. And what they demand of you in sacrifice is your blood, your heart. Their images are loathsome. On the other hand (and here I translate, for the passage is not without beauty), the true and universal God, Our Lord, Creator and Dispenser of being and life, as we have been telling you in our sermons, has a character different from that of your gods. He does not deceive; He lies not; He hates no one, despises no one; there is nothing evil in Him. He regards all wickedness with the greatest horror, forbids it and interdicts it, for He is perfectly good. He is the deep well of all good things; He is the essence of love, compassion, and mercy. And He showed His infinite mercy when he made Himself Man here on earth, like us; humble and poor, like us. He died for us and spilled His precious blood to redeem us and free us from the power of evil spirits. This true God is called Jesus Christ, true God and true Man, Dispenser of being and life, Redeemer and Savior of the world. Being God, He has no beginning; He is eternal. He created heaven and earth and hell. He created us, all the men in the world, and He also created the devils whom you hold to be gods and

86

whom you call gods. This true God is everywhere; He sees all, knows all; He is altogether admirable. As Man, He is in His royal palace, and here below, on earth, He has His Kingdom, which He began with the beginning of the world. He would have you enter it now, and for this you should consider yourselves blessed.

The terrestrial Kingdom of Jesus Christ is the Catholic Church. No one can enter His Heavenly Kingdom without having been His subject in this world. The Holy Father is the head of the Church, and the kings and the Emperor owe him obedience. He has given the religious the power to receive into his Church those who desire to belong to it and are ready to renounce the cult of false gods. Then, after a polemic that I shall examine below, the Twelve return to the definition of God. They repeat in greater detail what they have already said. They explain the creation of the angels, the revolt of Lucifer, the part played by the devils and the good angels, the creation of the world and men. The full text stops here, but we have the titles of the missing chapters. The missionaries then spoke of original sin, the death of Abel, the confusion of tongues, the Church, and divine justice. If one may believe the summary, the decisive argument was the observation made by the religious during a digression on the favors granted by God to His servants, to the effect that the Indians had not been supported in the slightest by their deities, while the true and omnipotent God had allowed His faithful servants, the Spaniards, to conquer Mexico. It is after the two chapters on the subject, indeed, that the discourse occurs by which the lords and "satraps" declare themselves servants of the true God.[20]

Of Book 2, which contained the catechism proper, we have only the summary, but this summary is singularly precious, for it contains the details of the instruction given the pagans before baptism. The first eleven chapters, in fact, are devoted to the following matters (that which treats directly of God having been summarized in the preliminary discourses): the immortality of the soul, free will, obedience to the Church, the seven Articles of Faith relating to the divinity of Jesus Christ, the seven concerning His humanity, God's love, and the three Commandments of the Church, the love of one's neighbor and the seven commandments that define it, the works of grace, hope of the joys of heaven, baptism, the

Mass, the Eucharist, the sign of the cross, the *Pater* [*Noster*] and the *Credo*. Then follows the sermon preached to all the catechumens on the day of their baptism. The catechism continues: marriage, communion, repentance, the deadly sins, confirmation, the enemies of the soul. Two parts of this *Doctrina* can be distinguished: everything not absolutely necessary to the proper and valid reception of prebaptismal instruction has been eliminated; the rest is reserved for later instruction. Since no one could marry, take communion,[21] confess, or be confirmed without having been baptized, there was no difficulty in delaying the instruction relating to these sacraments.

If Motolinía's preliminary instruction represents a minimum, the *Pláticas* of the Twelve, on the contrary, doubtless represent a maximum. Some instructions about the various categories of angels, seraphim, cherubim, thrones, and dominations seem even to be superfluous and, for a primer, excessively complicated. Nothing is more probable than that Sahagún, who doubtless had access to odd notes, arranged them,[22] but it is difficult to believe, given his known scruples as a historian, that he allowed himself to make important additions. This was the first great public manifesto of the Twelve and their contact with the natives. Moreover, they were addressing an elite. They knew it, and perhaps they exaggerated the philosophical knowledge and intellectual capacity of the chieftains and priests. They probably thought also that if they could confine themselves to giving the common people a rudimentary training, it was necessary, on the other hand, that, before taking the decisive step, the elite should be very completely informed about the religion they were about to practice. [The missionaries] spared neither the precautions designed to dispel fears, nor the explanations necessary to overcome intellectual resistance, nor, finally, the precise and indispensable details, so that [the intellectual capacity of the Indians] might be dedicated in full knowledge of the subject.

It goes without saying that the question of prebaptismal teaching could apply only to adults, and to children of some maturity. Also, it arose only in the first years [of the Conquest]. In a country which was almost entirely under the domination of a Christian power, and in which the ecclesiastical authority could concern itself without difficulty to the task of necessary control, there was no objection to baptizing babies and very young children, even though they were not yet capable of receiving any instruction whatever.[23] As a rule the Franciscans baptised babies only on Sunday after Mass, when the Indians had to bring their new-born to the church. The Augustinians followed the same procedure in Michoacán, except when there was danger of death. In very populous regions, nevertheless, the Franciscans, conforming to the decision of the *Junta Eclesiástica* of 1524,[24] designated two days for it, Sunday after Mass and Thursday after vespers. But the Indians often preferred other days or other hours, or, more exactly, did not have these days or hours [free], and even came at night. It was, therefore, frequently necessary to depart from the rule, but not so much that it would shock them, or discourage those of good will, so they were assured of a welcome at all hours.[25]

Despite the concern and zeal of the missionaries, it might happen that adults were not baptized, or that children reached maturity without having received baptism. Difficulties arose from this situation which the religious solved ingeniously. Many such Indians, in fact, who were swept along in the general movement, did not dare admit they were not Christians, and took [Christian] names, confessed, took communion, and married as if they truly and regularly belonged to the Church. When an inquiry was made, or when the Indians, tormented by remorse, admitted [they had not been baptized] and their sacrilege was revealed, it was necessary to proceed with great tact and prudence, to avoid hopelessness and scandal. Far from scolding them for their negligence and prevarication, [the missionaries] joyfully received these timid or foolish souls, and to humor the self-respect of the false Christians, willingly baptized them in secret when requested. But if, to vanquish the fear that held others back, they preferred to be baptized in public, an effort was made to lend the ceremony the greatest solemnity, like the father celebrating the return of the prodigal. When the Indians were married, and one of the couple had not been baptized, the matter was still more delicate, if the unbaptized wished to keep the wife or the husband in ignorance. In such cases the religious, on one pretext or another, arranged for the husband and wife to join hands by mutual consent. Thus they were remarried, and the one who was a *bona fide* [Christian] did not suspect that the other had not been baptized when they were married *in facie Ecclesiae*. "And," the chronicle adds, "in this way it is done without difficulty, for by such good artifices these people are easily persuaded and induced to do whatever is proper." [26]

This, however, was only a small practical difficulty. Two others arose, one theological, the other ritualistic. The first was not anticipated. Were the Indians sufficiently reasonable creatures to be admitted to baptism? This objection, however absurd it may seem, was made [27] by the Dominican Fray Domingo de Betanzos, or, at least, it was attributed to him, doubtless mistakenly. Father Betanzos appears to have been an impetuous character, not well balanced, but not without intelligence. It is difficult to ascribe to him an opinion so contrary to good sense. Besides, there is nothing in his life to justify our thinking that he raised this objection in bad faith or from lack of zeal. Zeal was what he least lacked. But his passionate temper made him enemies. He was apparently the victim of false reports, or at least of involuntarily inexact ones. If the Indians had been merely irrational animals, it would have been legal to take their goods and reduce them to slavery. A few greedy Spaniards perhaps found it convenient to believe that the theology of Father Betanzos was on the side of their rapacity. The men who had not hesitated to drag the Augustinian Fray Alonso de Soria down from his sacred chair because he preached against the servitude of the natives,[28] were not ones to shrink from calumny. Besides, the idea was in the air, and [Francisco de] Vitoria, in 1532, thought it his duty to refute it.[29] However it was, Sebastián Ramírez de Fuenleal, in two letters addressed to the Emperor from Mexico, May 11 and 15, 1533, said that, according to information received in America, Father Betanzos, then in Spain, had declared to the Council of the Indies that the natives were incapable of assimilating the Christian doctrine, and he repeated the charge on August 8 of that same year. Bishop Garcés of Tlaxcala, himself a Dominican, wrote to Pope Paul III urging him to take up the defense of the Indians. Somewhat in the vein of Las Casas, he painted an enthusiastic picture of them, too uniformly laudatory to be true. He maintained that the accusations made against them were owing to lack of zeal among the religious and, among laymen, to a wish to enslave them and confiscate their lands.[30] The [Dominican] Order dispatched Fray Bernardino de Minaya to Rome and charged him to obtain from the Holy See a definitive resolution of the question.[31] Pope Paul, in his bulls *Veritas ipsa* and *Sublimis Deus,* early in June, 1537,[32] recollected that Christ had commanded His Apostles to teach all nations without exception, and declared that nothing justified depriving the Indians, who were reasonable men, of the blessing of liberty and the light of the Christian faith.

Parallel with this conflict, in which interests were hidden having nothing apostolic about them, there developed another, which the Holy See also resolved at about the same time, [a conflict] that had set the Augustinians and the Dominicans at odds with the Franciscans. [The Franciscans] had been the first to arrive and had enormous stretches to evangelize. Their numbers, especially at the beginning, were extremely small. Consequently, each one had veritable multitudes to baptize. A few figures will give a notion of the matter. According to a letter written by Zumárraga to the general chapter of Tolosa, on June 12, 1531, and one sent on that same date by Martín de Valencia to Father Mathias Weynssen, the Franciscans had baptized more than a million pagans by 1524.[33] Martín de Valencia, writing to Charles V on November 17, 1532,[34] indicates a minimum of 200,000 between 1524 and 1532. Pedro de Gante, in a letter of June 27, 1529,[35] speaks of 14,000 baptisms daily. Finally, in 1536, when Motolinía was composing the last chapter of his *Tratado Segundo,* 300 to 500 infants were being baptized every week in Tlaxcala, and he puts at about five million the number of Indians baptized between 1524 and 1536.[36] This figure, which is much greater than those of Zumárraga and Martín de Valencia, even if one allows for the difference of four or five years, is not inadmissible, because we know that around 1529 evangelization made an immense jump,[37] and it is certain that the average number of baptisms was much greater between 1532 and 1536 than between 1524 and 1532. What should be borne in mind in all this is that the Franciscans had a very large number of baptisms to administer, and that, for the baptism of adults and older children, they habitually limited themselves to the strictly essential. Motolinía tells us that they assembled all candidates for baptism and placed the children in the front row, upon all of whom they performed [the rite of] exorcism.[38] Thereupon they selected only a few upon whom to perform the ceremonies preliminary to the essential rite: the insufflation of the Holy Ghost (*flato*), the sign of the cross (*cruz*), the introduction of salt into the mouth (*sal*), and the rite of ephphatha (*saliva*). The [the candidates] were dressed in a white robe (*alba*), the symbol of innocence, which normally was not done until after baptism by water. When these ceremonies were completed, the infants were baptized one by one with holy water and were sent away. Then the adults were given a second instruction in the significance of the sacrament they were about to receive and the obligations it implied, and in their turn were baptized one by one.[39] At first there was neither chrism nor oil.[40] Zumárraga wrote in 1537 that he had been obliged to administer them to a crowd of confirmands who had not received them.[41]

It is apparent that we are not concerned here with baptism by aspersion, of which some examples are to be found in the history of missions.[42] The two other Orders thought that the multitude of candidates was not a sufficiently grave reason for legally abridging the ceremonies, and some men went to the length of claiming that the Franciscans, by acting in this fashion, were committing mortal sin. Others thought that adults should be baptized only at Easter and Pentecost, and that only the imminent danger of death justified reducing [the ceremony] to the strictly essential.[43] In 1534, a year after their arrival, the Augustinians initiated the custom of baptizing adults only four times a year: at Christmas, Easter, Pentecost, and St. Augustine's Day [August 28]. The administration of the sacrament was celebrated, not only with all the ceremonies, but with the greatest solemnity. All inhabitants of the neighboring villages were summoned to the chosen village for the administration of baptism, and its church, houses, and streets were decorated with greenery. The neophytes, in their cleanest garments, formed a line, and the two ministers (two priests were brought in for the occasion) performed the preliminary exorcisms. Then one of them walked before the catechumens and anointed them with holy oils, after which they went to the baptismal fonts, where the second priest administered the sacramental ablution.

Then followed the other rites, the two priests dividing the task between them in the same way. Music and bells accompanied the ceremony, which ended with a sermon to remind the new Christians of the obligations they had just assumed. In the afternoon there was dancing (*mitote*) and much rejoicing.[44]

Since the matter could not be settled in New Spain, it was also sent to Rome, and the Dominican Fray Juan de Oseguera was especially charged to defend his Order's point of view. Pope Paul III in his bull *Altitudo divini consilii* of June 1, 1537,[45] ignoring the problem of the validity of baptisms administered without the complete ceremonies (doubtless because their validity was not open to question, since the essential rite had been respected), found the Franciscans to be at fault in principle, although he recognized the righteousness of their intention. For the future, he insisted, except in cases of urgent necessity, they should not omit the slightest part of the ceremony, except the rites of salt, the ephphatha, white robes, and candles, with some neophytes, but the sacrament had to be administered with holy water, each [neophyte] had to be catechized and exorcized, and anointing with the chrism had to be performed with all of them. This meant in effect—and this information had very likely been given him by some Mexican missionary—that the Indians were to be impressed with the grandeur of the sacrament, and not tempted to confuse it in the slightest degree with their pagan baptism.[46]

The execution of this bull was ordered by the synod of 1539, which was composed of a large number of religious, Bishop Zumárraga of Mexico, the bishops of Michoacán and Antequera (Oaxaca), the commissary general of the Franciscans, and the provincials of the three Orders.[47] It gave special attention to the definition of cases of urgent necessity, which the bull had not made clear. It listed four: siege, shipwreck, grave and dangerous sickness, and insecurity of the country, with imminent peril of death. It shortened the exorcisms and left to the minister the care and responsibility of determining whether the candidate was sufficiently well prepared; but it prescribed the observance of all ceremonies within the limits of possibility, the anointing of every one with the chrism and holy oils, and avoidance of baptizing adults except in the Paschal season.

Finally, it ordered the publication of a *Manual de adultos* for the guidance of missionaries. This *Manual* was published in 1540. Unfortunately, only the last two folios of the original are extant.[48]

The bull and the decisions of the synod were resented by the Franciscans, some of whom wished that, in conformity with the usage they had followed, the large number of candidates and the dearth of missionaries should be counted among the cases of urgent necessity. Meanwhile, they submitted, and suspended the baptism of adults. But this lasted only a short time, four or five months, according to Mendieta.[49] In fact, by the end of three or four months, the religious of Quecholac (Puebla), in spite of the bishops' prohibition (these are Motolinía's own words), decided to admit to baptism all those who presented themselves, who were soon a numberless crowd.[50] No sanction, it seems, was invoked. Did this mean that the bishops were helpless in the face of the immunities of the regulars? Perhaps they thought it preferable not to renew a conflict, the causes of which would inevitably multiply. In the following years the growing number of missionaries made it possible for them to baptize with all prescribed ceremonies, and, especially, with the passage of time and the progressive Christianization of the natives, only exceptionally did they have to baptize crowds, or even adults, for the Indians by now were from birth admitted individually to the Church of Jesus Christ.

It has seemed proper to shorten the review of these difficulties that arose in the matter of baptism, for they did not influence in a really profound way the course and development of evangelization. Once free of all this parasitical growth, the procedures of the Mexican missionaries seem to have been wisely simple and very bold: not to baptize too quickly, helter-skelter, no matter whom, unconditionally; not to close the gates of the Kingdom of God to those who sincerely wished to enter; not to make them wait indefinitely for their admission to the Church, since [the missionaries] had all the means to control their perseverance.[51] Hence the lack of a catechumenate in the strict meaning of the word, but only a brief training in essential things, followed by an elementary examination. As has been justly observed,[52] this system, that is, the suppression of a long preliminary catechumenate and the administration of baptism *en masse,* had the great advantage of forming compact Christian communities within a few years. It may also be observed, besides, with what care the Mexican missionaries avoided, instinctively or consciously, extreme solutions: hasty and unprepared baptism, indefinite waiting during a prolonged preparation, the former clearly dangerous, the latter extremely controversial.[53] In this one sees that character of moderation and common sense, that defiance of systematic and absolute theology, that eclecticism, which seem to me to be the dominant traits of the Mexican mission.

5 The Catechism

BAPTISM, as we have seen, was never administered without preliminary instruction, except in cases of urgent necessity; but since the catechumenate hardly existed, this instruction was summary and limited to essentials. It was out of the question to abandon the neophytes to the risks and difficulties of the Christian life with such a precarious religious training. It was therefore necessary to organize a supplementary instruction, for adults and children both.

As always, thanks to the abundance of Franciscan sources, we are best informed about the work and procedures of the Friars Minor. In the convent villages the catechism was held on Sundays and feast days.[1] Early in the morning the monitors (*merinos*) of each quarter of the large towns, and the *alcaldes* of the villages, summoned their people. Each quarter or each village assembled at the church, bearing crosses and reciting prayers; roll was called at the church, and the names of those whose absence could not be explained by the *merinos* or *alcaldes* were noted. This control was exceedingly severe, and in the beginning rigorous sanctions were applied. In 1539, for example, the bishops had to forbid beating the Indians with rods, imprisoning them or putting them in irons, "to teach them the Christian doctrine."[2] This prohibition, however, does not seem to have been strictly observed, for in 1570 it was still customary to give delinquent Indians half a dozen strokes on the outside of their clothing, for they knew no other punishment.[3] In any event, a strict discipline seemed necessary for the guidance of indolent neophytes, many of whom were ready to forget or neglect.[4] Generally, they were all assembled in the cemetery (*atrio*) that surrounded the church, and groups were formed around the crosses (which can still be seen in some places),[5] the men and women were carefully separated[6] and obliged to repeat aloud a part of the catechism two or three times,[7] after which the sermon was preached and Mass said.[8]

The Franciscans were two few in number to undertake a regular and general instruction, [so they had recourse to] the aid of trustworthy natives, who assisted the friars and the civil officers at the same time. The natives, called *fiscales* or *mandones* in Spanish, and *tepizques* or *tequitlatos* in Nahuatl, had not only the duty of assembling the people and bringing them to Mass and the catechism, but also, at the time of the bishop's visit, the duty of presenting the children and adults who had not been confirmed. In addition, it was their responsibility to see that everyone received baptism and confessed during Lent, that marriages were lawful, and that couples lived in peace. They denounced adulteries and concubinage, impenitent drunkards, and the wine merchants who encouraged vice for their own profit; and they denounced poisoners, sorcerers, and, in general, all those who still practiced paganism. In the *pueblos de visita,* that is, villages that lacked resident priests, the *mandones* policed the churches, kept the baptismal records, performed baptisms themselves in case of necessity, comforted the dying, buried the dead, and announced feasts, vigils, and fasts, and so forth.[9]

Naturally, the Franciscans trained their own *mandones*. In 1550, Fray Rodrigo de la Cruz wrote to Charles V from the convent of Ahuacatlán in New Galicia, that the Order had opened schools, in which a few Indians from each village were gathered and taught to read, write, count, and say the Hours of the Holy Virgin. Which done, they were sent home to repeat this service and the catechism, since the Fathers could make the rounds of the villages only infrequently.[10] It seems probable that these visits were for the purpose of prebaptismal instruction, which was the

97

procedure a few years later in that same region. There, in 1554, Fray Francisco Lorenzo and Fray Miguel de Estevales were converting the Texoquín Indians, some of whom they brought to the convent of Ahuacatlán, taught them the catechism, and then sent them back to their own people to teach the others, particularly the children, what they had just learned.[11] In short, they organized a group of catechist-censors, entirely like that organized by St. Francis Xavier in the East Indies in the same period.[12] Unfortunately, although we are quite familiar with the functions of the Mexican catechists, we have no document on the number of these precious helpers, or how many there were in proportion to the religious.

One matter worthy of note (and I shall frequently have to make observations of this kind), is that the institution of catechists has survived down to this very day with hardly a change. Every Mexican parish priest is still flanked by a *fiscal,* who even substitutes for him in villages that have no priest. The *fiscal* has charge of the whole religious and moral life of the community; he looks after the maintenance and decoration of the church, presides over the organization of *fiestas,* asks for the hands of young women in the name of their suitors, attends the dying and buries the dead, chooses the names of the new-born, and collects the money necessary to the functioning of services.[13]

Although the Franciscans did not neglect the adults, they directed their principal effort to the instruction of children, whom they usually divided into two categories. The children of the lower class (called *gente baja*) were assembled every morning after Mass in the *atrios* of the churches and separated into groups, depending on their knowledge of the catechism, which they were taught, along with the principal prayers. And that was all. At the end of the lesson in the catechism they were sent home to work with their parents. In each quarter, or each village, an old man was carefully selected to assemble the children, bring them in a group to the church, and take them home again after the catechism. In this the Franciscans were only following a native custom, which was to entrust the old men with this kind of duty.[14] The sons of the *principales,* or native aristocracy, were handled differently and with particular care, for they were the future leaders of the country.[15] These boys lived in the convents as boarders, and in this [also] the Franciscans did no more than conform to native usage, for before the Spanish conquest some Aztec youths were reared in this fashion.[16] Morning and evening they attended classes in the convent schools, studying not only the catechism, but also reading, writing, and singing. They were taught, besides, to serve at Mass and, in a general way, to assist the religious in the monastery. They were trained in the practice of silent prayer and forced to discipline themselves. Every day they attended Mass and vespers; they got up at night to chant the matins of Our Lady; twice a day, before breakfast and toward the end of the afternoon, they recited the catechism aloud and in chorus. "These are the two things," concludes the *Códice Franciscano,* "the habit and practice of which cannot fail to be most useful to their Christian training." [17]

Nevertheless, some boys of humble parentage benefited from this more careful instruction. In fact, at the beginning, many chiefs, unwilling to see their sons confined with the priests of the new religion, substituted sons of their subjects or slaves for them.[18] A few religious also, for obscure reasons, did not respect the native hierarchy, but instructed and trained sons of manual workers, who as a consequence became the governors of the sons of those who had formerly been their chiefs.[19]

If the Franciscans devoted themselves especially to the teaching of youth, it was not solely because these represented the temporal and spiritual future of New Spain, but also because the Franciscans realized, and events proved them right, that these youths would be their surest and most active helpers in the work of evangelization.[20] Thus, these young-sters were used for the instruction of girls, whom they assembled in groups in the *atrios,* each group being entrusted to a lad who had mastered the catechism and who was named as teacher. Moreover, when a few of the girls had advanced beyond their teachers, they were put to work teaching their companions, and the boys disappeared.[21] The boys, however, particularly those educated in the convents, had other duties, for in their own families and among the other Indians they were the least distrusted missionaries; their disinterestedness could not be doubted and their inquiries were not resented. They taught the catechism to adults; [22] they revealed to the religious the secret superstitions of their relations; [23]

99

they acted as interpreters when the need arose, repeating the missionaries' sermons with the most profound conviction and persuasive warmth,[24] for these youngsters had at times the souls of true apostles. Motolinía tells us the story of two young Indians of Tlaxcala who on their own volition, without revealing their intentions, after having confessed and taken communion, traveled more than fifty leagues away from home to convert and instruct other Indians, facing all kinds of difficulties and hardships.[25] Muñoz also tells us of two youths of Michoacán, Lucas and Sebastián, reared by the Franciscans, "who preached for many years among the Indians, the converted as well as the pagans, and won many souls for Our Lord." They went with the friars to Cíbola and were extremely useful to them.[26] Several of them did not recoil [even] from martyrdom. One such was the young Cristóbal who, at the age of thirteen, was killed by his father for trying to make him give up idolatry and drunkenness. Two others were the young Tlaxcalans who paid with their lives for their ardor in finding and destroying idols.[27]

In this they sometimes went too far and acted without discretion. The pupils of the school at Tlaxcala joyously stoned to death a native priest who, in reply to their questions, had said there was a god of wine, Ometochtli. They were convinced that they had slain the devil in person.[28] And then, among the apostles and martyrs, one finds hypocrites and precocious rascals. The young missionaries were not always worthy of the confidence placed in them. Some of them took advantage of their authority to rob those who came to them, to seduce women and girls, and bring disorder wherever they went. It also happened that others, either because of their pretentious vanity, or plain folly, twisted the Christian doctrine and taught dreadful heresies.[29] Nevertheless, in a general sort of way, this system of monastic education seems to have yielded good results. In 1531 the Licenciado Salmerón and the Audiencia of Mexico acknowledge as much,[30] and the use of child missionaries received in 1558 the implicit approval of Viceroy Luis de Velasco.[31]

Meanwhile, the method of internship had its inconveniences. Many of these pupils, much better fed, deprived of their accustomed physical activity, began, if we may believe Sahagún, "to show signs of sensual ardors and to instruct themselves in lascivious practices." It was therefore necessary to take away their internship and send them to sleep at home.[32] The Franciscan historians, however, did not hesitate to attribute to their young collaborators the greater part of the merit in the conversion of New Spain. Without these lads, wrote Motolinía, the religious would have been [as helpless as] molting falcons, and Mendieta went so far as to entitle one of his chapters: "How the conversion of the Indians was done through children."[33] The girls, moreover, showed almost as much apostolic zeal as the boys. Those who had been reared in the schools especially designed for them devoted themselves, when they had graduated from the internship, that is, at the age of twelve, to the teaching of the catechism. Others did not wait until graduation, but went out from time to time to teach the Christian doctrine in the *atrios,* or in private houses, and we are told that they made many converts.[34]

What precisely was the nature of the religious instruction that the Franciscans gave the Indians, children and adults? On this point one may take the *doctrina* as typical, that is, the catechism of Fray Alonso de Molina, one of the best known, which the Franciscans, as well as the secular clergy, seem to have used most generally.[35] It is also, very probably, the *doctrina breve* recommended by the bishops after the *junta* of 1546, which had ordered the composition of two *doctrinas* for the Indians, "one short, the other more extensive."[36] The Nahuatl-Castilian text of Father Molina's catechism is preserved in the *Códice Franciscano,*[37] and is divided into two quite distinct parts: first, the prayers and the essential verities, which were taught in church and which everyone was obliged to learn. All candidates for baptism, confession, communion, and confirmation were interrogated in them, that is: the sign of the cross, the *Credo,* the *Pater Noster,* the *Ave Maria,* and the *Salve Regina;*[38] also, the fourteen Articles of Faith, of which seven concerned the divinity of Jesus Christ and seven His humanity; the Ten Commandments of God, the Five Commandments of the Church, and the Seven Sacraments; the venial and mortal sins; the seven deadly sins; and the general confession —this last, exceptionally, being placed at the end of the *doctrina.* The second part is devoted to the complementary virtues, knowledge of which was not regarded as indispensable. It was only taught to the children of

101

the convent, who repeated it aloud every day. The book was also put into the hands of adults, who could repeat it [aloud], or have it read to them, thus acquiring a more advanced doctrinal training. This second part also included the cardinal and theological virtues, the works of mercy,[39] the gifts of the Holy Ghost, the senses, the faculties of the soul, the enemies of the soul, the Beatitudes, the company of the Blessed, and the duties of godparents.

Essentially, the *doctrina* of Alonso de Molina has nothing original in it, being evidently only a copy of the catechism then in use in the Peninsula. Besides, on the title page Father Molina appears only as translator, not as author. His catechism brings to mind the *Doctrina Pueril* of Raymond Lully.[40] But, above all, the plan adopted is almost identical with that of the *doctrina* which, in the closing years of the fifteenth century, the Jeronymite Fray Pedro de Alcalá had written for the benefit of the Musulmans of the Kingdom of Granada.[41] By and large, it is the same as the catechism approved by the Council of Lima in 1583.[42] Finally, it is, with insignificant differences, the same as the classical *Doctrina Christiana* of Father Ripalda, published in Burgos in 1591, and a catechism printed in Pamplona in 1606,[43] both of which were written for Spanish children. Since we are concerned with the most widely circulated Franciscan *doctrina*, this is the clearest proof of what I stated in my first chapter, namely, that in the missions of New Spain there was no general and systematic effort at adaptation in the presentation of the dogma. This effort is hardly discernible except in the *Pláticas* of the Twelve, where it was imposed by the force of circumstances, since they were not addressing converts [as in Spain], but people whom they had to convert, people particularly attached to their [old] religion. It also appears in the *doctrina* of the Dominicans, which I shall take up later on. In short, the Franciscans, in their teaching of the catechism, treated the Indians more or less like Spaniards, for whom they were content to transcribe or adapt the catechism published in the Peninsula. Is not the *doctrina* published in 1544 or 1545 under the patronage of Zumárraga based on the *Suma de doctrina* of the famous Spanish Lutheran Constantino Ponce de la Fuente, which had not yet been condemned? [44]

One may discern [in it], nevertheless, certain features that apply particularly to Mexico. Thus, the Franciscans, fearing the appearance of a new form of idolatry which would replace pagan idolatry pure and simple, insisted very strongly that the worship of images was not directed to the material substance, but to what it represented. Fray Maturino Gilberti, for example, in his Tarascan catechism, expresses himself in this way: "We do not worship any image, even though it be that of the Crucifix or St. Mary, for, when we represent the Crucifix or St. Mary or the Saints, it is only to remind ourselves of the great mercy of God, who gave us His Son for our redemption, and . . . although we kneel before the Crucifix in an attitude of worship, it is nevertheless not the Crucifix that we worship, for it is only made of wood, but God Himself, Our Lord who is in Heaven." [45] At the time of his trial he testified that he had expressed himself in this fashion to make it clear to the Indians that the wood of the image was not worshiped—this to root out their former idolatry and to make them understand that, when Christians adore or venerate images, their gesture goes beyond the image to the God or Saint it represents.[46] He insisted, besides, that this was why he was suspected of Protestantism, and why his propositions and explanations were described as scandalous or erroneous.[47] Fray Francisco de Bustamante, for his part, railed violently against the cult of Our Lady of Guadalupe [of Mexico] and the miracles attributed to her, for, he said, we have had plenty of difficulty in making the Indians understand that images should not be worshiped, for they were made of wood and stone, and here they were being told that the image of Our Lady was performing miracles! [48]

The religious were not prisoners of the printed text, here or elsewhere. It was meant to be committed to memory by the children in the monasteries, and to be read by the Indians at home. From the moment a missionary had finished teaching the essentials he was free to adopt whatever plan he liked, to add such and such considerations, or to suppress others; he would let himself be guided by the nature, the capacity, and the curiosity of his listeners, and would organize his teaching in the way he judged most favorable to the health of his parishioners.[49] It was in these familiar discourses that such an adaptation, banned from the books, had its place. Since it was less methodical, it could not help being less cold, more supple, more living; but its effect would doubtless have lost nothing if it had been more frequently prepared and amplified by that of the printed catechism.

This adaptation was marked by the use of two important devices: pictures and music, both of which are classical in the history of missions. Several religious, inspired by native manuscripts, adopted the custom of teaching the Christian doctrine by means of pictures (*pinturas*). For example, they had one canvas painted representing the Articles of Faith; another, the Ten Commandments; a third, the Seven Sacraments, and so on. The priest placed behind him the canvas concerning the subject he wished to expound, and with a pointer indicated to his listeners the things he was talking about. Experience proved that the Indians thus acquired a more intelligent and more profound knowledge of the faith.[50] To mention but two great names: Sahagún and Mendieta used this system. Mendieta had the rosary painted in order to awaken the devotion of the natives.[51] Some missionaries even composed catechisms in pictures. Pedro de Gante composed a whole *doctrina* in this fashion, in which were pictured the sign of the Cross, the *Pater*, the *Ave*, the *Credo*, and various other prayers; the mystery of the Holy Trinity, the Commandments of God and the Church, the sacraments and the works of charity.[52] Fray Luis Caldera, who, like Father Testera,[53] did not know the language of the Indians he was evangelizing, also used this method. Carrying large pictures representing the sacraments, the catechism, heaven, hell, and purgatory, he went from village to village. He added even more eloquent inventions. To inspire in the Indians a salutary horror of hell, he had a kind of oven brought in, had dogs, cats, and other animals thrown into it, and then lit the fire. The cries of pain of the unlucky animals naturally filled the Indians with a great fear.[54]

Since singing had also been very important in the pre-Conquest religion, the natives' love of music was also used. The Commandments of God were translated into Aztec verse, which they were taught to sing, along with the *Pater*, the *Ave*, and the *Credo*.[55] Pedro de Gante, whom one encounters everywhere, composed verses on the Christian doctrine for his pupils. Writing to Philip II on June 23, 1558, he said that in view of the fact that before their conversion the Indians were always dancing and singing during their religious ceremonies, "I have composed verses in which they can see how God made Himself man to save the world; how He was born of the Virgin Mary without sin; and in them they learn the Commandments of this God who saved them." [56]

If the *doctrina* of Fray Alonso de Molina, because of its diffusion and the confidence it inspired in the episcopate, may be taken as typical of the Franciscan catechisms, its sequel, the more highly developed catechism, which had also been anticipated by the ecclesiastical council of 1546, may be taken as typical of the Dominican catechisms. Indeed, the *doctrina* published in Spanish in 1544 by the Dominican Fray Pedro de Córdoba, in collaboration with Zumárraga and Betanzos, was designated by the bishops as the *doctrina larga,* which seemed to be necessary for the instruction of the natives whom they wished to train more seriously. The Dominicans, therefore, translated it into Nahuatl, and early in 1548 they got out a new edition, which contained both the Spanish and the Mexican texts. Only one copy, now in the National Library of Madrid, is known, and I was fortunate enough to examine it.[57] It contains all elements common to the *doctrinas* of the period: the principal prayers, the Articles of Faith, the Commandments of God, the sacraments, the works of mercy, the deadly sins. But it differs from the *doctrina* of Father Molina, not so much in its more precise explanations [58] and its division into forty sermons, as in an effort toward adaptation, which was absent from the Franciscan catechism. The author begins by emphasizing the disinterested love of the missionaries, the dangers they have faced, the sufferings they have endured—all this solely for the [spiritual] health of the Indians, who without the religious would go to hell like their ancestors. The Christian doctrine, which has now been brought to them, is the only thing that will make it possible for them to go to heaven. It teaches the existence of an omnipotent God of infinite perfection, very different from the pagan idols, who have no power or dignity. This God is supreme goodness: He does not accept blood offerings, and would be offended if men were sacrificed to Him. He is also supreme wisdom: He knows everything, sees everything; nothing escapes Him, even one's most secret thoughts. On the Day of Judgment He will reveal all hidden acts, good and bad. It is not to

105

be believed, moreover, that sin is not committed just because it is not seen, for one can sin in thought. The author, who, perhaps like Sahagún and his companion Father Lucero, may have noticed the Indians' penchant for hypocrisy,[59] and who doubtless feared that a pharisaical formalism would appear among them, gives great emphasis to the sin of intent.

As for individual procedures, the program adopted by Fray Gonzalo Lucero among the Indians of the Mixteca, many details of which are described by Dávila Padilla, seems to me the most interesting. Father Lucero began by teaching the Christian doctrine with the greatest simplicity, as if to children, and advanced very slowly, for the Indians, in his view, progressed only step by step, and it would not do to hurry them. At first he adopted a purely negative approach. To prove to the Indians that it was absurd to worship the sun, moon, and stars, he gave them a kind of course in cosmography; he brought a sphere and showed them how the stars only obeyed the commands of God. Then he demonstrated, in effect, the necessity of the existence of God as Prime Mover, the Creator of heaven, earth, and living beings, Author of the laws which one must respect in order to be rewarded, and the infraction of which brought rigorous punishment. As he enlarged on these aspects, he spoke of the immortality of the soul, paradise, hell, and redemption. He also made use of large pictures on which all this was represented.[60] He mounted them in a public place in the villages, to excite curiosity and awaken in the natives a desire to know their meaning. In one of the paintings they saw God in all His glory, surrounded by angels and saints, among whom were several Indians—a noteworthy feature, for the Father explained that these were converted Indians who had lived to the time of their death in obedience of the Commandments of God. In the same picture the torments of hell were painted, the hidden fire that devours the devils and the damned, among whom there were also some Indians who, the Father explained, were those who had not accepted the Christian faith, or who, after having accepted it, had not respected the Commandments and had died unshriven. Another painting represented, in the form of a river or a lake (*grandes aguas*), the changes and transitory nature of our present life. In it two canoes could be seen, the first full of Indians, men and women, with rosaries around their necks or in their hands, some holding scourges, others in the attitude of prayer, all accompanied by angels who carried branches in their hands and offered them [to the Indians]. This canoe was sailing toward glory, the beginning of which was painted at the top of the picture and continued on the one already described. Devils were clinging to the canoe and attempting to stop it, but the angels were protecting the Indians, and the Indians were defending themselves with their rosaries.

In the second canoe, on the other hand, the devils were sailing merrily in the company of Indians, men and women, who were getting drunk on large tumblers of wine, quarreling, killing each other, or embracing each other dishonestly. Angels were flying above them, offering rosaries and trying to arouse good thoughts in them; but the wretches disdained all that, unable to drag their eyes and thoughts away from their sad pleasures, away from the tumblers of wine and the women the devils were offering them. The devils [also] carried branches; they were hastening on their way to hell, the beginning of which could be seen at the bottom of the picture. The Father did not fail to show the greatest pity for the victims, or to inspire in his hearers a holy envy of those who were led to paradise by the angels and the rosary.[61] The Indians who had understood the pictures then interpreted them to the others, whereupon the missionary preached a sermon on the same subject, explaining the Ten Commandments, which had to be obeyed if one wished to obtain the joys of paradise and escape the torments of hell. Knowing that the Indians were what St. Paul termed *ad oculum servientes,* who hardly ever did good or avoided evil except when they felt they were being watched, he insisted that God is everywhere, that He sees everything, and that for Him there is no darkness or secret.[62]

Among the Augustinians the teaching of the catechism does not seem to have been appreciably different from what it was among the Franciscans and Dominicans. The people of the village were summoned to the church every day by a bell, and for an hour, either in the church or in the *atrio,* they were taught the catechism. Then the adults were sent home, the missionary keeping only the children, whom he set to studying the various prayers translated into the native tongue. At first there were two daily meetings for catechism, two hours in the morning, two in the afternoon; but this system was abandoned as soon as the Indians had advanced somewhat. Like the Franciscans, the [Augustinian] friars had the help of old natives in this task, and their control over absences was also very severe. In the *pueblos de visita* they were also represented by catechists (*fiscales*), who had charge of maintaining spiritual order. The Augustinians, again like the Franciscans, in their convent schools gave particularly careful instruction to the few children who struck them as more interesting. In addition to the catechism, they were taught to read, write, and sing, to play musical instruments, serve at Mass, and were also employed as sacristans or secretaries.[63]

The Augustinians did not go so far as to raise them to the priesthood or admit them to monastic life; but they were the only Order of the three that had much confidence in the spiritual capacities of the Indians. In the next chapter it will be shown that the Augustinians were the firmest believers in allowing them to partake of communion and even supreme unction, which the Franciscans, except at the beginning, were unwilling to do. [The Augustinians] therefore had high ambitions for their neophytes, which is what distinguished their teaching very decidedly from that of the other two Orders. They [even] attempted to initiate the natives into the contemplative life. Escobar tells us that in his day he had seen a painting representing *la vida mística* in the convent of Cuitzeo, Michoacán, in which the "meadows of the contemplative life" were represented, as he says elsewhere, which the religious explained to "the multitude." The terms he uses [64] make one think that it probably pictured the *Echelle spirituelle* of St. John Climacus, which is known to have enjoyed a certain vogue in Mexico. It was translated into Spanish by the Dominican Fray Juan de Estrada (or, de la Magdalena). His translation, of which no copy is extant, is generally accepted as the first book printed in Mexico, between 1535 and 1540, before the *Manual de Adultos,* which I mentioned in my discussion of baptism.[65] Unfortunately, we do not know what effect this teaching had. It was a curious experiment, no longer practiced in the time of Escobar, who wrote at the beginning of the eighteenth century. Nor do we know why it disappeared, whether because of the incapacity of the pupils or the masters' lack of zeal.

6 The Administration of the Sacraments

bAPTISM brought the Indians into the Church. They were [now] Christians. They had to live as Christians, and the missionary had the moral obligation of furnishing them the means to do so. These means were the other sacraments: marriage, confession, communion, and confirmation. To administer them, the religious had received the most extensive powers from the Holy See, in the bull *Omnimoda,* of May 9, 1522,[1] which were confirmed after the Council of Trent by Pope Pius V, in the bull *Exponi nobis,* of March 24, 1567.[2] Before the Council of Trent, in fact, it had been the custom in the Indies for the religious to retain the spiritual guidance of the regions they had converted, with no condition other than nomination by their superiors and the assent of the secular authority representing the *Patronato Real.* This is why the Indian parishes were called *doctrinas,* and not parishes or custodies. The *doctrinas,* as distinct from the parishes, were given only intermediate, not perpetual, titles. The Council of Trent upset this simple and flexible organization by putting the parish priests under the control of the bishops. The regulars, therefore, had either to give up their *doctrinas* or submit to the jurisdiction of the bishops. They rejected the latter solution as contrary to the privileges of the religious Orders, while the former was inadmissible because of the insufficiency of the secular clergy, in numbers as well as in competence.

Thus Philip II was obliged to beg the Pope not to trouble the Indies with any modification [of the custom]. The bull *Exponi nobis* was the answer to this request and this situation. So the religious retained the rights and privileges of parish priests, as well as the power to preach and to administer the sacraments without the express authorization of the bishops, "ordinariorum locorum et aliorum quorumcumque licentia minime requisita"[3] [without the express consent of the bishops or anyone else].

The one sacrament which from the beginning was beyond all question necessary and indispensable, was marriage, the administration of which came up against the immense obstacle of polygamy.[4] It was all the more serious in Mexico, for it was almost exclusively the chiefs (*principales*) who habitually lived with several women. Polygamy, therefore, was an obstacle to the conversion of the elite, and a beginning could not be made until this difficulty was disposed of. The Bishop of Tlaxcala, Fray Julián Garcés, in a letter to Paul III, wrote that it had been overcome with great ease: "Quodque adhuc difficilius existimatur a nostris (qui ne in abjiciendis quidem concubinis dicto pareant praelatorum) tanta facilitate uxorum pluritatem abjiciunt, quas in paganismo habuerunt, unicaque contenti, ut miraculi instar sit" [whereas theretofore it had seemed most unlikely to us that they would submit to the order of the bishops and put aside their concubines, on the contrary they got rid of the numerous wives they had had while they were pagans—indeed, they were so cheerful about it that it had the look of a miracle].

But Garcés was writing in defense of the Indians, who had been accused of being irrational animals, and he felt obliged to present things in an optimistic light; his letter was a special pleading, but was not, however, altogether false. In 1531, in a large village of New Galicia, Fray Martín de Jesús de la Coruña had experienced no difficulty in suppressing polygamy out of hand. The petty king of Cutzalán and his subjects, after having been instructed in the Christian faith, did not object to having to choose one of the women they had been living with, and marrying her according to the rites of the new religion.[5] But this appears to have been an exception. Besides, such seeming ease is suspect, for the natives had either misunderstood the obligations of Christian marriage, or they had renounced polygamy only outwardly, having firmly decided not to change their custom. Did not the bishops, in 1537, complain of seeing the Indians marry, rather to conceal their adulteries or vices than to accept one legitimate wife?[6] Tello does not conceal the difficulties that Fray Martín de Jesús, Fray Juan de Padilla, and Fray Antonio de Segovia had with that same chief [of Cutzalán] in New Galicia. For the same reason Fray Juan de Padilla failed to convert the cacique Cuixaloa and his subjects, and Fray Antonio de Segovia met with so much resistance that he was obliged to abandon [any thought] of imposing monogamy all at once, and was unable to reform [marriage] customs except by easy stages and with great precautions.[7] Other authors, no less trustworthy, such as Motolinía and La Rea, emphasize the magnitude of the difficulty,[8] and we know that it was the principal obstacle the Augustinians had to surmount at Ocuituco,[9] and that it was the main topic of discussion at the meeting they held on June 8, 1534.[10]

The difficulty was all the greater because polygamy, as practiced there and in most of the country, was owing less to the sensual temperament of the natives than to economic and social factors.[11] It was much more an institution than an abuse. Women were servants as well as wives; they performed all kinds of labor and represented a capital outlay that was hard to give up. Without polygamy many chiefs could not have made a living.[12] Moreover, the example set by the Spaniards was not one to inspire in the natives a high idea of conjugal life and the relations between the sexes. Too many of them led an irregular life and practiced polygamy in fact. Most of the married men, it must be said in their defense, had had to leave their wives in Spain, and many took Indian concubines. So, when the missionaries tried to prevent the natives from living in concubinage, the latter had a ready answer in the conduct of the Europeans.[13] In Spain the gravity of the problem and the resistance of the natives were so well realized that a *cédula* of June 26, 1536, recommended that the Bishop of Mexico use the greatest indulgence in this matter, bearing in mind that he was dealing with recent converts.[14]

In practice, the delinquents could be treated with indulgence, but it was impossible to tolerate the principle of polygamy, which in itself was incompatible with the Christian institution of marriage, and which at the same time brought the risk of an awkward influence on the morality of those who did not practice it. In fact (and this was the regular consequence of polygamy), the chiefs had a monopoly of all the women, and the Indian of modest means who wished to marry, often had a deal of trouble in finding a companion.[15] Although the missionaries agreed about the principle, they had in fact to employ different means [to put it into effect], depending upon the region, for when the assembly of delegates from the three Orders met under the presidency of Zumárraga in 1541 for the purpose of adopting common methods, one of the decisions they took was that polygamists be admitted to baptism only after they should undertake to live with a single wife. After their meeting of 1534 the Augustinians made it a rule to impose monogamy upon the Indians before baptizing them.[16] They met with great resistance. In the Franciscan missions the natives began to limit themselves to one wife only after 1531.[71]

It would not apparently be true to state that polygamy had been eradicated in Mexico. It continued to be practiced unofficially, so to speak; that is, it frequently happened that certain Indians, who had been married in church to a single wife, kept a number of concubines. And, since the Crown had recommended indulgence, it was difficult for the ecclesiastical authority to deal severely with abuses and repress them with the necessary energy. Zumárraga complained loudly of this state of affairs,[18] and we have seen how, in 1537, the bishops admitted that the Indians showed slight respect for the obligations of Christian marriage, or knowledge of them. But—and here we can see all the advantages of mass conversion, when it was possible—if polygamy was not in fact completely uprooted, little by little it disappeared of itself through the force of circumstances, which took one or two generations. There came a moment when the majority of Indians of marriageable age had been baptized at birth, or at least while very young, had received a Christian education and had been nurtured in a Christian environment. They did not have to shake off the heavy yoke of old habit, and readily accepted marriage with a single wife. The contrary, perhaps, would have seemed shocking to them and abnormal. Nevertheless, abuses still existed. Does not Fray Juan Bautista, writing in the last years of the sixteenth century, frequently complain that before marriage the Indians had illegitimate relations with their future wives? From the moment that they sincerely intended to marry, they did not think they were committing a grave sin in so doing.[19]

From the canonical point of view, the marriage of polygamists presented several difficulties. Should the interested party be given the freedom to marry the wife of his preference, or should he be forced to keep only the one whom he had first married according to pagan rites? The synod presided over by Martín de Valencia in 1524 decided to allow the Indians to marry the wives of their choice. This, however, was only a provisional solution, adopted pending better knowledge of native marriage customs.[20] The first question gave rise to a second, that is, did natural marriage really exist among the pagans? For we know that Catholic theology recognizes the existence of natural marriage, which, to be valid, requires that two fundamental conditions be met: mutual consent and the intention of accepting marriage for life.

Now, natural marriage, like the sacramental contract, cannot be dissolved. The Franciscans thought they could distinguish among the Indians two kinds of union: one performed with certain rites which could be unmade only by judicial decision; the other without ceremony, which could be broken by mutual consent. The latter, in short, was simple concubinage, while the former could pass for true marriage.[21] When an Indian had practiced only concubinage, the matter was simple: he was free to choose. In the other case there was a natural contract, which could be fulfilled only with his earliest wife, and he would have to give up all the others. When, however, the matter was examined more carefully, it became apparent that the situation was infinitely more complicated. It brought into being a whole literature, in which theologians and canonists vied with each other in displaying their ingenuity.[22] Roughly, there were two opposing opinions: the regulars maintaining that the pagans had had a true marriage;[23] the secular doctors, that they had not. Once again an appeal had to be made to the Holy See. In the bull *Altitudo divini consilii* of 1537, already cited, Paul III took a middle position, confirmed by Pius V in 1571, eight years after the close of the Council of Trent.[24] He ordered

113

that the Indians should marry the first wives they had taken and not be allowed freedom of choice unless it was impossible to determine this point. Those who had had only one wife at a time, but who frequently put them aside, were to keep the one they were living with at the time of their conversion.[25]

This was evidently a wise decision. In particular, it averted the danger of having these polygamists turn Christian only for the purpose of getting rid of old wives who had become a bore and burden.[26] But it was not perfect. No decision could be fully satisfactory in the circumstances, especially since it opened a wide gap for fraud. In fact, it was necessary to depend upon the testimony of interested parties and their friends and relatives, none of whom hesitated to lie, for it was more tempting to keep a young and pretty wife than to saddle oneself for life with an old one.[27] To meet this danger, the Franciscans had to exercise great caution. Each polygamist was obliged to present himself, bringing his whole family and all his wives, to the end that each one [of the wives] might plead her own cause. This took place in the presence of certain natives who knew all the inhabitants of the parish, and who were given the duty of examining the various claims. The difficult cases, moreover, were looked into by native specialists, whose learning was so much admired by the Spaniards that they were called *licenciados*. In the matter of pagan marriage customs and questions of consanguinity, they guided the religious and helped them to reach a suitable decision. Otherwise, the more obscure cases were referred to the episcopal authority.[28]

The bishops, however, were quick to accuse the religious of marrying and unmarrying the Indians with excessive ease, except in the diocese of Mexico, where abuses were less frequent. Such, at least, was the charge of Dr. Anguis, provisor of the Archbishop of Mexico. He gives as an example what he had observed in Michoacán. Pedro and María had been married in church. But Pedro takes a mistress and wants to marry her, so he calmly takes her to see a religious and says that he had married her before marrying María in the Christian fashion. Without verification or investigation, the marriage of Pedro and María is at once dissolved, and he is married to his mistress. A new husband is found for María, and all is well. But, lo and behold, Pedro gets tired of his new wife and wants to have María back again. So he hurries off to his religious, humbly confesses that he has lied, and that María is his real wife. And the religious at once unmarries and remarries him. Pedro leaves his former mistress; María, her new husband, and off they go together. An effort will be made to marry the two who are unaccounted for.[29]

This witty story smacks of the music hall; things are exaggerated and simplified as in the theater. Besides, Anguis seems to have been an extremely partial man. As Archbishop Montúfar's provisor, he accused the religious of infringing his authority and continually quarreled with them. A secular himself, he did not love the regular clergy. So he singled out a religious of Michoacán, whom he accused of being a Frenchman. It is quite likely that he had Maturino Gilberti in mind. The letter of Anguis is dated 1561, and the long trial that had set Gilberti and the seculars by the ears had been going on for two years.[30] Such testimony, therefore, must be viewed with the greatest caution, but it is evident that it should not be considered fantastic in all respects, for it is confirmed up to a point by a *cédula* dated at Monzón, December 18, 1552, which reminds [the religious] that matrimonial cases are exclusively in the jurisdiction of the bishops.[31] And we know that in 1538 an Indian, called Francisco in the suit, was prosecuted by the Holy Office for the crime of bigamy. Now, his two marriages had been performed in the same place, Coyoacán, and by the same religious, a Franciscan known only as Fray Juan.[32] The story of Anguis, therefore, can be accepted as evidence of the many difficulties following the marriage of polygamists and the inextricable confusion to which it often led.

On the other hand, for Indians who reached a marriageable age after some years of Christian life, things were made very simple. The Franciscans, for example, named one day a week when those who wished to get married should present themselves. They were asked whether they were unmarried, free, baptized, and confirmed, and a sufficient knowledge of Christian doctrine was made sure of. Not much weight, however, was attached to this [last] point. When, either from old age or natural simplicity, the interested parties had not been able properly to learn the catechism, nothing was required of them other than the *Pater Noster,* the *Credo,* and their acceptance of the Articles of Faith. To refuse to marry

115

them might drive them into concubinage, so the betrothed were given all necessary practical instructions. The ceremony was performed generally on Sunday. The priest asked whether the future spouses were qualified, gave them a short talk on the meaning and grandeur of the sacrament, and then married them.[33]

The first native marriages celebrated in Mexico were those of Don Hernando, brother of the lord of Texcoco, and seven of his companions, October 14, 1526. Motolinía describes the ceremony with his usual precision. Many illustrious personages, particularly Alonso de Avila and Pedro Sánchez Farfán, came from Mexico City to attend it, bringing presents for the couples, jewels, and also, adds Motolinía, with sly good nature, a large quantity of wine, "which was the jewel most appreciated." Since these weddings were meant to serve as an example for all New Spain, the ceremony was especially solemn. After Mass, the sponsors, accompanied by the principal personages of Texcoco, led the couples to the palace, that is, to the lord's house, with singing and dancing. There a banquet was spread and, in the patio, a grand ball was held, attended by the Indians called *netatiliztli,* some two thousand of them. After vespers, following in this the Castilian custom, the notables and relatives of Don Hernando brought gifts to the newlyweds, and the Marqués del Valle [Cortés] himself had one of his servants offer them magnificent gifts.[34]

The Franciscans administered the sacrament of penitence, which had been introduced in 1526,[35] in a very methodical fashion. Every Sunday afternoon they gathered up the Indians who were to confess during the following week, examined them in the Christian doctrine (it is noteworthy that they did not administer any sacrament without an examination of this kind), and instructed them in the necessity and efficacy of penitence, and the three conditions required for the remission of sins: repentance, acknowledgment, and restitution, after which they gave them practical instructions about confessing. On the morning of confession day they read them a list of all sins that man can commit. During Lent, the season especially designated for the administration of the sacrament, the friar-interpreters devoted themselves solely to confessing the Indians. During the rest of the year they confessed all who expressed a desire for it, those who had not confessed during Lent, and those who were to be married.[36] The Augustinians were more expeditious in their procedures. For example, the village of Tiripitío, in Michoacán, had been divided into quarters [barrios], each of which had its own confession day. The inhabitants were summoned to the church and collectively given absolution for venial sins and ordinary lapses, after which came individual confessions for graver faults.[37] But among them also Lent was the preeminent season of the Christian confession, as established by the Church.[38] The sick, of course, could confess at any time of the year.[39]

Pettazzoni, in his study of the Mexican [Aztec] confession, thinks that this custom may have facilitated in part the introduction of the Christian confession.[40] It could, indeed, have facilitated its introduction and also, possibly, its practice, but certainly not the understanding of it. Moreover, Pettazzoni himself soon makes some very judicious reservations in correction of his thesis. Penitence in general and the sacrament that bears its name are closely connected with the notion of sin, and are incomprehensible to anyone ignorant of that notion. We have seen that the Mexicans thought of sin as a material soiling. They had no conception of the sin of intent. We have also seen the great concern of the missionaries to emphasize this point. Moreover, although certain acts, such as homicide, were reprehensible from a legal point of view, the pagan confession concerned only sexual life and drunkenness. Besides, the faults committed in a state of drunkenness were not imputed to it, but to the god of wine, and to wine itself. "They even write, not unreasonably," adds Sahagún, "that they got drunk in order to commit a desired act, without exposing themselves to accounting for it as a crime, thus avoiding punishment for it." In this fashion many Christian Indians made excuses for their sins, saying they were drunk when they committed them, and it was difficult to get them to see that drunkenness, far from reducing their responsibility, was only one more sin added to the others.[41] Another difficulty was that the pagan confession formed a part of temporal justice. It frequently happened that the Indians, after having committed some crime, took refuge in a convent, where they confessed and did penance, whereupon they asked for a note to the authorities, [to the effect] that they had nothing further to account for. Many missionaries, through

117

ignorance of this custom, did not suspect this fraud, or know that repentance, most frequently, had nothing to do with the procedure of the penitent.[42]

Difficulties of another order were encountered, attested by Franciscan and Augustinian documents. Indians would present themselves before the tribunal of penitence without showing any pain or regret for their sins. Did one have the right [in such cases] to absolve them? Many confessors were perplexed. It was extremely hard at the same time to get detailed confessions out of the Indians, so hard that the Augustinians of Tiripitío reached the point of thinking that [the Indians] knowingly gave them false information. A closer examination showed that their penitents were generally sincere in acknowledging their actual sins, and that their fantasy applied only to the number of times they had sinned. [The Indians] did not often clarify the matter. If the confessor suggested a number they accepted it an once and applied it to all their other sins, meaning, perhaps, that they had committed them a certain number of times. Some religious wondered whether they were capable of confessing properly and whether they should be admitted to the sacrament any longer. They consulted their colleague Fray Juan Bautista de Moya, who was renowned for his theological learning and his knowledge of the natives. He answered that the errors and omissions of the Indians should not be given an excessive importance, for they were almost always attributable to faulty memory; that one should only ask them to acknowledge their sins with complete sincerity, to repent of them truly, and to resolve not to repeat them.[43] The Franciscans who faced the same problems came to the same conclusions.[44]

The explanation given by Fray Juan Bautista de Moya was clearly just. Illiterate people generally have an excellent memory, but it is a specialized memory,[45] and the Tarascans had not yet had time to train their own with respect to this wholly strange Catholic confession. But the explanation of Father Moya is only a partial one. Let us leave to one side, as too easy a solution (although it may not be entirely negligible) that invincible and almost pathological love of lying that has been observed at times among primitive peoples.[46] One should, moreover, guard against taking uncertainty for lying, lack of precision for fantasy, as Europeans frequently do when dealing with noncivilized people.[47] The Tarascans, who had no complicated system of numbers like that of the Aztecs, had, in common with other primitive peoples, a profound distaste for all arithmetical operations, however rudimentary. *Mutatis mutandis,* one could doubtless apply to them these two passages from Dobrizhoffer, one of which concerns the Abipones, the other the Guaraní:

They are not only ignorant of arithmetic; they reject it. When one tries to get them to perform unfamiliar operations, their memory fails them. They cannot abide having to count; it bores them. Consequently, in order to avoid answering the questions that are put to them, they will hold up several fingers —this either to deceive themselves or their questioners. . . . In general, we had less trouble teaching them music, or painting, or sculpture, than arithmetic. They can pronounce all the numbers in Spanish, but when it comes to counting they are so often confused that one cannot be too careful when trying to follow them in such matters.[48]

As has been said as a marginal note to the studies of Lévy-Bruhl, most primitives count only by "a faculty of visual intuition." [49] Sins that are localized in time but not in space, especially sins of intent and sins of thought, were beyond the visual intuition of the Tarascans, at least in the counting of them. The Tarascan penitent, pressed and tormented by the embarrassing questions of a confessor, who seemed to him extraordinarily meticulous, could not make the effort of memory and arithmetic demanded of him, and so ventured a guess, or accepted at once the number suggested by the religious and stood by it to the end. Thus he avoided a painful task, and thought that his meekness would satisfy the missionary.[50]

Escobar, who relates these difficulties in Tiripitío, says that the Augustinians had the same experience in the Cortés estate.[51] The Indians of the Nahuatl civilization, on the other hand, seem to have had a sharper feeling for exactness—which is not astonishing, given the precision and complexity of their system of enumeration and their calendar. Some of them made written lists of their sins, complete with details.[52] Others had recourse to pictures analogous to their ideographs. Motolinía made use of this procedure at Toluca one day when he was besieged by penitents.

119

Confessor and penitent each held a straw, with which they pointed to the figures representing the sins. The confession was thus made very short, all the more so, adds Motolinía, since the pictures were so accurate and detailed that the confessor rarely had to ask further questions.[53] The Indians, with a scrupulous exactness and sincerity that deserve mention, did not altogether trust their recollections and memory to establish [the accuracy of] the pictures, but proceeded as follows: As they read the list of all possible sins (noted above), they indicated their sins with grains or little pebbles, together with the circumstances and number, after which they had only to transcribe all this in their fashion.[54]

This system, Motolinía tells us, had an advantage other than precision, for it reduced considerably the length of the confession, an advantage that was appreciated because the Indians were fond of confessing.[55] Since the number of confessors was small, the Indians did not hesitate—fifteen, twenty, twenty-five at a time—to manufacture excuses to receive absolution, and when they found a confessor anywhere they immediately formed an interminable line, like ants, one might have said. The worst trouble these Indians gave, Motolinía says finally, was in the confessions, for they appeared at all hours of the day or night, in the churches or on the roads, so that the whole year became a Lent.[56] Unfortunately, there were not enough religious, nor were all of them suitable for hearing the natives' confessions. In 1556, Archbishop Montúfar of Mexico stated that he would consider himself very happy if three or four thousand Indians, out of the fifty or sixty thousand of his diocese old enough to confess, should receive absolution every year. Some of them, he added, go for twenty years without confessing; others never confess at all. Motolinía tells us, indeed, that many sick [dying] confessed for the first time,[57] although the Christians of the diocese of Mexico, concludes the archbishop, are the most fervent and best organized. [If this was true there], what must the situation have been in places where a priest was seen only at long intervals?[58] Should this insufficiency be attributed to the imperialism of the Franciscans who, with a small number of missionaries, wanted to keep for themselves three-fourths of the territory, and who prevented the Dominicans and Augustinians from establishing themselves in regions that had no priests? The testimony of the Dominican Fray

Andrés de Moguer, who makes this accusation in a letter to the Council of the Indies, does not inspire confidence. He risks being too partial, and his tone is peevish, venomous, and altogether disagreeable.[59] And, although we know of the conflicts between the three Orders, and between the regulars and the seculars, it seems to me that in this one we must recognize a phenomenon that was inevitable in vast territories served by a limited number of priests. I have encountered examples of it elsewhere.[60]

The religious cannot be reproached with narrowing the gateway to regeneration. They realized that, given the Indians' timidity, it was necessary carefully to avoid everything which in the penitents' eyes might have the appearance of criticism or reproach, and, above all, to show, as did the Dominican Fray Domingo de la Anunciación,[61] a profound sorrow at the sins that had just been confessed. The Franciscans gave absolution with an indulgence and breadth of spirit which scandalized Montúfar, who was already inclined to smell heresy on all sides.[62] At the same time, in order not to discourage the new converts, or turn them away from a sacrament, or tempt them to conceal their sins for fear of what they regarded as a punishment,[63] the religious ordinarily imposed only very light penances.

Some [of the Indians], nevertheless, with the advice or authorization of the religious, imposed upon themselves, in addition to their penances, the most austere mortifications of the flesh, such as fasting and scourging. Scourging in particular seemed to them a very meritorious thing, and the penitents were frequently disappointed when the confessor did not impose it. "Why do you not order me to be whipped?" Many of them, especially at Tlaxcala, adopted the custom of scourging themselves every Friday in Lent, and during droughts or epidemics.[64] We shall see later on how the Spaniards introduced processions of flagellants.[65] López de Gómara not unjustly observes that the Indians, because of the sanguinary practices of pre-Conquest paganism, were well prepared to accept the scourge. He adds that some [religious] objected to this form of corporal penance, convinced that the Indians would give themselves up to it in a pagan spirit.[66] Besides, I am morally certain that these flagellations, if performed under the supervision of the missionaries, could not have degenerated into dangerous practices, as happens today in Tzintzuntzan, where the natives are allowed to scourge themselves for several hours with nail-studded straps until they fall in a faint, or become sickly or infirm for the rest of their days.[67]

According to Motolinía, when an Indian had taken the goods of his neighbor he was not at all hesitant about making restitution, preferring to take his punishment in this life, even at the risk of extreme poverty. They freed the slaves they had owned before conversion, marrying them off and helping them to make a living, and they tended to restore the inheritances they had received, if they thought them unjustly acquired.[68]

It is not surprising that at a time when the most pious laymen only rarely took communion, the administration of the Eucharist to the Indians should have been viewed with many doubts and misgivings. Some religious were of the opinion that they could not be admitted to the communion table, that they had been too recently converted, that they were incapable of knowing the value and grandeur of the sacrament, and that it should be denied them lest they fall into frequent sacrileges. Others thought that it was impossible to take a general and fundamental decision, that this was a theological question, and that it was reasonable to give communion to the Indians who asked for it, when they had been confessing frequently for four or five years and were able to distinguish between ordinary and sacramental bread, between an unconsecrated and a consecrated wafer, and when their confessor was satisfied with their conduct and piety.[69] Motolinía, who thus summarizes the two positions, and who, after a solid experience among the Indians, favored the second solution, concluded moreover that the priest who refused communion to a properly disposed Indian would be committing mortal sin.[70] The bull *Altitudo divini consilii* and the synod of 1539 supported him and his colleague Fray Jacobo Daciano, who was the first to admit the Tarascans of Michoacán to communion.[71] The Augustinian Fray Nicolás de Agreda, member of an Order that had always shown particular confidence in the spiritual capacities of the Indians, presented the assembly with a *Dictamen sobre que a los indios se les debe ministrar el Sacramento de la Eucaristía*,[72] and the assembly agreed with him. It began by treating with some irony the objections that had been offered. The reason for refusing

122

communion to the Indians, goes the decision, is not that they are bad Christians, but that they are Indians and new converts. This is not a serious objection. Communion was instituted not only for the weak and the sick, but for the strong and healthy; it is a remedy, not a reward. And from the moment that the Indians were trusted and had been baptized, there was no authority for depriving them of the Eucharist, which would help them meet the engagements they had undertaken when they entered the Church. It was enough that they should approach the sacrament in the proper frame of mind and with the approval of their confessors.[73] The synod of 1546, as was to be expected, confirmed this decision.[74]

One suspects, unfortunately, that these decisions of the synods were not obeyed everywhere and by everyone. Why does it happen, indeed, that at a very late date, 1573, another Augustinian religious, Fray Pedro de Agurto, thought it his duty to publish a treatise demonstrating that the sacrament of the Eucharist must be administered to the Indians? [75] The fact is that, despite the formal orders of the ecclesiastical authority, obstacles to [admitting the Indians to] the communion table continued to pile up. The Indians were pictured as public sinners, and most of them as incorrigible drunkards, not capable of understanding the value and meaning of the sacrament. In a word, they lacked the knowledge to receive it properly. These were pretty frivolous arguments, and the opponents of this bit of Jansenism had no trouble in showing that the first objection could apply only to certain individuals; that no sin, unless it was inveterate and rooted, could systematically exclude a Christian from the Eucharist, that, moreover, there were graver sins than drunkenness, and no one dreamed of denying the Eucharist to those who committed them; that the only two conditions necessary to receiving the Eucharist were reason or discretion, and [the ability] to distinguish between the bread of the Eucharist and ordinary bread; that it could not be argued that the Indians did not fulfill these two conditions; that in this respect a great many Spanish peasants were not superior to them; that only an extraordinary mental incapacity could justify depriving a Christian of the sacrament; and, finally, that if the Indians did not have the necessary knowledge, it was their pastors' duty to teach them, which was, after all, a minor matter, for it only amounted to knowing the *Pater,* the *Ave,* and the *Credo*. Are we waiting, concluded Fray Juan Bautista, for the Indians to be perfect before we admit them to the Eucharist?

Nevertheless—and this point must be emphasized, for many have held the contrary opinion—some did not wait; the confessors merely proceeded with considerable caution. It frequently happened that they refused communion to Indians who very insistently demanded it. Mendieta himself was not in favor of systematically denying the Eucharist to the Indians; nor was he in favor of admitting them all.[76] But the religious little by little tried to bring to the sacrament Indians who did not demand it, but whose virtues and piety they recognized. It was these Indians who held back, on the ground that they were not yet worthy. In any event, many Indians of the sodality of the Holy Sacrament, which was under the direction of the Franciscans, took communion during Lent. There were villages in which as many as five thousand persons were seen at communion [in Lent], but in the course of the year it was rarely administered except to the sick. The principal reason for this parsimony was that the Franciscans were badly overworked, for they did not admit Indians to the Eucharist without a preliminary confession. Not only that, but the religious prepared them in minute detail for the reception of the sacrament. After confession, they gave a special badge to those they judged properly prepared and then gave them a short examination in the meaning of the Trinity, the unity of the Divine Essence, the Incarnation and Passion of the Son of God, the Eucharist, and consecration, preaching them a brief sermon on this last point.

Fray Maturino Gilberti, if we may believe a document presented at his trial, made clear to his faithful the meaning and importance of consecration by having them adore a consecrated wafer, after which he crushed unconsecrated wafers under foot.[77] Finally, on the eve of the day designated for communion, they were briefly instructed in the necessary physical procedures—fasting and conjugal abstinence—and were told, out of respect for the Holy Sacrament, to dress themselves in their best and cleanest garments.[78]

The Dominicans divided their converts into two categories: the first, after examination, receiving permission to take communion whenever they wished—these were called "graduados" or "communiotlacatl," that is to say, "those who commune"; the second, taking communion only at Easter, or when they were gravely ill, and then only with the consent of their confessors.[79]

The Augustinians adopted the custom of giving all their Indians a general instruction in the Eucharist; the dogma of the Real Presence was explained to them, that is, that Christ was present in the least particle of the wafer; they were told that they had to be in the state of grace, and were not to eat or drink anything after midnight. Then, on each Sunday of Lent, they were given more detailed instructions and subjected to a brief examination on the catechism, after which the religious designated those who would be received for communion on the following Saturday— Saturday being selected doubtless because Sunday, with its services and catechism, was too full. On Friday the communicants had to listen to a special instruction on the sacrament before admission, and the preparations necessary to its proper reception. The Indians had to arrive at seven o'clock, dressed as for a wedding, and remain silent up to the moment of communion, which they performed with great piety, some of them crawling to the altar on their knees, a custom that is still observed. Then, under the guidance of a religious, they consummated their act of grace. Before communion, according to Grijalva, they recited in chorus in Nahuatl the prayer of St. Thomas Aquinas, *Omnipotens sempiterne Deus,* and the prayer of the act of grace by the same author. At first, the Augustinians did not bring the viaticum to the sick, because of the squalor and filth of their huts. Later, when the dwellings of the natives were more decent, they gave communion to the sick in their own houses. The priest was accompanied on that occasion by a numerous party of cantors, musicians, and candle bearers.[80]

According to several sources, the Augustinians were not excessively severe in their selection of communicants. At Tezontepec [for example] they admitted almost all Indians to the Eucharist.[81] At Atotonilco they gave communion to all Mexicans, that is, to all Nahuatl-speaking Indians, with very rare exceptions. On the other hand, they admitted only a minority of the Otomí, whom they held to be of inferior intelligence, while they educated them to increase their number of communicants.[82] At Pahuatlán, where there was still a large majority of Otomí, many natives

125

received the sacrament at Easter.[83] Elsewhere, as in the Sierra de Meztitlán, [the Augustinians] had to be more circumspect, for they were dealing with a people still rough and coarse in spirit, so the Eucharist was administered only in a few large villages.[84] The same was true in the region of Tlalchinolticpac [Hidalgo], where, along about 1570, hardly more than four hundred, out of about eleven thousand, Indians were taking communion.[85] The religious, nevertheless, raised the number of communicants to a thousand.

At the end of this account I hope I may be permitted to point out the incorrectness of the current statement, [to the effect] that the Spanish missionaries refused to admit the Indians to communion. The question is truly complex, obscured by conflicting opinions and practices, and wrongfully settled by recourse to a partial and insufficient documentation, which does not permit all aspects of the problem to be seen.[86]

We are very badly informed about the administration of confirmation. A brief of Leo X had authorized the religious to confirm in the absence of a bishop. With the exception of Motolinía, however, who had performed confirmations before the arrival of [Bishop] Zumárraga, they did not avail themselves of this privilege, but only prepared the natives to receive the sacrament,[87] which beyond a doubt was administered rather generally. Zumárraga, four days before his death, in a letter to Charles V, stated, with evident exaggeration, to be sure, that he had been confirming for forty days on end, and that the number of confirmands exceeded four hundred thousand.[88]

In the early days there was difficulty in procuring consecrated holy oils for extreme unction,[89] but, since it was not essential to salvation, it was rarely administered, at least by the Franciscans. The huts of the Indians, we are told, were not sufficiently clean to allow a proper administration of the sacrament, and to bring the dying to the church might have meant their death before arrival. Besides, the scanty number of priests were overworked, so they administered supreme unction on demand only to leading citizens whose houses were fit for the ceremony.[90] The Augustinians, on the contrary, whose two principal chroniclers are quite clear on this point, administered this sacrament generally and habitually.[91] It is likely that there were disagreements between the two Orders [in this matter], for in 1573 [the Augustinian] Fray Pedro de Agurto argued that the Indians should be given supreme unction as well as the Eucharist.[92] Here one encounters again in this Order that sympathy for the spiritual needs of the Indians, which I have already had occasion to mention.

7 *Virtues of the Founders*

tO found the Church in a pagan land and bring into being a new Christendom, it is not enough to learn the native languages, baptize the inhabitants, teach them the catechism, preach the Christian doctrine, and administer the sacraments. All this difficult and complex task could lead only to illusory results if it did not rest upon the authority of the missionary, and if his acts did not conform to his teaching. It is hardly conceivable, indeed, that the apostolic work can be accomplished by a missionary without zeal, love of souls, a [holy] interior life, and a spirit of self-abnegation and sacrifice. And it is even less conceivable that the pagans will recognize the superiority of a new religion, if the missionaries of that religion fail to demonstrate by their daily example that superiority in a living and palpable fashion. The religious of Mexico, like the others, understood that they had to prevail by their unselfishness, their poverty, and the austerity of their habits. They were, to be sure, already dedicated to all this by the vows of their Orders, but they also realized that living among the Indians they had to observe their vows more scrupulously than elsewhere. As I approach the end of the first part of my study, in which I have attempted to summarize the thankless labor of founding the Mexican Church, I may be permitted to devote a few pages, in the words of one of the great historians of that heroic period, "to the exemplary life that the servants of God, the first evangelizers of the country, led among this great multitude of infidels, a life that was a living sermon for their conversion." [1]

To set an example, to teach and preach by example, was almost an obsession among the missionaries of Mexico, especially while they were ignorant of the native languages. Thus Martín de Valencia attempted to compensate for this lack by the grandeur of his example,[2] by prayer above all. Knowing how much the Indians were influenced in their conduct by what they saw others do, he prayed in places where he could be seen by everyone, "so that, by imitating him, they might come to God, because the Indians are very prone to do what they see others doing." [3] Fray Antonio de Maldonado, who went to Mexico in 1529 with Fray Antonio de Ciudad-Rodrigo, did the same. "Although he had not learned the Mexican language well enough to be able to preach in it and confess the Indians, the work he did in the provinces was of very great importance, for by his saintly and exemplary life he converted the idolatrous pagans and strengthened the faith of the new converts." [4]

Even the most eminent linguists, naturally, were not exempted from setting an example by their way of life, nor did they believe themselves to be exempted. As Muñoz writes about Gilberti: "Everyone in general uses his printed books and their sound doctrine, to preach to and instruct the natives, for which he was extremely beloved and respected, and [the Indians] readily put into practice the virtues he recommended in his sermons and good advice. Such was the credit that his edifying life won for him in their eyes, a matter of great importance among the Indians, who are much influenced by appearances." [5] If Gilberti had been wanting in charity, and if he had not preached by example, he himself, despite his knowledge of languages, would have been "as sounding brass or a tinkling cymbal."

He was a model of disinterestedness, and no one, perhaps, could have reaped a greater spiritual harvest. We have seen how the *Pláticas* of the Twelve and the *doctrina* of the Dominicans emphasized this point, that is, that the missionaries desired souls, not gold, not silver, not precious stones. The cupidity of so many Spaniards made this disinterestedness all the more necessary and set it in relief. "The Indians marveled," writes Dávila

Padilla, "at the perseverance of the preachers, and even more at their scorn of the gold and silver to which the Spanish laymen gave such value, and the religious' contempt of worldly riches strengthened their belief in spiritual riches." [6] Fray Domingo de Betanzos refused to accept the four villages that Alonso de Estrada offered the Dominicans,[7] and the religious of the three Orders always opposed requiring the Indians to pay tithes, lest they might think that the missionaries had come among them for personal profit.[8]

Viceroy Luis de Velasco paid them this tribute on February 1, 1558: "It cannot truthfully be said that the religious seek temporal goods, for to my knowledge they have not thus far owned any private property. They wear garments of monk's cloth and coarse stuff, and their eating is so moderate that they are hard put to sustain themselves, and if on any day of the year they have something left over, they give it to the poor." [9] They combined poverty of living with their disinterestedness. The Augustinians, whose convents were famous for their magnificence, led a very poor life among their sumptuous surroundings.[10] In 1545, Zumárraga called the Emperor's attention to the extreme humbleness of the Franciscan convent in Mexico City, which Cervantes de Salazar, in fact, calls "mediano." "The monastery," he writes, "receives only a few alms, the religious there live in the greatest poverty, and it is so damp that they all get crippled with rheumatism." [11] It is told of the Twelve that when they arrived at Mexico City, they heard the Indians whispering "Motolinía, motolinía." Fray Toribio de Benavente asked what the word meant, and when he learned that it meant "the poor one," he declared that such would be his name thenceforth.[12] A symbolic story, which could be applied to many missionaries of New Spain. *Motolinía,* the poor one, had come to evangelize the poor.

In a difficult country of rigorous climate, where roads and inns did not exist, where work never stopped, poverty was necessarily accompanied by suffering. To preach the Gospel in such trying conditions, men had to be trained to expect every deprivation. In New Galicia Fray Martín de Jesús could give the children their catechism only at night,[13] and Fray Rodrigo de la Cruz wrote that in a journey of more than eighty leagues he often had nothing to live on but water.[14] Did not Zumárraga say that Martín de

Valencia died of pure want?[15] His case is not unique. Privations and fatigue caused a heavy mortality among the Dominicans, who had to cover too vast a territory. "Since the religious of this Order of St. Dominic," Viceroy Velasco wrote Prince Philip in 1554, "eat no meat and travel on foot, their suffering is intolerable, and this is why they live such a short time."[16] Dávila Padilla and Franco record the sufferings and austerities of Fray Domingo de Santa María, Fray Domingo de la Anunciación, Fray Gonzalo Lucero, and Fray Jordán de Santa Catalina.[17] The same was true of the Augustinians. Fray Juan Bautista de Moya "would not allow anyone to procure food from the Indians for him, and would only accept the *tamales*[19] which were offered to the religious as well as *camotes*[18] and at times a bit of *atole* prepared for the sick in the hospitals, and he took so little that the Indians, who themselves got along on a very small amount, were dismayed and wondered, they said, how he sustained himself."[20]

All that, however, was as nothing compared with the asceticism of Fray Antonio de Roa, who, we are told, seeing the Indians barefoot and naked and sleeping on the ground, would wear nothing but a coarse robe and sleep on a board. Seeing that they ate roots and were so miserably nourished, he gave up all pleasure in eating and drinking, and for a long time drank no wine and ate no meat or bread. By thus identifying himself with his poor Indians he succeeded in winning and converting them very rapidly. When, however, he thought they were not sufficiently regretful for their sins, he tried by his example to inpire them with a spirit of repentance and a horror of the slightest fault. As he preached, he had himself scourged in the sight of all, and, as the Indians, he said, give little weight to words without deeds, once, while speaking of hell, he threw himself upon some burning coals, where he stayed for some time, and then arose abruptly, calling their attention to the fact that, if he could not stand such pain any longer, what must be the pain of eternal fire! To demonstrate that the body is a slave, he had his skin burned by bits of torch. Every time he saw a cross he had himself cruelly scourged, insulted, and spit upon. All that, he told the Indians, God had suffered in order to redeem the sins of men. In this fashion he fixed in their minds the recollection of his teaching.[21]

Self-abnegation, poverty, and asceticism were not only necessary and salutary examples; for the missionary they were the only possible means of identifying himself with his flock, of making himself an Indian among his Indians, who were strangers to cupidity and who for the most part had led a hard and miserable existence. The natives really understood that the religious, in heart and soul, had become one of them. In this, perhaps, rather than in their good works, one can explain the veneration in which they were held, and, as Suárez de Peralta could say, "they are almost worshipped by the Indians." [22] And, doubtless, many of the Indians, whether their missionaries were Franciscans, Dominicans, or Augustinians, would have answered as did those who were asked why they so loved the Franciscans: "Because they go about poor and barefoot, like us; because they eat the same food as we do; because they establish themselves among us; because they live peacefully with us." [23] This is the key to souls, the key without which all evangelization comes to an immediate and definite stop, and without which it may seem to be only a deceitful and empty façade.

In all these anecdotes and tales it is evidently important to make some allowance for hagiography, so it would not be well to make imprudent generalizations. In Mexico there were some holy missionaries and excellent religious. Others were less worthy of their cloth and of the task that had been entrusted to them. Others had passing weaknesses, and still others, whose lives were irreproachable, committed errors. Saintliness may give to some a clairvoyance superior to that attained by the ordinary run of Christians, but it is not always and necessarily a synonym of infallibility. It is the duty of the historian not to conceal these unworthy acts, failings, and errors. Respect for the truth has forced me, and will force me again, to point them out. But I should be equally failing in respect for the truth if I neglected to record the eminent virtues of so many of those who founded the Church in New Spain.

II THE STABILIZATION
OF THE CHURCH

8 *Social Organization and Public Works*

IF one leaves out of the reckoning the large city of Tenochtitlán and the Zapotecs of the valley of Tlacolula, who formed compact groups,[1] pre-Hispanic Mexico was not a country with a concentrated urban population. Even today the villages are made up mostly of scattered houses.[2] This dispersion was much more marked in the sixteenth century. In some parts it was even more accentuated after the coming of the Spaniards, for in 1551 the Franciscan Fray Francisco de Guzmán pointed out that the natives of the Jilotepec region had been obliged to take refuge in the mountains because of the ravages committed on their lands by the cattle of certain civil officers and rich Spaniards. He added that this prevented the religious from visiting and teaching as they should.[3] The arrangement of the villages and even the houses was in fact a formidable obstacle to methodical evangelization, and for the missionaries was a source of hardships and dangers, as Motolinía complained. "Some of the villages," he wrote, "are on top of mountains, others on the floor of valleys; so the religious are obliged to climb up into the clouds, for the mountains are so high that they are always covered with clouds, and at other times they must descend into the abyss. Since the country is very rough and because of the humidity is covered with mud in many places and slippery spots where it is easy to fall, the poor religious cannot travel

135

over these roads without suffering great hardship and fatigue."[4] And so, he concluded, in a letter to Charles V, it would be necessary to gather the Indians into villages, like the peasants of Spain, in order to evangelize and civilize them more easily.[5] The Dominicans made the same request in similar terms,[6] and one of them, Fray Domingo de la Anunciación, remarked that the situation was full of difficulties from the physical point of view alone, for the Indians who lived in these scattered [villages], in remote and inaccessible regions, were fleeced with impunity by their caciques.[7]

It was an extraordinary and noteworthy thing that the Crown, the episcopacy, and the civil authorities were in general agreement on this point among themselves and with the missionaries. The only notable exception to my knowledge was Fray Pedro de Ayala, Franciscan bishop of New Galicia, whose pessimism is well known. According to him, when the religious founded villages they sought to build in them the most sumptuous convents that their rules permitted,[8] and he thought that the dispersion of the Indians was better for work in the fields. But in 1503 the royal instructions to Nicolás de Ovando had already envisaged the gathering of Indians into villages, with a church, a native *cabildo, regidores,* hospitals, and so on.[9] In a *cédula* dated at Valladolid, June 26, 1523, Charles V looked forward to the development of native life in organized villages.[10] He issued another letter, dated at Palencia, September 28, 1534, in which he prescribed in an oversimplified way the concentration of the scattered Indians of Michoacán in a single town.[11] He returned to the same subject at Valladolid, August 23, 1538,[12] and *cédulas* of the same tenor were continuous from 1550 to 1570.[13] Zumárraga, on his part, strongly and frequently insisted on the necessity of gathering the natives into villages.[14] The episcopal *junta* of 1537, the *junta eclesiástica* of 1546, and the synod of 1555 made the same recommendation.[15] Viceroy Luis de Velasco was resolutely in favor of this system, although he, better than anyone else, saw all the difficulties in it,[16] and a high civil officer, after reporting to Philip II that he had given the order for congregating the Indians in villages, in the regions he had visited, ended by saying it was the most necessary thing in the world, because before [his coming] the patrimony of God and the King was beyond all control.[17] The spiritual advantages of the system were complacently listed in a letter written by the native *regidores* of the municipality of Huejotzingo: "Your Majesty should know," they wrote the King, "that the good that has been done to us all, in soul and body, by congregating us is beyond description. In fact, since our congregation, if anyone falls sick he can confess and receive the sacraments, and his neighbor can help him, and, if he dies, he is buried in the church and the religious and the others pray for him, and we can come to hear the sermon and the Mass, and live together like men. All these things, or even one of them, were impossible while we lived scattered in the mountains." [18]

In the circumstances it is not astonishing that the three Orders competed in the founding of Indian villages, a task that required them to undertake the whole work of material organization and civilization. Among the Dominicans the most remarkable instance was that accomplished by Fray Francisco Marín among the natives of the Mixteca. He had found them a barbarous people; he taught them to dress, feed themselves properly, and live in communities, and he initiated them into civilized life. He set up a common chest for the expenses of a general nature, and he directed the construction of churches and public buildings. [19] A similar work among the Tarascans was accomplished by the Franciscan Fray Juan de San Miguel. His predecessor, Fray Marín de Jesús, had only had time for the preliminary task: destroying idols, putting a stop to pagan ceremonies, and building churches. Fray Juan had to reassemble the Indians, who were living in the mountains "like a flock without a shepherd," as La Rea said, and, the chronicler continues, he was the lawgiver expected by [King] David, who was to teach these hordes that they were men, not beasts. He founded towns and villages, the sites of which he selected with meticulous care, laying out the squares and streets, and marking the locations of the principal buildings. His masterpiece was, beyond a doubt, the little town of Uruapan, in the most delightful part of Michoacán, which Father Ponce's secretary was later to describe so enthusiastically. Its balmy quietness, cooled by innumerable brooks, makes an unforgettable impression on the traveler. Here also [Fray Juan] laid out streets and squares, and indicated the quarters, following a plan "worthy of the Roman nobility." [20] He had valuable collaborators, such as Fray Jacobo Daciano, one of the great apostles of Michoacán and founder of the village of Querécuaro.[21] Their fellows did even more, creating a completely artifical village, the population of which had no unity at all. For fear lest the children reared in the monasteries would revert to paganism when they returned to their families, [the Franciscans] founded a special village for them, four leagues from Mexico City, not far from Coyoacán, near a convent, to keep their Christian faith intact.[22] At times they removed entire villages whose situation offered difficulties. Thus, during the very first years—the convent dates from 1529 —the famous Franciscan architect, Fray Juan de Alameda, who later (1539) laid out the village of Tula, transported the community of Huejotzingo (which had at the time more than 40,000 inhabitants) from an exceedingly rough location to the site it occupies today, where the monastery was built.[23]

But it was the Augustinians who seemed to be masters of the art of founding villages, and policing and administering them.[24] Like the Franciscans, they gave their principal attention to the region of Michoacán, which was really the chosen theater of the early evangelization. There Fray Diego de Chaves organized the village of Yuriria (Guanajuato);[25] Fray Francisco de Villafuerte, that of Cuitzeo;[26] Fray Juan Bautista de Mora, that of Pungarabato.[27] The people of the vicinity of Tiripitío had been living scattered about in poor huts. The Augustinians gathered them together, laid out squares and streets, brought in water, erected a hospital and a convent, built houses all on one level, following the custom of the country. Most of the houses had, however, besides the bedrooms, a common room, a kitchen, and a chapel where the holy images were kept, and where the family came to pray. They built, moreover, wide and solid causeways over the swamps to the south in order to connect Tiripitío with nearby towns.[28]

Michoacán was not the only [province] to benefit from this civilizing activity, as attested by the urbanizing work successfully carried out at Atotonilco and in the province of Meztitlán (Hidalgo) by Fray Alonso de Borja and other Augustinians;[29] in the region of Chilapa and Tlapa (Guerrero), by Fray Agustín de la Coruña and Fray Gerónimo de San Esteban;[30] and the work of Fray Pedro de San Jerónimo among the

Piranda of Charo, whom he brought down from the mountains of Zurundaneo and settled in a village divided into four quarters, each with its church; [31] and as is proved above all in the administration of the village of Santa Fe by Father Alonso de Borja, who was in charge there before taking over the government of Atotonilco. This village of [Santa Fe], inhabited only by converts, was founded two leagues west of Mexico City, where it still stands. [It was founded] by the future bishop of Michoacán, Vasco de Quiroga, while he was a member of the Audiencia, and he entrusted its direction to the Augustinians. They put Father Borja in charge; he founded a convent, a school for young people, and an asylum for children, and forced the inhabitants to lead an almost monastic life. Under his direction the village attained a population of 30,000. [32] I shall return to Santa Fe when I discuss hospitals.

These villages were entirely in the hands of the religious, even their temporal affairs. They administered justice, decided questions of succession, distributed the goods of the dead among the various heirs, and took care of widows and orphans. [33] The missionaries thus became true political authorities. We are told of a Franciscan named Fray Bernardino (not Sahagún, for he came from Alcalá de Henares), who governed a territory of forty [square] leagues, obeyed punctually by the Indians in all things. [34]

Like the villages of Spain and those of pre-Conquest Mexico—the two traditions are in agreement— [35] these "villages of evangelization" were grouped and organized around a vast space which served as a *plaza mayor* and a market place at the same time—the *tianguiz,* as it was called in Mexico. This square was the heart of the village, the center of community life, and it still is. Here one found the fountain and the gibbet (*horca*). It was surrounded by public buildings: the church, the schools (usually placed near the church), and the town hall, which housed the court and the prison. Here the community funds (*caja*) were kept, and travelers were lodged. These buildings were usually constructed of good stone, "ex calce et immensis saxis," says Valadés. [36]

In detail how was the founding of native villages done? The documents give us only vague phrases. Luckily, Beaumont, in his *Crónica de Michoacán,* has an exact description of the founding of Acámbaro

(Guanajuato). First a large wooden cross was erected; then the streets were marked out; a chapel was built near the cross, with a kind of wooden door frame in which two bells were hung; and, on Sunday, September 20, 1526, the priest of the village of Tula celebrated the Mass of the Holy Ghost there, which was followed by the Rosary, the chanting of the *alabado,* and a recitation of the *doctrina,* for the edification of the pagan Chichimecs, a great number of whom attended the ceremony. Then followed the distribution of lots for the building of houses and the laying out of gardens. The operation was somewhat complicated, because this agglomeration was entirely artificial—"una congregación de indios"— and included Otomí and Tarascans. The formalities of the founding ended with a great Indian military parade; but this was not the end, for there had to be an election of the administrators of the new community: *gobernadores, alcaldes, regidores, fiscal mayor,* this last being charged with the control of religious life. Then a small monastery had to be built for the two Franciscan Fathers who had the duty of governing the village. One of them, Fray Antonio Bermul—who, with his companion, Fray Juan Lazo y Quemada, is otherwise quite unknown—organized the water supply and founded the neighboring village of San Mateo de Tocuaro. The construction of houses at Acámbaro took up the whole year of 1528, and in 1529 the Audiencia ordered the erection of a large convent, which was finished in 1532. The native hospital was founded that same year. Thanks to the apostolic activity of the two Franciscans, the village of Acámbaro was completed later, with the founding of a large village of Chichimecs on the far bank of the Lerma River opposite the Otomí-Tarascan community.[37]

The work of congregating [the Indians], which seems to have been very active when these reports were made, was nevertheless inadequate. In 1556, if we may believe Archbishop Alonso de Montúfar, some houses of [only] two religious [each] had to visit as many as twenty villages thirty leagues distant, and at times more than 100,000 souls. Since only one of the two religious could be absent at a time, the visits were very few and extremely hasty. The missionary said Mass, baptized, married, and took himself off. Some villages in the archdiocese of Mexico, although they were the least badly served, went five years without seeing a priest.[38] One must allow for the habitual exaggeration of the prelate [Montúfar]; but we know that in 1570 the Indians of as central a diocese as Tlaxcala were insufficiently grouped.[39] Mendieta, writing in the last years of the sixteenth century, complains that not enough attention had been given to congregating the Indians in villages and to establishing various Spanish villages separate from them.[40] This situation was the result of several factors. First among them should be mentioned the terrain, which was often too broken to admit of the establishment of large communities. The Augustinians made the same complaint about Tlalchinolticpac.[41] On the other hand, as we have seen in one of the early chapters of this study, too often the Orders demanded or accepted the direction of immense territories, which they lacked the resources to evangelize properly, but in which they would not admit other religious or secular priests. We have also seen how the monasteries multiplied and how the missionaries crowded into certain more agreeable or healthier regions, while others were neglected. It will be recalled that for this reason New Galicia and the high plateaus of the north were especially passed by.[42] There is no doubt that, in 1556, Fray Juan de Tapia journeyed through parts of the present states of Jalisco, Nayarit, Sinaloa, and Durango, where he taught, baptized, and gathered the Indians in villages, or got their promise to do so. Four years later, the work of Christianization and civilization began to take form among these warlike and nomadic hordes of the north, which were swept together under the general name of Chichimecs. By 1533, Fray Juan de Padilla had founded the village of Zapotlán, into which he had gathered the Indians of the vicinity. By 1542, Fray Miguel de Bolonia had founded Juchipila (Zacatecas) in the same way, and it at once became a large center of evangelization. By 1554, Fray Francisco Lorenzo and Fray Miguel de Estivales had traversed the region of Ahuacatlán congregating the Indians in organized villages, and building churches.[43] But this was a small affair in these immense stretches.[44] An extremely numerous personnel would have been necessary [to carry it through], and most religious were not attracted to these sterile lands.

At the same time it would be unjust to accuse the missionaries alone, for some difficulties were chargeable to the natives themselves. It

141

frequently happened that the Indians, to avoid the proximity of churches and convents, and to be free to practice their own customs and vices, would make off and install themselves in remote corners; and, since at least two royal *cédulas* had recognized their right to live where they pleased, the administration was helpless [to prevent it].[45] In 1554, Viceroy Luis de Velasco begged the King to give him the power to force the Indians to stay in their own villages; otherwise, the congregation might prove impossible.[46] The Crown's reception of this request is unknown.

In any event one thing is certain, which is that about 1570 the Indians were not sufficiently concentrated to allow the religious to restrict the celebration of the services and the administration of the sacraments to the villages where they usually lived. The [religious] were also obliged, during part of the year, to act as itinerant missionaries. Thus, every Sunday the Augustinians of Atotonilco had to visit the dependencies of their convent; each religious said two masses, in two different villages, baptized and confessed the sick, ministered to the dying, gave communion, blessed the marriages, preached and taught. As Lent approached, they traveled about among the dependent villages to confess all the Indians who had reached the prescribed age, a task that kept them busy from Christmas to Easter.[47] In Meztitlán the situation was the same. The dependent villages were regularly visited by two religious, who went off in opposite directions, said Mass, and administered the sacraments. At the end of their tour they returned to the convent, and two others at once set out to cover the same ground. In this fashion the dependent villages were visited by the missionaries at least eight or nine times a year.[48]

It was not, however, merely a question of congregating the Indians in villages; they had also to live in them. "To preach to a savage," said the Spanish missionary, the Benedictine Salvado, evangelizer of Australia, three centuries later, "to preach to a savage is not difficult, but neither is it very fruitful. In the middle of the sermon the savage turns to the missionary and says: 'Everything you tell me may be very true, but I am very hungry. Will you give me a bit of bread, yes or no?' If you don't give it to him, he turns his back and goes off into the woods to satisfy his hunger. But let's suppose that you do give him something to eat and that the savage settles down and becomes a Christian. Who then will clothe him? Who will provide for him? Hence the need of labor." [49] This labor must be essentially the cultivation of the soil. Now, the religious have always kept up the tradition of kitchen gardens and cool *huertas* [orchards]. The Franciscan monastery at Tlaxcala had a most beautiful *huerta,* watered by a very clear stream, planted with Spanish and native fruit trees; the Augustinian convent at Acolman, the same; in Mexico City also, the Franciscans and Dominicans had vast kitchen gardens, and Dávila Padilla boasts of the fruit orchards of the Dominicans at Tepetlaoxtoc. [50] Motolinía states that almost all orchards of New Spain had been planted by the Friars Minor, and that he himself had successfully raised dates at the convent of Cuernavaca. [51] In this the missionaries were excellent teachers of the Indians. In the hospitals of Santa Fe, which I shall discuss in the next chapter, the children were taught agriculture as a recreation or pastime, which did not interfere with the hours of catechism, "for it was also a kind of catechism and a training in good habits." [52] It was the Dominican Fray Domingo de Santa María who taught the Indians of the Mixteca the systematic cultivation of the prickly pear for the production of cochineal. [53] The Augustinians brought fruit trees from Castile, grew flowers and legumes, taught the Indians to grow wheat, and improved the cultivation of maize. [54] At Tarascan Uruapan Fray Juan de San Miguel had numbers of fruit trees set out: bananas, *ate* [possibly quince], *chicozapote* (Acras Sapota L.), mamey, oranges, and various kinds of citrons. All Indian houses of the village were thus surrounded by small kitchen gardens and little orchards, well-watered; besides, abundant harvests of wheat were gathered at all seasons. [55] The religious were also interested in raising cattle. Fray Domingo de Santa María established a certain number of cattle farms (*estancias*) among the Mixtecs, and the provincial of the Dominicans, Fray Pedro de la Peña, wrote Philip II, on July 25, 1561, that the Dominicans were encouraging in every way the development of farms and the raising of sheep and goats. [56]

One of the most interesting experiments in this kind of co-operation was silk culture, which was especially developed in the Mixteca and encouraged by the Dominicans. [57] Icazbalceta has pointed out the contra-

143

dictions in the documents concerning it. According to him, an examination of the dates shows that, either the Mixteca was not the first province where silk was raised, or that it was not the Dominicans who introduced it there.[58] The matter has only a secondary importance here, for one thing seems to be certain, namely, that although Fray Domingo de Santa María may not perhaps have introduced silk in that country, he had the Indians of Yanhuitlán, who were in his charge, plant mulberry trees, and he taught them to raise silk worms. Fray Francisco Marín did the same.[59] And Burgoa tells us that the people of Achiutla planted more than two [square] leagues of mulberry trees under the direction of his companion. Zumárraga showed the keenest interest in the development of this industry, even requesting that Morisco specialists be sent to New Spain who would be distributed among the villages and teach the natives the cultivation of mulberry trees and the manufacture of silk. This request was favorably received, but the Moriscos never came. At the same time [Zumárraga] ordered the clerk of the Oaxaca cathedral, Alonso de Figuerola, to write a book about the industry for the instruction of the Indians.[60]

Silk culture grew important enough to persuade the Crown to issue a *cédula,* on August 1, 1539, ordering the Indians to pay a tithe on silk, as [the Moriscos did] in the archdiocese of Granada.[61] In 1542, according to Bartolomé de Zárate, *regidor* of the City of Mexico, who does not attempt to conceal his astonishment, more than 9,000 pounds of silk were produced in the diocese of Oaxaca.[62] Motolinía has left us a famous description of the prosperity of the silk industry in the Mixteca. He does not, to be sure, distinguish between the Spaniards' share and the Indians' share, but it seems to me useful to repeat his essential passages here:

This is a very rich and populous region, where there are mines of gold and silver, and very many good mulberry groves, . . . and although this culture is very recent in New Spain, it is said that this year more than 15,000 pounds of silk will be harvested. And this silk is so good that the artisans who work in it say that their *tonotzi* is better than the lustrous silk of Granada, and the lustrous silk of this New Spain is extremely good. . . . It is noteworthy that silk is produced [here] in all seasons of the year, whatever the month. Before writing this letter, in the present year of 1541, I traveled for more than thirty days through the region I am speaking of, and in the month of January in many places I saw many silk worm eggs, some of which were already hatching, some of black worms, some of white, of one, two, three, or four moultings; others already hatched and on the screens; others about to spin; still others in their cocoons, and moths laying eggs. Three things should be noted in what I have said: one, that the eggs can be made to hatch without putting them in one's bosom, or in soiled linen, as is done in Spain; two, that the worms do not die [here] in any season from cold or heat; finally, that the mulberry trees stay green throughout the year—all this owing to the mildness of the climate.[63]

Unfortunately, this prosperity was short-lived, lasting at most some fifty years.[64] Despite the testimony of Fray Domingo de Santa María and despite the authority of Zumárraga, some religious were hostile to this industry, alleging that the raising of silk worms led the Indians to neglect the Lenten services.[65] A Flemish Augustinian, Fray Nicolás de San Pablo (Witte), had a large number of mulberry trees cut down in the valley of Meztitlán.[66] Burgoa tells us, moreover, in veiled language, of the greed of certain *justicias,* who caused the disappearance of the cultivation of mulberry trees and the raising of silk worms. The truth is, however, that it was Chinese competition that definitely killed the silk industry of New Spain, after the colonization of the Philippines. Although imported Chinese silk was of inferior quality, its very low price ruined the Mexican industry.[67]

The development of agriculture is necessarily linked to irrigation. Indeed, it would have been astonishing if the Spaniards had not kept their veneration for water which is still today so striking in the Peninsula. The perpetual fruits and greenery of Uruapan were the work of Fray Juan de San Miguel, who captured and canalized the water of the nearby streams; [68] and in the Mixteca, a dry country of scanty rainfall, the cultivation of the prickly pear for cochineal would have been impossible without the irrigation system directed by Fray Francisco Marín.[69] The Augustinian Fray Antonio de Aguilar, "vir incredibili multarum rerum cognitione insignis," [a man outstanding for his incredible knowledge of many things], as Pamphilus writes admiringly, transformed the village of Epazoyuca, "cum antea esset sterilis," into "oppidum salubre et gratum, propter irriguam aquae copiam" [70] [hitherto sterile, into a healthful and pleasant town by means of an abundance of irrigation water]. We have

145

seen how each village had a fountain in its central square. The Augustinian Fray Pedro Juárez de Escobar built an especially celebrated one at Chilapa.[71] At Tiripitío his fellows brought water in from a distance of two leagues and built canals to feed the public fountains, the hospital, and the convent.[72] They also built aqueducts at Yuriria and Charo.[73] The fountain still to be seen at Tepeaca is fed by canals constructed about 1543 under the direction of the Franciscans, who had brought water in from the mountains.[74]

In this domain, however, one name stands out above all others, that of Fray Francisco de Tembleque. Father Tembleque resided in the convent of Otumba, not far from Mexico City, in an arid region. Fifteen leagues [about forty miles] away, he found water at Zempoala and although untrained in architecture, built an aqueduct, the construction of which occupied him for seventeen years. It was finished in 1571, and is generally known as *los arcos de Tembleque,* after its builder.[75] It is almost intact today; it is about forty-five kilometers in length [thirty miles, more or less], and consists of three series of arches, the first of forty-six, the second of thirteen, the third of sixty-seven. A large ship under full sail could easily pass under the arches of the third series, the construction of which took five years. The commissary general of the Franciscans, Fray Alonso Ponce, at the time of his visit [1585], admired this already famous masterpiece, and Madame Calderón de la Barca, three centuries later, described it as "the work of a giant." This exploit so struck the imagination of his contemporaries that Father Tembleque became a legendary figure almost immediately. During the whole time the work was in progress, we are told, his only companion was a gray cat, which spent the nights hunting and brought him rabbits or quail for his day's ration.[76] Later, old, sick, and blind, when he had retired to the Franciscan convent of Mexico City, the lay brother who had care of him tried to murder him by cutting his throat. Father Tembleque lost an enormous amount of blood, but, in spite of his age and infirmities, a skillful surgeon cured him completely in a few days. Everyone was astonished and some cried miracle! As for the assassin, he stated that he had been made mad by the devil.[77]

It has been difficult to determine with any exactness the nature and characteristics of landed property in the native villages founded and governed by the religious. According to various documents which shed light on this point, and to which I have already referred, it seems that we can assume the parallel existence of two kinds: individual and collective. Absolute collectivism seems to have been practiced only in the hospitals of Santa Fe, the organization of which will be described in the next chapter. Heads of families generally owned their little houses, as well as the plots of ground surrounding them or situated outside the village. These plots supported them and their wives and children. According to Grijalva, the Augustinians distributed the goods of the dead among the heirs, a bit of testimony that proves, at least, the existence of individual landed property, since it is probable that the personal goods of almost all natives were insignificant. Along with individual property, it cannot be doubted that collective landed property existed, to which Escobar gives the name of *ejidos.* The very valuable pages that Robert Redfield devotes to the present-day form of property (in his monograph on the village of Tepoztlán, Morelos) may give us a notion of what it was at the beginning of the colonial period. We cannot be positive about it, but there is every likelihood that it has changed little since then. In Tepoztlán individual and collective property exist side by side. Individual property consists of:

1. The house, or, more exactly, the lot (*sitio*) that it occupies, the *corrales* behind the house, and the attached cultivated land (*milpa*), which may be remote from the house, but is legally a part of it.

2. The *milpas de labor,* or vacant lots which the municipality cedes to individuals, but which are not, strictly speaking, private property, for the municipality can reclaim these lots if they are not cultivated. Nevertheless, those who have the use of them consider them to be private property.

3. The *tlacololli,* like the *milpas de labor,* but set apart in the mountainous common lands, the soil of which is quickly exhausted, which cannot be cultivated continuously for very long.

Collective property is the land unsuitable for cultivation which surrounds the private *milpas;* that is, pasture land (*pastales*) and *cerriles,* or mountainous wooded land, which is part of the collective lands of the

147

Indian village, the *altepetlalli*, which have not been transformed into private property, and today are the *ejidos*.[78]

Collective lands were bound up with the institution known as *cajas de comunidad*, or the municipal treasury. This term may cause some confusion, which should be dispelled at once. There were in all Spanish America *cajas de comunidad*, officially and purely civil in nature. In the sixteenth century they were managed by the *corregidores*, and were particularly numerous in Peru, where they were organized by Viceroy Toledo. Their prosperity in that country is doubtless owing to the existence of pre-Columbian native communities.[79] Despite their identity of purposes (public works, support of the clergy, religious services, care of the poor, widows, orphans, the sick and helpless), these civil and official *cajas* were sharply different from those of the Mexican missions of the sixteenth century. In Paraguay, moreover, the Jesuits invented a kind of private *caja de comunidad*, which had nothing in common with the state institution. In Mexico, the *cajas*, although not managed by the religious, were at least controled by them. They established [the *cajas*] to spare the poor Indians the payment of excessive tributes, in view of their ordinary taxes and their support of the missionaries. Formerly, when a village lacked the money to meet common expenses, the chiefs assessed each family for a contribution, the amount of which they fixed themselves, and which took precedence over the needs of the community. They pocketed the difference and got rich at the expense of their subjects. To remedy this situation in the Mixteca, Fray Francisco Marín constituted *bienes de comunidad*, creating for the purpose plantations of mulberry trees and prickly pears, the product of which went into the common treasury.[80] But these *bienes de comunidad* naturally assumed other forms, and the *cajas* received the profits from quarries, flocks, and work stints of one kind or another.

If one may believe the report of Archbishop Montúfar, from which I am taking these last items, the *cajas de comunidad*, established with the purest and most praiseworthy intentions, toward the middle of the sixteenth century, had degenerated into an extremely tyrannical institution. In short, this system was infinitely more ruinous for the unlucky Indians, who were [already] crushed under corvées and taxes, on the

148

pretext of filling the village treasury. These abuses multiplied in proportion as the *cajas* increased in number beyond all control in villages where there were no religious. In its working the institution revealed other weaknesses, whether the *caja* was kept by the native nobility or by the religious. In the former case the [Indian] nobles, after allowing for the support of the clergy and public works, spent what was left in the treasury for their personal use, most often in debauches and drink. This at least is what most frequently happened. Afterward, when their accounts were examined, they claimed that the treasury had been exhausted in the support of the missionaries and churches, and in the purchase of sacred vessels and priestly ornaments. At times their cynicism went to the length of their showing indignation at this waste. Thus, the Indians of San Francisco de Tlaxcala swore to the treasurer general, Hernando de Portugal, contrary to all truth, that they had spent 30,000 pesos for the [support of the] religious, while the 40,000 pesos that the Indians of Izúcar (Puebla) charged to the support and expenses of the Dominicans, had in fact been stolen by a *cacique* of the neighborhood.[81] On the other hand, it would have been unwise for the religious to have kept a watch on the treasury themselves, for it would have aroused suspicions and easily led to scandals. And then, above all, the principal vice of the institution, in the eyes of Montúfar, was that the religious disposed of these sometimes considerable funds as they pleased, and no one could prevent them. Once more Montúfar thought it was evident that the power of the religious went beyond the authority of the bishop, and that their influence was free from all control by the hierarchy. One must take into account his personal interest and prejudices in his criticism of the *cajas de comunidad,* but none of the features he mentions is in itself unlikely, nor is it contradicted elsewhere.[82] The existence of abuses was partly confirmed by the report of the visitor Valderrama (1565), who demanded that the religious should not be allowed to touch the money in the *cajas de comunidad,* or keep them in their convents.[83]

It is no less certain that, in a general way, the presence or the visitation of the missionaries was for the Indians the source of unquestionable benefits. And, if one may believe the provincial of the Dominicans, Fray

Pedro de la Peña, the natives were sufficiently shrewd to realize it. "Since the natives," he wrote to Philip II from Mexico City, July 25, 1561, "see that their resources would diminish if the religious did not constantly come to their aid, they have frequently offered some mill or farm in certain villages for the support of the religious, so that in their hands their capital would be conserved and increased." [84] The religious even had the notion of having their converts exempted from paying tribute, this either to strengthen them in their new faith, or because they had suffered some calamity.[85] Thus the missionary appeared at times as the Providence of the Indians, and it was under this aspect that the Augustinian Fray Pedro Juárez de Escobar described him in a passage that is not without a certain eloquence:

> All these Indians are like nestlings whose wings have not yet grown enough to allow them to fly by themselves; they still need to have their parents lovingly provide their food and nourishment, so they will not suffer from hunger and die. They must always, so long as they live, have near at hand their encouragement and presence, their aid and their support, for fear lest they, flying without strength, be lost, and that deprived of wings they fall. The religious, as Your Majesty should know, are their true fathers and mothers, their advocates and representatives, who take for them all the blows of adversity, who are their physicians and nurses, for their bodily ills as well as for the sicknesses which their weaknesses and misery cause them to fall into, for their faults and sins. The [religious] are the ones to whom they appeal in their sufferings and persecutions, their hunger and needs, as children do with their mothers. Where the religious are, there is a Christian life and knowledge of God, dignity and order, satisfaction and joy, peace and harmony, justice and good administration, and great care and vigilance, lest the Lord be offended; and the air resounds night and day with the chants and praises that these poor naked Indians sing for the glory of their Creator and Redeemer.[86]

The work of the missionaries was salutary from the material point of view, but did it have equally happy results in the social and spiritual domain? We may first observe, with Raoul Allier, that "if evangelization is regularly accompanied by material advantages it works against itself." [87] It runs the risk of making conversions for self-interest. But surely such [conversions] are not always to be condemned, especially if care is taken not to administer baptism too rapidly, because one who has adopted a new

150

religion for purely material reasons can later be sincerely convinced in the course of his instruction; transforming himself under the influence of baptismal grace and education, he may become an excellent Christian. It may be that he had selfish interests at the moment he became a catechumen, but it will no longer be true at the moment when he becomes truly a Christian through the sacraments. The whole question is to determine at what moment of his evolution the term conversion should be applied to him. Strictly speaking, conversion cannot take place during prebaptismal instruction. Self-interest, indeed, is often found to be the occasion, but not the cause, of conversion.[88] Nevertheless, if some individual cases prove that one should not condemn *en bloc* conversions made from self-interest, it does not seem wise to favor them. In my opinion, this is only one unimportant aspect of the question, and we are not interested here in the method of recruiting catechumens, but in the stabilization of the Church. Now, the case of the Mexican mission especially poses the problem of the Christian villages, considered as instruments of that stabilization, one of the most complex in missionary methodology. I shall not examine it thoroughly or in all its aspects, but it is necessary to say a few words about it.

This system, we know, has been followed everywhere and at all times, from the Brazilian mission of the sixteenth century[89] and the famous Jesuit reductions of Paraguay in the seventeenth and eighteenth, down to the Kabyle missions of Cardinal Lavigerie and the White Fathers of our day. In many cases it was imposed by circumstances. Sometimes the missionaries were too few to visit a scattered population frequently enough; sometimes life in their old habitat was impossible for the new Christians; sometimes they formed groups by themselves, instinctively, to practice their common religion with more freedom and with less risk of apostasy.[90] It should be noted, however, that the problem varies according to whether nomad or sedentary peoples are involved. Whenever living conditions permit, it is to [the missionary's] interest to tie nomad peoples to the soil and to transform hunters and herdsmen into farmers. This, for example, was what had to be done in the north of Mexico, at the beginning of the Tarahumara mission.[91]

When, however, sedentary peoples were concerned, whom the missionaries could attend or visit without much difficulty, they tended more or less, it seems, to give up the system of founding Christian villages, the inconveniencies of which experience had shown.[92] There seems to have been only one advantage in it, that of teaching the spirit of work, for it had been proved that the spiritual level of the Christian villages was not always very high. The elite, lost in the crowd of the mediocre, had no incentive, while in a pagan environment they would feel the need of affirming their faith more strongly and to live it more deeply; it would act as an example and a leaven. So they let themselves fall willingly into routine and tepidity. At times they even went further, and then the missionary was obliged to take severe measures and throw out the trouble-making Christians, which gave rise to anger and resentments, and created around him and the Christian community an atmosphere of hostility. Another danger, akin to the former, was the spirit of administration, even of bureaucracy, which threatened to replace the spirit of religion and progress. The letter destroyed it. To repeat a remark of Raoul Allier, somewhat modified, the neophyte reasons in this fashion: One must become a Christian to be a member of a village; hence, to be a member, to share its life, even in a purely mechanical way, is to be a Christian. And that is again what engendered spiritual laziness. For the missionary himself the danger is perhaps greater. He risks letting himself be absorbed in his temporal duties, in material cares, in administrative routine, and giving up to the insidious temptation of cutting a figure of importance in the secular world, and of governing a state within the state. Nothing is more dangerous for him, who thus risks losing his zeal, his self-abnegation, and his spirit of the supernatural. Nothing is more dangerous for the community that he governs, for this temporal influence can awaken the mistrust and the jealousy of the state, and lead to sharp conflicts with the civil authorities, in which his converts would have nothing to gain.[93]

In fact, in New Spain the government of the deferential and docile Indians had given some religious a taste for, and the habit of, domination; their absolute government of the native villages gave them a redoubtable temporal power. In many places the religious were the sole masters, and doubtless, as at the time of the revolt in New Galicia [1541], they gladly used their influence in the service of peace and order, as did a certain Fray Gonzalo Lucero at Mixtepec.[94] But they did not always bow before the authority of the viceroy, or even that of the bishops, against whom they vigorously invoked their pontifical privileges. Later on we shall see how conflicts arose from this situation, responsibility for which was not always chargeable to the religious, but these collisions were certainly not favorable to the progress of the apostolic work. Besides, the system was the result of practical considerations. It is true that the missionaries acted from a desire to protect their Indians from European influence, but there were practical reasons also for grouping the faithful in villages. Because of their relatively small number, this was perhaps the necessary condition for the stabilization of the Church. Their error was to forget that they should have dreamed, before all else, of training Christians who would be capable of governing themselves; it was even more of an error to seal off these groups from all contact with the outside, and to prevent, with a too minute solicitude, the development of individual personalities. Some of them thought it would be a good thing to settle married and well-known Spaniards among the Indians, to set a good example.[95] Such Spaniards were not sufficiently numerous for the relatively large number of native villages. Moreover, the general opinion was not favorable to this reform, for it seems to have been [the missionaries'] preoccupation to protect the Indians at the same time from the bad examples and the abuses of the Europeans. Legislation, with a jealous care, closed the native villages to the Spaniards; travelers who stopped there had to leave on the third day at the latest.[96] No European, no Negro, no mestizo, no mulatto, could reside there.[97]

This concept of tutelage, the formula for which we have just seen in the writing of Father Juárez de Escobar, kept the Indians in a perpetual status of minors, and at the same time implied the indefinite presence of the missionary. When he disappeared, the Indians had not served their apprenticeship in liberty, and, bewildered, were ready to follow the first leader. At the same time, they had lived in an almost absolute isolation; they had little contact with their racial brothers, and none at all with the Europeans, who were excluded from the native villages, and whose language they did not understand. They were strangers to the life of the

153

country. From this point of view, the Christian village was an unfortunate and unwise institution.[98] But this unwisdom seems painless four hundred years later, in the light of all the events that have occurred since then. The missionaries would have needed a gift of prophecy to discern it. This gift they did not have, and, if we wish to be just to them, let us recognize that it would not have been easy to anticipate the independence of New Spain, and that the fundamental problem of an independent Mexico would be the incorporation of the Indian into national life.

9 The Hospitals

"**P**HYSICIANS and healers of bodily wounds and infirmities," wrote Father Juárez de Escobar. He might have cited as examples the devotion of the Dominicans during the epidemic of 1545, and especially the death of the Franciscan Fray Agustín de Deza, guardian of Zapotlán, who in 1551, at the bedside of an Indian, contracted the disease that was to carry him off.[1] The religious who actually practiced medicine were, however, very few, and none of them seems to have devoted himself more to the Indians than to the Spaniards. The best known is Dr. García Farfán, who took his degrees at the University of Mexico (1562–1567). He joined the Augustinian Order in 1568 upon the death of his wife, and professed the year following under the direction of Fray Diego de Vertavillo. Fray Agustín Farfán wrote a treatise on surgery and two on medicine, well known to bibliographers.[2] His *Tratado Breve de Medicina* was addressed to Indians who had no physician at hand.[3] We also have records of several Franciscan lay brothers who practiced medicine and surgery. One of them, Fray Pedro de San Juan, seems to have been an unedifying character. In 1543 Viceroy Mendoza had him investigated for running away from his convent and throwing his habit into the nettles. The surgeon Fray Juan de Unza, who died at Acapulco in 1581, was a different type. Whenever one of his patients died, he scourged himself cruelly, in the belief that he had been negligent. Fray Lucas de Almodóvar, a nurse at the convent of Mexico, was considered a saint. He had, we are told, "the gift of healing," and became famous for having cured the illustrious Augustinian, Fray Alonso de la Vera Cruz, and especially Viceroy Mendoza, who had been given up by the physicians.[4]

The list is rather short. It was especially by founding and organizing hospitals that the missionnaries strove to relieve and attentuate the miseries of the Indians, a work that was all the more necessary because of the murderous epidemics that constantly ravaged New Spain. "Since this country was discovered," wrote Sahagún, after the month of August, 1576, "there have been three violent and universal epidemics, not counting many other less fatal and more local ones." In his opinion the inhabitants for this reason were on their way to extinction.[5] If this prediction was not fulfilled, it may have been owing, in part at least, to the activities of the religious. In such a vast country, however, this task, added to so many others, was heavy and slow. Archbishop Montúfar, on December 15, 1554, again stated that hospitals were the most important thing in Mexico,[6] and in 1555 the synod of Mexico, in which, naturally, a great many religious took part, ordered hospitals to be erected in all villages, alongside the churches, to receive the poor and sick, so that the priest could easily visit them and administer the sacraments.[7] It may be assumed that at this time the number of hospitals was inadequate. It is likely, however, that the decision of 1555 was put into effect and bore fruit, for in 1583 Montúfar's successor, Moya de Contreras, could write: "In all the Indian villages with the rank of head towns (*cabeceras*) there are hospitals built with the labor, money, and alms of the Indians themselves."[8]

The only hospital to my knowledge founded by the Dominicans was the famous one at Perote, which Fray Julián Garcés built at his own expense while he was bishop of Tlaxcala. Situated on the Vera Cruz-Mexico road, it received fewer Indians than Spaniards, who were ill from their long crossing and their journey to the capital.[9] It was the Franciscans and Augustinians who distinguished themselves in the founding and operation of hospitals, but the Franciscans were everywhere the great builders. In 1543, following an epidemic, they built several hospitals in New Galicia.[10] Fray Miguel de Bolonia, for example, was responsible for the one at Juchipila (Zacatecas); Nombre de Dios had one by the end of 1553; Topia, by 1555,[11] and Zacoalco, by 1558.[12] These hospitals also served as refuges for travelers—an important institution in an enormous and scantily populated country—and they were supported by what was called the brotherhood funds.[13] The hospital at Querétaro, planned for Indians and poor Spaniards, was founded by Hernando de Tapia at the urging of a French Franciscan, Fray Juan Jerónimo.[14] The descriptions of villages published by Paso y Troncoso in the *Papeles de Nueva España* include many localities with hospitals that had been founded before 1572: at Tepeaca and in each of the four villages of its jurisdiction; at Jalapa and Tepeapulco.[15] The hospital at Jalapa was intended for Spaniards fatigued by the journey to Mexico City, and for the Indians [bearers] who fell sick from the traffic. In Mexico City itself, the royal hospital of San José for Indians was founded about 1530 by Pedro de Gante,[16] and in the quarter of San Cosme Zumárraga founded a hospital for Indians from out of town, putting it under the protection of San Cosme and San Damián.[17] In Tlaxcala also the Franciscans had a celebrated hospital, the Encarnación, which was inaugurated with great solemnity in 1537. It could accommodate as many as four hundred persons; it had its brotherhood for the [burial] service and interment of the poor, and the celebration of feast days. Its principal support was the Indians, who never ceased making offerings and giving alms of every kind: linen and clothing, fowl, sheep, pigs, peppers, maize, and beans. After seven months the hospital's goods were evaluated at a thousand gold pesos. It was the Indians who kept most of the hospitals going, this in spite of their extreme poverty; although they gave little, they gave often, and, since there were many of them, the hospitals survived without difficulty.[18]

One Franciscan, however, stands out above all others in the history of the first hospitals of New Spain, Fray Juan de San Miguel, who is credited with having founded most of the hospitals of Michoacán. "In all the villages [of Michoacán]," writes Muñoz, "administered by our Order, as well as in those administered by other Orders and by the seculars, he founded hospitals next the churches. There travelers are entertained, and the sacraments of penitence and supreme unction are administered." [19] These hospitals were served by the brotherhood of the Immaculate Conception, to which all the Indians belonged if they so wished. They took turns in attending the sick; they divided their women into parties of five or six, each party serving a week, during which they made offerings to the hospital according to their means. These benevolent nurses were obliged to confess and take communion regularly; they assembled in the chapel every morning and evening to repeat the *doctrina;* on Mondays, Wednesdays, and Fridays services were held for the dead; and every Saturday there was a service in honor of the Immaculate Conception, patron of hospitals. Some of these hospitals were very large. Several of them accommodated more than four hundred patients during the great epidemic of 1576. Their funds were minutely budgeted. Some of these establishments had incomes, but generally it was the Indians who supported them, each village donating one or two days' work [a week], more if necessary. Half of what was collected was set aside for the support of the patients and staff; the other half was used for the purchase of medicines, linen, and the like. [Their income] was augmented by the voluntary contributions of the Indians and the profit from the part-time work of the nurses. [20]

There were hospitals also in almost all villages administered by the Augustinians, especially in Michoacán, where charitable institutions seem to have had a very singular growth in the hands of the religious. [21] I am best acquainted with those of Charo, Huango, Cuitzeo (which was founded by Fray Francisco de Villafuerte [22]), and Tiripitío. The last-named was famous for its comfort and pleasantness, even luxury. The happy arrangement of its rooms, and the abundance and variety of its medicines were boasted of. In the central *patio* a garden had been laid out filled with roses and health-giving herbs, and lined with luxuriant orange trees; in the middle, a fountain with musical jets of water; the hospital itself surrounded by gardens. [23] In all hospitals the Indians of the villages, men and women, without exception, were obliged to serve in turn for a week. Their life was extremely austere, truly monastic, especially for the women, who were not allowed to wear any ornaments and had to dress in the most severe fashion. According to Escobar, they had to abstain from the "licit uses of holy matrimony." They were obliged, moreover, to observe long hours of prayer, and to get up at night to chant matins on their knees.[24] This was a singularly audacious regime, by which the Augustinians once again made their attempt to raise high the level of spiritual life among the Indians.

Like the Franciscans, the Augustinians did not establish hospitals solely to shelter and care for sick natives, but also to receive and entertain travelers and passers-by—this to keep the houses of the villages from being filled up with more or less discreet strangers. They tended to protect private citizens from a hospitality that might become a heavy burden, even a danger. The hospitals were, moreover, free provisioning centers, where the natives found everything they could want: meat, oil, wine, lard, and sugar, not to mention the advice and instructions of all kinds that they demanded of the religious.[25]

The most famous of the Mexican hospitals, the two at Santa Fe, were founded by the [future] bishop of Michoacán, Vasco de Quiroga, while he was still an *oidor* of the Audiencia of Mexico. One of them was two leagues [west] of the City of Mexico; the other, in Michoacán, on the shore of Lake Pátzcuaro. [The history of these] two establishments, if only because of the person of their founder, would take me beyond the limits I have set for myself. Since, however, it was an Augustinian, Fray Alonso de Borja, who had the spiritual direction of the village and hospital of Santa Fe de México, this circumstance allows me to summarize its curious organization.[26]

The hospitals of Santa Fe (which may be spoken of in the plural, since both were conceived and organized in the same way), were of a very special kind, being, as Father Cuevas has observed, veritable phalansteries. Besides the buildings reserved for the sick and the administrative offices, they included schools, workshops, storehouses, and dwellings for members of the congregation and their families. These dwellings, called *familias,* were all surrounded by small kitchen gardens. The hospital itself owned land and cattle, its principal resources. The central unit, reserved for the patients, had four parts, grouped about a square *patio;* a room for

159

contagious diseases, and, facing it, a room for the noncontagious; the quarters of the administrator, and, opposite it, those of the steward. In the center of the *patio* was a chapel, open on two sides so that the patients could follow the Mass from their rooms. Seven or eight couples with their children lived in each *familia*. A rotation had been set up for work in the exterior properties of the monastery, and the rector of the hospital designated the families [that were to serve in them] every two years. There were six hours a day of common and obligatory labor. After the harvest, the members received whatever they needed for their year's supply, the shares being strictly equal. The rest was destined for the hospital and the community, as much as they needed. What remained was set aside for the poor, or against famine, drought, or any other calamity. The clothing of the members, men and women, had to be of the greatest simplicity. The offices were all elective, but no one could be elected twice to the most important. There were no lawsuits; all disputes were settled amicably. Members whose conduct left something to be desired were pitilessly expelled.[27]

In the beginning, medical care may have been a tool for conversion, a means to attract the Indians and teach them the existence of Christian charity.[28] But the multiplicity of hospitals came from the most diverse interests among the missionaries. In the very first rank, evidently, [was their desire] to protect the physical life of the Indians, whom they saw constantly decimated by epidemics. Sahagún could not have been the only one who feared the disappearance of the native races. The [friars] could not meet this danger by teaching the rules of a hygiene that was entirely unknown at the time. Their only recourse was to found hospitals where the sick could at least receive a few attentions and some comfort, and where the contagious cases could be isolated. But other and different purposes were envisaged. The reader has certainly been struck by the singularly austere life that the nurses were forced to lead in these hospitals, where an effort was made to render more assiduous the practice of religion, and more profound and elevated the spiritual life. Thus the hospitals appear to have been asylums for the sick and infirm, and a kind of retreat at the same time, where at regular intervals the Indians would come to seek refreshment in solitude, peace, mortification of the flesh, and the spirit of charity.

This brings me to another aspect. If the Franciscans founded hospitals, says the *Códice Franciscano,* it was for the purpose of giving shelter to the sick, and teaching those in good health "the exercise of charity and the works of mercy that one must practice toward one's neighbor." [29] The missionaries' part was only that of management and control. The staff was Indian, and support was provided mostly by Indians. Thus, in the eyes of the religious, care of the sick had the good effect of teaching the daily practice of humble, silent, and patient devotion. Alms, especially the donation of one or several days' work, nurtured a spirit of solidarity along with frugality; it taught the individual the need of self-abnegation in the service of the community, and little by little inculcated a spirit of fraternity, which is necessarily the foundation of the Christian city. Even if we leave to one side the curious phalansterian organization of the hospitals of Santa Fe, the Mexican hospitals, which were at the same time asylums for the sick, and retreats and centers of edification for the healthy (this is especially true of Michoacán), were among the most original creations of the Mendicant Orders, and one of the most ingenious devices for making Christian ideas a part of daily life.

10 Missionary Conditions and Church Architecture

I N a community governed by religious, religious life held first place, and the heart of the village was necessarily the convent and its church, most frequently situated on the main square. The general plan of Mexican convents is very simple: the church, often of a single nave, is oriented east and west, with the altar at the east end. It has two doors, the main one at the west end, the other on the north side. At the right of the main door, usually, that is, on the south side of the church, stands the convent, the entrance to which is masked by a portico, which itself leads to the cloister. The cells of the religious are on the upper floor; on the ground floor, the refectory, the kitchen, the chapter room, the library, the stables, and the cellars. Almost all sixteenth-century monasteries include a stage. But an archaeological study of the convents and monastic churches of New Spain would be out of place in this work. Not only do I consider it more prudent to leave it to specialists, but also the characteristics of these structures are mostly owing to factors other than purely missionary ones. It seems to me indispensable, on the other hand, to study here the influences that these missionary conditions had on monastic architecture, and on certain details of plan, arrangement, and decoration of the convents and their churches.

When one travels through Mexico today in search of colonial convents, and tries to fill out personal impressions with reading the accounts of travelers and with examining photographic records, one's first impression is that the convents are most often situated on high spots, sometimes within, sometimes without, the villages which they dominate and even at times seem to crush, and frequently appear to be the strategic [military] key to them.

How did this situation come about? When we studied the distribution of the missionaries in New Spain and the geographic dispersion of their convents, we saw that the religious, for the purpose of disorganizing and overthrowing pre-conquest paganism, installed themselves preferably in built-up areas which were at the same time political and religious centers, such as Texcoco, Tlaxcala, Huejotzingo, Cholula, Tula and Huexotla. These religious centers necessarily included one or several *teocallis,* or sanctuaries on the summits of pyramids, and is seemed most opportune to build churches and convents on these same pyramids, a choice which completed the political disorganization and initiated a policy of substitution. Thus many convents may be mentioned which were certainly built on former *teocallis,* such as the Franciscan convents of Tlaxcala, Huejotzingo, and Huexotla.[1]

These *teocallis* also had strategic importance, which is one of the reasons they were destroyed. It is certain that this consideration was taken into account when they were chosen as sites for convents, for in the sixteenth century monasteries had to serve, not only as fortresses to help keep the natives in subjection, but also as refuges for the Spanish population in the event of rebellion.[2] Here also the spiritual conquest completed and reinforced the military occupation—which explains the military strength of many convents that were not erected upon *teocallis.* Some of them were in the outskirts of the villages that they held (if one may dare so to express it) under their threat. Such, for example, was the Franciscan monastery of Atlixco (Puebla), built outside the village on the lower slope of the *cerrito* of San Miguel, which dominates the town from its pointed mass. In this respect the convent of Atlixco resembles that of San Francisco de Tlaxcala, which was also built apart from the main square on the slopes of the rugged hills that frame the loyal city. Others were built in the very center, such as the Dominican convent of Etla (Oaxaca), and especially Santo Domingo de Oaxaca, the enormous mass of which crushes the whole city. Indeed, its strategic importance, during the turbulent history of Mexico, has made it the scene or the object of innumerable combats.[3] In their situation both of them may be compared to Huejotzingo and Huexotla. The Franciscan church at Cuernavaca, another at Zempoala (Hidalgo), and the one at Tepeaca, could all be included in this comment.

Nevertheless, it is evident enough that there were not always natural or artificial high places suitable for the strategic location of a monastery, but it was always possible to make it a center of resistance by building it like a fortress. Among the convents already mentioned, that of Huejotzingo has this form, which is repeated in a startling fashion at Acolman, Cholula, Actopan, Yecapixtla, and many other places. It attained its highest form at Tepeaca and Tochimilco (Puebla), and at Tula (Hidalgo), which are veritable fortress-monasteries. Louis Gillet describes them: "Crenelated masses of steep forms, with a single rank of windows, placed rather high to discourage scaling, supported by a series of square buttresses, topped by turrets to prevent flanking. The roof is a platform for guns. The gargoyles imitate the mouths of cannons. Sometimes a second platform runs around the building, half way up, like a sentry walk, to insure a double fire platform."[4] Does not Tello inform us that the convent of Etzatlán (Jalisco) was built to serve as a fortress against the mountain people of that region?[5] Fray Servando Teresa de Mier[6] mentions the viceroy who said that the best defenses of the royal domain were the convents and churches, and he was not speaking figuratively.[7] If many of these convents seem to have been too small to hold all the Spanish population in the event of a native uprising, it should be borne in mind that they had an exterior enclosure within the walls of the *atrio,* where the Spanish families, their livestock, provisions, and indispensable objects could be kept in safety. Often, as at Tlaxcala[8] and Huejotzingo, they were surrounded by a crenelated wall. When the inhabitants of Oaxaca begged Viceroy Antonio de Mendoza to build a fortress to shelter them and their wives and children, he replied that all they had to do was to close the wall of the cemetery, that is, the *atrio* of the church.[9]

Plate I. (*Above*) Franciscan church at Tepeaca, Puebla. Plate II. (*Below, left*) Augustinian church at Actopan, Hidalgo. Plate III. (*Below, right*) Franciscan convent at Tula, Hidalgo. (*All photographs courtesy of Archivo Fotográfico—Instituto Nacional de Antropología e Historia, Mexico.*)

Plate IV. (*Above*) Augustinian church at Acolman, Mexico. Plate V. (*Below*) Augustinian convent at Yecapixtla, Morelos.

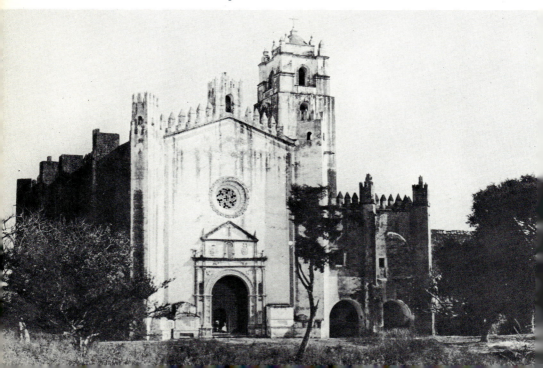

Plate VI. Augustinian church at Yuriria, Guanajuato.

Plate VII. (*Above*) Augustinian cloister at Actopan, Hidalgo. Plate VIII. (*Below*) Franciscan cloister at Tlamanalco, Mexico.

Plate IX. (*Above*) *Atrio* of the Franciscan convent at Cholula, Puebla. Plate X. (*Below*) *Atrio* of the Dominican convent at Atzcapotzalco, D. F.

Plate XI. (*Above*) Cloister of the Dominican convent at Atzcapotzalco, D. F. Plate XII. (*Below*) Franciscan church at Cholula, Puebla.

Plate XIII. (*Above*) *Capilla real* of Franciscan church at Cholula, Puebla. Plate
XIV. (*Below*) Open-air chapel of the Franciscan convent at Tlamanalco, Mexico.

Plate XV. (*Above*) Dominican cloister at Cuilapan, Oaxaca. Plate XVI. (*Below, left*) Dominican cloister at Amecameca, Mexico. Plate XVII. (*Below, right*) Dominican church at Oaxaca, Oaxaca.

The *atrio,* also sometimes called the *patio,* was a vast enclosed court that extended widely across the front of the church and the porch of the convent. (Plates IX and X give two typical examples.) The *atrio* commonly opened upon the principal square of the village by a more or less crude gate, which was almost always approached by several steps, for, when the convent was not built on a high spot, it was most frequently slightly raised. These *atrios,* which are among the most characteristic features of convent architecture in New Spain, and among its charms, did not always have the political and military uses of which I have just spoken. Their proper function was a purely missionary one.

One of the great difficulties faced by our religious was that the conversion of Mexico was not gradual, but massive. They were, therefore, suddenly confronted with an enormous crowd of neophytes and converts. How were these multitudes to be taught, when only a tiny fraction of them could be accommodated in churches? The invention of the *atrio* was the solution to this problem. It was, and still is, very frequently a cemetery where the dead were buried by *barrios,* the name usually given to the subdivisions of the village, and each *barrio* had the right to a certain portion of the *atrio.*[10] But [the *atrio*] was above all the place where the religious heard or directed the catechism, where men and women gathered to hear the *doctrina,* and where little girls and boys taught each other. It was the place where the missionaries assembled their parishioners whenever it was necessary. Finally, it was the place where some of the processions were held, on feast days or in open air ceremonies. Some of these *atrios,* such as those at Huejotzingo, Cholula, and Calpan, even had a sort of small chapel, called a *posa,* which was probably used for a resting place during processions, and possibly for saying Mass.[11]

[The *atrio*] was only a partial solution. Mass, the service, and the administration of most sacraments could be performed only in the church proper. So the *atrio* was supplemented by another and even more original invention, the open chapel, which derived from it and was conditioned by it. Its plan was very simple. At one side of the church, generally on the north opposite the convent, a kind of large niche was constructed, in which was placed a true chapel with its altar. There the priest celebrated Mass and the faithful could follow the ceremony from the *atrio* without difficulty. There is a chapel of this kind in the Augustinian convent of Actopan, on the north side, [so placed] that the church stands between the convent porch and the open chapel.[12] There is a much smaller one in the Franciscan convent of Otumba, near Mexico City, built on the very porch of the convent.[13] Still another is in the Dominican convent of Coixtlahuaca in the Mixteca. It is on the same side of the church as that of Actopan, but it is square and opens upon the *atrio* by means of a large flat arch.[14] It is evident that all three Orders followed this plan, and Motolinía, in his *Memoriales,* was probably alluding to such chapels when he wrote: "In this country the *patios* are of a very remarkable size, for the faithful cannot be accommodated in the churches, so that everyone may attend Mass on Sundays and feast days. The churches are used only during the week." [15]

The open chapels have yet another and more complicated aspect. To the north of the church—the convent being on the south side—another sanctuary is placed, which opens upon the *atrio,* so that the faithful there may easily follow the ceremonies being celebrated in the chapel. Open chapels of this kind are of two distinct types. In one, the axis of the chapel is parallel to that of the main church; it has a large number of naves that open upon the *atrio.* Such was the plan of the famous Franciscan chapel of San José de los Naturales in Mexico City, no longer extant, which had seven open naves. And such was the plan of another Franciscan sanctuary, the Real Capilla de las siete Naves, at Cholula (Plate XIII). This last, to be sure, dates from the seventeenth century, but it seems quite likely that it had the same plan as its predecessor, which had collapsed in the sixteenth century. Unfortunately, its naves were sealed up on the side of the *atrio* at a later date.[16] These chapels, with their columns, give a very decided impression of mosques; but what I have just said is sufficiently indicative that there was no question of Hispano-Moorish influence here, at least in its general concept.

In the second case, the axis of the chapel is perpendicular to that of the main church, and its naves do not open on the *atrio,* but the bays do. Chapels of this type are naturally much shallower than the first. One of the jewels of colonial art is in this category, the unfinished chapel of the Franciscan convent at Tlamanalco, on the way to Amecameca, built during the last years of the sixteenth century (Plate XIV).[17] The Dominican convent at Teposcolula in the Mixteca also has a chapel of this kind, the *capilla vieja,* hugging the north side of the church. It has two naves, the bays of which open on the *atrio*.[18] In my opinion, the chapels of the ruined sanctuary of Cuilapan, near Oaxaca, on the flank of the enormous Dominican convent, belong in this latter category. This chapel of three naves is striking because of its prodigious length. Unless I made a mistake [in counting them] in my visit there, it has no fewer than thirteen bays. Manuel Toussaint sees it only as a simple church in the form of a basilica, but Burgoa has left us a sufficiently detailed description of it, in which he says that in former times the bays opened on the *atrio,* but had been sealed off before he composed his *Geográfica Descripción.* The only difficulty here is that he states that the system of open bays was adopted in order to make the entrance easier for the crowds attending the services. But it is not impossible that by his day the origin of the open chapels had been forgotten.[19] It is noteworthy that this type of chapel, either parallel or perpendicular to the [axis of] the main church, seems to have been unknown in Augustinian architecture.

It is easy to grasp the plans and general disposition of the old Mexican convents, but it is more difficult to get a precise notion of the details of their arrangement and decoration. Many of them have been remodeled or restored in a frequently clumsy way. Many, after long neglect, or after earthquakes, particularly in the Oaxaca region, have been confiscated by the state and put to new and sometimes startling uses, which makes them more or less unrecognizable. One such is San Francisco de Puebla, now a military hospital; another is Santo Domingo de Oaxaca, which, by a decision beyond my understanding, was turned into a cavalry barracks. So it is just as well to suppress one's personal impressions of today and examine those of their contemporaries, on whose testimony I have principally drawn. It may be that in studying them we shall succeed in distinguishing between the truth and the exaggerated tradition which makes these old convents out to be symbols of a very unmonastic pomp and luxury.

It is clear that the Indian multitudes were extremely sensitive to the pomp of ceremonies.[20] Zumárraga, for example, writing to Charles V on the subject of music in the churches, says: "Experience teaches us how much the Indians are edified by it, for they are great lovers of music, and the religious who hear their confessions tell us that they are converted more by music than by preaching, and we see them come from distant regions to hear it." [21] And we read in the *Códice Franciscano*: "Ornamentation and pomp in the churches are very necessary to uplift the souls of the Indians and bring them to the things of God, for by nature they are indifferent to internal things and forgetful of them, so they must be helped by means of external appearances." [22] One gathers, then, that one of the best devices for attracting the Indians to the Church, retaining them, and making regular practice easy for them, was the celebration of divine services with all possible splendor.[23] Besides, before the Spanish conquest, feasts and ceremonies were continuous and extremely brilliant. They had to be superseded, at first to keep the new religion from being compared unfavorably with the old, and then so that it would itself be a source of joy and beautiful spectacles; also, so that the Indians, deprived of their customary pleasures, might not be tempted to revive their ancient festivals in secret, or to give themselves up to a dangerous idleness.[24] An effort was made, therefore, to interest and charm the new converts by splendid services, processions, and festivals of all kinds, which were celebrated in the most solemn fashion.

Is it necessary to attribute the proverbial sumptuousness of the Mexican convents to missionary zeal? Probably. On February 8, 1537, Zumárraga wrote the Council of the Indies that beautiful churches helped in the conversion of the Indians and strengthened their devotion. Twenty years later, on February 1, 1558, Viceroy Luis de Velasco made the same observation to Philip II.[25] It is quite evident that if one insisted upon luxury and pomp in ceremonies, the setting in which they occurred could not be overlooked. It is my belief that this reputation of the old monasteries is partly unearned. It is true, nevertheless, that their size and sumptuousness are frequently remarked by contemporaries and attested moreover by the statements of certain religious. Along with prejudiced witnesses, violently hostile to the regular clergy, such as Montúfar and his provisor, Dr. Anguis,[26] an impartial and thoughtful man like the

Licenciado Lebrón de Quiñones wrote Prince Philip, in 1554, that the works begun for the construction of certain monasteries were "of an extreme splendor and sumptuousness." [27] In fact, in the various¹ descriptions of Mexico one is struck at every turn by the mention of "sumptuous" monasteries, the common epithet. Despite their spirit of poverty, the Franciscans were not always free of this concern. Their convent at Tlaxcala was "exceedingly sumptuous and ostentatious." It was approached by a staircase of sixty-three steps of cut stone, which were so wide and inclined so gently that one could climb them on horseback.[28] And the retable of their church at Cholula had cost more than 10,000 pesos.[29] In Mexico City the Dominicans had an enormous house. "Their monastery is vast," wrote Cervantes de Salazar; "it has a church of a single nave, one of the largest I have seen." [30] Even today one is greatly impressed by the dimensions of some of their convents in the south, such as that of Cuilapan (Plate XV), and especially that of Santo Domingo de Oaxaca, in which Porfirio Díaz was able to house an army of 10,000 men.[31]

In what looked like a kind of race in gigantic construction the Augustinians were accepted as masters. They did not conceal their love of ostentation in their churches. "We have founded," one of them wrote to Philip II, "a large number of monasteries, which reflect our tastes and customs, our rule and manner of life. The churches are adorned with bells, statues, and retables, and have [musical] instruments and organs in the choirs. The sacristies are filled with jewels, silver, and ornaments; they are clean and well cared for, offered and consecrated to the King of Heaven, to honor Him in divine worship." [32] Gonzalez de la Puente even compares the convent at Yuriria to the Escorial. It had been built by his colleague, the great architect Fray Diego de Chaves (Plate VI). This project provoked the wrath of Viceroy the Marqués de Falces, but Father Chaves answered him so ably that he succeeded in obtaining authorization to complete his Escorial.[33] It filled Pamphile, by hearsay, with the keenest admiration.[34] At Ucareo, in Michoacán, the civil government attempted, just as vainly, to curb a zeal it considered excessive. Viceroy Luis de Velasco had insisted upon a "moderate" house. The architect, Father Utrera, interrupted the work, but in appearance only, for he continued to have the stones cut in the quarry, and the necessary beams shaped. Then he reassured the viceroy by promising that the construction would not take more than a year. And in one year, thanks to this stratagem, he built an enormous monastery, the dimensions of which caused general stupefaction.[35] The Augustinians especially were the target of Montúfar, Anguis, and Lebrón de Quiñones. In the single province of Meztitlán they had two very sumptuous convents, never occupied by more than four or five religious each.[36] Their house at Valladolid (Morelia) is one of the largest in Mexico. Nothing is left of their first convent in Mexico City, but it also was "sumptuous" and had the reputation of being the richest in New Spain, in income, ornaments, and silver. Pamphile describes it, with innocent pride, as "facile primas tenet"[37] [easily the first]. Zumárraga, who was generally moderate in his opinions, himself considered that the church at Ocuituco begun by the Augustinians was much too sumptuous, and excessively large for the resources of the village.[38]

These enormous edifices were, of course, built by the Indians. For them it was a heavy burden, whether they had to pay the workmen, or whether, more frequently, they had to do the work themselves, while they neglected their fields or trades.[39] But one must accept with reserve the testimony of the Indians who complained of abuses by the Dominicans during the construction of the convent at Puebla, claiming they were exhausted from work, and that one of the religious had loaded them with large stones and then beaten them over the head with a stick. This testimony is recorded by a Franciscan chronicler.[40] Nevertheless, brutalities of this kind among the Augustinians at Ocuituco are attested by as trustworthy a personage as Zumárraga himself.[41] Moreover, such excesses are complained of elsewhere. In 1549 the civil officers of New Galicia wrote to Charles V, informing him that the natives were crushed by the work they were forced to do in the construction of enormous and pretentious monasteries.[42] On April 1, 1570, the cathedral chapter of Guadalajara went so far as to write Philip II: "When the Augustinian friars built . . . a new monastery, the few natives who were left [alive] disappeared because of the sumptuousness that [the Augustinians] aspire to in the construction of their churches and houses." [43] The Crown, however, had long since adopted a fixed policy [in this matter]. In 1531, a *cédula* severely criticized the Dominicans for having built in Mexico City a too-sumptuous and too-costly monastery,[44] A little later this magnificent structure tumbled down and had to be rebuilt at the expense of the royal treasury,[45] for these imposing piles were not always solidly built. In 1561 Anguis stated that the Augustinian church in Mexico City which had cost "an infinity of silver," was slowly falling to pieces,[46] and that the vaulting of the *capilla real* at Cholula, which had just been completed, collapsed one fine night, a few hours after a festival attended by more than four thousand.[47] Before 1550, this weakness was undoubtedly owing to the lack of skill of the religious architects and masons. In the instruction that Viceroy Mendoza left for his successor, before leaving for Peru, he stated that many mistakes had been made in the construction of convents, and that a very large number of them had been very badly built, for lack of skilled workmen.[48]

Finally, at times there was no hesitation in abandoning these convents and churches for new ones. Thus the Franciscans abandoned their first convent at Cholula, which had been built at the expense of the natives, although, to be sure, it was turned into a hospital.[49] It even happened that the old convents, and even private houses, were pillaged and stripped for the benefit of the new ones. The bishop of New Galicia, Fray Pedro de Ayala, loudly denounced to the Council of the Indies the abuses committed by a Franciscan religious named Fray Miguel de Diosdado, "who built a monastery at Poncitlán and tried to bring there virtually all [the people of] the region for this purpose. He has wrecked and pillaged nineteen churches, stripped them of their ornaments and bells, and demolished the houses of a like number of villages, the least important of which had more than fifty dwellings, while others had a hundred or a hundred and fifty, and has torn them all down, of which the Indians . . . have complained." [50]

How much truth is there in all this? Fray Pedro de Ayala, like Father Diosdado, was undoubtedly a Franciscan, but he was also a passionate man, readily heated, as is evident in his correspondence, which is full of recriminations, complaints, protestations, and angry accusations. The

171

Licenciado Oseguera, on the other hand, who, like most civil officers, had little sympathy for the religious, spoke favorably of Fray Miguel de Diosdado.[51] It is possible that the Indians who complained exaggerated matters, consciously or not, and that Fray Pedro de Ayala in his turn exaggerated them also. In any case, the destructive fury of Father Diosdado seems to have been exceptional. It usually happens, indeed, that it is the exception that makes the noise and shocks people, and it is the exception that it is emphasized in the documents.

This is a fact that must not be forgotten when one studies the testimony affirming the sumptuousness of the old Mexican convents. Assuredly the Augustinian monastery at Morelia and the Dominican monasteries at Cuilapan and Oaxaca, the vast dimensions and imposing mass of which we can still appreciate, confirm the opinions of Montúfar and Lebrón de Quiñones, and the splendor of the [vanished] Augustinian convent in Mexico City is too unanimously emphasized to allow one to doubt it. It is difficult also entirely to accept the opinion of Zorita, that is, that there had never been any excess in the matter.[52] On the other hand, alongside these sumptuous houses, which attracted attention by their size and richness, one should bear in mind the poor ones also. In the preceding chapter we have seen the extreme humbleness of San Francisco de México, which was so unhealthful that the religious there all suffered from rheumatism.[53] In [the convent of] Pahuatlán the Augustinians had only four cells covered with thatch, while the church was constructed of wood and unburned brick, and was slowly collapsing.[54] In 1552, Fray Angel de Valencia complained that the Franciscan convent in Guadalajara, which had been described to the King as a replica of San Pablo de Valladolid or of Santo Tomás de Avila, was a miserable heap of earth and raw brick.[55] One must bear in mind, above all, the unglorious multitude of modest little convents, discreetly poor, which no one ever dreamed of mentioning at all. The Franciscan convents at Huexotla and Otumba, in the valley of Mexico, seem to me to be the perfect type of them, and, so far as one can judge today, the [convent] at Cuernavaca and those of the environs of Puebla (always excepting San Francisco de Tlaxcala), do not seem to exceed reasonable limits. By and large, it cannot be said that the Franciscans of New Spain violated their rule, which prescribed the construction of exceedingly poor (*paupérrimos*) convents.[56] Nor can one accuse Motolinía of exaggeration when he writes that the Friars Minor were building smaller and smaller, and poorer and poorer, monasteries.[57] There is no doubt that the Order of St. Francis has always observed the spirit of poverty, but Motolinía's assertion cannot be applied to the other two. Even so, one should not exaggerate about them either. The Augustinian convents at Acolman and Actopan do not, it seems to me, deserve their reputation for sumptuousness, a reputation that is perhaps owing to the myopia of Mexican historians. Compared with the great monasteries of Europe, they are only of moderate dimensions (Plates II, IV, and VII). It is not to be believed that all Dominican monasteries were as large as that of Cuilapan. Atzcapotzalco (Plate XI), Amecameca (Plate XVI), Oaxtepec, and Etla are suitable structures with no striking excesses.[58]

In 1564, the Dominicans attempted to justify themselves with the Council of the Indies. Their letter is a pleading, to be read and judged as such, but, since I have cited at length the documents that accuse the missionaries, it is only fair to give them a hearing. "According to information that we have received," they wrote,

one of the things we are accused of and reproached for before Your Highness is the sumptuousness and excess (it is said) of the buildings we have erected to serve as our monasteries. It is easy to verify these things exactly, because walls cannot be hidden, and Your Highness can have them visited and inspected, and take whatever measures that are fitting for your royal will and service. One thing we can assure Your Highness in all truth is that of the forty-eight monasteries and houses that we have in New Spain, not three have been finished, for we see to it that the Indians work on them with their full consent and at their pleasure, without abuse or vexation of any kind. Besides, although there are a few houses of reasonable size, the others, that is most, are very humble and simple, with no pretentions, elegance, or excess, and in their construction we have done no violence to the Indians, who, indeed, wish to honor their villages, because they have no churches in them other than the monasteries. And even among these houses there are many that cannot be lived in without danger to our health. And, finally, these houses do not belong to us, but to Your Highness.[59]

One point in this pleading should be borne in mind, that is, that in certain villages it was the Indians themselves who insisted, in their local pride, on having a handsome monastery. Nothing is more likely, and it must be recognized that especially in a young Christian community it would not have been wise to discourage this sentiment. For the same reason it was doubtless not a bad thing to force the Indians to build their own churches. The missionaries were obeying the same principle applied by the [present] federal authorities in their task of "incorporating" the Indians through the schools. The *Secretaría de Educación Pública* insists on the cooperation of the native communities in rural education. This policy, which was necessary at first because of lack of money, has had the advantage of creating among the natives a genuine attachment for their schools. One always has a fondness for the work of one's hands,[60] an observation that applies equally well to the churches. The Mexican missionaries understood it, and here also they appear as precursors.[61] So it seems quite likely that the seven naves of the chapel of San José de los Naturales, its seven altars, its porch, its multitude of columns, and its vast dimensions inspired in the Indians a high notion of their new religion.[62] Such arguments are not without persuasive power for the ordinary run of people. Have there not been countries whose natives measure the value and truth of their religion by the number of its churches?

The tradition of the Church, doubtless, has been hostile to overly luxurious buildings. Four centuries later, in his encyclical *Rerum Ecclesiae* (February 28, 1926), Pope Pius XI was to say to the missionaries: "Avoid erecting buildings and churches that are too sumptuous and costly." And three great Spanish saints, born, like our missionaries in countries of golden altars and vast monastic buildings, that is, St. Francis Xavier, St. Francis Borgia, and St. Theresa, denounced the construction or purchase of overly imposing and overly splendid houses.[63] Here, however, as in so many things, it is a matter of proportion. As much as it is important not to fall into a luxury incompatible with the religious life, not to exhaust the finances of a mission, and not to crush the Christian community with costly and ill-considered works, so it is just as important to make the new Christians as proud of their churches and convents as of their pastors. In the eyes of the Catholic missionary, the Church is not only the mystical body of Christ, but also a society of men sharing a visible institution. She must cling to the earth and at the same time cling to souls and strike her roots deeply. Above all it is necessary for Christ to rule over hearts, but the Church is stabilized only when His Kingdom is visible to the eye, and when the bells of a strong and beautiful church announce the Mass, the services, and the Angelus, and give rule and rhythm to daily prayers and work, telling of the joys and sadnesses of life.

11 *Pomp and Magnificence*

t HE same motives that led the religious to construct vast and beautiful churches and decorate them luxuriously led them also to surround the Mass and the services with the most solemn pomp. This had a double advantage. It maintained the enthusiasm of the Indians, who were very sensitive to external spectacles, and it enhanced their devotion and their respect for the ceremony at the altar.

For the celebration of the Mass, on Sundays and feast days, the church and especially the altar were brilliantly illuminated, and, at the same time, were decorated with all possible ornaments: tapestries, green boughs, gladioli, iris, and mint, with which the floor was covered also.[1] On Christmas Eve the natives illuminated the *atrios,* and for Epiphany, which they observed with great solemnity, they set up a crèche in the church, and in it placed all kinds of offerings, such as wax, incense, doves, and quail. On Palm Sunday they filled all the churches with greenery, especially those in which the benediction was to be held. To avoid all confusion, jostling, and accidents, the priests blessed the branches (probably palm leaves) in the hands of the faithful. A day or two before Ash Wednesday the Indians brought branches to the church and burned them for the coming ceremony.[2]

176

The ceremonies were almost always accompanied by singing and music. The Indians generally chanted plain-song, sometimes to the accompaniment of the organ, sometimes of instruments. And the choir, we are told, could bear comparison with those of Spain.[3] The orchestral part must have been very rich, and one is struck by the great variety of instruments: flutes, clarinets, cornets, trumpets (both *real* and *bastarda*), fifes, trombones, *jabelas* (Moroccan flutes), *chirimías* (the *chalumeau,* or ancient *chalemi* of France), *dulzainas* (similar to the *chirimías*), *sacabuches* (a kind of trombone), *orlos* (a kind of oboe), *rabeles* (or *rebec,* or *vihuela de arco,* a kind of guitar played with a bow), and finally the *atabales,* or drums.[4]

For the desired sumptuousness of masses and services, it was not enough to have a great number of different instruments, but to have good performers and singers. They were easily recruited. Native Mexicans are great lovers of music, and they came from a distance to learn it.[5] In certain regions, indeed, such as Michoacán, the natives are especially noted for their musical gifts,[6] and in the villages of Michoacán the tradition of the purest untaught plain-song has survived down to our time.[7]

Singing schools were founded in Mexico by three Franciscans: Pedro de Gante, a pioneer in all fields, Fray Arnaldo de Basaccio, and a very old religious by the name of Fray Juan Caro. Motolinía tells us that this last-named hardly knew Nahuatl, but delivered long sermons in Castilian to the Indian children, who listened to him open-mouthed and made strenuous efforts to understand what he was saying. The sight was so amusing that his assistants were hardly able to keep a straight face. He, however, although he had no interpreter, little by little succeeded in making his pupils understand him, and taught them the Mass of the Holy Virgin, the *Salve,* and the *Sancta Parens,* and they profited so well by his lessons that they took to composing, and one of them even wrote a whole Mass.[8] This should not be regarded as anything out of the ordinary. Others learned in a month to perform a Mass and vespers, omitting nothing.[9] There was a Spaniard in Tlaxcala who played the rebec. An Indian began by making a copy of it. After three lessons from the Spaniard, he had absorbed everything the other knew, and before ten days had passed he was playing his rebec among the flutes, executing a counterpoint for them. Another [Indian], in Mexico City, played the *vihuela de arco* and composed several four-part pieces for it.[10] Fray Juan de San Miguel, one of the great apostles of Michoacán, trained some remarkable organists and groups of musicians.[11] At Zapotlán, in New Galicia, the Spaniard Juan Montes taught music and church-singing to the Indians.[12]

The Augustinians had the same principles and practices. Each convent had an organ. To supply organists, they chose the most gifted musicians from among the Indians and sent them to Mexico City to study. The community supported them and paid their instructors. The other musicians trained each other. Every morning the cantors sang the *Te Deum* and the Hours of the service of the Holy Virgin. In the afternoon they sang vespers and complines in the same service, except on feast days, when they sang the first vespers of the solemn ceremony. Every Friday after vespers and complines they sang the *Benedicta,* and on Saturdays the salute to the Holy Sacrament. All this they performed in the nave, the choir being reserved for the religious.[13] In order to keep the number of examples within reason, I shall limit myself to the results obtained by Fray San Pedro de Jerónimo in Charo, Michoacán. His Indians sang very well in their language, not only the prayers, the *Te Deum,* and all kinds of hymns, but also, in Latin, the Mass, the Hours, the hymns of the great feasts, the litanies and their prayers, the *Miserere,* and the service for the dead—all this with a "pretty pronunciation" and generally from memory, to the great astonishment of Basalenque and all who heard them.[14]

Except for Motolinía's reservation about the Indians' playing of the *chirimía,*[15] there is nothing but enthusiastic eulogies and admiration for them among the missionaries.[16] The missionaries were no less enthusiastic than their Indians for beautiful and melodious services. They were delighted to encourage musical fervor among their parishioners. They welcomed cantors with open arms and multiplied the number of instruments and musicians. Excesses necessarily arose from this community of tastes. Instead of controlling the flood, the missionaries joyfully let it run, and soon their difficulties did not arise from a paucity of cantors and players, but from their multitude. "There is not an Indian village, even of twenty inhabitants," says Grijalva, "which is without trumpets and a few flutes to enrich the services."[17] At first the purchase of

178

instruments was a very costly business, and, besides, not everybody paid his assessment, which finally fell upon the native communities, and especially upon the poor. And then the cantors and musicians became insufferable. When not engaged in the services they had nothing to do, so they got into the habit of loafing, and used their leisure to seduce the women and girls. Besides, they became so swollen with self-importance— in some missions they wore magnificent costumes in church—[18] that they believed themselves to be great personages, affected an air of independence, and stirred the Indians up against their chiefs.

The synod of 1555 thought it had to take severe measures, such as forbidding the playing of trumpets in church—this instrument would be allowed only in processions outside the sanctuary; forbidding flutes and *chirimías,* except in the principal towns; an absolute prohibition of *vihuelas de arco* and other noisy and complicated instruments, for all of which the organ, "the ecclesiastical instrument," must be substituted, "so that the noise and clamor of the other instruments may cease"; and finally the religious and the parish priests are begged to reduce the number of cantors in each village to the strictly essential.[19] In a *cédula* of February 19, 1561, Philip II himself attempted, unsuccessfully, to stop this abuse.[20] Actually, his reform seems to have been motivated by a single consideration, to oblige the Indian cantors to pay their assessments [tributes], like everybody else. Another difficulty, however, arose at this point. Their salaries, which were very small, two pesos a year, would be almost entirely eaten up by the tribute, and the unfortunate cantors would be forced to neglect their duties to supplement their incomes. In 1565, the bishops also demanded a reduction in the number of cantors, so that they might be paid sufficient salaries and thus be able to perform their duties conscientiously.[21] In that same year the visitor Valderrama, in his report to the Council of the Indies, concluded that there were too many cantors and musicians in some convents, and this multitude should be reduced. He also requested the suppression of trumpets and *atabales,* which he thought were unsuitable in religious services.[22]

Processions were the natural and necessary complement of the religious services. In this matter also the traditions and tastes of the missionaries could not but coincide with the desires of the Indians. [Processions] were held on almost all Sundays and feast days, accompanied, it goes without saying, by singing and playing, and also, if I may be forgiven the expression, by a complete theatrical setting. The way was covered with flowers and boughs, and decorated with arches; brilliantly illuminated resting places were erected; the Indians carried floats. On Palm Sunday each bore a frond in his hand. This was the occasion for a vast overflowing of joy and enthusiasm. The children climbed trees along the route of the procession, sang, cut branches and tossed them down, and even threw down their clothes as the procession passed.[23] But, although the Palm Sunday procession was a solemn one, the [other] great processions seem to have been above all processions of mourning and penitence. At the church of San José de los Naturales in Mexico City, which was especially reserved for the natives, there was a procession on every Friday of Lent, and every day of Holy Week. On Monday, it was the procession for the souls in Purgatory; on Tuesday, St. John the Baptist; Wednesday, San Diego de Alcalá; Thursday and Friday, days of great emotional excitement, the Trinity and the Crucifixion, and the Virgin and the Entombment.

All processions, evidently in the Spanish tradition, carried floats: St. Francis leading the souls out of Purgatory by his girdle; the *Ecce Homo;* the life of the Precursor; the death of St. James. In the second procession of Holy Thursday, which was especially famous, more than 3,000 crucifixes were counted in the early days: many Indians carried them.[24] Others had candles. Zorita was dismayed by the consumption of wax. Still others lashed themselves with scourges, singing the *Pater,* the *Ave,* the *Credo,* and the *Salve Regina.* The crowd was vast, as many as 10,000 to 12,000, we are told. The procession took up the whole length of the street. Women took part in it, as well as children, the smallest in the arms of their parents, the largest on foot, also carrying candles.[25]

Less showy and less solemn processions were organized on other occasions, such as those held in the native quarters of Mexico City (Santa María, San Juan Bautista, San Pablo, and San Sebastián), to celebrate the feast days of their patron saints.[26] Others were more intimate, like that of the hospital of Tiripitío, directed by the Augustinians, which they had placed under the protection of the Virgin. Her image was carried to the church every Friday and brought back to the hospital on Saturday morning. It was the occasion for very brilliant and very devout processions, accompanied by carillons, singing, and concerts, amidst triumphal arches, flowers, and banners. On Saturday morning the Indians chanted the litanies of Our Lady of Loreto as they escorted her image.[27] The processions held in the Augustinian villages filled strangers with admiration. Each village had a wooden statue of its patron saint, carried on a gilded litter, and each quarter or parish had its own image as well. On days when general processions were held, all people of the neighboring villages flocked in, with their banners, floats, and bands. All these bands, floats, banners, and the burning sea of candles, made these processions "the gayest and showiest thing" that could be imagined. The Lenten processions had a different character, but were no less striking because of their order, their silence, and their severe and profound devotion. Everyone recognized that, despite the Spaniards' passion for processions, the Indians were their masters.[28]

In exceptional circumstances, extraordinary processions were staged. In 1529, in the convent of Santo Domingo in Mexico City, a silver vessel containing the consecrated wafers was stolen. A solemn procession of penitence and reparation was organized. It is not known how great a part the Indians had in it, but they attended it, and beyond a doubt it made a vivid impression on them.[29]

These examples show that processions were continuous, as they had been in pagan times. They were much more frequent during certain religious seasons, but they were held throughout the year and brought together all classes and all ages. Like the pagan festivals, they were a part of life, and with them and by them Christianity penetrated that life a little more deeply.

As in Spain, the processions depended in general upon another institution, the effect of which upon Christianization was no less profound. I refer to the confraternities. The apostolic activity of Pedro de Gante was also responsible for their beginning, before the arrival of Zumárraga. He it was who founded, in San José de los Naturales, the confraternity of the Very Holy Sacrament.[30] All the great processions of

Holy Week, just mentioned, were organized by a confraternity based at San José: the confraternity of the Souls in Purgatory, that of St. John the Baptist, that of San Diego de Alcalá, that of the Trinity, that of the True Cross, that of La Soledad, and that of the Entombment.[31] All these confraternities were directed by the Franciscans in charge of the parish of San José de los Naturales. The other two Orders directed them also. Fray Tomás de San Juan, O.P., founded a confraternity of the Holy Rosary, which grew mightily, but it was apparently not limited to Indians.[32] The Augustinians founded in each of their convents a confraternity of the Souls in Purgatory, which celebrated a Mass for the Dead every Monday; a confraternity of Our Lady, which celebrated a Mass for the Living every Saturday—Saturday being, as we know, a day of prayer especially consecrated to the Holy Virgin. They also had confraternities "de sangre," that is, of flagellants, who organized the Lenten processions with floats, candles, and banners.[33] We also know that there were confraternities of Indian women, who, if one may believe the *Códice Valderrama,* which gives us no details, offered certain difficulties.[34]

The confraternities, indeed, did not have the single purpose of organizing processions. More accurately, the processions were only the expression of pious feeling that the confraternities sought to bring into being and develop. Thus, the confraternity of the Holy Sacrament had been founded to increase the Indians' devotion to the Eucharist, and those of Our Lady, to strengthen the love and trust for the Virgin. In fact, it was noted that in villages that had confraternities not only were the processions more brilliant, but the services were better attended and more faithfully followed. In general, the spiritual level was higher in them, for the confraternities kept an eye on and controlled each other.[35] But there was a danger in this, too. Such spying ran the risk of encouraging hypocrisy among some, with everything that it might imply, and among others habits of malice and tale-bearing. There is no institution, however well conceived, that is without risks; and by the processions they organized, as well as by the religious practices they encouraged, the action of the confraternities prolonged, happily and usefully, the solemnities of worship.

However solemn the services, however brilliant the processions, however joyful they all were, thanks to the familiarity and good fellowship characteristic of Spanish piety, it is still true that while they were diversions, they were also manifestations of some austerity, or at least of gravity and seriousness. Now as Acosta says at the beginning of his chapter on Indian festivals, a wisely governed state should, when convenient, allow for recreations and pastimes.[36] Did not the Pope himself impose upon the Carthusians a weekly period of relaxation? Between services and processions the Indians had need of a rest, which it would have been imprudent to deny them. There was another reason for it. [Christian] services and processions might replace the religious ceremonies of paganism, but the [pre-Conquest] Indians had also had festivals of a religious nature—religion was part of their life—but of less liturgical significance. These festivals, the essence of which was dancing and singing, had also to be replaced, or, rather, to be Christianized. The guiding principles followed here more or less consciously by the missionaries, have been well summarized by Acosta. Speaking of the Mexican dances, he says: "It is not good to deprive the Indians of them, but one should take care to see that no superstition is mixed with them. In Tepotzotlán, a village seven leagues from Mexico, I have seen the *mitote* I have mentioned danced in the patio of the church, and it struck me as a good device for keeping the Indians occupied and amused on feast days, for they need some recreation, and, since this dance is public and harms no one, there are fewer objections to it than to others, which would be performed in secret if this one were taken away from them." The only thing necessary, he concludes, is to strive to see that these festivals and merry-makings, many of which had formerly been celebrated in honor of some idol, should redound to the greater glory of God and His Saints.[37] In this fashion the missionaries Christianized the native songs and dances. We do not know the details of their method, but what we do know, and what is the best proof of their skill and success, is that the songs and dances which they thus transformed are today still very much alive in the form the missionaries gave them.

Two procedures were employed in singing. The simplest, which had

183

little value in religious education, consisted of translating Spanish *octavas, canciones, romances,* and *redondillas* into native languages. The Indians sang these translations in the original tunes, with great pleasure and success. The second, which evidently had a much greater significance, was to adapt the new Christian words, in the native tongue, of course, to native tunes.[38] The most characteristic effort was certainly the *Psalmodia cristiana* of Sahagún, which, although not published until 1583, was composed by that famous Franciscan and used by the religious during the reign of Luis de Velasco—hence before 1564—as is brought out in the author's prologue.[39] The title, however, is misleading in its shortened form. It must be cited at length to allow one to seize the character and significance of the collection: *Psalmodia christiana, y Sermonario de los Sanctos del Año, en lengua Mexicana, compuesta por el muy Reverendo Padre Fray Bernardino de Sahagún, de la Orden de Sant Francisco. Ordenada en cantares o Psalmos: para que canten los Indios en los areytos, que hazen en las iglesias.* These are pious songs, in fact, written in the spirit of Sahagún, destined to replace the pagan songs of the pre-Hispanic period. There are songs for each of the principal feasts of the year. The book begins with prayers and a shortened *Doctrina,* which was meant to be sung also. Unfortunately, I cannot affirm that native tunes were used here. The new converts, however, supplied the Spanish and native words, and it is also possible that pre-Conquest songs, unconnected with the worship of idols, have thus been preserved, although it seems unlikely. In the Banco Nacional de México there is a collection of more than sixty native *cantares,* some of them before, others after, the Conquest. Miguel O. Mendizábal has studied them and believes they were collected by order of Sahagún, and were composed for Indian festivals, or used in them.[40]

Of all the works of the missionaries, this is perhaps the one that has best survived the vicissitudes [of time]. To them must be ascribed the greater part of the religious songs one hears in the most famous sanctuaries of Mexico: Chalma, San Salvador el Seco, Los Remedios, and Cholula, the origins of which are generally unknown. Moreover, doubtless by a kind of contamination, they must be considered the sources of certain popular songs. One of the first to be composed in Spanish by natives was sung at the *Fiesta del Pendón* [41] by a student of the College of Tlatelolco, which was directed by the Franciscans. Now, this song has all characteristics of the *corrido,* then called a *tocotin,* which is one of the commonest forms of the popular song in Mexico.[42] One other example, although it takes me beyond the limit I have set for myself: The *Alabado,* a hymn in honor of the Holy Sacrament taught to the natives by Fray Antonio Margil de Jesús in the eighteenth century, became a kind of national anthem in Mexico.[43]

With respect to dances, it was attempted at first to tie them in so closely with divine worship that they were performed at times inside the churches, as is proved by a decision of the *Junta Eclesiástica* of 1539, which I shall take up later. But dancing was performed also in the squares and in the *patios* of houses. Motolinía describes one, at a time of the festivals, in which the upper-class Indians, clad in white shirts, and blankets decorated with feathers, holding roses in their hands, danced and sang into the night, in the midst of illuminations.[44] These dances have also survived. At San Miguel de Allende (Guanajuato), for example, the feast of the Archangel [St. Michael], patron of the village, is still celebrated with dances and merry-making that go back to the evangelization of the sixteenth century.[45] According to a tradition which, unfortunately, I have not been able to verify, the festival called Altepe-ilhuitl, which is celebrated in September every year at Tepoztlán (Morelos), was introduced by Fray Domingo de la Anunciación as a substitute for a pre-Hispanic seasonal festival.[46] And the *danza del tigre* of Taxco is perhaps a Christianization of the ancient hunting dances of pagan times.[47] But the type that one encounters most frequently is the one called *Las Morismas,* that is, the *danzas de moros y cristianos.* These well-known and often described dances, of which, however, I have no methodical list, were observed all over the central part of Mexico: among the Totonacs of Vera Cruz; in the state of Tlaxcala; in the environs of Mexico City; in Michoacán; in Jalisco; even in the states of Zacatecas and Chihuahua.

Stripped of all adventitious elements, the *morismas* are built about a very simple theme, essentially a mock combat, with dialogue, supposed to represent a battle between Moors and Christians, who are divided into two groups of opposing dancers. St. James is almost always the leader of the Christians, and Pilate generally the leader of the Moors. It regularly ends with the victory of the Christians and the triumph of the Cross. *Morismas* were very frequent during the colonial period, among Creoles as well as Indians. They must have originated in the feasts celebrated in Mexico City in 1538, and in Tlaxcala in 1539, in which Moors and Christians were engaged. In the former, the taking of Rhodes was performed; in the latter, the capture of Jerusalem. These plays must have been connected with the cult of the Cross and the cult of St. James, and, also, in the Indian communities, with the cult of the village patron. In literature, they seem to be connected with the traditional themes of the Chansons de Geste, the romances of chivalry, the *Crónica General de España,* the *Romancero,* and the Hispano-Moorish romances. The missionaries did not originate the *morismas* in New Spain, for the first one, celebrated in Mexico City in 1538, was conceived and organized by Europeans for Europeans. But there is no doubt that the missionaries brought them to many Indian communities and worked very actively to spread them. This view is supported by various characteristics of the *morismas:* the importance given to the cult of the Cross; the many speeches, or rather sermons, on the catechism; and the baptism of the Moslems which was usually the denouement of the festival, which ends with the triumph of Christianity. Moreover, this was not merely a military and political triumph, but was above all a spiritual and religious triumph. The infidels recognize the supremacy of the Christians, and especially they accept the religion of Christ.[48]

The persistence and popularity of all these christianized *mitotes* prove how deeply their tradition was rooted among the natives and how wise the missionaries were in not trying to suppress them. The episcopate, however, was not disposed to favor these merry-makings. At the *Junta Eclesiástica* of 1539 and the synod of 1555, the bishops looked into the matter of *areitos*—a term borrowed from the Arawak of the Antilles and usually applied to the *mitotes*—and prohibited them in the Indian festivals honoring the patron saints of villages; they also prohibited their performance in churches, which were evidently not fitting places for them, but what the bishops seem especially to have feared was the survival of pagan forms, and they also feared that the *mitotes* would encroach more and more, and end by taking the lead over the Christian services.[49]

In 1555, they forbade the performance of *areitos* before sunrise and after High Mass, and allowed them only between morning services and vespers, and then on condition that the Indians stop the dance when the bell announced the latter service.[50] For many Indians it was surely more amusing to dance than to attend vespers, but, although [vespers] were not obligatory, it would not do to allow the accessory to become the principal, and to allow a partly profane festival to take the place of the divine cult. It seems doubtful that the bishops were altogether successful in stemming the flood. Jourdanet, the translator and commentator of Sahagún, saw Indians at Guadalupe, "dressed in their ancient style, form a circle, bound together by ropes of flowers, dance in the very middle of the church dedicated to the miraculous Virgin, while they hummed a monotonous tune which doubtless reminded them of their past." In 1853, the archbishop of Mexico prohibited these dances; but, with the tenacity which is their dominant trait, they did not disappear, but were only removed to the great square in front of the church, where they still go on.[51]

The general impression one gets from all the religious and quasi-religious festivals, is that the clergy was defeated little by little, as I have already noted in the matter of cantors. The Indians had such enthusiasm for all these manifestations of religion that they could hardly do without them, and, in case of need, they did not hesitate to play the priest's part. The prohibitions of the synods of 1555 and 1565 are revealing in this respect. In villages that had no priests the Indians might not recite the canonical Hours or say Mass on their own (*en seco*), as had happened in several places, but were authorized only to recite (*par dévotion*) the service of the Holy Virgin on feast days. Also, the Indians might not hold funeral services by themselves when priests were available.[52] Again, Indians might not organize processions on feast days without the attendance of a priest.[53] The excessive liberties enjoyed by present day *fiscales,* which I mentioned in the first part of this book, go back to these abuses and are owing to the tendency of which they are the expression.

In many countries the organization of pilgrimages is considered the normal and necessary complement of conversion. Their efficacy is undeniable.[45] In Mexico, however, the part played by the Mendicants in

187

the development and diffusion of this kind of worship seems to have been very slight. Mexico abounds in sanctuaries, especially Marian sanctuaries, which are the objects of pilgrimages, the origin of which goes back to the sixteenth century. Two of them, however, both near the capital, lead all the others: Nuestra Señora de los Remedios and Nuestra Señora de Guadalupe. The chapel of the Virgen de los Remedios is on the Cerro de Toltepec, near San Bartolo Naucalpan, in the Federal District and the state of Mexico. In its origin, as in its history, it is essentially a Spanish cult. It goes back, indeed, to an episode of the Conquest. After the evacuation of Tenochtitlán during the *Noche Triste,* the Virgin appeared to the Spanish army there to give it courage.[55] She even dazzled the Indians who were pursuing the fugitives.[56] Nuestra Señora de los Remedios, moreover, has always been considered the patroness of the Spaniards, and, during the war of Independence, they chose her as the protector of their armies, which is what gave her the name of *La Gachupina.* The religious, however, do not seem to have been much interested in this cult, at least at its beginning.

The case of Nuestra Señora de Guadalupe is very different, in the sense that the *Virgen Morena,* whose portrait was embroidered on Hidalgo's banner, is considered to be the special patroness of the Mexican Indians. According to tradition, it will be recalled, she appeared many times in the month of December, 1531, on the hill of Tepeyac, near Mexico City, to a converted Indian named Juan Diego. When he begged her for a sign that he might show to Bishop Zumárraga, she told him to pick all the flowers on the summit of Tepeyac and take them to him. In the presence of the bishop Juan Diego unfolded his cape, in which he had put the flowers, and the portrait of the Virgin was found miraculously painted on it. The cult of Our Lady of Guadalupe has continued to grow since that time, in Mexico and in all Spanish America. Its origins, however, are obscure.[57] It is especially difficult to determine the attitudes of the three primitive Orders toward the new cult and the part they played in its diffusion. Their part appears to have been very small. During the period covered by this study, neither the Dominicans nor the Augustinians—I speak of them, of course, as groups—appear in the history of the cult of Guadalupe, which their chroniclers do not even mention. The question is more complex with regard to the Franciscans. In 1544, to abate a grave epidemic that was devastating Mexico City and its vicinity, they organized a procession of children to the chapel of Our Lady of Guadalupe.[58] But this, to my knowledge, was the sole gesture of their concern and support of the cult of Tepeyac, and even here the evidence is late and untrustworthy. There is no reason to accept Torquemada's version, which attributes the founding of the primitive chapel to [one of] the first Franciscans, that is, to Motolinía.[59] On the contrary, the hostility of the Friars Minor is proved by altogether indisputable testimony. On September 8, 1556, the provincial of the Franciscans, Fray Francisco de Bustamante, formerly commissary general of the Indies, in a sermon he preached in the Franciscan chapel of San José during the celebration of the Nativity of the Holy Virgin, violently denounced the cult of Our Lady of Guadalupe. He declared that it had no foundation and that the picture had been painted by an Indian. He took Archbishop Montúfar severely to task for tolerating such an ill-founded cult, which moreover was dangerous, because he saw in it a disguised idolatry, and lamented that the efforts of the religious should thus be thwarted, for they had been at great pains to inculcate among the Indians precise notions about the cult of images.[60]

This sermon, which openly attacked an already popular cult, and which treated the episcopal authority with such scant respect, stirred up an enormous scandal. Montúfar, who was not present, was naturally very unhappy about it and ordered an investigation, the text of which I have. The testimony of the witnesses proves that Bustamante was not alone in his Order. One of his colleagues deposed that the sanctuary [of Guadalupe] was frequented by great numbers of Indians, but that the cult had cooled among some of them by order of the religious.[61] It does not seem too daring to think that there were Franciscans among them. Two other witnesses, moreover, reported a conversation they had had with the Franciscans Fray Antonio de Huete and Fray Alonso de Santiago, and with other Friars Minor. The two Fathers were hostile. Fray Alonso said that the cult of Our Lady of Guadalupe was dangerous, because the Indians believed that the painting at Tepeyac was the Virgin herself, whom they worshiped as an idol.[62] Finally, the first witness also deposed that a religious of the convent of Santiago Tlatelolco, a certain Fray Luis,

189

had told him that all the Franciscans were opposed to the cult of Our Lady of Guadalupe, "a cult which we all deplore." [63]

It is to be noted that the parish of Guadalupe was served by secular priests.[64] Actually, before 1572, the cult of Our Lady of Guadalupe seems to have been a secular and episcopal affair, fomented and favored by the two bishops, or archbishops, of Mexico. According to tradition, the appearances took place during the episcopate of Zumárraga, to whom Juan Diego had presented the flowers of Tepeyac; the picture was at first kept at his house; he it was who, in 1533, had it brought from the cathedral to a little chapel at Tepeyac; and, finally, it was he who, with Cortés, organized a collection for the construction of a decent shrine.[65] His successor, Montúfar, showed an equal interest in the cult. In several documents he is mentioned as "patron and founder" on the first sanctuary, and, in fact, it was he who had it built.[66] On September 6, 1556, two days before Bustamante's sermon, Montúfar himself preached solemnly in favor of the cult of Our Lady of Guadalupe.[67] Ten years later, he presided at the offering of a silver statue, which the celebrated Alonso de Villaseca had made for the shrine.[68]

In all this, perhaps, one should not look for the cause of the hostility of the Friars Minor. Montúfar, during almost all his episcopate, had stormy relations with the regular clergy, particularly with the Franciscans. Did not one of the religious concerned in the investigation of Bustamante's sermon go so far as to say that the Order should have the archbishop sent back across the sea? And did not the provincials of the three Orders actually write the King demanding his recall?[69] On the other hand, to suppose that the Franciscans' opposition to Our Lady of Guadalupe was owing solely to the fact that the cult was patronized by Montúfar, and that the quarrel over the tithes and privileges of the regulars had embittered their relations with the archbishop, would be to attribute to them a very narrow and petty spirit. They had more serious motives, and I do not believe that Bustamante and his colleagues spoke in bad faith when they brandished the scarecrow of idolatry. I have noted in this study the precautions taken by one of them, Fray Maturino Gilberti, to avoid such a perversion, and the care with which he reminded the Indians that one did not worship the material image, but God, or the saint it represented.[70] Sahagún, who was very mistrustful in such matters, was particularly uneasy about the cult of Guadalupe. He was acutely afraid lest the Indians, on the pretext of honoring the Holy Virgin, whom the preachers had erroneously given the name of Tonantzin, would really continue to render homage to the pre-Hispanic goddess Tonantzin, whose shrine had been at Tepayac itself.[71] A like fear, although less precise, is manifested by Bustamante and his colleagues. The missionaries, said Father Bustamante, have had great trouble in preventing the Indians from worshiping material images. Certain Indians adore the Virgin so devoutly that they worship her images. The religious are constantly obliged to remind them that images are made of wood and stone, and they are not to be venerated, but only what they represent: Jesus Christ Our Lord, the Holy Virgin, and the Saints in Paradise. To favor the cult of Our Lady of Guadalupe and spread the belief that the image at Tepeyac, the supernatural origin of which Bustamante denied, and attributed to an Indian, that this image worked miracles would mean the destruction of the edifice so painfully built by the stubborn teaching of the religious. Besides, it would risk disturbing the faith of the new converts, who were always on the lookout for prodigies, in the expectation of which they would be frequently disappointed. The provincial of the Franciscans thought, therefore, that this cult would be fatal to the progress of evangelization. The objections of the other Franciscans agree on the whole with those of Bustamante,[72] who may properly be considered in this matter as the standard bearer, if not of the whole Order, at least of the Fathers in the region of Mexico City.

The cult of Our Lady of Guadalupe and the pilgrimage to Tepeyac seem therefore to have been born, grown up, and triumphed with the support of the episcopate, in the face of the indifference of the Dominicans and Augustinians, and the turbulent hostility of the Friars Minor of Mexico. The part of the Orders is more certain in other and less important pilgrimages which, nevertheless, still enjoy today an extreme popularity. The best known, perhaps, is that of the Sacromonte, on the summit of a height overlooking Amecameca, at the foot of the great snow-covered volcanoes, in one of the most beautiful landscapes of Mexico.[73] This sanctuary goes back to Martín de Valencia. We know that toward the end of his life he delighted in retiring to pray in a grotto at the top of this hill. In 1584, the Dominican who had charge of the parish of Amecameca deposited there several relics of this servant of God and arranged them in a chapel, where he placed a great reclining figure of Christ, *El Señor del Sacromonte,* which ever since that time has been the object of an uninterrupted veneration, in particular on Good Friday, when the sanctuary and the admirable road that leads to it are invaded by crowds of Indians.[74] El Sacromonte thus appears as a Franciscan sanctuary in its origin, and Dominican in its history. Ocotlán, Zapopan, and San Juan de los Lagos, on the other hand, are entirely Franciscan. It may be of interest here to mention the legend of Our Lady of Ocotlán, near Tlaxcala, whose appearance is fixed by folklore in 1541, toward the end of the episcopate of Garcés.[75] In any case, it occurred in the Franciscan house at Ocotlán, and the statue was placed in the Franciscan chapel. At Zapopan, the Marian sanctuary very near Guadalajara, the action of the Order seems to have been more positive, for, if we may believe the local tradition picked up by Tello, it was Fray Antonio de Segovia himself who gave the miraculous image to the village at the moment when he and Fray Angel de Valencia were engaged in the conversion of its inhabitants.[76] It was also a Franciscan Father, either the same Father Segovia, or Fray Miguel de Bolonia, who gave the village of San Juan de los Lagos (Jalisco) the statue of the Holy Virgin which is still today the object of an extremely popular yearly pilgrimage in November.[77]

None of the sanctuaries I have mentioned appears to have been a substitution for a native shrine. Chalma, on the other hand, is a substitution, rivaling Guadalupe [in popularity]. Next to the pilgrimage of Tepeyac, that of Chalma is the most frequented by the natives of Mexico. It is not so widespread, but neither is it entirely a local cult. Indians attend it from Querétaro, Michoacán, Oaxaca, Guerrero, and even from the Huaxteca of San Luis Potosí. There is no better testimony for the success of the method of substitution, which was used by the Augustinians at Chalma. Otherwise, the origins of the sanctuary are confused. We know them only from traditions collected in the seventeenth century by Father Florencia.[78] The Augustinians, as we have seen, established themselves in Ocuila, southwest of Toluca, in the present state of Mexico. The place is most often called today Chalmita, and is attached to the municipality of Malinalco. Not far from the village there is a grotto, where the natives used to go in crowds to worship a very famous idol, the identity of which has not been established. The Augustinians learned of the existence of this sanctuary. In 1540, probably, they removed the idol in unknown circumstances, and replaced it by a crucifix that has become the celebrated *Señor de Chalma,* or even, as the Indians call it, the *San Señor de Chalma.*[79]

Whatever the attitude of the regular clergy, the pilgrimages I have just spoken of have a double character common to them all, which must be brought out, and which explains why I have given only a few pages to them. All of them are of uncertain or obscure origin, and all were instituted after the end of the sixteenth century and during the remainder of the colonial period. The actual establishment of the pilgrimage of the Sacromonte dates from 1584, and it is, along with Guadalupe, the most ancient in popularity. From this fact, and from the hostility or indifference of the three Orders toward the cult of Tepeyac, one may conclude that they attached only a secondary importance to pilgrimages. Even at Chalma it seems that the religious were more interested in the substitution of cults than in the development of pilgrimages, which occurred only as a side product, possibly independently of [the religious]. In other words, our missionaries were hardly acquainted with this policy of [fomenting] pilgrimages which some of today's missionary advocates recommend. In this field, Fray Alonso de Montúfar, by his perseverance in spreading and propagating the cult of Our Lady of Guadalupe, showed more clear-sightedness and boldness. In a day when the unanimous veneration of the *Virgen Morena* is perhaps the only tie that persists among the Mexicans, one must admire the perspicacity of the second head of the Mexican Church.

12 *The Edifying Play*

tHE teaching implicit in religious ceremonies, and the influence of singing, festivals, and processions were completed and extended by another kind of teaching, no less effective in charming and keeping up the somewhat childlike spirit of the Indians. I refer to the educational play. We are not concerned here, of course, with the plays introduced by the Spaniards for their own pleasure, which had a magnificent career in Mexico, but with the plays staged by the religious in the native language for the Indians alone, in which only the Indians took part.[1] These plays, like the festivals, were substitutions, for the Aztecs had also had theatrical performances, of which, unfortunately, we know little.[2]

No text of a sixteenth century *auto* has survived. All that have come down to us, at least in the form in which we know them, belong to the following century,[3] or to the eighteenth.[4] To judge by several documents, however, I think it likely that a study of the seventeenth-century *autos* may be combined with that of those staged in the sixteenth. There is every indication that the seventeenth century *autos* had been played for a long time—I have definite proof for one of them—and that the written text at my disposal is only a late fixation of an ancient oral tradition. In other words, it is probable that the *autos* written or copied in the seventeenth

194

century had been composed long before.[5] Besides, even if we admit that the date of the copy is quite close to that of the original, the *autos* invented in the seventeenth century could not have been very different from those of the sixteenth. If there was a difference, it is probable that the first *autos,* written at the beginning of the conversion, contained longer and more numerous moral and dogmatic admonitions, and had a clearer and more obvious educational purpose.

The two oldest plays of which I know are to be credited to the Franciscans, Fray Luis de Fuensalida and Fray Andrés de Olmos. I am acquainted with the work of Father Fuensalida only through Beristain, who claims to have seen the original manuscript. The text reveals a profound knowledge of the Mexican language, but, from the dramatic point of view, it seems to have been a very rudimentary affair, consisting of dialogues in Nahuatl between the Virgin Mary and the Archangel Gabriel. The Archangel, according to Beristain, presents the Virgin with several letters from patriarchs in Limbo, begging her to receive their ambassador and give her consent to the Incarnation of the Word.[6] We do not know that these dialogues were really staged, and we know as little of the date of their composition, but it is difficult to place them after 1535. Fray Luis de Fuensalida, in fact, left for Europe to report to Charles V on the religious situation in New Spain at an undetermined date, which could hardly have been after that year, for he does not appear again in Mexico—died, indeed, on his return voyage in Puerto Rico, in 1545. It is quite unlikely, also, that he wrote these dialogues during his stay in Europe.

The famous polyglot Fray Andrés de Olmos wrote, also in Nahuatl, an *auto* entitled *El Juicio Final,*[7] which is a little later than the other. It was staged in the chapel of San José de los Naturales before Viceroy Mendoza, who arrived in 1535, and before Zumárraga, who died in 1548. According to Las Casas, some eight hundred actors and supernumeraries participated in it and played their parts to perfection.[8]

We are better informed about the *autos* staged by the Indians of Tlaxcala, in 1538 and 1539. Motolinía has recorded them for us in his *Historia de los Indios de la Nueva España,* in a famous chapter.[9] On St. John the Baptist's Day [June 24], 1538 four *autos* were staged: the

Annunciation to Zacharias of the birth of St. John, which lasted an hour; the Annunciation of Our Lady, which lasted the same; [10] the Visitation of Our Lady to St. Elizabeth; and then, after Mass, the Nativity of St. John the Baptist. During the Easter celebration of 1539 the Fall of Adam and Eve was played, with a great deal of theatrical apparatus. Our first parents are seen in the terrestrial paradise, in the midst of plants and flowers extremely well imitated, surrounded by all kinds of animals, some of them played by Indian boys. Even the four rivers of paradise are successfully represented. Motolinía describes the setting in detail. Its exterior pomp must have greatly flattered the taste of the natives. The *auto* apparently had four scenes: the Temptation, the Fall, the Divine Curse, and the Expulsion from Eden as an apprenticeship for hardship and pain. This *auto,* says Motolinía, was performed by the Indians in their own language.

To celebrate the ten years' truce between Francis I and Charles V (June 18, 1538), several other plays were performed at Tlaxcala in 1539.[11] In Mexico City the Spaniards staged the Capture of Rhodes; in Tlaxcala the Indians staged the Capture of Jerusalem, on Corpus Christi Day. This was a kind of great spectacle in pantomime, rather than an *auto* proper. Just as the Spaniards had done in the Capture of Rhodes, in Mexico City, the [Tlaxcalans] built a fortified city, with donjon, towers, and crenelated walls decorated "with roses and flowers," a very characteristic trait of the Mexican natives, as recorded by Motolinía. Facing the city, to the right of the Spanish camp, were the Emperor's quarters; to the left, those of the different tribes of New Spain. In the middle of the square stood Santa Fe, which the Emperor was to occupy with his army. This being Corpus Christi Day, the play was staged in the presence of the Holy Sacrament, which was placed on a rostrum surrounded by personages representing the Pope, the cardinals and the bishops.

First appears the Spanish army, in which all countries of Europe are represented; the rear guard is of Germans and Italians. Then the Mexican army makes its entrance, at its head the men of Tlaxcala and Mexico, with their royal standard and that of their captain-general, Viceroy Antonio de Mendoza. The body of the army is made up of the natives of the Huaxteca, Cempoala, the Mixteca, Acolhuacán, and Peruvians and natives of the Antilles. Its rear guard is composed of Tarascans and Guatemalans. The Spaniards at once begin the assault on Jerusalem. The Moors, under the command of the Sultan, sally forth, but they are defeated and retire within the city. Then it is the Mexicans' turn to attack. The Moors make another sortie, suffer another defeat, and again retire. Thereupon Galilee, Judea, Samaria, Damascus, and all Syria send reinforcements to Jerusalem, and the Moors, encouraged at once make a new sortie, jostling the Spaniards and Mexicans so roughly that the Emperor, informed of the situation, decides to set out in person with a third army for Jerusalem, where he arrives flanked by the kings of France and Hungary, "with crowns on their heads."

All of them together occupy Santa Fe. The Moors are at first terrified, but they recover their courage and even gain the advantage over the Spaniards. Then the Emperor sends a messenger to the Pope begging him to help with his prayers. The Pope at once orders prayers throughout Christendom and grants a plenary indulgence. Then, accompanied by his cardinals, he kneels before the Holy Sacrament and begins to pray. The Spanish army does the same. An angel appears and comforts them, announcing that God has only wished to test them, that their prayers have been heard, and that the Lord is sending the Apostle St. James to them. As soon as he appears, mounted on his white horse, in the midst of the acclamations of the Spaniards, the panic-stricken Moors retreat into the city. Then the Mexicans try to take it, but are repulsed, and fall to praying in their turn. Another angel appears and makes them a speech like that of the first: God only wanted to test them and prove to them that without his aid they can do nothing; but He has heard their prayers and is sending them St. Hippolytus, whose feast is celebrated on the day that the Tlaxcalans and Spaniards, now united in brotherhood, took the City of Mexico [August 13, 1521]. St. Hippolytus, in fact, does arrive, mounted on his black horse. He takes his place at the head of the Mexicans, while St. James takes his at the head of the Spaniards, and the assault begins. The battle is very stubbornly fought up to the moment when the Archangel St. Michael appears and speaks to the Moors, [saying] that God has forgiven them all their sins because they have spared the Holy Places, but they must be converted and do penance. The Sultan and the

Moors, suddenly seeing the light, decide to surrender. The Sultan sends the Emperor his letter of submission, signed "The Great Sultan of Babylon and Tetrarch of Jerusalem." Then he renders homage to the Emperor and the Pope. In his company are many Turks, (that is to say, adult Indians, whose baptism has been planned for that day), who publicly demand of the Pope that they be admitted to the Sacrament. The Pope makes a sign to a priest, who baptizes them on the spot.[12] After which the Temptation of Our Lord Jesus Christ is played, by the Indians, naturally; then St. Francis preaching to the birds; and finally, after Mass, the Sacrifice of Abraham.[13]

The *auto* published by Paso y Troncoso under the title of *El Sacrificio de Isaac* [should be] correctly entitled *Del Nascimiento de Isaac Del Sacrificio que Habraham su Padre quiso por mandado de Dios hazer*. In fact, only the second half of the subject is treated, the Sacrifice of Isaac. The persons appearing in it are: God the Father, an angel, Abraham, Sarah, two *caballeros*, Agar and Ishmael, two servants, and a devil.[14] Later I shall take up the characters of this play. We are better informed about the *Comedia de los Reyes*, also published by the Mexican scholar [Paso y Tronscoso]. Its exact title is *Comedia de los Reyes, conpuesto a noestro padre Fray Joan Vauhtista guardia de santa teulogia de Santiago Tlatelolco Mexico del y sietecientos y siete (sic) años*. Contrary to what this document says, the date of the piece is probably 1607, not 1707. In 1606 Father Juan Bautista was reader in theology at Tlatelolco. The author is probably an Indian, possibly Agustín de la Fuente, secretary to Father Juan Bautista and assistant to Sahagún. The *comedia*, therefore, by its date as well as by its author, belongs in the tradition of the sixteenth century. The piece is probably raw material, which had not yet been submitted to review by the religious editor. In fact, errors, not only of history and geography, but of prophecies and passages incorrectly ascribed to the Holy Scriptures, are found.[15] The persons of the play are: the Virgin Mary; an angel; the Emperor; two of his vassals; the three Magi, Gaspar, Balthazar, and Melchor; their captain; King Herod; four Jewish priests; a Jewish captain; a notary; six Jews; and a farmer. The *comedia* is divided into four scenes: the Appearance of the Star and the Departure of the Magi; the Arrival of the Magi at Jerusalem; the Adoration of the Magi; and the Slaughter of the Innocents.

The play *La Adoración de los Reyes,* which I shall now examine, is incomplete, but we have more information about it than about the *comedia.* It is the only play that can positively be dated in the sixteenth century. The *comedia* is known to us on two occasions. It was played at Tlajomulco, near Guadalajara, on January 6, 1587, that is, on Epiphany, before the Franciscan visitor, Fray Alonso Ponce, and more that 5,000 Indians. The religious who wrote the account of his journey recorded the play in some detail.[16] Paso y Troncoso discovered another copy of it that he published in 1900, together with a Spanish translation. The text of Ponce's *Relación* proves, moreover, that the piece had been played since at least 1550, for Father Ponce was assured that the old Indian who brought the presents of the Magi had been playing the part for more than thirty years, that is, since before 1557.

The characters are the Child Jesus, the Virgin Mary, St. Joseph, the three Magi, their messenger, King Herod, his majordomo, and three Jewish priests. The first three are silent. Ponce describes the setting in broad strokes. The Indians had built a crèche in the *atrio* of the church, almost at the foot of the bell tower; the Holy Virgin and St. Joseph are standing near it. A little way off Herod is seen on his throne surrounded by his courtiers. The cortege of the Magi descends from one of the hills that surround the village. The way is long, the progress slow and majestic. It takes almost two hours, according to the account, for it to reach the church. Meanwhile, the eyes and spirits of the faithful are occupied with edifying intervals of various kinds. Angels come to sing and dance before the crèche. They are replaced by shepherds. An angel appears at the top of a little wooden tower, sings the *Gloria,* and announces the birth of the Child. The shepherds at once bring their offerings to the crèche, and then all dance and sing. The royal cortege finally arrives. Gaspar remarks that he no longer sees the marvelous star that has guided him thus far, which means they have reached their destination. He sends one of his servants to salute Herod and beg an audience for him and one of his two companions. Once admitted to [Herod's] presence, Melchor recites his story and asks him where to find this King of the Jews who has just been born and whom they wish to adore. Herod is angry and uneasy. Is this an unknown rival? He orders his priests to come and explain all this mystery to him. They look into the Prophecies, to the greater uneasiness and anger of Herod, for he discovers that the Child is to be born in Bethlehem. He drives away his priests and then, after apologizing, begs the Magi to come to see him when they have adored the Child, so that he may adore Him in his turn. Then the Magi, again guided by the miraculous star, go to the God Child and adore Him.[17] Each offers Him his gifts and does Him homage in a short speech. Then an angel appears and commands them to go home by a different road without going to see Herod.[18]

The educational theater is generally characterized by a very strict and careful attention to the temperment of the natives and their attitude toward the new religion. It was exclusively native, not in inspiration, but in language and actors. All sources agree that the participants, the actors proper, the supernumeraries, singers, and dancers, were Indian, and that everything spoken or sung was in the native language, most frequently Nahuatl, which was the most widely used and the one the missionaries tried to spread still more. The texts recovered by Paso y Troncoso are evident proof of this characteristic, which very forcefully struck the writer of Ponce's *Relación*. In his description of the Tlajomulco play he emphasizes the fact that the angels sang in the Mexican language, that the angel exhorted the shepherds in the Mexican language, that the shepherds also sang in the Mexican language, and that the Magi addressed the Child in the Mexican language, as did the old Indian who brought the gifts. "Lengua mexicana" occurs like a refrain. Motolinía gives similar details. The missionaries, moreover, did not hesitate to adapt the action of the play to the traditions of the native festivals, such as having the animals acted by young boys, in the *auto* of the Fall of Adam and Eve.[19] But, to make these plays comprehensible to the native audience it was not enough to have them played by Indians in the native language. The indications I have given show that all these *autos* had an extremely rudimentary structure. Facts were represented more or less as they must have occurred. There was no research involved, for the question was less how to interest than how to instruct and edify. And it was important that the mass of spectators should be instructed and edified without effort [on their part], that they should have the least possible amount to comprehend and interpret, and that above all they should have something to look at. Hence the sumptuous and complicated staging, which attracted and held the eyes of the Indians.

It is no cause for surprise, therefore, that the plays were closely tied in with religion and had a strikingly liturgical character. It may have been noticed that at the time of the feasts of St. John the Baptist at Tlaxcala in 1538, the Mass was celebrated after the first three *autos* and before the last one, the nativity of the saint. The following year, on Corpus Christi Day, the plays were put on in the presence of the Holy Sacrament. The Christian army, as we have seen, kneels before it and begs for victory, after which the Holy Sacrament is thanked. Even the administration of baptism is inserted in the play, in the place of the circumcision of St. John the Baptist. The baptism is a very real one, of a baby eight days old, who is given the name of John. In like manner, at the end of the *Capture of Jerusalem,* baptism is administered to a number of make-believe Turks.

In this respect, however, the most characteristic play is still the *La Adoración de los Reyes,* because of the intimate connection in it between the liturgy and the theater. According to the notes on the setting in the copy published by Paso y Troncoso, which differs slightly from Ponce's *Relación,* the crèche is inside the church, where the Magi enter to adore the Child, at the moment Mass was beginning, or had just begun. After the *Credo,* the three Kings present their gifts, while the holy sacrifice is being performed, so that it ends almost at the moment when the angels tell them to leave by a different road. Then everybody, actors and spectators, all the faithful, in short, leave the church. Paso y Troncoso is correct in saying that this *auto* is a Mass, preceded and accompanied by theatrical scenes.

One should not be astonished either by the fact that the missionaries took all kinds of precautions to keep their plays from being diverted from their purpose and becoming the occasion of disorder or scandal. Their first precautions were of a practical order. Women were completely excluded from the stage. The dancers, actors, and singers were all men or youths.[20] Other precautions were of a somewhat doctrinal nature, and these are the most interesting. In the *Sacrificio de Isaac,* for example, the episode of Agar is told in Nahuatl in such as way that it is impossible to learn that she had been Abraham's concubine and that her son Ishmael

201

was Isaac's brother. The missionaries had had too much trouble in eradicating polygamy to give the natives an argument, however weak, for their ancient custom.[21] Another striking example: the *auto* of the *Destrucción de Jerusalén* derives from a Valencian romance of St. Pierre Pascal, save only that the episode of the mothers who, pressed by hunger, devoured their children after seasoning them, has completely disappeared from the Mexican version, for [the representation of the episode] would have been singularly dangerous in a country where human sacrifice and ritualistic cannibalism were still recent.[22]

All this, however, has only a negative character. Each of the plays of which I know had, directly or indirectly, in the ensemble and often in detail, a positive value for teaching and edification. It is probable that Fray Luis de Fuensalida, in his dialogues between the Virgin Mary and the Archangel Gabriel, was trying to show the natives the grandeur of the mystery of the Incarnation, since only the incarnation could open the doors of heaven to the holy persons of the Old Testament. It is also probable that he wished to augment in this fashion their love and veneration of the Virgin Mary, especially since she was the patroness of his Order. As for the *auto* of the Last Judgment, it seems useless to emphasize its evident purpose, the moral value of thinking about judgment and hell, especially among souls that are a little rude or childlike. For one should not expect of them that perfectly selfless virtue that is almost one with saintliness, the fear of God being their only path to wisdom. As Luis de Granada was to write a little later, in his brief treatise on the teaching of the Christian doctrine to infidels: "This subject, when well presented, contributes greatly to terrify the hearts of men. . . . And this terror disposes many hearts to accept the Faith."[23] In fact, as we learn from Motolinía, this play "greatly edified everyone, Indians and Spaniards alike, and persuaded them to give themselves to virtue and renounce this wicked life; and this terror, and the compunction that it brings, leads many sinful women to God."[24] The Fall of Adam and Eve was an equally excellent subject for meditation. It reminded the Indians of the lamentable consequences of sin and the punishments incurred by man when he rebels against divine law. Thus, many Indians, Motolinía tells us, in his account of the festivals at Tlaxcala, "shed tears and showed great sorrow, especially when Adam was condemned to exile and sent out into the world." [25] The lesson of the *auto* of the Capture of Jerusalem was the humiliation of the infidels before the Christians, and that of the Sultan before the Pope, the Emperor, and the all-power of God, represented by the triumph of the Holy Sacrament, the true conqueror of the enemies of the faith.

In the Temptation of Our Lord Jesus Christ, and in the preaching of St. Francis to the birds, certain vices of the Indians are slyly or severely rebuked, as when the devil offers Our Lord all Castile, its riches and wines, "very good wines, and thus touched everybody, Indians as well as Spaniards, because the Indians are mad about our wines." [26] St. Francis has just begun his sermon to the people when he is interrupted by a drunken Indian, who is singing, Motolinía tells us, just as the Indians sing when they have had too much to drink. The saint begs him to be silent, but the drunkard persists, whereupon St. Francis summons the devils, who come running, very ugly, and noisily drag the wretch to a horrible hell near by. Then St. Francis resumes his sermon, but this time he is interrupted by witches, in whom one recognizes the old wives who perform abortions for pregnant women. They also are dragged off to hell. Motolinía adds: "This hell had a secret door by which all those who were within could emerge, and as soon as they had come out it was set on fire, and it burned so fiercely that it seemed no one had escaped, and that everyone, demons and the damned, was burning; and all the souls and devils groaned and screamed, which filled with horror and fright even those who knew that no one was [really] burning." [27] By such devices the missionaries strove to inculculcate the fear of hell among their Indians.

The desire to instruct and edify is especially apparent in the *Sacrificio de Isaac*. It could even be said that the play is a perpetual sermon, at times dogmatic, at times moral. The angel who appears at the beginning, speaking of the Son of God, does not fail to say that He it is who will really open the gates of paradise by His blood and death. The *auto* aims on the whole to teach all the duties and responsibilities of parents toward their children—in short, the obedience that all men owe to the expression of the divine will. The duties of parents toward their children are evoked in the person of Ishmael, who represents the spoiled and obstreperous child. The obedience of children to the parents is embodied in the person of Isaac, all of whose acts and attitudes are inspired by this virtue. Finally, as one might expect, Abraham symbolizes obedience to the commands of God. He never ceases from reminding us, not without complacency, of the respect and docility with which we should receive and obey them. "Assuredly," he says somewhere, "one will do whatever may be the will of God, for He thus commands me." And, speaking to Isaac: "Approach and kneel thou here; this is what God has commanded me, and I will do His will." And Isaac replies: "Let the sovereign command of God be done, as He and thou wish." [28] Then the angel who speaks to the public at the end of the play, summing up his teaching, says: "All ye who are here have seen this prodigy. So then make your way of life conform to the divine commandments. Violate not a single one; see that your children live not according to the flesh; that they live in wisdom; and that they serve God our Lord, that they may deserve the Kingdom of Heaven. So be it." [29]

The same desire for edification and teaching is found in the Magi plays,[30] but they had, besides, a meaning peculiar to themselves. Epiphany, in fact, is the manifestation of the true God to the gentiles. It is the feast of the gentiles called to the faith, the feast of the summons of the pagans to Christianity. It was, therefore, the Indian feast *par excellence*. "The feast of the Magi," writes Motolinía, "is celebrated by them with great rejoicing, for it seems to them that it is their own feast, and on that day they frequently stage the *auto* of the gifts of the Magi to the Child Jesus." [31] He adds that the Indians' devotion to that feast did not stop growing. We have seen that the play witnessed by Fray Alonso Ponce was attended by more than 5,000 Indians. All those of the vincinity, we are told, had come to Tlajomulco for this celebration.[32] Hence, it may not be too daring to think that the dogma of the redeeming Incarnation was one of the main points of the missionary theater. Were not the patriarchs, invoked in his dialogue by Fray Luis de Fuensalida, the image of the very gentiles for whom the Son of God opened the gates of heaven with His blood and death, as the angel in the *Sacrificio de Isaac* says? And Epiphany, the first manifestation of the Word Incarnate to the pagans, is one of the principal themes of the edifying theater.[33] But it would have been dangerous to allow the Indians to believe that the Incarnation and the Redemption alone assured the salvation of each one, doing away with the necessity of human collaboration. Man was free not to profit by the fruits of these mysteries. He was free to disobey God. He was free to go to hell. And, since one could hardly demand of the great mass of Indians that they practice a purely selfless virtue, the dogma of ultimate purposes and the dogma of hell became one of the favorite themes of the edifying theater.

It is evidently impossible to gauge the effect of the spiritual influence that this theater may have had. Mendieta tells us of all the good accomplished by the presentation of the *auto* of the Last Judgment. In 1599, the Franciscan Fray Juan Bautista expressed himself in a similar way in an appreciation of the whole: "I have had a long experience," he said, "[in appreciating] that, by means of these plays I have had put on during Lent, concerning these and other subjects, Our Lord in His mercy has harvested much fruit, and has cleansed and converted consciences which for long years had been hardened in enmity." [34]

It should be noted that, like the feasts and dances I have spoken of, the theater created by the missionaries has survived through the storms. In the last years of the nineteenth century, Mexicans and Indians, in Texas and New Mexico, were still playing a kind of *auto* that represented the Adoration of the Shepherds. [35] Along about 1900 the Tarascans of Michoacán were still staging *coloquios* on religious subjects (Adam and Eve, the Birth of the Messiah), which were performed sometimes in Spanish, sometimes in the native tongue. Dr. León has published the text of one of these plays, in which he believes he sees the hand of the first missionaries, and which may have been transmitted orally from generation to generation. [36] And in different parts of Mexico, particularly at Tzintzuntzan, on the shore of Lake Pátzcuaro, episodes of the Passion are still played today during Holy Week. Frances Toor attended them. She writes: "I am beginning to understand why the most ignorant Indian has the episodes of the drama so deeply engraved on his consciousness." Could one demand a better proof of the pedagogical value of this theater? [37]

It should again be noted that, although we have the account of a play staged by the Dominicans in 1575, [38] the genre appears to be almost exclusively Franciscan. To be sure, most of the themes treated (the Fall of Adam, the Sacrifice of Abraham, the Nativity of St. John the Baptist, the Adoration of the Shepherds and the Magi, the Temptation of Our Lord, the Last Judgment), are extremely banal. They are found as frequently in the iconography of the end of the Middle Ages as in the French and Spanish religious theaters. It should be added, nevertheless, that although the teaching is very theatrical in form, it still seems to be in the Franciscan tradition. Remember the episode of the crèche of Greccio in the life of St. Francis;[39] also, the altogether dramatic character of the *Meditations on the Life of Christ,* by the pseudo-Bonaventure.[40] Another theme besides, the sermon of St. Francis to the birds, is exclusively Franciscan. In the *Capture of Jerusalem,* played at Tlaxcala, the allusion to the Moslems' respect for the Holy Places, which were in the charge of the Franciscans, seems to have been a Franciscan trait.[41] And if a profound study of the matter should be made—which would go beyond the scope of this work— one would find, perhaps, that the most banal themes of this repertory were those exploited by the Franciscans, or written under their inspiration.[41]

13 Primary and Technical Schools

a MISSION without schools," said Pope Pius IX one day to an apostolic vicar,[1] "is a mission without a future." Nothing is more evident than the importance of the school in the stabilization of the Church. The instruction given in the schools by the religious, or under their direction, completed the training begun with the catechism. It gave the young Christians the instruments necessary to carry forward the study of their religion, if they so desired. It created bonds of affection between the pupils and their teachers, who were often the religious themselves. The stabilization of the Church was also bound up with the temporal progress of Christianity. Without primary schools, which gave the members of the community a modicum of useful knowledge, and without the technical schools, which gave the Indians a sure and honorable means of support, the Church might have become the victim of the slightest disorder, because it would not have been based upon an organized society.[2]

I shall not consider here the primary instruction given to boys, for I spoke of it already when I discussed the catechism. In the type of society called theocratic by general consent, teaching could not be separated from indoctrination. Consequently, the Christian doctrine and reading and writing went side by side. They were closely bound together and were frequently taught by the same teachers. This is what happened then, and this is what happens today in many mission countries. There are only a few notes to be added here. The first two schools of the New World were founded in Mexico by the Franciscans: that of Texcoco, opened by Pedro de Gante in 1523, before the arrival of the Twelve, and that of Mexico City, organized in 1525 by Martín de Valencia. The first school in Tlaxcala was founded in 1531 by another Franciscan, Fray Alonso de Escalona.[4] It would be tedious to list the rest, from the College of San Juan de Letrán, which received the orphans of Indian and Spanish women, and which was at first an ordinary school directed by the Franciscans,[5] to the school at Ahuacatlán in New Galicia, founded by Fray Francisco Lorenzo and Fray Miguel de Estivales.[6] But this whole undertaking is dominated by one celebrated name, which I have so often mentioned, Pedro de Gante.

Born about 1480, probably at Ayghem-Saint-Pierre, near Ghent, Fray Pedro arrived in Mexico in 1523, and remained there until his death in 1572, at an extremely advanced age, without ever returning to Europe. He spent his life in the most widely diverse fields and taught generations of Indians to read and write. He it was who founded the great school of San Francisco in Mexico City, behind the chapel of San José de los Naturales, and directed it for more than forty years, and had as many as a thousand pupils.[7] Even today no name is more revered in Mexico. I should have liked to sketch a portrait of this great figure, but his humility makes it impossible. Pedro de Gante, despite his eminent qualifications, would never accept ordination, and consequently could never accept a place or fill an office. His person is obscured by his work, and his extraordinarily modest letters tell us nothing about himself, except when, in a gesture of approaching despair, he gives evidence of a passionate love for his Indians, on the day he begged Charles V to send several religious of Ghent to Mexico. "In this wise," he wrote, "when I die the Indians will not miss me too much."[8] Archbishop Montúfar paid him an involuntary tribute, when, in a moment of exasperation, he exclaimed: "Pedro de Gante is Archbishop of Mexico, not I!"[9]

When the Franciscans taught the catechism they divided the children into two classes: those of the *gente baja,* and those of the Indian aristocracy. Although the children were commingled, according to Motolinía,[10] [the two classes] were under different rules. The former were day pupils and came regularly every morning to attend classes, and were free in the afternoon. The latter were boarders. We are told that they lived at times in the school, at times in the monastery, which comes to the same thing, for the school was a dependency of the convent and church, with which it was connected on the north side; that is to say, in general, on the side opposite the convent and church. Children in this category had classes morning and evening, but what was especially emphasized was their religious training. Nonreligious training was the same for both groups: reading, writing, numbers, and singing. Spanish was not taught, and all instruction was in the native tongues, generally Nahuatl. Now, most native tongues were not written at all, and, even in Nahuatl, the only writing available was picture-writing, which was entirely inadequate, so the missionaries taught their pupils the Latin alphabet. But the abstract letters were completely foreign to the Indian spirit, so [the missionaries] tried to link the forms of the letters to concrete objects, and even, as much as possible, to things the pupils could comprehend. Thus, "A" was represented as a double ladder, or a compass; "B" as a pair of andirons, or a guitar; "C" as a horseshoe, or a horn, and so on, relatively easy objects to manipulate. "I" was represented as a tower; "X" as a boat. Valadés has preserved for us an alphabet of this kind. Most of the representations are very arbitrary, or extremely stylized; but that could hardly have bothered the Indians, for the Mexican manuscripts have the same conventional character.[11] The religious put either the objects themselves or pictures of them into the hands of their pupils, and the pupils thus learned to group and assemble them, as European children of today do with blocks. Along with this ideographic instruction, the missionaries had recourse to another system, which was strictly phonetic. Its alphabet was made up of a series of animals or objects, the names of which were well known, each of them representing the initial letter of its name.[12] Many Indians thus got into the habit of using Latin characters. [The missionaries] also invented another system of mixed writing, in which sentences in Latin characters were intermingled with hieroglyphs and pictures.[13] In whatever way it was done, the introduction of the Latin alphabet for the transcription of native tongues was a revolution in the intellectual history of Mexico, the importance of which cannot be exaggerated.

I have taken the Franciscans as an example because of their justified reputation in pedagogy. It would be wrong, however, to conclude that the other two Orders neglected primary instruction. At Yanhuitlán [the Dominican] Fray Jordán de Santa Catalina founded a school in which he taught reading, writing, and the catechism to more than four hundred pupils.[14] All Augustinian monasteries had schools with regular instruction in attending Mass, reading, writing, singing, and the playing of musical instruments.[15] In the schools of Tiripitío, which were considered to be well organized, the children were beginning to read and write at the age of eight.[16] The programs were evidently the same as those of the Franciscans, and their methods of instruction do not seem to have been essentially different.

The education of girls, the future mothers of families, was no less important than that of the boys.[17] Zumárraga was aware of it, and in 1530, with the approval of Cortés and the Empress Isabel of Portugal, who took the project to heart, he had six nuns sent from Spain and put them in charge of the education of Indian girls, who, up to that time had been gathered up and taught by the Franciscans. After his consecration, in 1534, he brought eight pious women from Spain for the same purpose,[18] and in 1535 one of the nuns of the 1530 group, Catalina de Bustamante, in her turn sent from Spain three new fellow workers. All of them were active, and by 1534 there were already eight schools for girls in New Spain: Mexico City, Texcoco, Otumba, Tepeapulco, Huejotzingo, Cholula, and Coyoacán. Although they are called colleges in many documents, these establishments were hardly even primary schools, where the teaching of manners took precedence over [other] instruction. Their purpose was not to turn out even slightly educated women, but to protect Indians girls from exploitation by their own fathers and prepare them for marriage and their duties as wives and mothers. It is not certain that they were taught reading and writing. They learned the catechism and the Hours of the Holy Virgin, sewing, embroidery, and all household tasks. They were kept strictly indoors, but were allowed to go out from time to time, always accompanied. They were taken very young, at seven, or even at five or six, and kept until they were twelve, when they were married to pupils of the missionaries. Zumárraga and the religious generally were in favor of these early marriages, by means of which they thought to prevent certain abuses and vices.

For this reason the founding of girls' schools lasted only ten years. Given their purpose, they could only be temporary, for they were meant to protect girls from the dangers and corruption of the pagan environment and make good mothers of them. Since a Christian education was given at the same time to the boys, the danger of the pagan environment, or, more exactly, the pagan environment itself, disappeared automatically, owing once more to massive conversion. The daughters of the former pupils of the colleges were born in Christian homes and reared by Christian parents, from whom it would be useless and perhaps dangerous to separate them. On the other hand, it seems that the schoolmistresses did not give entire satisfaction. There were two classes of them. Those of 1534 were secular, what would be called today "working women," with no religious affiliation; the others, those of 1530 and 1535, were *beatas* of the Third Order of St. Francis, who were considered to be practically nuns, although, strictly speaking, they did not deserve the title, for they did not take religious vows. So they, like the secular teachers, were not bound by [the vow of] obedience, and the bishops complained loudly of both groups. Most of them, in fact, left when they pleased and ended by abandoning the schools entrusted to them, finding in private households more interesting employment.[19]

The lack of cloistered [personnel in the schools] was another cause of their failure, for a different reason. The Indians had been accustomed to rear their girls very rigidly in an almost absolute confinement,[20] and it seemed to them the girls enjoyed an excessive liberty in the schools. Although an effort was made to impose compulsory attendance, they sent their children to them unwillingly and as little as possible, and they refused to help them with money, in the hope that [the school] would have to send them home. So Zumárraga and the other bishops insisted, in 1536 and 1537, on getting real nuns, preferably cloistered ones, but they failed.[21] When Bishop Ramírez de Fuenleal of Santo Domingo was made

211

president of the Audiencia of Mexico, the Crown regularly consulted him about all these matters, and he wrote that he did not think it opportune to send cloistered nuns. We do not know the basis for his opinion, but the decision was certainly unfortunate. It would doubtless not have been a long-term affair, but it would have been of capital importance. The part played by women and especially by mothers in the stagnation or progress of societies is obvious, and Zumárraga, who had sought to Christianize native society by giving its women a new training, was clearly aware of it. But he realized too late that he had used inadequate means for this heavy and delicate task, which could not be accomplished with seventeen devout women of good will, but undisciplined, of mediocre culture, and without a vigorous personality. It would have required a whole army of cultivated and active cloistered nuns, accustomed to obedience and directed by superiors with a feeling for government. This army was denied him. He was even denied the simple monastery he asked for. And so, because the counsel of good common sense was ignored and the means disapproved of, the purpose was not accomplished.

If primary instruction was directed particularly to the moral education of young Indians, their technical instruction had a predominantly practical end. It was not enough to lecture the new converts about the necessity and dignity of work, and to fill them with a taste for it; it was also necessary to give them the opportunity. It is a truism to observe that when one doesn't know how to do anything, one does nothing. It was indispensable, therefore, to give the youngsters a trade. Manual labor would prevent their falling into vicious idleness,[22] and at the same time it would be an instrument of moral uplift.[23] Technical instruction, moreover, would give the Indians a sure and honest way to earn a living, and it contained an element of social stability, which could not help but strengthen the Church.

The beginning of the technical schools was once again the work of Pedro de Gante, of whom Valadés wrote: "Omnes artes illis ostendit; nullius enim nescius erat"[24] [He taught them all the arts; he was, indeed, ignorant of none of them]. He it was who took the initiative in introducing instruction in the arts and trades in the school installed beside the chapel of San José de los Naturales. He gathered adults there and trained blacksmiths, carpenters, masons, tailors, and cobblers. He formed a whole group of painters, sculptors, and jewelers, who fashioned the statues and retables for the churches, and furnished them with ornaments, crosses, candelabra, holy vessels, and the like.[25] The teacher of design at the school may have been Valadés himself.[26] There is no doubt that the school had an Italian lay brother, known only as Fray Daniel, who got together a famous team of embroiderers. They made ornaments for the different parts of the service.[27] In Michoacán it was a secular bishop, the celebrated Vasco de Quiroga, who earned the glory of making handicrafts flourish among the natives, although no small part of it belongs to Fray Juan de San Miguel, one of the great apostles to the Tarascans.[28] The Franciscan chronicler La Rea boasts of the maunal skill and artistic talents of the Tarascans trained by his Order who painted and carved, and manufactured furniture, bells, trumpets, *sacabuches,* and even organs, all out of wood.[29] It was also the Franciscans who taught the natives the art of building vaults. The first one they built was the nave of the Franciscan church in Mexico City, the work of a Spanish mason. Nothing could have astonished the natives more, for they thought that when the scaffolding and the truss were removed, the whole thing would collapse.[30]

We know little of Dominican activity in this field, but they are credited with the introduction of ceramics at Puebla de los Angeles, imitating Talavera ware.[31] We do know, however, that the Augustinians gave their full attention to the training of good craftsmen. When their villages had need of indispensable technicians, they sent several Indians to Mexico City for training. Grijalva boasts of their workers' skill in mosaics and inlays. Their embroiderers rivaled those of Fray Daniel. They were used, continues Grijalva, for making ornaments for convents and churches, to the profit of everyone, for the Indians loved the work and found an honest occupation in it.[32] In Tiripitío, the opposite system was used, and workers were brought in from outside to train the Indians there. Thus, Spanish workmen, very carefully recruited for the construction of the convent and church, taught the Indians the art of quarrying and stone-cutting, which they did with such success that the pupils came to equal their teachers.

Natural conditions influenced the development of trades. Tiripitío was surrounded by woods, and many of its inhabitants, therefore, chose the carpenter's trade and succeeded in making "very good chests of drawers and pretty things." On the other hand, the region produced no cotton, of which the ordinary clothing of the Indians was made. It had to be brought in and manufactured, so the Indians preferred [woolen] stuffs, the use of which spread throughout the province, and tailors' shops multiplied. They also learned the trades of potter, dyer, sculptor, and painter, although they did not equal the Spaniards in them, and that of blacksmith, in which they did exceedingly well, thanks to their natural talent. Tiripitío became the technical center for all Michoacán, and the people of other villages came there for instruction, or brought in its workmen to instruct their own.[33]

Thus an elite of native craftsmen was created, the skill and talent of whom aroused the admiration of Las Casas. The famous Dominican went into ecstasies over the crosses, chalices, curtains, and altar cruets fashioned by the gold- and silversmiths, the crucifixes carved by the woodworkers, the ease with which the Indians made musical instruments, and the talent of the calligraphers. They had not all been trained by the missionaries, however. Some were self-taught. Indians, muffled to the eyes in their blankets, would stand beside a goldsmith's shop and watch him without seeming to do so, and then would reproduce his work, just as fine and delicate.[34] Motolinía boasts of the talent of a young Indian who reproduced so perfectly a papal bull that had been given him to copy that it was next to impossible to distinguish the copy from the original. He was the first of his kind, and an enthusiastic Spaniard took him off to Europe. [Motolinía] adds that many natives learned to illuminate, bind, and engrave. And he praises again in happy detail the skill of the painters, goldbeaters, leather workers, bell founders, gold- and silversmiths, and embroiderers, and even so I have shortened his list. The speed and ease with which the Indians learned all these trades very soon forced the Spanish craftsmen, who no longer enjoyed a monopoly, to lower their prices.[35] Romero de Terreros credits a native with the fresco in the Franciscan convent at Cholula which represents the Mass at the moment of the Elevation. According to Paso y Troncoso, the large retable in the old chapel of San José de los Naturales was executed in 1554 by the Indian painter Marcos de Aquino, assisted by other native artists. He was known as Cipac by his compatriots.[36] It is quite probable that the portrait of the Dominican Fray Domingo de Betanzos, now in [the church of] Tlazcantla, Tepetlaostoc (Mexico), was painted on maguey paper by one of the friar's pupils.[37] Lumholtz attributes to the missionaries the floral design of Tarascan pottery, which replaced the former symbolic and religious decoration.[38] Although definite pre-Conquest influence in monastic architecture cannot be pointed out, native workmen left their mark on the decorative sculpture. They frequently used European subjects in their own way, as, for example, at San Agustín Acolman and in the open chapel at Tlamanalco,[39] and especially in the church at Tlaxcala, which is decorated with coats of arms, where, as Father Cuevas wittily observes, the lions have turned into Mexican squirrels; chateaux have become Indian huts (*jacales*); the eagles have become vultures (*zopilotes*); and the heralds two cowering natives.[40] In the Dominican church at Coixtlahuaca (Oaxaca) the symbols of the Passion are handled entirely in the native manner, like figures in a pre-Conquest manuscript, where the Nahuatl sign for speech issues from the mouths of two human heads.[41] Elsewhere true Mexican motifs are introduced by the workmen, or under their influence. The organ cactus appears in the Augustinian convent at Yecapixtla.[42] It occurs again in the Franciscan convent at Calpan, in an almost symbolic union with a maguey blossom.[43] The portal of the Augustinian church at Yuriria records the triumph of an Indian craftsman, who uses his own figure as one of the principal motifs of the decoration.[44]

A more exhaustive study of sixteenth-century monuments will undoubtedly permit archaeologists some day to give us fuller and more precise information about this interesting aspect of the clash of the two cultures. On the other hand, the missionaries' instruction in the moral and spiritual field did not yield such happy results—this in spite of their training of women in the duties of mothers, and their training excellent craftsmen to be able to earn an honest living. Work, to be sure, is a factor in spiritual progress, but I must repeat here the observations I made on the subject of native villages: that the education given to young Indians removed them from contact with Europeans, and even from other Indians. It withdrew them from life, instead of preparing them for it: the boys more or less cloistered in the convents, the girls shut up in boarding schools. Even the training of craftsmen allowed native groups to live by themselves in closed societies, without access to the outside world. Here again we find the system of tutelage operating, which was undeniably successful in its application, but which kept the Indians in a perpetual minority. And it sharply diminished the range of the admirable activity of the missionaries and prevented them from crowning their work by giving their Christian community a [native] priestly class.

14 *Training an Elite: the Problem of a Native Clergy*

a NEW Church cannot live without leaders. The humble mass of peasants, craftsmen, and all those who worked with their hands in New Spain, to whom the missionaries had brought security for the future—this humble mass must be directed, trained, and nurtured by an elite: a lay elite, and a priestly and monastic elite. Its necessity does not have to be demonstrated. It is theological, for the priest is the necessary intermediary between the faithful and God. He alone, in the name of the God whose place he is filling and whose words he pronounces, can preach, absolve, and consecrate. A monastic elite, although, strictly speaking, not indispensable, is also almost a necessity, because of its stronger or more flexible organization, its example of putting evangelical teachings into practice, the spiritual influence of its convents, the power of its prayers in intercession and expiation, its austerities and its self-denials. Even so, a Christian community can hardly do without a lay elite. The layman can concern himself with matters which convention and canon law deny to a priest; he can penetrate freely into places that are closed, or only half-opened, to a priest. In certain cases, at the same time, he can serve as intermediary and link between the clergy and the mass of the faithful, and between the religious and civil authorities. The lay elite is the counselor and collaborator, free yet obedient, of the priestly and monastic elite. This double necessity was apparent to the missionaries of New Spain, especially to several Franciscans; but, although they were thoroughly and happily successful in the formation of a lay elite, they met a complete check in the formation of a priestly elite. This attempt and its two very different consequences are worth examining.[1]

The Dominicans did not found a single secondary school in their missions in New Spain. They were hostile to the notion, particularly to the teaching of Latin to the natives. The Augustinians did not share their misgivings, and their famous house at Tiripitío seems to have been a primary school, in which instruction was given side by side with musical and technical training.[2] But, in 1537, [they had] in Mexico City a college to which, we know for certain, natives as well as Spaniards were admitted, where a professor (*letor*) taught Latin, that is, grammar. The Augustinians considered this work very necessary, and they believed it induced the Indians to gain a more solid knowledge of the Christian doctrine. And then, since the income of a hundred and fifteen *pesos de minas* [a year] donated by its founder, a certain Bartolomé de Morales, did not suffice to pay the teacher, they supplemented it with thirty-five pesos from the income of their convent, in order to assure him a salary of a hundred and fifty pesos. Also, to facilitate the life of the college and assure its continuance, they founded the *Cofradía del Nombre de Jesús,* which was to elect two majordomos and four alternates. In spite of all this, their college had a hard time surviving. They did not wish to abandon the project, so on December 15, 1537, they begged Charles V to give them [an Indian] village or grant them a sum of money.[3] I do not know where or how they recruited pupils for their college, which had been founded for teaching reading, writing, and Latin "to willing persons, Spanish or Indian." Did the teaching of Latin mean that this was to be a true seminary?[4] The words are vague. It would be hazardous to conclude that the Augustinians had a wider concept of secondary teaching, more democratic, as we should say today, than the Franciscans, who admitted to the somewhat more advanced studies only the sons of the native aristocracy, the *principales,*[5] thus restricting their secondary and higher College of Santiago Tlatelolco to the sons of great families.[6]

This college, established near Mexico City in the *barrio* of Santiago Tlatelolco and placed under the patronage of *La Santa Cruz,* was opened on January 6, 1536, Epiphany, which symbolizes the call of the gentiles to the true faith, and which the Indians considered to be more or less their national feast day. The first viceroy, Antonio de Mendoza, who arrived soon afterward, presided over the extremely solemn ceremony. After a sermon preached by a certain Dr. Cervantes in their church, the Franciscans went in procession from their convent in Mexico City to Tlatelolco, where Mendoza, Bishop Zumárraga, and the president of the Audiencia, Sebastián Ramírez de Fuenleal, surrounded by a great crowd, were awaiting them. During Mass a sermon was preached by Fray Alonso de Herrera. The inauguration ended with a banquet in the refectory of the religious given by Zumárraga to the first pupils, attended by the Franciscans and invited guests. Fray Pedro de Rivera preached the concluding sermon.

Nevertheless, the building inaugurated with such great pomp was very modest. For lack of money, and because it was not thought desirable to test the intellectual capacities of the Indians too soon, it was considered enough to erect a small building of rough stone.[7] Later, the Indians built a stone house, which perhaps had a stage. On the day of the inauguration the college had sixty pupils, chosen from among the best of the convent of San Francisco de México. They belonged, consequently, to the native noble families.[8] By the following year they numbered seventy, and the bishops would have liked it if there had been three hundred, for they were well aware of the resources and needs of New Spain.[9] Hence the recruiting was expanded by choosing two or three boys of ten to twelve years in each important town of Mexico, so that the whole country might have the advantages of the institution, but the recruiting was still restricted to the aristocracy. The pupils, who lived in the college, led an almost monastic life. They wore a kind of cassock called a *hopa;* they regularly recited the services of the Holy Virgin; they arose with the sun; and, before going to work, they heard Mass in the chapel. They took their meals in common in the refectory and slept in a dormitory where the beds were arranged in two opposite rows, separated by a central aisle. The beds were only a mat and a blanket, in the Indian fashion, raised upon wooden trestles because of the dampness. A lamp was kept burning all night, and silence, calm, and respect for decency were assured by the presence of a monitor. Each pupil had a small locked box, in which he kept his clothing and books.[10]

In the beginning the Franciscans had the direction of the college. Zumárraga and the provincial, Fray García de Cisneros, had participated in its founding, and its administration was entrusted to the guardian of the Franciscan convent of Santiago Tlatelolco.[11] It was a Franciscan who wrote (very much later, for his book was not printed until 1559) the Latin grammar used by the pupils.[12] The European staff was also completely Franciscan, chosen, moreover, with great care, for the list contains the names of only the religious of the elite: Fray Juan de Goana, Fray Bernardino de Sahagún, Fray Francisco de Bustamante, Fray Andrés de Olmos, Fray García de Cisneros, Fray Arnaldo de Basaccio, and Fray Juan Focher.[13] The subjects taught were reading, writing, music, Latin, rhetoric, logic, philosophy, and Indian medicine.[14] We know that Basaccio, Sahagún, and Olmos taught Latin, in which all courses were given; [15] Goana taught rhetoric, logic, and philosophy.[16] All these religious, however, did not teach simultaneously, probably no more than two at a time,[17] for it was fairly frequent in the religious orders for the teachers to be overloaded in this way. They had helpers besides. Motolinía, speaking of the college, says that the Indians had two religious as teachers, with an Indian *bachiller,* who taught grammar,[18] and who, without doubt, was that "Miguel," professor of Latin at Tlatelolco, mentioned by Mendieta.[19]

Teaching was always in the hands of the Franciscans, but they soon relinquished ownership of the college, for lack of resources to keep it going. On November 24, 1536, Zumárraga wrote to Charles V that they had just given it to the Crown, represented by His Majesty and the viceroy.[20] Ten years later they even gave up the management of the house, which they abandoned. It seemed to them the moment to turn the task over to those who had been trained for it, their former pupils, who wrote a system of rules, elected a rector, counselors, and professors. This regime lasted twenty years, but was not successful. By 1550 the house was falling into ruin, and ten years later pupils could no longer sleep in it because it had almost entirely tumbled down. All of them, therefore, became day pupils, which greatly hindered the progress of studies.[21] Sahagún lays the blame for this decadence equally on the Spanish majordomo, the rector, the native counselors, and the religious, who were negligent in their management of the establishment.[22] The religious had to take things in hand again and reform the rules and the college. This kind of second founding, about 1570,[23] did not save the project, which never recovered its first splendor, for it had hardly been reconstituted when the students were decimated by the great epidemic of 1576. In the seventeenth century the building was again in ruins, and at the time Vetancurt was writing, only two rooms had been reconstructed to accommodate a primary school.

The idea of such a foundation was evidently born on the spot, in New Spain itself. It had been in the air for a long time. In 1525, the *Contador* Rodrigo de Albornoz, with a clear vision of the spiritual needs of the country, demanded the foundation of a college for the training of the sons of a few noblemen and chiefs for the priesthood. In substance he was saying that one native priest would make more conversions than fifty European priests.[24] The next year an unknown person, probably a religious, wrote to Charles V: "It will be necessary to establish in Tenochtitlán a general college for the teaching of grammar, arts, and theology, for the training of the natives of this country. All the sons of nobles and chiefs of the land should be admitted." [25] At the time the college was founded, Fray Arnaldo de Basaccio had been teaching Latin at the school of San José de los Naturales for several years.[26] It was very likely the success of his teaching and the good that the Indians derived from it that led to the project of founding and planning a college for secondary studies.

These circumstances make it clear why everyone, with remarkable enthusiasm, collaborated in the founding of the new establishment. Viceroy Mendoza, who had a high opinion of the Indians' intelligence, greatly encouraged the project; [27] a royal *cédula* of September 2, 1536, gives Zumárraga credit for the original decision,[28] and we have seen the part played in it by the Franciscan Order, particularly by the provincial, Fray García de Cisneros. In this friendly rivalry, the Bishop of Santo Domingo, Sebastián Ramírez de Fuenleal, was especially active. In a letter of August

8, 1533, to Charles V he clearly gives himself credit for initiating the teaching done by Fray Arnaldo de Basaccio. "I have urged the religious of the Order of St. Francis," he wrote, "to teach grammar to the natives in the common language of Mexico. They liked the idea and have named a religious to take charge of the matter. And the natives are showing such intelligence and capacity that they are a great deal better at it than the Spaniards. Without any doubt whatever, within two years there will be fifty Indians who will know grammar and teach it. I am watching the project closely because of the great good that will result from it." [29] He urges the King to furnish the necessary means for the founding and support of the college. Moreover, Zumárraga himself, despite the undeniably important part he had had personally [in the project], expressed himself as follows: "This college for Indian grammarians, which Monsignor the Bishop of Santo Domingo, in the name of Your Majesty, had built. . . ." [30] Evidently, the authority of three such considerable personages as Mendoza, Zumárraga, and Fuenleal, who were known for their sober judgment, could not fail to have a happy effect at home, and their agreement was enough to convince the Crown of the utility of the enterprise. [The Crown], at least during the first years, showed its interest in a college for Indian students in the most tangible and appreciable ways. On August 23, 1538, in a letter to the bishops, the King rejoiced in its founding, expressed his gratitude and satisfaction to the professors, authorized the construction of a solid building, and gave [an Indian village] to the institution, although its resources proved inadequate. On the same day he begged the provincial of the Franciscans and the viceroy to take all necessary steps to ensure the progress and perpetuity of the establishment.[31]

The college, which aroused so much enthusiasm, as well as so much criticism, did succeed in creating among the Indians a remarkable elite. From this point of view its success was complete and seems undeniable today. Fuenleal has told us that the Indians far surpassed the Spaniards in the study of Latin. Jerónimo López, whom we shall meet again, a strenuous opponent of the college, declares that the Indians speak Latin with the elegance of Cicero—"hablan tan elegante el latín como Tulio"— and says besides that it is astonishing to see what they write in that tongue.[32] Motolinía tells the story of a priest, a recent arrival from Castile, who was vanquished in a grammatical argument with a student and was at loss to answer a question that the latter put to him.[33] Miguel, *el bachiller indio,* who taught at Tlatelolco, was so familiar with the language that when he lay dying he conversed in Latin with Fray Francisco de Bustamante, who had come to administer spiritual comfort.[34] The most famous of the Latinists turned out by the school at Santiago Tlatelolco was Antonio Valeriano, already mentioned among the collaborators of Sahagún. Even in his declining years he spoke and wrote Latin with ease, and with such elegance and propriety that "he resembled Cicero or Quintillian." (Comparison with classical writers was indispensable). The Franciscan Fray Juan Bautista, who also praised Valeriano, in the "Prólogo" of his *Sermonario en lengua mexicana,*[35] has preserved the text of the last letter that Valeriano wrote him. The reader may be grateful to me for reproducing it below.

His litterarum gerulus ad vestram paternitatem portat id quod mihi traducendum jussisti. Nescio profecto, an in traductione ejus sim felix. Multa quippe in eo sunt praegnantia, ut nesciam in quem sensum meliorem verti debeant. Si quid est erratum, parcas obsecro. Et tuam gravem censuram adhibeas, et his litteris tam male formatis simul et ignoscas, illiteratae enim videntur potius quam litterae; nec mirum vestrae paternitati videatur, manus namque vacillant, oculi caligant, et aures occlusae. Iterum atque iterum parcas. Deus optimus maximus longaevam tuae paternitati vitam concedat. De Mexico. Tui amantissimus etsi indignus. Antonius Malerianus.

[The courier will deliver to Your Paternity the translation you ordered me to make. It, to be sure, is full of difficulties, and I know not how they could be better solved. If there are errors I beg you to overlook them. Give me your frank opinion of the characters, which are so misshapen that they seem to be nonletters rather than letters. And be not astonished thereat, Your Paternity, for my hands are trembling, my eyes are clouded, and my ears closed. Forgive me again and yet again. And may the Good and Great God grant a long life to Your Paternity. From Mexico. Your most loving, but unworthy, Antonius Valerianus.]

The text of this letter shows that one of the principal services rendered to the missionaries by the pupils and former pupils of Taltelolco was translation. Sahagún, the great Mexicanist, acknowledged their collaboration. "If," he writes, "there are sermons, critiques, and explanations of the doctrine in Indian languages worthy to be published, free of all heresy, they did it themselves. Since they are already instructed in the Latin language, they explain to us the true sense and figures of their own language, as well as the incongruities that we sometimes [are guilt of in] our sermons and writings. They correct all that, and nothing translated into their tongue would be free of mistakes if it were not read by them." [36] Fray Juan Bautista gives us a whole list of these translators, who were perfectly grounded in Latin, Nahuatl, and Spanish: Juan Berardo, Diego Adriano, Francisco Bautista de Contreras, Esteban Bravo, Pedro de Gante, Agustín de la Fuente, and Hernando de Ribas. The last-named had helped Fray Alonso de Molina in the composition of his *Arte* and *Vocabulario* of the Nahuatl language, and helped Fray Juan de Goana in his dialogues on the peace of the soul. Agustín de la Fuente had taught Fray Pedro Uroz and Sahagún. We have already seen the enormous part played by the pupils and former pupils of Tlatelolco in the composition and editing of the great work of Fray Bernardino [de Sahagún]. In like fashion, the *Pláticas,* which I have discussed above, were written with the aid of the native collaborators of Sahagún, all of them trained at Tlatelolco.[37] To Fray Juan Bautista's list should be added the name of Zorita's informant, Pablo Nazareno,[38] who translated the Epistles and the Gospel into Nahuatl.[39] The religious also found in the college copyists and typesetters for the printing of their books.[40] It should be further remarked that, although all collegians seem to have known Spanish, that language was banished from the curriculum. Along with Latin, which had first place, as Fuenleal had desired,[41] only Nahuatl was admitted and practiced. In one aspect, therefore, the College of Santiago Tlatelolco was a kind of center for Mexican studies, whose pupils, in exchange for their instruction, contributed their knowledge to the special training of the missionaries.

This dazzling success, however, was only partial, for its brilliance concealed a failure; that is, the College of Santiago Tlatelolco gave the Mexicans not a single priest of their own race—this in spite of the fact that the college had been founded not merely to train translators, copyists, and Latinists, but above all to train priests. It was to have been the first native seminary of the New World. The costumes of the students, and the kind of life they were obliged to lead, are enough to prove it. We also have these revealing lines of Zumárraga, who, now disillusioned, wrote to Charles V on April 17, 1540: "We do not know how long the College of Santiago will last, for the Indian students and the best grammarians *tendunt ad nuptias potius quam continentiam"* [42] [are inclined more toward marriage than continence.] When it is recalled how insistently Zumárraga had demanded this college, the enthusiasm with which he had promoted it, and his perseverance in getting funds for it,[43] such a rapid disillusionment is somewhat astonishing. But the fact is that, despite the rank and influence of its sponsors and the favor of the Crown, the college met with extremely violent hostility on all sides.

The antinative party, such as exists in every colonial country, was infuriated by this singular and dubious institution. An unfortunate incident occurred which gave their campaign an unexpected argument. In 1539, a former student of Tlatelolco, the *cacique* Don Carlos of Texcoco, was accused of spreading among his people certain heretical propositions and inducing them to abandon the practice of Christianity.[44] At once the cry was raised that the college was nothing more than the home of heresies. The *escribano* Jerónimo López had declared from the beginning, as he states in his letter of October 20, 1541, "that it was an error fraught with dangers to teach sciences to the Indians, and still more to put the Bible and all the Holy Scriptures into their hands to be read and interpreted as they pleased. Many people in our Spain have been lost in this way, and have invented a thousand heresies because they did not understand the Holy Scriptures at all and, because of their malice and pride, were not worthy of the spiritual light necessary for their understanding. Thus they have ruined themselves and many others." [45] He returns to the attack in a letter of February 25, 1545, in which he reveals at length and furiously his animosity toward the friars and his contempt for the Indians, two themes that frequently coincided at the time. He complains of the insolence of the natives, that is, those who did not accept being treated as slaves, and he states that it is owing, among other things, to their having been taught Latin and the sciences.[46] The Dominicans, to whom Sahagún was doubtless alluding when he spoke of "the hostility of the monks of other Orders" toward the college,[47] on their part mounted a vigorous offensive [against the college] at court. On May 5, 1544, the provincial Fray Domingo de la Cruz and Fray Domingo de Betanzos wrote to Charles V to convince him that the Indians should not be educated [for the clergy]. In fact, they said, this would lead to nothing; the Indians could not preach for a very long time to come, because they lacked the preacher's necessary authority; because those who had studied were even more vicious than the others, and were not different enough from the common run. Besides, the Christian doctrine had not yet sufficiently penetrated their spirit, and it was to be feared that they would spread heresies, as had already happened. Finally, they were not capable of properly understanding the dogmas of the Christian religion and explaining them in a fit and precise fashion.[48] They also objected that the knowledge of Latin would allow the natives to expose the ignorant priests.[49] Their passion against the college must have been boundless to allow them to advance an argument so weak and pregnant with admissions!

Mendoza, Mendieta,[50] and Sahagún complained vigorously of this narrow and violent opposition, which had halted the development of the college. Sahagún's words deserve to be quoted in full:

The Spaniards and the monks of other Orders who witnessed the founding of this institution laughed loudly and jeered at us, thinking it beyond all doubt that no one could be clever enough to teach grammar to people of such small aptitude. But, after we had worked with them for two or three years, they had attained such a thorough knowledge of grammar that they understood, spoke, and wrote Latin, and even composed heroic verses [in it]. The Spaniards, both laymen and priests, were astonished. It was I who worked with these pupils for the first four years and who initiated them into all matters concerning the Latin language. When the laymen and the clergy were convinced that the Indians were making progress and were capable of progressing still more, they began to raise objections and oppose the enterprise. As I was concerned in the dispute, since it was I who taught grammar to the pupils of the college, it will be easy for me to speak truly of this opposition and the answers made to the opponents. They said that since these people were not to be ordained, what was the use of teaching them grammar? It would only put them in danger of becoming heretics, for, reading the Holy Scriptures, they would learn that the old patriarchs had had many wives at the same time, just as they themselves used to have. This would result in their refusing to believe what we now preach to them, namely, that no one may have more than one legitimate wife *in facie Ecclesiae*. Other objections of the same kind were raised, the answer to which was that, even if [the Indians] were not ordained, we still wanted to know their aptitudes, knowing which, we could say what they were capable of, and in holy justice could act accordingly, just as we are obligated to act toward our neighbor. As for the accusation that we might expose them to heresies, we replied that, inasmuch as that was not our aim, but rather to put them in the way of a better understanding of matters of faith, for it would always be possible to check deviations that might occur (for we are, after all, subjects of a Most Christian Prince). As for the women, the Gospel tells us of the punishment the Redeemer inflicted upon the man who, following ancient custom, took many wives. This passage of the Scriptures, therefore, will be preached to the Indians, who must believe it, and, if they do not, they will be chastized as heretics, since the ecclesiastical and secular authorities have the power to do so. There were many other disputes over this matter which it would take too long to enumerate here.[51]

It should be added that, although the college enjoyed the favor of Zumárraga, it is most probable that his successor, Montúfar, did not look upon it with a benevolent eye. Montúfar was a Dominican, a former prosecutor in the Holy Office of Granada, and smelled heresy on all sides. I do not imply that the college seemed to him a dubious institution and a source of errors and abuses, but, on the other hand, when the commissary general of the Franciscans, Fray Alonso Ponce, was received at Tlatelolco in 1584, a kind of small symbolic play was put on for him, singularly revealing of the atmosphere in which the college lived and languished, after the enthusiasm of the early years had been extinguished. Father Ponce was received by one of the pupils, who recited a short speech of welcome in Latin and Spanish, after which their professor, evidently a religious, begged the commissary to forgive them, for his pupils were only "parrots and magpies," who recited what they had learned but did not understand at all. Then another pupil spoke, also in Latin and Spanish, like the first. He allowed that in fact they were considered by many to be magpies and parrots—"a non paucis estimemur tamquam picae et psittaci"—for indeed their aptitudes were slight—"certe tenuissima habilitate dotati sumus"—but he adds that for that very reason they needed

227

more help and sympathy. At this juncture, a grown Indian, dressed as a Spaniard, interrupted. He mocked the others in Spanish, saying it was a waste of time to help them, only to have them turn out as drunken and ungrateful as the rest. The professor gave him the lie, saying that his pupils were excellent lads, studious and virtuous. "But you," he concluded, "can never open your mouth except to speak ill of them, and everything good that happens to them strikes you to the heart, for you would like to see them always with their backs bent under burdens, working in your service." [52] Could there be a more eloquent commentary on the complaints of Sahagún and the letters of Jerónimo López, for whom the Indians were at best good only for slaves and carriers? It is easy to see how the college could only vegetate over the years, surrounded as it was by such persistent malevolence.

The sterility of the institution has quite likely another source. The recruiting was too narrow, being limited to the sons of the aristocracy. This seems to have been a mistake, especially at a time when the immense territory of Mexico had not been completely explored or conquered, and when the missionaries had been able to penetrate only a small part of the country. It lessened the chances of awakening deep and lasting vocations [for the priesthood], which would have multiplied if there had been a wider [base of] recruiting. Besides, the college was a Franciscan institution, which makes it almost certain that the Augustinian missions did not recruit pupils for Santiago [de Tlatelolco]. I do not know what the Dominicans thought of the matter. For this very reason the choice was reduced and the possibilities of vocations were limited. [53]

The College of Santiago met with violent opposition among the [secular] clergy and the public, for the greater part of the Spaniards in Mexico, to tell the truth, did not wish to see the natives elevated to the priesthood. So from the moment that the Indians were excluded from it the college lost all reason for being, as Sahagún was told. Cervantes de Salazar devotes a few scornful lines of his chronicle to the College of Santiago, the need for which escapes him. "The Indians," he says, "cannot and should not be ordained, because of their incapacity, and outside of this retreat [Santiago] they make little use of what they know." [54] And

228

the Dominicans end their letter of 1544 by declaring that the incapacity of the natives for teaching the Christian faith implies *a fortiori* their incapacity for the priesthood, and that consequently there is no reason to educate them. Even among the Franciscans, and likewise among the professors of the college, some religious were against the ordination of the Indians. On a date that I have not been able to fix, but probably between 1550 and 1553, a Franciscan, Danish according to some, eastern European according to others, known by the name of Fray Jacobo Daciano, who had taken the initiative in admitting the Indians of Michoacán to communion,[55] attempted, with astonishing clear-sightedness, to demonstrate that the Mexican Church had not been properly founded, because it did not include native priests.[56] Although a few had dreamed of training them, up to that time no one had dared clearly to state such a revolutionary thesis—revolutionary for the time and the place, especially for the place. The documents tell us nothing of the matter, or next to nothing, just as they tell us nothing of the scandal provoked by Fray Francisco de Bustamante when he attacked Archbishop Montúfar and the cult of Our Lady of Guadalupe. But it is not difficult to imagine the feeling aroused by such a statement. Nevertheless, one would be equally inclined to imagine a vehement protest by the Dominicans or the secular clergy. Contrary to all expectations, it was a Franciscan, a Franciscan clearly pro-Indian, a professor at the College of Santiago, Fray Juan de Goana himself, who undertook, or was ordered, to refute the thesis of Father Daciano.[57]

Should one not conclude that the builders of the college had gradually lost faith in their work, or that they had let themselves be insensibly shaken and then convinced by the arguments of their enemies? Zumárraga had been quickly discouraged. The notions of his friend Fray Domingo de Betanzos had perhaps rubbed off on him. Mendoza, before leaving office, wrote his successor, Luis de Velasco, that he should not definitely consider the Indians to be brutes, for many of them were honest men of sound judgment,[58] and that it was a great mistake to look upon them as unfit for studies. But he soon added, as if fearing that he had gone too far: "I do not mean to say by this that they must immediately be admitted to the priesthood." It should be noted, nevertheless, that with his keen sense of reality he recognized at the same time that the task of Christianization would be achieved only when a truly Mexican clergy was available, Creole as well as Indian.[59] Mendieta, who was open-minded, declared that the Indians were made to be commanded, not to command.[60] And even Sahagún wrote: "This vice (of drunkenness) has caused a great number to be thought unfit to exercise the ministry, especially since the Indians who get drunk do not seem able to observe the rules of continence and chastity necessary to the true practice of the priesthood." [61] Lack of authority, drunkenness, ineptitude for intellectual effort [necessary] in the government of souls, and [lack of] celibacy— such were the characteristics that rendered the Indians unworthy of the priesthood. This state of mind could only lead to the abandonment of the training of native priests at the College of Tlatelolco. Having thus lost its seminary character and its essential purpose, from that time forward the institution was condemned, if not to death, at least to a languishing and difficult life, so its rapid decline is no cause for astonishment.

The doors of the priesthood were closed to the Indians. The synod of 1555 forbade the ordination of mestizos, Indians, and Negroes,[62] and, in 1570, one reads in the *Códice Franciscano* that the sacrament of [admission to] the Order is not administered to the Indians, even for minor orders, because they do not yet have the necessary qualifications.[63] The *Junta Eclesiástica* of 1539 did indeed decide to allow a few mestizos and Indians to enter the minor orders. They were selected with particular care from among the former pupils of the colleges and convents who knew reading, writing, and, if possible, Latin. These Indians were to be given the duty of assisting priests in the ministry of the parishes. The bishops judged the experiment to be without serious danger, since the minor orders did not lead to irrevocable commitments, so the auxiliaries who should turn out to be incapable of celibacy might resign their duties and marry.[64] But this decision, which the religious accepted without protest, was apparently not put into effect. The monastic life, even in its humblest form, was equally denied to the natives. The first regulations of the Provincia del Santo Evangelio forbade Indians and mestizos to wear the habit.[65] The Dominican chapter of September 27, 1576, forbade it also.[66] Muñoz, in his report on the Indian Lucas, tells us that because of his virtue and exemplary life it was thought he might be admitted into the Order, but that it was not done "because he was an Indian." [67]

It should be borne in mind, nevertheless, that not only opinion and prejudice were behind this interdiction, but also an experiment. Sahagún relates that at the beginning it seemed the natives had aptitudes "for the things of the Church and the religious life." Two young Indians, who had helped the missionaries in the preaching of the Gospel, and who had attracted attention by their intelligence and modesty, were dressed in the habit of St. Francis. "But the experiment demonstrated," he adds, "that they did not have any of the necessary qualifications, so it was decided to unfrock them. Since then we have not admitted any Indians into our Order, for they have been judged incapable of exercising the priesthood." [68] A similar experiment was made with women, for it would have been a happy thing to recruit cloistered nuns, bound by perpetual vows, from among the natives. It seemed all the easier because certain women in pre-Conquest times had lived in chastity in the pagan temples. So some of them were given special religious training. They were taught to read and write, the best of them were selected to take charge of the others, and they were formed into a kind of community. "At first," writes Sahagún, "we thought that the women would make respectable nuns, all the more since we had believed that the men would make good religious and good priests. But we were mistaken. Experience taught us that neither the men nor the women were at that time capable of such perfection, so we gave up the communities and monasteries we had at first dreamed of. Even today we must still admit that the time has not arrived to try the experiment again." [69]

But what were these experiments worth? Motolinía also speaks of an early attempt made in 1527, specifically to recruit Franciscans from among the natives. He deplores its failure, but does not attribute it to the ineptitude of the Indians. With his usual good sense, he judges the experiment to have been premature. The novices, after going back into the world, got married and lived like good Christians, and they said, upon

231

abandoning the religious life, that they had not realized what they were doing, and that if they had it to do over again they would have stayed with it, even if they died for it.[70]

It seems, therefore, that these experiments were made somewhat hastily and despaired of too quickly. They went from one extreme to the other. The religious at first exaggerated the spiritual capacities of the Indians and, when they were disappointed, exaggerated their incapacities. In so doing their lack of missionary experience was unhappily manifest, reflecting the lack of it in Europe at that time. They had too many preconceived notions. They operated on the principle that men, all created in God's image and all redeemed by His blood, are all called to be perfect. In the beginning they do not seem to have considered the conditions that influence the development of such a possibility. To recruit native religious in 1527, four years after the arrival of Pedro de Gante, three years after the arrival of the Twelve, among people who had barely emerged from paganism, seems to us today like almost foolish audacity. In that mysterious domain in which, according to the doctrine of the Church, divine grace and individual liberty act with invisible and equal force, nothing is more dangerous than absolute rules, and it has been possible to make holy priests and excellent religious out of pagan children, born of pagan parents, and reared in paganism by a pagan family. But it seems difficult, if not impossible, that only a few years after the beginning of the apostolic labor the populace, however gifted, could produce priests and monks in an intensive and regular fashion. Such a thing cannot happen except in a Christian community already partially organized and stabilized. Before such time, calls to the priesthood can only be exceptional and spontaneous, and it is preferable and more prudent to allow them to occur of themselves, without an attempt at systematic recruitment.

It is easy enough today to make these remarks, in the light of more than four centuries since the missionary apostolate. The religious of New Spain necessarily felt their way along, and it is remarkable that this is perhaps the only point in which their lack of experience was regrettable. But this point, unfortunately, is of capital importance. The excessive boldness of the beginnings is balanced by an excessive timidity, which was extraordinarily harmful to the spiritual interests of the Mexican Church.[71]

There were, nevertheless, admirable spiritual riches among the Indian races of Mexico. I have mentioned Motolinía's story of the young Indians who died for their faith. The vocation of martyrdom, however, is not necessarily the same as the vocation of the priest or the religious. Other examples [of these riches] are more convincing. Motolinía tells us of certain devout persons who dedicated themselves to the care and protection of young Indian girls, accompanied them to their catechism, and prepared pagans for baptism. [He also tells us] of the young matrons who attended the chapel of Our Lady every morning to recite the service of the Holy Virgin.[72]

These devout women were doubtless going to marry, or were already married, or had been married. But, does this mean that a young woman who becomes an excellent mother would have made a bad nun? There was at Texcoco another house where young women and widows lived in seclusion and cloistered, under the care of a Spanish lady. Zumárraga wrote of it with admiration to Charles V.[73] Ponce's secretary realized that, although Indian women were on the whole not fitted for the religious life, many of them individually led most virtuous lives and preferred virginity to marriage. The convents of Mexico, he adds, present a refuge for a good many widows and young women, who seclude themselves of their own free will in order to serve the nuns, and in some cases remain there to the end of their days.[74] And what of the famous *beatos* [holy men] of Chocamán? An Indian of Cholula, Baltasar by name, had gathered together in this solitary spot, "the place of tears and penitence," (which was the meaning of the name they gave it), a certain number of Indians, men and women, who wished to live in pious seclusion. There they led a communal life under strict rules, with severe mortification [of the flesh]. Fray Juan de Ribas, one of the Twelve, got interested in them and assumed their direction. They left behind them a reputation almost of saintliness.[75]

Motolinía also tells us the admirable story of a young *cacique* of Michoacán, Don Juan de Turécato (probably Tarécuato), who was converted to a life of perfection by reading the biography of St. Francis of Assisi. He promised to become a religious and dressed himself in coarse serge. He freed his numerous slaves and taught them the Christian doctrine, and exhorted them to love one another and conduct themselves as good Christians. Then he gave away his goods and jewels, renounced the duties and prerogatives of a *cacique,* and lived in humility and poverty. It was also in Michoacán, which was peopled by a singularly noble and gifted race, where the two brothers, Lucas and Sebastián, were born. The missionaries had never had, perhaps, more precious and devoted helpers, who made innumerable converts among the savage Indians of the north of Mexico. Sebastián was the first to die, "in a very holy way." Muñoz tells us that both of them conducted themselves like "very perfect religious," and were considered to be such. Nevertheless, they were never allowed to advance beyond the rank of *donados;* that is to say, they lived with the religious and wore the religious habit, but were never permitted to take vows. We have seen how some would have liked to see Lucas admitted, but it could not be done "because he was an Indian." The humility and perseverance of Juan de Turécato were not enough to bend this too-rigid rule. After having voluntarily renounced everything, he demanded the habit many times in Michoacán, but it was denied him. He then went to Mexico City, forty leagues from his country, demanded it again, and was again refused. Then he went to see Zumárraga, whom he won over, and "who would have given him [the habit] if he had been able to do so," writes Motolinía. At the beginning of Lent he went home to take part in the exercises and confess. After Easter, he returned to Mexico City and again asked the Franciscan chapter for the habit; but the chapter decided only to authorize him to live among the religious and wear his serge robe, and to admit him later if he gave satisfaction in his attitude and piety.[76] These are not isolated cases. Many convents included *donados,* who lived like monks, but did not take vows. I could cite many other examples if I did not fear to weary the reader.[77]

In the dispute over the College of Tlatelolco and [the formation of] an Indian clergy, which has too often been mistakenly oversimplified, and the complexity of which has not been understood, we find once more the two [conflicting] opinions that have already been remarked. One party was composed of those who realized that in a colonial country more than elsewhere it is necessary "to know in order to plan and provide," and that an exotic people cannot be properly governed and converted if they have not been studied from the beginning with method and sympathy. For them the native problems were fundamental; they understood that the Mexican Church could not live and flourish upon a purely European foundation. Opposed to them was the mass, unfortunately always large in colonial lands, too often including their very leaders, who misunderstand, despise, and at times are totally ignorant of, the native, his life, his civilization, and his sufferings, and who would keep him perpetually inferior. They content themselves with empirical solutions and a day-to-day policy. One cannot regret too much that this party triumphed in New Spain. Missionaries and civil officers alike committed this gross error, which was exposed in the eighteenth century by the Creole Ribadeneyra,[78] and which weighed terribly upon the destinies of the Mexican Church.[79] Is it not symptomatic that the famous impostor, William Lampart, promised the Indians the religious habit in order to conciliate them? [80]

This error prevented the Church from striking deep roots in the nation, gave it the appearance and character of a foreign institution, and kept it strictly dependent upon the mother country. Izquierdo, speaking of Mexican institutions, justly remarked that it was the Church that suffered most from the political rupture between Old and New Spain, because it was so closely identified with the former. There were some Indian priests, to be sure, after the beginning of the seventeenth century, for a Church cannot get along indefinitely with foreign personnel. One may even speculate whether a Christian community living entirely upon outside support ever attained the rank, or deserved the name, of a Church.

These Indian priests, however, appeared only sporadically. They were not recruited according to any directing principle—it was against the rules.[81] Worst of all, they were relegated to inferior posts and the thankless work of rural parishes. Dignities and government places, in general, were denied to them, and colonial Mexico never got a complete native clergy. Had the College of Tlatelolco given the country even one [native] bishop, the history of the Mexican Church might have been profoundly changed.

III: CONCLUSIONS

15 *Internal Dissensions*

IN the course of this study I have many times touched upon the obstacles encountered by the Mendicants in their work of evangelization; but these occasional remarks do not give an exact notion of all difficulties they met: difficulties within the Orders and between the Orders, difficulties with the episcopate and the secular clergy, and difficulties with the civil authorities, and, along with these internal difficulties, the stubbornness of pagan religions and superstitions. In order to judge their work it is not enough to examine, as I have done, their positive accomplishments, but one must also recognize the negative elements, the forces of resistance, they had to overcome. I shall attempt here to give a general view of them.

The first difficulties were of the religious' own making. I shall not emphasize the moral and intellectual deficiencies of some of them. An incontrovertible source, a declaration of Pope Gregory XIII, of May 14, 1578, tells us that at times certain Franciscans of New Spain and Peru abandoned their Order to return to the Peninsula in secular dress, after having worked for their personal enrichment more actively than for the health of their flocks.[1] Such failures happen in every epoch and in every country. They are the normal obstacles that thwart the apostolic task. On the other hand, however, agreement within the [religious] communities was not always perfect. Cooperation in the beginning, when the apostolic team was small, may have been close and intimate, but successive additions little by little enlarged the early groups; custodies or missions were elevated into provinces; organization became more complex; the hierarchy also; duties and functions were multiplied. Divergencies of opinions appeared, opposing concepts or temperaments, personal rivalries, incompatibilities of character, and conflicting ambitions. Divisions split into rival clans and opposing parties, conflicts between young and old, between the pronative and antinative groups. Intrigues and quarrels, those perfidious enemies of the spiritual life, appeared, in which the missionaries wasted a part of their strength, talent, and time, and which thus became the hidden hobbles on the work of conversion. We have seen the dissensions among the Franciscans over the problem of a native clergy; we have seen an even more characteristic disturbance in the hostility within the Order itself which surrounded the desperate effort of Sahagún, almost completely smothering his work. I shall cite here only one example taken from another Order concerning some incidents that occurred in 1563 during the inspection of the Augustinian province of Mexico by the vicar general, Fray Pedro de Herrera. I was fortunate enough to recover part of the record.

Although it was a separate organization, the Provincia del Santísimo Nombre de Jesús de México was subordinate to some extent to the province of Castile and Andalusia. In 1562 the superior of the province ordered the Sevillian Fray Pedro de Herrera to visit Mexico as vicar general. Father Herrera arrived in New Spain probably that same autumn.[2] He met at once with violent resistance. Some religious rebelled against the jurisdiction that the provincial of Castile claimed to have over the Mexican province. Others, of a low moral caliber, feared investigation and punishment. A small group headed by Fray Juan de San Román, provincial vicar in the absence of the provincial Fray Agustín de la Coruña, then in Spain, and [including] the chapter deputies Fray Antonio de San Isidro and Fray Antonio de los Reyes, refused to recognize [Herrera] as visitor, and stood their ground even in the face of insults and defamation. Father Herrera, nevertheless, supported by the majority of the religious, undertook his inspection and did not allow himself to be intimidated. He first visited the convent at Mexico City, the prior of which was Fray Antonio de San Isidro himself. Father San Román charged that the prior was the victim of some calumnies on the part of Fray Pedro de Herrera, and was particularly [the victim] of the perfidy of Fray Esteban de Salazar, "homo maledicus" [a scurrilous man].

Father San Román, however, is a dubious witness. All documents are extremely hard on Fray Antonio de San Isidro and agree that his administration was disastrous. He was, moreover, anything but an edifying character. His evil reputation was well established. He had been involved in some nasty affairs, such as bringing his mistress over from Spain and having a daughter by her. As Herrera reported: "He was a carnal man, a landowner and a great merchant, a man of evil reputation." Not only did he scandalize the city by his conduct, but he achieved dignities and promotion by intrigues. The visitor deposed him and decided to send him back to Spain, meanwhile keeping him in prison until the departure of the fleet. This caused a very involved conflict with the provisor of the diocese, the irascible Dr. Anguis, who demanded custody of the prisoner. In this conflict Fray Pedro de Herrera was naturally opposed by Fray Juan de San Román. Fray Antonio de San Isidro succeeded in getting out of jail and sailing for Spain in the company of Fray Antonio de los Reyes, who, it seems, was no more worthy than he, and whom the rebels had given the task of securing the recall of the vicar general and the complete autonomy of the Mexican province.

Meanwhile, Father Herrera had to struggle against innumerable obstacles. The viceroy and the Audiencia were hostile to him, and their attitude encouraged the rebels. One of them, whose life was not irreproachable, and who was aware that his faults were known to the vicar, although the vicar had not yet mentioned them, entered [the vicar's] cell and slashed his face furiously with a knife. We do not know how far he would have gone if he had not been interrupted by other religious, who made him see reason. The visitor persevered in his task nonetheless. In January, 1563, he presided over a meeting at Totolapan, where he had Father San Román suspended from his duties as provincial vicar. On May 8 he presided over the provincial chapter at Epazoyuca and had him proclaimed ineligible for any office whatsoever.

Nevertheless, it was Fray Juan de San Román who won out. He appealed to the general of the Order, with the support of the viceroy, who demanded the recall of the visitor and the separation of Mexico from the province of Castile. So the general named Fray Diego de Salamanca and Fray Miguel de Alvarado, then in Spain, as visitors to replace Father Herrera, who left Mexico in 1564. The sanction taken at Epazoyuca against Father San Román was rescinded. Where were justice and law in all that? In the light of new documents I believe that Fray Pedro de Herrera was treated too severely and that he was innocent of the gravest charges. It is not up to me, however, to distribute blame and praise.[3] I shall only remark that these internal discords were relatively rare. Disputes between the Orders, and especially their differences with the bishops and the secular clergy, were very much more frequent and serious.

Quarrels between the Orders occurred early. In the Queen's instructions of 1536 to Viceroy Mendoza, she was already urging him to put an end to them.[4] Relations between Franciscans and Dominicans were soon strained. At the time of the conflict between Zumárraga and the first Audiencia (1529-1530), the Dominicans opposed him and his [Franciscan] companions, possibly because they were jealous of the Franciscans and the relatively large number of their converts. The close friendship between Zumárraga and [the Dominican] Fray Domingo de Betanzos did nothing to smooth things over. On the contrary, Father Betanzos, rendered suspect within his own Order by this friendship, got into difficulties with his prior and had to leave for Guatemala and a less hostile atmosphere.[5] The Dominicans blamed the intrigues of the Franciscans for their bad reception by the Indians, when they took possession of a convent ceded to them by the Friars Minor.[6] A characteristic memorial of this friction is a letter from the Dominican Fray Andrés de Moguer to the Council of the Indies, in which he accuses the Franciscans of trying to monopolize three-fourths of the territory [of New Spain], despite their very reduced numbers, and of not permitting the Dominicans and Augustinians to establish themselves in regions that had no priests.[7] The

Augustinians themselves were not above reproach on this score, because at the time they released the parish of Ocuituco, following their quarrel with Zumárraga, they threatened that if he should replace the secular priest with Franciscans, they would drive the Franciscans out at the point of the lance.[8]

In 1556 the Crown was obliged to repeat its order to the viceroy, Luis de Velasco, to settle the disputes among the three Orders, "because of the great conflicts," wrote Montúfar, "among those who occupy most of the provinces, towns, and villages of the natives."[9] The Orders ended their dispute in an unexpected way, deciding that no Order might penetrate a village served by another without the formal consent of the latter. Montúfar, not unreasonably, denounced the treaty in vigorous and picturesque language. "Could there be," he wrote, "a more diabolical decision than this? There is nothing Christian in it, for none of the Orders is capable of teaching the catechism or administering the sacraments to the fifth, tenth, or twentieth part of its territory. What kind of Christian law is this, which does not allow one Order to go to the relief of another, which does not permit a bishop to furnish men to help out an Order . . . ? They act as if they were disposing of their own vassals! And sometimes they even confront each other with battalions of Indians![10] But he was too late. A royal *cédula* of August 1, 1558, confirmed the agreement.[11]

This kind of imperialism had the most vexatious consequences for the apostolate, and was the basis for another reproach that the bishops made against the religious. Dr. Anguis, who was very hostile to the Orders, but who for that very reason summarizes faithfully enough the complaints of the bishops (against whom he inveighs severely elsewhere), stated that the main concern of the religious was to [be allowed to] administer the sacraments without the authorization of the Ordinary, to build houses and monasteries, and to occupy all the territory possible.[12] Montúfar was specific in his memorial of 1556. Some convents [he wrote] housing no more than two religious had to serve, at a distance of thirty leagues, as many as 100,000 souls, with the result that some villages did not see a priest for months on end. He himself knew of villages in his archbishopric which had not been visited in five years. And these rare visits were at the same time extremely hasty, with only time to say Mass, administer a few baptisms, and bless a few marriages. Moreover, the religious quarreled over the fertile and pleasant regions, crowded into them, and built monasteries there, avoiding the sterile or unhealthful places, the inhabitants of which were consequently neglected. In the archdiocese of Mexico, which was the best provided for and converted, the Indians went for many years without confessing, and some never confessed at all. What, then, must be the situation in regions where the natives did not see a priest or a religious but once in thirty years? [13]

To the accusation of negligence Montúfar added the reproach of ignorance. He affirmed that the prior of the Augustinians brought him one day twenty-four religious to be ordained as deacons and priests, but that they were so ignorant that only two of them knew Latin, and that many could not even read it.[14] Anguis went further and blamed Montúfar himself for having too frequently ordained religious who were completely incapable of saying Mass. He affirmed that many of the candidates were retired merchants, or men without intelligence and education, who at the end of their novitiate were ordained and sent out to hear confessions.[15]

Another accusation [made against the religious] concerned their brutality toward the Indians. The *Junta Eclesiástica* of 1539 forbade the imprisonment and whipping of the Indians. One example: In 1561 Montúfar and Vasco de Quiroga, bishop of Michoacán, brought suit against the Franciscans, Dominicans, and Augustinians for usurpation of jurisdiction and the abuse of Indians.[16] The religious, wrote the bishop of Michoacán, "have inflicted and are now inflicting many mistreatments upon the Indians, with great haughtiness and cruelty, for when the Indians do not obey them, they insult and strike them, tear out their hair, have them stripped and cruelly flogged, and then throw them into prison in chains and cruel irons, a thing most pitiable to hear about and much more pitiable to see." [17] Two Franciscans in particular, Fray Francisco de Ribera and Fray Juan Quijano, had an Indian arrested whose words had annoyed them, had him tied to a post by his hands and feet, and cruelly whipped. The wretch was set free by the *teniente de alcalde mayor* of Toluca.[18]

244

Meanwhile, what most set the Mendicant Orders and the bishops at odds was the struggle for power. The essential cause of the animosity of the episcopate lies in the situation created by the bull *Exponi nobis fecisti* of Adrian VI, and later papal orders. The popes had granted the rights and prerogatives of parish priests to the Mendicants, and authorized them to administer the sacraments. When the Council of Trent organized parochial life in the form in which it exists today, and in principle gave parish priests alone the right to administer sacraments to the faithful, Pius V, in a new bull, *Exponi nobis* (1567), confirmed the decisions of his predecessors and, realizing the insufficiency of the secular clergy, permitted the regulars to administer the sacraments without the authorization of the Ordinary.[19] The religious, naturally, were strongly attached to these privileges, which gave them enormous power. They dreamed of extending them and, since they enjoyed great prestige among the Indians,[20] they began gradually to abuse their rights and to set themselves up independently of the bishops. Such at least was the situation according to the incessant complaints and accusations of the prelates, particularly Montúfar. In 1532 the calm and thoughtful Fuenleal wrote that the Dominicans and Franciscans were claiming the functions of bishops. [21] In 1537 the bishops of Mexico, Oaxaca, and Guatemala declared that the religious were acting in cases in which the bishops did not dare to act, and that it was very troublesome and subversive of episcopal dignity that the religious seemed to wield more power than the bishops. They added that the religious, not satisfied with the appearance [of power], proclaimed that they were above the bishops, brandished their privileges when the bishops sent visitors, and threatened to imprison them when they tried to prevent abuse of the Indians and the building of needless monasteries. And they concluded: "Now that they have ceased quarreling with the Audiencia, they want to quarrel with us—all this to make themselves masters." [22] The bishops, to be sure, remarked that only a minority [of the religious] were involved; but, two years later, they burst forth implicitly against the indiscipline of the regulars, who [they said] were more given to annoying the Ordinary then to helping him,[23] and against the marks of respect, excessive in their eyes, which the Indians showed for the religious. [The Indians should not be allowed, they demanded] to sweep the roads or raise triumphal arches except for processions and receptions of the bishops; and they should kneel only to receive the episcopal blessing, and should only kiss the hands of simple priests, or the robes of the religious.[24]

Dr. Anguis records all complaints of the bishops, to wit: the religious administer the sacraments without permission; they build sumptuous monasteries without permission, and even at times against orders; they seize for their quarters houses in which the Ordinary has installed secular priests; they judge and decide suits, often in a very ridiculous fashion; they marry and separate [couples] capriciously; they grant dispensations in the gravest cases; they do and undo things that the bishops dare not even think of; they proclaim they are the masters and thrust forward their pontifical privileges in the most provocative manner.[25] The correspondence of Archibishop Montúfar is filled with—even made up of, one might say—complaints of this kind; that is, the religious name the native *alcaldes* and *regidores,* give orders to the [Spanish] *corregidores,* imprison and release [from prison], and violate the King's justice whenever they please.[26] Their purpose is to have the dioceses delivered over to them and reduce the bishops to the simple role of prelates *in partibus, obispos de anillo,* who would have no jurisdiction and would be limited to administering sacraments and performing ceremonies which did not require episcopal consecration.[27] They sow rebellion among their parishioners and tell them not to obey the bishops. They fail to publish the letters, censures, and other official documents sent out by the Ordinary.[28] The result of all this is that the Indians do not recognize their prelate, that a Franciscan lay brother is more powerful than the archbishop of Mexico, and that, finally, a bishop has hardly as much influence as a sacristan.[29] The bishop of Michoacán states, in 1561, that the religious have set themselves up as absolute spiritual and temporal lords.[30] Fray Juan de Medina Rincón, now bishop of Michoacán, makes this admission: "When I was a religious and the simple prior of a convent, I was more courageous and bolder in making decisions than I am now as bishop." [31] It is likely that one of Montúfar's concerns, upon deciding to convoke the first two Mexican synods (1555 and 1565), was to attempt to regulate the activity of the religious and limit their independence.[32]

The religious, naturally, did not lack grievances against the prelates, whom they reproached with failing to visit their dioceses,[33] with ignorance of the language of their flocks, with being unaware of their needs and wretchedness,[34] with exhausting their Indians by having themselves carried in litters over mountains and valleys, with slandering the religious,[35] with trying to take away their Indians and give them to the secular clergy,[36] with refusing to ordain the religious who aspired to the priesthood,[37] and with preventing them from administering the sacraments.[38] The principal target of the religious, along with Montúfar, was doubtless Quiroga. The commissary general of the Franciscans, Fray Francisco de Mena (1553–1556), left a list of sharply hostile charges against [Quiroga], so hostile that it loses all value as evidence.[39] On January 24, 1560, [he wrote], the Franciscans of Michoacán complained to Philip II that the bishop [Quiroga] would not allow them to continue administering the sacraments and so badgered them that many religious preferred to return to Spain,[40] to the great deteriment of the apostolic task; and in that same year the Augustinians filed suit against [Quiroga] and his [secular] clergy for the ill-treatment and persecutions they had suffered.[41] Finally, in 1563, Fray Maturino Gilberti circulated a manifesto of extreme violence against Quiroga, accusing him of destroying the Indians in the labor on his cathedral, which would never be completed, and which, moreover, was excessively sumptuous; [and accusing him] of imprisoning and abusing the Indians, of doing justice to none, of favoring the pagan Chichimecs, the fierce enemies of the Christians, of failing to respect the pontifical privileges of the religious, of filing suits against them without a hearing, on the hearsay evidence of servants, of ordaining incompetent candidates (*mancebos idiotas*), and of making insulting remarks about the religious in public.[42]

In all these bouquets hurled at one's head there is quite likely as much to ignore as to accept. We know hardly anything of these ructions but what is supplied by interested parties, judges and advocates at the same time. In all these diatribes, therefore, we must set aside the rancors, susceptibilities, exaggerations, and illusions of each person and each group. Likewise, it is not up to us to settle their differences, in which, as generally happens, there are wrongs on both sides. It is certain that the

247

religious' pride in their Orders and their spirit of anarchy, on the one hand, and, on the other, the captious, fussy, and touchy intransigeance of the bishops (whom Anguis himself reproaches with scarcely ever seeking peace),[43] were not conducive to an atmosphere favorable to loyal and harmonious cooperation. It was all disputes, complaints, quarrels, and lawsuits. And, since it involved such robust and hot-headed personalities, the struggle at times reached the point of frenzy. Anguis, as was his habit, told the whole story baldly, without mincing his words: "The construction of buildings and convents, more than anything else, has provoked scandals, especially in this archdiocese (of Mexico) and the diocese of Michoacán. The religious and the bishops have come to blows many times, the former wishing to occupy more territory, the latter to drive them out . . . , and they squabble so much that the whole country is scandalized by the conduct of both parties." [44]

We have seen how the Augustinians threatened to receive the Franciscans at Ocuituco at the point of the lance. Details of the same sort occur in the tragicomic dispute which, in 1565, set the Augustinians at odds with the tempestuous bishop of Michoacán, Fray Pedro de Ayala. The Augustinians wished to found a monastery at Guadalajara, where the Franciscans were already established. The bishop refused his authorization on the ground that there was a sufficient number of priests in the city; also, that it was forbidden to allow an Order to install itself where another was already working. The Augustinians, resolved not to yield, took up quarters in a *posada,* to which they gave the name of convent, and, contrary to the dispositions of the Council of Trent,[45] set about celebrating Mass, and preaching and confessing, without the authorization of Father Ayala. He was for expelling them by force, but the Audiencia [of Guadalajara] refused to cooperate. So the Augustinians, barricaded in their *posada* and surrounded by a lay army, brandished arms and arquebuses, and snapped their fingers at the fulminations of the bishop.[46]

It should be added that a little later Fray Pedro [de Ayala] favored the installation of more Franciscans, himself being one of them. This detail shows that, behind the rivalry between religious and bishops, there was also at times rivalry between the Orders. Many of the bishops of New

Spain in the sixteenth century belonged to one or another of the three Orders. For example, Zumárraga, Ayala, and Fray Martín de Hojacastro were Franciscans; Garcés, Montúfar, and Alburquerque were Dominicans; and Fray Juan de Medina Rincón was an Augustinian. However hostile they may have been to the privileges of the religious, at times they were tempted to give their own Order the edge over the others. This did not promote harmony either. Among the secular prelates, such as Quiroga and Ruiz Morales, the same spirit prevailed—this not only out of their concern for their dignity and episcopal rights, but out of a feeling of solidarity with the secular clergy, who, besides, were more pliable, and over whom they had better control [and whom they could count on] against the encroachments of the regulars.[47]

Now, this was not an element of peace either, for there was no love lost between regulars and seculars. In their criticism of the seculars the religious were just as vehement as they were against the bishops. The seculars (they said) did not know the native languages and imagined they were fulfilling all their apostolic duties merely by saying Mass; they ruined the villages by their manner of life, entertaining friends and guests, engaging in commerce, and closing their eyes to the faults and vices of their Indian helpers;[48] they were more interested in hunting and amusing themselves than in teaching the catechism.[49] Besides, they were accused of incompetence and simony, in the letter of the Franciscans of Michoacán to Philip II,[50] and in the memorial of Gilberti.[51] Gilberti, moreover, was carrying on an extremely sharp campaign against the secular clergy, telling the Indians (if one may believe the fragmentary documents of his trial) that they would soon see the arrival of priests who would try to deceive them and pervert their faith, and that only those Indians who remained faithful to the Franciscans, Dominicans, and Augustinians would be saved.[52]

It seems certain that most of the secular priests were less than worthy. One cannot, of course, base such an opinion upon the trial of Diego Díaz, the parish priest of Ocuituco, who, not content with debauching Indian women and sleeping with his own daughter, made mock of the Mass, tried to ruin an Indian by accusing him of idolatry, and by trying to make him preach a false sermon on the Gospel to the Spaniards.[53] Such a mountainous heap of infamies proves by itself that this was an extreme and exceptional case. Besides, it would be as imprudent and unjust to judge the clergy by trials of this kind as it would be to judge a people by the records of the law courts. But Viceroy Mendoza, who was neither a sectarian nor a man given to exaggerated opinions, judged [the seculars] severely: "The seculars who come here," he wrote, in the instruction he left for his successor, Luis de Velasco, "are bad priests. They are all looking after their own interests, and if it were not that they are under orders from His Majesty, and administer baptism, the Indians would be better off without them. What I am saying is applicable only to the majority of them, for there are some good individual priests." [54] This does not, however, excuse the really excessively violent measures that certain religious took against them to prevent their establishment in parishes that [the religious] coveted, or would not give up. There is the well-known story of Juan de Ayllón, who was mistreated and evicted from his house by force, with all his possessions, because the religious wanted to take over the village he was in charge of; [55] and there are other examples, just as characteristic, such as the affair at Ocuituco. The Augustinians, who were installed in this village, stubbornly insisted on having the Indians build them a monastery there, without even waiting for the completion of the church which was much more necessary. Zumárraga had twice ordered them to stop the work until the church was finished, and, failing to secure their obedience, installed a secular priest at Ocuituco, with orders to teach the Indians, administer the sacraments, and protect them from the excessive work stints imposed upon them by the Augustinians. At once the Augustinians decided to abandon the village. Furiously they stripped the church of its bell, ornaments, locks, and even the orange and other trees they had planted, and carried everything off to their convent at Totolapan. Zumárraga had the church completed and furnished it with everything necessary for worship. When they saw that they were out, the Augustinians told the priest that the church was theirs and that they would return, in spite of the bishop. Then it was that they threatened to receive the Franciscans at the point of the lance, in case [the Franciscans] should be sent to replace them.[56] This time, however, their violence stopped with words.

250

There are better, or worse, examples. Vasco de Quiroga, bishop of Michoacán, complained that the religious, to force the Indians to come to their monastery, made them demolish the churches they had erected at the bishop's order, and that they had carried off the bells, chalices, crosses, and all the ornaments. In the archdiocese of Mexico, the Franciscans, Fray Francisco de Ribera and Fray Juan Quijano in particular, gathered up six hundred Indians in the Toluca region, armed them with bows and arrows and shields, and one fine night demolished the church at San Pedro Calimaya, after which they burned everything that was left. In the same way they demolished the church at San Pablo de Tepamachalco. One of their companions, Fray Antonio de Torrijos, confessed that he also had burned a church.[57]

It should be added that the seculars also sometimes employed unedifying methods. They did not stop with telling the Indians that the religious lacked authority to administer the sacraments, nor with filing a suit for heresy against Fray Maturino Gilberti.[58] They gave blow for blow, and at times started things themselves. In 1550, during the dispute over boundaries that set the bishops of Michoacán and New Galicia by the ears, the seculars of Michoacán invaded the neighboring diocese, pillaged and plundered a church, arrested its priest, and forced the religious to decamp.[59] One night in 1559, at Puebla, they sacked the convent of St. Dominic, mistreated the religious, broke the teeth of the prior, Fray Andrés de Moguer, and stole everything in sight.[60] Gilberti, who, to be sure, is not always trustworthy, charges that at Pátzcuaro they smashed the baptismal fonts of the Franciscan convent and expelled Fray Jacobo Daciano by force.[61] Even in Mexico City they often went armed to certain chapels to which the Indians were accustomed to come in procession, under the direction of the Franciscans, and attempted to prevent their entering. Once the furious Indians took to throwing stones and a scandal was narrowly averted.[62] "Your Majesty should also know," wrote Dr. Anguis to Philip II, "what happened in the diocese of Michoacán between the Augustinian Fathers and the seculars of that province, in a dispute over the possession of the village of Tlazazalca, and how they reached the point of hating each other so fiercely that one fine morning the house of the religious was set on fire, and half a dozen religious who came to protect the house barely escaped burning." And he added: "I am assured today that they are hurling challenges at each other and acting as if they were at war." [63]

But the great quarrel that ranged the religious against the bishops and the secular clergy was about tithes. It was characteristic in that it included all their complaints. It is therefore worth repeating, at least for the incumbency of Montúfar, under whom it reached its greatest bitterness. At first it had been decided not to assess tithes against the Indians, for fear that the yoke of the new religion might prove too heavy for them. They contributed to the support of the religious who catechized them, and that seemed enough. But, with the founding of the bishoprics and [cathedral] chapters, and the introduction of the secular clergy, some means had to be devised to procure more resources and to make the natives pay tithes. Tithing was finally adopted,[64] over the strong resistance of the religious.[65] In May, 1544, under Zumárraga, they had already spoken out against it.[66] On May 15, 1550, the Franciscans, speaking through their provincial, Fray Toribio de Motolinía,[67] and, on September 15, 1555, the three provincials, Fray Bernardino de Alburquerque of the Dominicans, Fray Francisco de Bustamante of the Franciscans, and Fray Diego de Vertavillo of the Augustinians, protested tithing the Indians,[68] and on January 20, 1557, the religious of the three Orders drew up a new statement confirming their opposition.[69] These collective protests were backed by individual ones, such as the extraordinarily violent letter that Fray Nicolás Witte wrote to Las Casas.[70] The principal reason [he said] advanced by the religious is that in the beginning the missionaries had insisted that they were disinterested. "We have told the Indians," said they, "that we are giving them the things of our faith freely and without profit to us, and seek only the health of their souls—an attitude that has contributed no little to their conversion. If they are forced to pay tithes they will wonder whether it is for their profit or ours that we have brought them the Christian religion." They added that tithing would probably be a very grave obstacle for the conversion of regions that were still pagan.

The bishops, and Montúfar in particular, answered that the adoption of the tithe might have its difficulties, but that it would allow them to avoid a greater evil. They affirmed, in fact, that the regular clergy was much too

252

reduced to assure parishes of proper service because of the large number and dispersion of the new Christians; that many converted Indians were almost completely neglected, and that the only remedy for this situation was the development of the secular clergy. Now, the secular clergy could not subsist without the tithe of the Indians. Another argument was that the religious, partly relieved of parochial duties, could dedicate themselves more easily, if they wished, to the spiritual conquest of lands where the Church had not yet been founded.[71]

There was sincerity on both sides, but, after what I have said, the reader will surmise that considerations of a different kind were mingled with these spiritual motives. It seems likely that at heart the religious were less opposed to tithing than to the increase of the secular clergy. Not all of them had achieved perfect detachment or perfect obedience. Some had got used to parochial duties, heavy no doubt, but less laborious and certainly less dangerous than penetrating pagan and unknown lands. In others the government of gentle and complaisant Indians had developed a taste for domination, and they were reluctant to give up their power. Besides, some had given themselves wholly to their charming parishioners, and the mere thought of leaving them tore their hearts. Finally, most were convinced that the seculars, with their moral and intellectual inferiority, could not properly fulfill their duties. And then, if the regulars were replaced by seculars, would there not be a risk of making the Indians believe that the instruction they had received was bad, troubling their spirits and discrediting the first missionaries?[72]

The bishops realized that the religious, by their long ministry among the natives, by their experience in the administration of villages, and by the affection they had for their parishioners and their parishioners for them, had become the true rulers of the Indians. [The bishops] had been relegated to second place, and saw that the Indians were getting out from under their authority, like the religious themselves. This explains in large measure their desire to institute the tithe and give the Indian parishes to the seculars, whose activities they could more easily control and direct.[73] Thus it was this business of tithing, grafted upon conflicts of jurisdiction, personal rivalries, and quarrels of all kinds, which set the episcopate and the secular and regular clergy at sixes and sevens, and disturbed the

253

atmosphere in which the work of evangelization was being painfully carried on.

Many Crown functionaries, from the viceroy down, were hot partisans of the religious. The bishops felt they were being overwhelmed and reduced to the role of show pieces, for individual laymen and the civil authorities took an active interest in all these arguments, even in those of a purely theological character.[74] Jerónimo López had campaigned at court and even in Mexico against the founding of the College of Tlatelolco, the teaching of Latin, and the formation of a native clergy.[75] Others interfered in the apostolic task in an even graver way. In 1537 Zumárraga complained that the Spaniards, to advance their own interests, were allowing the Indians to practice idolatry and pagan ceremonies. It was a most discouraging thing for the religious, he said, to see that what they accomplished on one hand, the Spaniards destroyed on the other, that it was the Spaniards who prevented the conversion of the Indians,[76] and that if the religious reproached them for committing forbidden acts, they complained to the Audiencia, which found in their favor, so that the ecclesiastical authority could not count on the secular arm for the punishment of the guilty.[77] Some [Spaniards] forced the Indians to work on Sundays and feast days, or prevented their attending Mass.[78] Other [Spaniards] went further. Zorita denounced these bad Christians, who were trying by every means to ruin the religious with the Indians, not even stopping at false accusations.[79]

Nevertheless, generally speaking, it does not seem that the laymen obstructed the work of the missionaries consciously and systematically. When in their greed they carefully gathered up the fragments of valuable idols smashed by the Dominicans of Oaxaca, and when they followed the religious and asked the natives where the broken idols were to be found, it probably did not occur to them that the natives might think that the missionaries' sermons against paganism were for the purpose of making them produce their idols so that the Spaniards could seize them.[80] In Mexico, as everywhere else, the Spaniard interfered with the missionary indirectly, by his bad example, his debauchery, his insults, and his cruelty toward the natives, giving them a poor notion of the influence that

254

Christianity had upon the lives of its votaries. The Indians frequently had no recourse other than to run away, to avoid this fatal contact with the Europeans. One example: The Franciscans were twice obliged to abandon Michoacán because the natives, maddened by the excesses of Nuño de Guzmán, ran off to the mountains.[81] The bishop of New Galicia, Pedro Gómez de Maraver, writing to the King from Guadalajara on December 12, 1550, gave it as his opinion that the fundamental condition for the conversion of the Cascanes was to deny the country to the Spaniards for fifteen years, and to allow no one but the religious to enter it.[82] But this is the sad story of all mission countries, and there is no need to repeat it.

The supreme authority in New Spain, after the anarchy of the first years, rested first with the Audiencia, and then with the viceroy. The second Audiencia, under the presidency of the venerable Ramírez de Fuenleal, a man of years, solid virtue, and common sense, containing such men as Vasco de Quiroga, gave the missionaries no great trouble. Fuenleal, who was sympathetic to the Indians, was at times even the protector and valuable collaborator of the religious, taking an active part in the founding of the College of Tlatelolco.[83] Things had been very different under the first Audiencia, composed of Nuño de Guzmán, Juan Ortiz de Matienzo, and Diego Delgadillo. A violent conflict occurred between them and Zumárraga, who had been nominated as bishop of Mexico on December 12, 1527. By a *cédula* dated at Burgos, January 10, 1528,[84] Zumárraga had received from Charles V the title of "Protector of the Indians." As such he vehemently denounced the abuses and robberies committed by Nuño de Guzmán, his two *oidores,* and their accomplices, the *factor* Gonzalo de Salazar and the interpreter García del Pilar, this last an unsavory character who had barely escaped hanging two or three times. These worthies imposed a contribution upon the country; they forced the Indian nobles to cover them with gold and jewels; they used the natives without pay, stole their lands and flocks, and, one suspects, did not spare their women. One night Delgadillo violated the cloister of the College of Texcoco, which the Franciscans had founded to shelter a certain number of Indian women. There he kidnaped two young girls, whose beauty had caught the eye of one of his brothers. The position of

Zumárraga vis-à-vis these bandits was weak, for he had left Spain without waiting for his consecration, so it was easy to cast in his teeth the fact that he was only a religious like the others. And then his jurisdiction, rights, and powers as protector of the Indians were so vague and badly defined that he could always be told that he was meddling in things of no concern to him. His authority was further diminished by the Indians, who, not content with complaining when they had real grievances, abused his good offices, smothered him with excessive or baseless recriminations, and tried to avoid, thanks to his support, their proper duties and obligations. Moreover, the protector could not be in all places at once, or see everything, but had to send visitors [in his place]. Also, in order effectively to exercise his functions, he had to take cognizance of all suits concerning Indians and punish the Spaniards who were wronging them. In short, the protector, in order really to protect the Indians, would have had to assume the government of the country. This was an unconscionable burden, for which the Crown must take the blame, and which the Audiencia, having all military, political, and civil responsibility, could not allow. The protector was thus reduced to spiritual weapons only, and, whatever may have been their efficacy in that day, they were not strong enough to intimidate men like Guzmán and his friends.

Shortly after his arrival in Mexico, Zumárraga presented his title of protector to the Audiencia. He was told that he would be given all necessary support, but was sharply reminded that he had delegated his powers [as protector] to other religious, and that they had usurped the jurisdiction of the Audiencia by setting themselves up as civil and criminal courts. When he took up the matter of Indian complaints, he was told that this kind of suit was the concern of the Audiencia alone and that his only duty toward the Indians was to teach them the catechism like the other religious. He requested a hearing, to which Guzmán and his two *oidores* answered by threatening him with exile, confiscation of revenues, and lawsuits. At the same time they forbade the Indians, on pain of hanging, to file complaints in the court of the protector. The three of them inspired such wild terror that the bishop suddenly found himself isolated. No one could speak to him, and he was unable to find a lawyer with sufficient courage to act as his counsel. He did not get discouraged, but exhausted every means of conciliation, after which his only recourse was to denounce the Audiencia publicly in a sermon and to threaten to inform the Emperor of what was happening.

The *oidores* neglected their duties and spent feast days in promenading in the neighborhood gardens, to the great scandal of the parishioners. Then they presented Zumárraga with a scandalous document, in which they attempted to dishonor the bishop and the religious. Zumárraga vainly asked them for a copy of it; had a vain interview with the president [Nuño de Guzmán]; another no less vain with the whole Audiencia in the presence of the principal Franciscan and Dominican religious; and he vainly proposed a new solution, which would allow him to fulfill the duties of his office without usurping the jurisdiction of the Audiencia. Meanwhile, complaints kept coming to his court, and one of them started the conflagration.

It came from the Indians of Huejotzingo, in the *encomienda* of Cortés. They charged that, beyond the normal contributions which they regularly paid to their *encomendero,* they were forced daily to furnish certain produce for the household of each *oidor,* and that the interpreter García del Pilar demanded a special contribution for himself. Zumárraga begged them to keep their complaint secret, and, without disclosing his source, he referred the case to the Audiencia and demanded a schedule of the tributes. Guzmán answered that the Audiencia was not accountable to him and that, if Zumárraga insisted on defending the Indians, he would treat him as Don Antonio Acuña, the bishop of Zamora, had been treated, who had been hanged from the walls of the castle of Simancas for his part in the revolt of the *comuneros.* A little later Guzmán heard of the action of the Indians of Huejotzingo and sent an *alguacil* to arrest them. Zumárraga heard of it in time and warned the Indians, who took refuge in the Franciscan convent, while he set out for Huejotzingo, closely followed by the *alguacil.* But neither his presence nor the energetic protest of the guardian of the convent, Motolinía, prevented the arrest of the Indians, who were brought to Mexico City in the most ignominious fashion. Zumárraga remained at Huejotzingo, where perhaps he attended the meeting presided over by the custodian, held for the purpose of studying an answer to the libel of the Audiencia. It was unanimously

257

decided to send to Mexico City a preaching friar from the Franciscan convent to beseech the *oidores* to respect justice, and to proclaim before God that the religious had not committed the crimes they were accused of. The sermon was delivered on Pentecost during the pontifical Mass, which was chanted by the bishop of Tlaxcala. It ended in a frightful scandal. Guzmán, in fact, attempted to silence the preacher, Fray Antonio Ortiz. When Ortiz tried to continue, an *alguacil* and several partisans of the Factor Salazar, by order of Delgadillo, scaled the pulpit shouting and, seizing the Franciscan by the arms and robe, threw him down among the spectators. Meanwhile, Mass continued in the normal way, and Father Ortiz, who perhaps had expected violence, made no protest. The next day, however, the bishop's provisor, in the belief that the authors of the scandal were *ipso facto* excommunicated, decided that they could not be admitted to Mass until they begged absolution. The answer of the *oidores* was to exile him from New Spain and all the domains of His Majesty, and to ask an *alguacil* to arrest him and take him by force to Vera Cruz. The provisor took sanctuary in a church, in which the Audiencia besieged him and cut off his food supply. Zumárraga returned to Mexico City when he heard what had happened, and persuaded the Audiencia to come to [the convent of] San Francisco to do the trifling penance he had imposed on them, that is, to recite the *Miserere*. The *oidores* also made a gesture of appeasement by ordering the scandalous libel against the Franciscans to be burned.

The peace was short-lived. Soon afterward, in fact, Guzmán ordered the demolition of the chapel of San Lázaro, a pilgrimage center in the environs of Mexico City, and built on the site a magnificent country house, all at the expense of the Indians, whom he forced to work, even on feast days, paying them neither for the materials nor their labor. When Zumárraga mentioned this, Guzmán laughed in his face. The Audiencia, moreover, anxious to prevent word of these high-handed actions from reaching the court, intercepted correspondence for Spain and held up Zumárraga's letters especially. By the end of 1529, Nuño de Guzmán, now obliged to get away from his *oidores,* with whom he was no longer on good terms, thought to obtain the Emperor's indulgence by making a brilliant conquest, and set out for New Galicia. His absence did not improve the situation, for he had left Delgadillo and Matienzo in charge, and they were no better than he. Two months after the departure of their chief, they kidnaped two tonsured priests, Cristóbal de Angulo and García de Llerena, from the convent of San Francisco, where they had been imprisoned by order of the episcopal court. This stirred up a new conflict with Zumárraga. Angulo and Llerena were taken to the public jail, where they were at once put to the torture. Zumárraga, the bishop of Tlaxcala, and the superiors and religious of St. Francis and St. Dominic formed a procession and marched to the jail to demand the release of the two accused. Tempers got so heated—each group had its partisans—that the demonstration almost ended in a pitched battle. Zumárraga, losing his habitual patience, answered with insults the insults shouted by Delgadillo's bodyguard, who finally chased away the bishops and the religious at the point of the lance.

Zumárraga was driven to adopt the most rigorous sanctions. He blasted the *oidores* with an interdict and threatened to extend it to the whole city and suspend religious services if the prisoners were not released within three hours. The *oidores,* with admirable gentleness and spirit of conciliation, answered by ordering Angulo to be hanged and quartered, and Llerena to be given a hundred lashes and to have a foot cut off. So services were suspended, and the Franciscans abandoned their church and convent and installed themselves in Texcoco with their young pupils, leaving the empty tabernacle wide open, the altars stripped, and the benches upset. Innumerable negotiations, in which the city government played the principal part, with the bishop of Tlaxcala and the Dominicans discreetly supporting the Audiencia, failed to bring about a reconciliation. The conflict had begun in mid-Lent. At Easter the interdict was automatically lifted, and Zumárraga did not impose it again until Low Sunday. But he could not lift the personal excommunication of the *oidores* until they should beg him for absolution, and, since they were equally stubborn, there was no solution. The *oidores,* in fact, remained excommunicated until the arrival of the second Audiencia, and the penalty apparently was not removed until the beginning of 1531. We do not know what satisfaction was imposed upon them, but it seems to have been no great matter, for Motolinía was bitter on the subject, saying they did no penance and gave no satisfaction whatever, adding harshly that "they had been absolved by an idiot." [85]

I have felt obliged to retell the principal episodes of this famous conflict, which is one of the best known in the history of sixteenth century New Spain. Strictly missionary problems were doubtless in its background. If it is true that a missionary cannot abandon even the physical defense of his neophytes, and that the office of protector of the Indians was consequently a proper missionary function and that Zumárraga was fulfilling his missionary duties by defending the Indians of Huejotzingo, it is nevertheless certain that the basic course of the confusing struggle must be sought in the attitude of the first Audiencia, which assuredly was the most cynically despotic, dishonest, and vicious government that colonial Mexico ever suffered. It is easily understood how it exhausted the gentleness of Zumárraga, and how the bishop, exasperated by such rapacity, insolence, and cruelty, became so intransigeant that some have found it excessive. But these incidents cannot be entirely passed over, because, in the period I am covering, they were the only really serious conflict between the architects of the Christianization and the civil authorities. The second Audiencia cooperated whole-heartedly with the missionaries, and the first two viceroys, Antonio de Mendoza and Luis de Velasco, were noblemen, incapable of descending, even in matters of sharp disagreement, to the actions of Guzmán and Delgadillo.

The occasion did not arise. Mendoza encouraged with all his power the founding of the College of Tlatelolco. He was a close friend of Zumárraga. He was not sympathetic toward the secular clergy, in whom he would have liked to see more solid virtues, and he always supported the regulars. He wrote his successor, Luis de Velasco, that without them little could be done, and that he had always favored them, despite criticism of certain individual [regulars], and he advised Velasco to do the same.[86] Velasco did so and even showed himself to be a more decided and energetic partisan of the regular clergy. A letter of his to Philip II is an enthusiastic and unqualified defense of the religious. Without the religious [he wrote] the conversion and catechizing of the Indians would be impossible, for these holy Orders had founded the Church in the country and were daily extending their domain; the religious were living in the most absolute poverty, and, although they were given to erecting beautiful churches and celebrating the services with pomp, it was for the purpose of attracting the Indians.[87] From the beginning his attitude toward the Orders was so plain that in 1552 four Franciscans, Goana, Motolinía, Escalona, and Fray Juan de Olarte, wrote to Charles V begging him to strengthen the authority of the viceroy and increase his salary.[88] [Velasco's] attitude provoked the protests of the bishops, who, when they attacked the religious, at once found themselves blocked by the King's representative. The hot-tempered Montúfar complained of it with his habitual acerbity: "We are so little respected by the religious," he wrote the King, "and so badly regarded by the viceroy, that we have fallen lower than sacristans." [89] He begged him to give no credence to the reports of the viceroy, who was entirely under the thumb of the religious. Dr. Anguis, who is more trustworthy than Montúfar, in spite of his partiality, assures us that the viceroy completely backed the complaints of the religious, and that he had taken up arms against the bishops, whom he reproved for their litigious practices, their hostility to the regulars, and their refusal to ordain them; he also denounces Montúfar's indifference toward his flock and his violent character—to which the bishop replied with similar complaints. And when [Anguis goes on] the religious were asked why they had become so stubborn and furious in the lawsuits, they answered that it was by order of the viceroy, so they spent their time consulting and conspiring with him against the bishops.[90] Thus it happened that the viceroy did not play the part of arbiter to which he was called by his high office and lay character. He was imprudent enough to take sides in ecclesiastical quarrels, and by his interference contributed to the turmoil and disorder which at times slowed down the work of conversion.

This was perhaps inevitable. It is evident that occasions for conflict between the viceroy and the bishops, especially the archbishop of Mexico, who, being the spiritual head of the country, might be considered his equal in rank, were more numerous than between the viceroy and the simple religious. With the latter in particular there could not occur those finicking quarrels over etiquette and precedence which dot the history of

261

Spanish America, and which kept the high civil servants, the military, and the ecclesiastical authorities at each other's throats.[91] And then the religious Orders, especially as communities, wielded a power much greater than that of a bishop. In the first place they represented a superior authority in Spain and the Holy See; in Mexico itself their power was greater, for it was they who largely governed and administered it; and materially and spiritually they appeared as the chiefs and masters of the native population, upon whom the bishops, on the contrary, had no hold. How was a civil officer to control them? The tension between the episcopate and the regular clergy was too great for him to [attempt to] control the latter without running the risk of being thought hostile to the former. It was difficult for the viceroy to be neutral. If he tried to mediate he exposed himself to being treated as an enemy by both groups at the same time, and the situation would perhaps have got worse. Obliged almost in spite of himself to take sides, it was natural for him to range himself with those whose cooperation was indispensable for the accomplishment of his mission.

It may be that some of my readers will have received a painful impression from the story of all these quarrels, conflicts, and intrigues, and may think it was unnecessary to go into such wretchedness. I have thought it proper to give a picture of it because I thought I could not pass over it in silence without mutilating and falsifying my account of the apostolic task carried out in New Spain by the three primitive Orders. Their history would be misunderstood and badly appreciated if we did not know the moral conditions in which our religious worked and the obstacles they had to surmount. It must be added also that I myself give their difficulties only a secondary importance. [The difficulties] were merely in the background of the evangelization. They disturbed it and slowed it down, but they never dominated or stopped it. If they appear with such frequency in the correspondence, it is because the correspondence had that purpose, and because, when one wrote to the Council of the Indies, one seldom did so to express gratuitous praise of one's neighbor, but rather to defend oneself against critics, that is, if one was speaking of a friend, or, if one was speaking of an enemy, to denounce his actions roundly. The resistance of the natives was a more serious check. Unfortunately, it is much less well known, and the reason is easily explained. Nevertheless, it is all the more necessary to examine it since it poses the question of the efficacy of the early preaching.

16 Native Resistance

eVANGELIZATION encountered many obstacles among the natives. The peoples of the coast, the Anahuac plateau, and Michoacán did not violently oppose the coming of the missionaries or the preaching of the Christian faith. We only know that for the first five years they resisted mainly with the great force of inertia.[1] We do know, however, of several instances of open hostility. At Achiutla (Oaxaca) the Dominican Fray Benito Fernández was shut up in his cell and denied all food. It was not carried very far, for several Christians secretly sent him *tortillas,* and then the chiefs of the village, realizing they were being put in a bad light, released the missionary.[2] This kind of thing was exceptional.

On the other hand, in the vast plains of the northwest and the Sierra Madre Occidental, inhabited by ferocious tribes, there were numerous victims: the Franciscan Fray Bernardo Cossin, a Frenchman; Fray Pablo de Acevedo, a Portuguese; and Fray Juan de Herrera and Fray Juan de Tapia, among others.[3] But, however lamentable their consequences, these murders were only individual acts, or sporadic reactions. The rebellion of the Indians of New Galicia in 1541, the so-called Mixtón War, had a very different meaning and extent, because it was a general movement and brought in a large number of tribes, particularly vigorous tribes, like the Cascanes,[4] and it threatened to take the south and center of New Spain. It barely failed to put an end to the European occupation. There is no doubt whatever of the religious nature of this uprising. The insurgents were fighting, not merely for their liberty, but for their religion; they were fighting, not merely against Spain, but against Catholicism. It was evident [to them] that the two things were intimately connected. When the emissaries from the sierras of Tepic and Zacatecas arrived in the valley of Tlaltenango, they spoke to the inhabitants substantially in these words:

We are the messengers of Tecoroli (of the devil, translated the Spaniards). Accompanied by his ancestors, whom he has revived, he is coming to seek you. He will make you believe in him, not in God, on pain of never seeing the light again and of being devoured by beasts. Those who believe in him and renounce the teachings of the friars and follow him will never die, but will become young again and have several wives, not merely one, as the monks order, and, however old they may be, will beget children. Whoever takes only one wife will be killed. Then Tecoroli will come to Guadalajara, Jalisco, Michoacán, Mexico City, and Guatemala, wherever there are Christians from Spain, and slaughter them all. After which he will go home, and you will live happy with your ancestors, suffering no more hardship or pain.[5]

Among the leaders of the rebellion was a certain Tenamaxtle of Nochixtlán (Zacatecas), to whom the Franciscans had assigned the duty of gathering up the people and bringing them to the catechism. When the insurgents entered the village of Tlaltenango (Zacatecas), they burned the church and the cross.[6] In Tepechitlán (Zacatecas) they gave themselves up to sacrilegious ceremonies and parodied the Mass by pretending to worship a *tortilla*. In Juchipila (Zacatecas) they attempted to murder Fray Antonio de Segovia and Fray Martín de Jesús; they burned the monastery, defiled the cross, celebrated their sacrifices, and performed pagan dances. In Cuzpatlán (Cuspala, Jalisco?) they also burned the convent and the cross.[7] After the Spanish defeat [at Nochixtlán], in which Pedro de Alvarado was mortally wounded, the rebels became even more ferocious. When the Christian Indians abjured their faith, [the rebels] washed their heads to remove the mark of baptism and made them do penance for the time they had been Christians. In Tequila (Jalisco) they murdered Fray Juan de la Esperanza with arrows and stones, and horribly mutilated his mouth to prevent his speaking to them of his God and sending them to hell. Near Etzatlán they killed Fray Juan Calero, and between Etzatlán and Ameca, Fray Antonio de Cuellar.[8] This is not the place to tell how this dangerous uprising was finally put down, but only to emphasize its violence and anti-Christian character.

The struggle against Christianity rarely went to such extremes. The natives were not well enough united or organized to put up an effective resistance to the Spanish administration; nor did it often take the form of a free discussion. Neither the civil nor the religious authorities would have permitted the native priests or chiefs to trouble the souls of their brothers, spread heterodox ideas, and risk stirring up disorders by free public discussion of the philosophic and moral values of the new religion. The only discussion of which we have an echo took place at the beginning, upon the arrival of the Twelve. It will be recalled that the missionaries soon brought together the head men of the City of Mexico to explain the Christian doctrine to them. In their first *Plática* they spoke of the Pope who had sent them, the Holy Scripture, and the true God and His Church. The head men answered this lecture, after some very bombastic civilities—according to Sahagún, at least—that it seemed unjust lightly to give up and destroy the customs and rites that their ancestors had practiced and held to be good,[9] but that they were not learned enough to answer and discuss the propositions of the religious. So they called their priests together and repeated to them the discourse of the Twelve. "The priests," says Sahagún, "were greatly troubled and felt sad and fearful," and did not answer. The next day, however, accompanied by the chiefs, they sought out the Twelve. They began by saying they were extremely surprised and shocked to hear the religious affirm that their gods were not gods. And they repeated their trivial objection: that their ancestors had always considered [their gods] to be such, had always worshiped them, and were the very ones who had taught their descendants to honor them with certain sacrifices and ceremonies. It would [they said] therefore be a great folly and frivolity to set aside very ancient laws and customs left by the first inhabitants of the country. Then they told the

266

chiefs that it would be impossible to force all the old men to give up the customs in which they had been reared; and they threatened [the chiefs] with the wrath of the gods, and also with popular uprisings, if the Indians should be told that those whom they had always regarded as gods were not gods at all. They ended by saying that it was enough to have lost their liberty, and that they would die rather than cease to worship and serve their gods.

The missionaries answered all this by again explaining what the true God was, and, after speaking of angels, devils, creation, and the first man and his fall, they returned to their starting point by showing them that their gods had no real existence.[10] Unfortunately, Sahagún's text carries us only to the fall of the first man, after which we are obliged to be content with his summary at the beginning of his *Pláticas* which necessarily compresses the matter excessively. The religious told the Indians that their gods had been impotent to protect them against the Spanish invasion, a remark that provoked a dispute between the priests and the chiefs. A little later the Twelve returned again to this point, whereupon the priests and the chiefs expressed themselves as ready to serve the God of the Christians and to renounce their idols.[11]

This contradictory account is, I believe, a unique fact in the history of the evangelization of Mexico. Were there really many Indians capable of sustaining a theological controversy at the time of the arrival of the Spaniards? In any event, although it was doubtless difficult at first to avoid a discussion with the political and religious heads of the Mexican community, there was no reason to grant the Indians a freedom of speech and expression which the Holy Office did not concede to the Christians of Europe. The natives were unable to prevent by force the preaching of the Gospel, for it rested upon the political and military might of Spain. By their own ignorance and the pressure of the authorities they were prevented from publicly discussing the new religion and from opposing its doctrines and ceremonies peacefully but openly. They were faithfully attached to their ancient gods by their convictions and habits, and could make only a kind of sly resistance to the action of the missionaries by inertia and dissimulation. The tyrannical organization of pre-Conquest

Mexico had accustomed them to this kind of struggle. The form it instinctively took at the beginning was very simple: to retreat before the missionaries, create a vacuum, avoid contact with them, and hide. The first Augustinians were received in this fashion at Chilapa in the Sierra Alta.[12] But this tactic was only possible in distant regions hardly occupied by the Spaniards, and resistance could not last indefinitely, say, three months or a year, in the cases I have just cited. This warfare by sly inertia had other aspects. Thus, when the religious tried to gather up the sons of chiefs and rear them in monasteries, they ran up against a silent but almost invincible opposition. The parents either hid their children, or sent in their place young slaves or the children of their subjects, dressed in fine clothes and accompanied by many little servants, the better to deceive the missionaries, or they made shift to keep their first-born and favorite sons with them.[13] Similar difficulties were experienced with the girls. Indians of the lower class had the custom of offering them, willy nilly, to their chiefs, who kept them for concubines, locked them up in their houses, or concealed them in mysterious hiding places, not allowing them to attend catechism or receive baptism.[14]

I have already noted, when I discussed marriage, the trouble the missionaries had in uprooting concubinage and polygamy. In 1536 Zumárraga complained of the dissolute habits of the *caciques,* and said that at the date of writing they conducted themselves in secret even worse than before hearing of the Catholic faith.[15] Indeed, one could compile a long list of the Indians prosecuted by the Holy Office for debauchery, concubinage, or bigamy, and for declaring that concubinage was not a sin.[16] I have also pointed out that it frequently happened that one saw Indians removing their villages to more remote places, far from convents, churches, and the religious, so that they might give themselves in complete freedom to their customs and vices.[17]

There is nothing surprising in this, and, in the field of customs, one may wonder whether it would be just to speak of reaction or opposition. Everywhere in old Catholic countries, as in mission countries, human weakness, even in alliance with sincere faith, rebels against the severities and demands of Christian morality, and allows itself to be a party to acts which [Christian morality] does not countenance. Conversion does not cause one to cease being a sinner, and the Mexican neophytes had no monopoly on vice and debauchery. Nothing, unhappily, is more normal than that some of them should secretly retain their freedom of customs, such as they had enjoyed before the arrival of the missionaries—which does not imply a systematic resistance. What we have here is not religious arguments, but a sharp religious resistance, although invisible. Too much weight, however, should not be given to a letter of Fray Pedro de Ayala, according to which, after the Crown had forbidden the religious to inflict corporal punishment on the Indians, many of them, at least in New Galicia, had ceased attending catechism, Mass, and sermons.[18] Discounting Fray Pedro de Ayala's habitual pessimism, we have here, very likely, [the Indian's] laziness and indifference rather than organized hostility. It is certain that idolatry continued to be practiced secretly and was never to be completely eradicated. At times this was not owing to ill will on the Indians' part, but simply to ignorance. When the vigilance of the clergy relaxed, the Indians' ancestral paganism came unconsciously to the surface, and, in their feasts and dances, they mingled Christian elements with the practices and beliefs of their old religion.[19] At a relatively early date, it is true, the *Junta Eclesiástica* of 1539 thought it detected a survival of polytheism in the multitude of little chapels erected by the Indians, "just like those they had once had for their particular gods." [20]

Most often, however, it was a willful and conscious resistance, which the bishops never ceased lamenting. In their letter of November 30, 1537, the bishops of Mexico, Oaxaca, and Guatemala begged the King for authority to take extremely rigorous measures against idolatry, which the Indians had seemingly renounced, but continued to practice secretly at night, worshiping their gods and offering sacrifices.[21] What is particularly noteworthy is that the situation does not seem to have improved by 1565, for on October eleventh of that year the bishops of New Spain, with Montúfar at their head, addressed a memorial to the Audiencia of Mexico, as follows: "The great readiness with which these newly converted Indians revert to their idolatries, rites, sacrifices, and superstitions is notorious." [22] Sometimes, as at Chalma, the idolaters gathered in caves of difficult access, there to continue their cult; [23] at other times, with a refinement of dissimulation and an excess of caution, they hid their idols beneath the cross,[24] as at Cholula,[25] or in the altars of the churches,[26] where they worshiped them under the cloak of performing their [Christian] devotions.[27] Whenever their idols were discovered and destroyed, they made new ones.[28] The country, at least certain regions of it, was full of hidden idols and secret idolaters.[29] Nothing is more revealing of this than the records of the trials of idolaters published by the Mexican National Archives.[30] The data are relatively ancient (1536–1540), but they reveal that the Indians not only concealed idols,[31] but also practiced human sacrifice; that there were Indians who hid themselves when the Franciscans came to preach and baptize, Indians who refused to build churches, indulged in blasphemous jokes and sacrileges, and spread pagan propaganda among children and youths.[32] Moreover, it was an Indian judge, Marcos Hernández Atlabcatl, who, although baptized fifteen years before, made mock of the religious, rebelled against their authority, declared that they had invented the confession to learn the sins of others, and told [the Indians] to continue to live in concubinage and drunkenness.[33] Finally, we have the testimony of Fray Andrés de Olmos, to the effect that the *cacique* of Matlatlán, a drunkard surrounded by seventeen or eighteen concubines, had relinquished several idols, but had kept others to distribute to various natives. In addition, he hardly ever attended church, but spread propaganda for paganism. His followers, if one may believe Father Olmos, were no better. The Gospel had been preached among them for twenty years; there were more than eight religious in the region; he himself had visited every part of it for five or six years; and yet they continued obstinately attached to their idolatry and evil ways.[34]

This resistance was inspired and led, not only by the *caciques,* but by native priests and sorcerers,[35] who were even more implacable, because they were more threatened or convinced, or both. So they mounted a ferocious campaign against the religious, who, by their attire, their conduct, and their life, had at first taken the Indians by suprise. For example, seeing the humility and poverty of the Dominicans, they said to themselves that these must be great sinners to live in such a mortification of the flesh.[36] They considered the first Franciscans simply to be madmen, for, unlike other men, they sought only solitude and melancholy, and, at midnight and in the morning, when everybody else was making merry, they gathered together to weep and howl.[37] The sorcerers of Michoacán made skillful use of this lack of comprehension. They convinced the natives that the religious were dead men, that their habits were winding sheets, and that at night when they retired they disappeared and rejoined their women in hell, leaving behind them only their bones and their habits. As frequently happened, monastic celibacy was for them manifestly inexplicable. The sorcerers also convinced the Indians that the water used in baptism was blood and that the religious split the children's heads. For this reason the Tarascans did not dare bring their children to the Fathers for fear of seeing them die. It was apparently the sorcerers of Michoacán who circulated all the strange notions that hindered the beginnings of evangelization there, for the Indians were persuaded that the religious were born dressed in their habits, that they had never been children, and that when they said Mass they gazed into the water, just like the sorcerers themselves. So the Tarascans were very much afraid of the confession, for they imagined that the confessor would kill them, and if one of them, especially a woman, overcame this terror, all the others, having spied on her during the confession would beset her to learn what had happened, what questions she had been asked, and what she had been told. Finally, when they were told they would go to heaven, they did not believe it, but answered they had never seen anyone go there.[38] It also happened that pagan priests would slip in among the sick and dying to persuade them to give up Christianity.[39] We have the trial records of several sorcerers charged with campaigning against the religious. One of them, Martín Ucelo (or, more properly, Ocelotl), was accused of transforming himself at will into a tiger, lion, dog, or cat, and, like Mixcoatl, of turning the Indians away from baptism and inventing a blasphemous parody of the *Credo*.[40]

Sometimes these campaigns ended tragically. Certain historians attribute the [Mixtón] revolt of 1541 to the machinations of the sorcerers. The Indians had been celebrating one of their feasts by dancing around an empty pumpkin, when a gust of wind carried it away and they could not find it. The sorcerers, questioned as to the significance of the prodigy, answered that heaven had ordered the Indians to rise up against the

Spaniards and chase them away, just as the wind had blown away the pumpkin.[41] The revolts of the Indians of Oaxaca in 1547 and 1550 were infinitely less grave, but seem also to have been caused by the intrigues and preaching of the sorcerers.[42]

The famous trial of Don Carlos, *cacique* of Texcoco, may be thought of as the symbol of pagan resistance.[43] Don Carlos Mendoza Ometochtzin (or Chichimecatecuhtli, as he called himself), baptized by the Franciscans, former pupil in the College of Tlatelolco, was prosecuted in 1539 by Zumárraga, representing the Holy Office, for concubinage and idolatry. Evidence of pagan worship was found in his house: a manuscript, altars, and a large number of idols, a list of which is among the trial papers. His young son, ten or eleven years old—in the Inquisition trials one too frequently finds these unpleasant depositions of children against their parents—declared that he had not been reared in the monasteries and had not learned the catechism, because his father had forbidden him to go to church. Indeed, he was ignorant of any prayer and did not even know how to cross himself. According to other depositions, Don Carlos had in fact carried on a stubborn campaign against Christianity and the religious, had advised his compatriots not to learn the Christian doctrine, and had especially proclaimed that the Indians should live according to the religion and ways of their ancestors—the usual appeal. He pointed out the differences in dress, rules, and teaching among the Franciscans, Dominicans, and Augustinians, and secular priests, and concluded that everyone had his own way of life and that it was good, and consequently the Indians should not give up theirs. He added that the Spaniards were drunkards and debauchees who made mock of the interdictions and sermons of the religious, so why should the Indians not be allowed the same pleasures? [44]

Don Carlos, in the course of his trial, confessed only to living in concubinage with his niece, and consistently denied the other charges. His wife, who had some reason to complain of him and did not hide her complaints, nevertheless deposed that she had never seen the idols [allegedly] kept in her husband's house, and had never seen him celebrate sacrifices and pagan ceremonies. Moreover, the extreme weakness of the defense, the total absence of friendly witnesses, and the isolation of the accused, give the impression of a kind of conspiracy. Was Don Carlos a victim of obscure Indian intrigues, which the Spanish judges could not fathom or even suspect?[45] In colonial countries it happens that one sees the natives, with consummate skill, take advantage of European justice to satisfy their hatreds and personal grudges. On the other hand, Don Carlos, at the moment of mounting the scaffold, for he had been condemned to death, admitted that he well deserved the punishment he was about to suffer, because of his faults and sins, and he exhorted the spectators not to follow his bad example, but definitely to abandon idolatry. Was this the final weakness of a man wasted by a long trail, who lacked the strength to resist the suggestions of those who by his execution wished to shock the spirit of the Indians? Was it a spontaneous and genuinely sincere acknowledgment? It is hard to ferret out the truth. One thing, however, is suprising and that is the severity of the sentence, which is in singular contrast to the gentle punishments meted out to the idolaters I have mentioned. Doubtless, Don Carlos was stubborn in his denials, which was almost always an aggravating factor in inquisitorial trials. Even so, the sentence is still astonishing, all the more so since Zumárraga, who presided over the investigation and arguments, was definitely not a cruel man, or even a hard man. Was it his conviction that Don Carlos was at the head of a widespread pagan revolt? Since he had been worried for some time, as his correspondence reveals, about the survival of paganism and the Indians' attachment to their old ways, did he wish to make a salutary example? Was he the one who suggested those last words to the condemned? The fact is that the inquisitor general [in Spain] judged the sentence to have been too harsh, for he favored treating the newly converted with more indulgence. The death sentence could have been justified only in the case of human sacrifice, of which not a word was said during the trial. Don Carlos was denounced only as "a preacher of heresy."[46]

This patient resistance was often successful. In a study of the Mexican calendar in the National Library of Mexico published by Juan B. Iguínez a dozen years ago, Sahagún himself is revealed as having pronounced a terrible judgment on the evangelization of New Spain which amounts to a condemnation. He begins by doubting the eradication of idolatry by the first missionaries, and adds that in any case it is certain that pagan practices always tend to reappear and multiply in secret. So the Indians continued their sacrifices, but used only animals, whose hearts they tore out, as they had formerly done in human sacrifices. They worshiped idols hidden in Christian churches, and when a church was erected on the site of a vanished temple, what they worshiped there was the ancient god. What really happened, according to Sahagún, was that, although the pagans did indeed consent to become Christians and receive baptism, at the bottom of their hearts they never really meant to abandon their old ways, deny their traditions, or renounce their gods. They saw nothing contradictory in this attitude. When they were first admitted to baptism, which had not been fully explained to them, the early missionaries repeatedly assured their fellows that the natives had entirely given up paganism and accepted Christianity in all loyalty. Later on, various incidents revealed the secret survival of idolatry, but they were concealed [by the religious], as much to safeguard the official story as to avoid shocking the newly converted.[47]

Many examples confirm the observations and pessimism of Sahagún. Three hundred years later Humboldt wrote that the Spaniards had accidentally discovered the pyramid of Papantla, northwest of Jalapa (Vera Cruz), in the midst of a dense forest, where the Totonacs had for centuries succeeded in guarding this venerable monument from the curiosity of the Christians.[48] At Coixtlahuaca (Oaxaca), a native chief who knew of the location of a cave full of idols disappeared mysteriously, and, despite all the efforts of the Dominicans, was never found, nor were the cave and the idols.[49] Moreover, when Mexico City was occupied for the second time [1521], the Indians carried off the five principal idols of the great temple and took them to the house of an Indian named Miguel, who kept them for ten days. They were soon collected again and taken to a place which he, even under torture, declared he did not know. Indeed, they were so carefully hidden that, in spite of minute investigations, it was impossible to find them, and their resting place today is still unknown.[50]

From these examples, which could be multiplied, and from the observations of Sahagún, must one conclude that the early evangelization was a failure? Some have thought so, even in the sixteenth century. Motolinía, writing at a relatively early date, tells us that many Spaniards did not believe in the conversion of the Indians,[51] and, in the *Rhetorica Christiana,* Fray Diego Valadés vigorously refuted the opinion that the Christianization of the Indians was no more genuine than that of the Moriscos of Granada. Valadés remarks that the Indians have been better converted, by more numerous, more competent and particularly dedicated ministers, and that, as distinct from the Moriscos, they have suffered no violence. And he insists on their Christian qualities, piety, and faithfulness in attending services, their pleasure in liturgical pomp, love for the religious, and the sincerity and humility of their confessions. He reminds us especially that it is very difficult to render judgment in the matter, and that only God knows our loins and hearts.[52] We should keep his words in mind. To solve this thorny problem and avoid drawing conclusions from superficial and false appearances, one would have to live a long time, a very long time, among the Mexican Indians, win their confidence, and learn various native tongues. It is self-evident that an investigation in such detail, covering such a long period, is almost impossible for Mexican specialists to undertake, and is necessarily denied to European historians. In any case, it would lead only to an approximate solution. It should be added that it could not be made in all points of that vast territory, and would [therefore] admit of only local conclusions. The observations of Mgr. Vera y Zuria reveal a great diversity from one village to another in a single diocese; an apathetic indifference side by side with the liveliest fervor; hostility or ignorance, with the most genuine faith. In short, how much historical importance would such an investigation have? Three and a half centuries have passed since the end of the primitive evangelization, three and a half centuries of tranquillity, in which tepidity and routine have not been absent. And then there have been civil wars, anarchy, social upheavals, religious persecution, and conflict with the Church. A study of the present situation would not in any sense allow one to appreciate the religious state of New Spain at the time Motolinía, Sahagún, and Valadés were writing.

These reflections should induce an extreme caution in one's investigations. Nevertheless, a theory was circulated a few years ago which I must examine here, because it implies a judgment of the efficacy of the early evangelization, although it especially concerns the present. This is the theory of a "mixed religion," or, if one prefers, a syncretism of which [the late] Manuel Gamio is the chief exponent. [According to it] the Indians are not truly Catholic; they have not really accepted the dogma and moral system of Roman Christianity, but have contented themselves with taking over a certain number of foreign ceremonies and practices, and have mixed this entirely formal and superficial Catholicism with their ancient superstitions and traditional rites, which they have preserved by [thus] deforming them. The sixteenth-century missionaries realized that paganism was ineradicable, and were reduced to accepting this apparent conversion, to accomplish which they utilized the surface resemblances of the two religions.[53] This theory immediately arouses distrust because of the assurance with which it solves a problem, the delicacy and complexity of which should have been self-evident to all historians, whatever their personal philosophy might be. I should not like to fall into the same trap by flatly denying it all exactness and verisimilitude. There are some true elements in this obscure problem which one can retain, and upon which one can lean in an attempt to arrive at a general conclusion.

The survival of paganism in Mexico seems to be undeniable. Certain native groups, protected by their isolation, have not yet given it up. The Popolaca, studied by Nicolás León, still venerate their ancient idols and hardly have the idea of a Supreme God, whom they represent, moreover, as a material being. They do not believe in the existence of the soul, or in hell and eternal punishment. The future life [for them] is only an extension of the present, although a better one. They have many sorcerers, who are greatly feared, among whom the parish priest occupies only an inferior rank. Catholic marriage is celebrated several months after the pagan marriage.[54] The natives of the Sierrade Zongolica receive the sacraments, but still celebrate rites that are pagan in form and substance, like the invocation of the Dios Venado.[55] Among the Totonac of the Sierra de Puebla the situation is clear. They do not recognize baptism, they do not attend Mass, and they continue to worship their idols, which rest on their hearths in the company of a few images of Christian saints.[56] These communities live apart, in mountainous country difficult of access, and have been only slightly converted, if at all. But even among the Tarascans of Michoacán, one of the paradises of the early apostolate, one finds like conditions. Dr. León surprised the fishermen of Santa Fe in the act of offering incense to a stone fish, in order to assure an abundant catch. When the parish priest of Pátzcuaro remodeled the church of San Agustín, he discovered an idol behind the image of the Señor de Taretán. He gave it to the Museo Michoacano and thus killed the cult of the Señor de Taretán.[57] In Huejotla, just outside Mexico City, it was noticed that the natives came to the church to venerate the pagan symbol of the cardinal points, which their workmen had stylized in the form of a cross.[58] So we have a mass of evidence which cannot be doubted, and the interpretation of which is clear.[59] We are on less solid ground with the cult of the saints, which plays an enormous part, or possibly even an unfortunately predominant one, in the piety of the Mexican people. To what extent is this idolatry? Does this allow one to insinuate, with the "liberal" priest Agustín Rivera, or to affirm, with a contemporary ethnographer, that the Indians worship the saints in their own way, or, more precisely, worship their physical image? [60] On this point I shall follow the wise advice of Valadés. Who can flatter himself that he knows what takes place in the dark minds of the natives? They themselves certainly do not see clearly among the ideas and feelings that guide them.

On the other hand, the Indians are not always as far removed from orthodoxy as is claimed by the "mixed religion" school. The ethnographer I just mentioned, a collaborator of Manuel Gamio, has studied the religious concepts of the natives of the valley of Teotihuacán and, when all is said and done, he reveals only one clearly heterodox belief, to wit, that the Indians do not admit the eternity of hell; on the Judgment Day [they believe] some of the damned will be pardoned and admitted to heaven. This heterodox notion is, moreover, probably not of pre-Hispanic origin, and one may see in it a deformation born of ignorance and insufficient teaching, or perhaps a confusion with the disappearance of purgatory after the Final Judgment. As for the cult of the saints, the author affirms rather than demonstrates. What remains of the general concept that the Indians of Teotihuacán have of Catholicism? For them a Catholic is a person who goes to Mass, confesses, and takes part in the popular feasts, dances, and plays by which the village honors its saints—a concept that is dangerous in its oversimplicity, narrowness, and incompleteness. But up to what point can it be considered pagan, idolatrous, and pre-Hispanic? [61]

Naturally, no serious scholar can deny the multitude of superstitions that encumber Catholicism in Mexico and impede its progress. The essential question for us is to determine precisely the degree in which these superstitions may be considered survivals of pre-Hispanic paganism. For my part, I am fully persuaded that a good many of them are of European origin, or were born and developed in New Spain after the conquest. In his precious *Letters,* Mgr. Vera y Zuria cites many examples of superstitions that I do not hesitate to place in that category. In one instance it is the sacristan who marks the faithful with a spur from the statue of St. James—a Spanish superstition in all its aspects—; in another, the inhabitants of San Bartolomeo have a statue of the devil in chains, which they strike off in order to turn him loose upon their enemies. [62] A superstition is not necessarily a pagan survival, and pre-Hispanic paganism should not be considered to be the only origin of modern superstition. Superstition does not arise solely from paganism; it has no unique historical sources, but rather psychological origins above all. [63] It appears as a deviation from, or a perversion of, the religious sense, as inevitable as other perversions of the intellect or character. Hence it is not astonishing that it is found everywhere. And it exists—I must insist upon elementary facts, which the theory of the "mixed religion" does not take into account —it exists as much in the oldest Christian communities as elsewhere. Certain examples of Mexican "pagan-Catholicism" appear as superstitions of an extreme triviality, such as the case of the Apache of Tepito who prays to the Virgin de la Soledad for victory in his next combat, and that of the young girl who hangs St. Anthony up by his feet, [64] the equivalents of which may easily be found in Europe among uneducated Catholics. If they had been better acquainted with European religious life the defenders of the "mixed religion" would not have given the features they mention such excessive importance. [65]

Mexican superstition, like pre-Hispanic paganism, seems to be the offspring of religious ignorance, which has permitted imaginations, without guidance and without support, to work upon vague and insufficient notions, and to distort as they please the legacy of preceding generations. When the Indians of Tepetitlán (Puebla) put a hat on the statue of the Child Jesus and then give him the name of St. Ignatius of Loyola; [66] when others, out of respect, confer upon their bishop the title of the Holy Trinity; when an old Indian woman takes communion three times running, in the name of the Father, the Son, and the Holy Ghost, one can attribute it to ignorance, but only to ignorance. Sometimes a different story is told, how an Indian comes to confession, and the priest begins by asking him how many gods there are. Two, replies the Indian, or ten, or twenty, and so on up to fifty, to the rising indignation of the priest, who ends by sending him to relearn his catechism. At the church door the Indian meets a friend and asks him the same difficult question. The friend answers correctly, and the other exclaims: "Very well, but don't go and confess to that *padrecito*. He's not happy even with fifty!" Is this a survival of polytheism? This can only be crass ignorance. One must add the meaning that the question has in Spanish for a coarse intelligence. It seems to imply, in fact, that there are many gods, and it is not surprising that it causes the poor Indian, who is already worried about appearing before the tribunal of penitence, to forget all his theology.

Still, the more or less conscious work of the imagination in an ignorant head is not always the cause of these gaps or deformations, which also result from confusion or misunderstanding. Fray Juan Bautista explained the origin of two errors about the dogma of the Trinity which, he said, were extremely common among the Indians. The first had to do with Divine Unity and came about from the missionaries' use of an ambiguous sentence in Nahuatl: "There is only one God, who is Father, Son, and Holy Ghost, three persons, only one of whom is the true God." Almost all Indians, according to Fray Juan Bautista, interpreted the proposition in its last sense, and believed that only the Son was God. The second error arises from separating the persons [of the Trinity]. Some missionaries made a precise statement on the subject of the Father, Son, and Holy Ghost, "three in person, but one in essence." But this sentence is also obscure, and many Indians understood that God was only one person who appeared in three different guises. "And," adds Fray Juan Bautista, "in spite of all that, many preachers have even preached and taught the true doctrine against these two errors, which are manifest heresies, and there are many Indians who do not succeed in thinking or responding according to the true and pure doctrine of our Holy Catholic Religion." [67]

What is left is that in their celebrations the Indians frequently honor Jesus Christ, the Holy Virgin, and the saints, especially in their dances, the form of which is probably pre-Conquest. I have already discussed the feast of *moros y cristianos* and the dances at Guadalupe. The theory of the "mixed religion" commits the error of sticking exclusively to the form of these celebrations, in which a survival of paganism is naturally detected.[68] Now, a dance, unless it is immoral, is neither pagan nor Christian. If it should be immoral it would be anti-Christian, but not on that account necessarily pagan. What really counts is the intent. In this the theory of the "mixed religion" borrows from Catholicism a formalism which can assuredly be found in individual abuses, but which in no respect is within the spirit of the Church. It attributes a "magic" value to the Catholic rite which that rite never had, for it loses all meaning if it is not given life by the one who performs it. There is no consecration if the priest has no intention of consecrating the act of the Church. This is where one should seek the basis for the method of substitution, the theory of which Acosta explained in his treatment of dances, and which has no meaning if it is only the form that determines the significance of the act.[69] A Christian meaning was substituted for the pagan meaning of the pre-Conquest feast. What does it matter, then, that the Indian of today, to honor the Virgin of Guadalupe, makes the same gesture that his ancestors made in honor of Tonantzin, if he really means to honor the Virgin and not Tonantzin?[70] In my opinion it is as frivolous to consider these feasts of substitution as pre-Conquest survivals as it would be childish to consider the use of Latin in the Church a survival of Roman paganism.

For all these reasons I believe that if there is some substance to the theory of the "mixed religion," there is even more to be ignored. Some of the facts that it alleges cannot be denied, but I think others can be differently interpreted. I especially think it errs in its generalizations. Its formula, or what could be its formula, that is, "the survival of paganism within Catholicism," which is valid, for example, among the Tarascans and the natives of Zongolica, should be corrected by a parallel formula, namely, "the survival of paganism at the side of, and outside of, Catholicism," which is valid for the Popoloca and Totonac, and doubtless for most of the mountain people of the north and south. But this second formula should not be regarded as exclusive either. It is interesting to observe that these people, who have remained almost purely pagan, are those who, by reason of geographic obstacles, dangerous climates, or difficulties of language, were hardly touched by the early evangelization. And if, as I have said, it would be imprudent to judge the intensity of Christian life in the sixteenth century by a study of the present situation, in the wide view it is no less true that the spiritual geography of contemporary Mexico, as far as one can determine, corresponds to the area of early missionary expansion. Leaving out of the reckoning the salient made by the Franciscans toward Zacatecas and Durango, which was an exploration rather than a methodical apostolate, the main thrust of the sixteenth-century missionaries occurred in the central plateau and its prolongations, to wit, the regions of Puebla, Mexico and Pachuca, Michoacán-Jalisco, and Oaxaca. The coasts were extremely unhealthful, and the vast territories of the north were inaccessible. I deliberately excluded from this study the regions of Chiapas and Tabasco, but I may remark that the least Catholic states of Mexico are those of the coasts: Vera Cruz, Guerrero, and the great northern states of Sinaloa, Sonora, Chihuahua, Coahuila, and Tamaulipas.[71] Sonora is even considered to be a state without churches. I may also add that most of the anticlerical personnel of the Mexican Revolution came from these last-named states: Carranza (Coahuila); Generals Obregón, Calles, and Amaro (Sonora); Portes Gil (Tamaulipas). I may further remark that at the time of the religious conflict of 1926 [the Cristero revolt], the policy of General Calles was opposed by the central states, not counting the old Creole cities of Puebla, Morelia, Guadalajara, and Oaxaca, where there is still a Catholic bourgeoisie. It was opposed particularly by the Indians of Michoacán and Jalisco, while the states on the periphery remained neutral or favored [the anticlerical policy of General Calles.] Finally, with the exception of Morelos, these central states, especially Guanajuato, are the ones that have the largest number of priestly vocations.[72] I say once again that the activity of the religious of the sixteenth century heavily influenced the destinies of Mexico. The summary and general examination of this activity which I shall now undertake will affirm the truth of this observation.

17 The Early Evangelization and the Religious Evolution of Mexico

tHAT the framework I have adopted for this study seems contrived and artificial is as apparent to me as to anyone else. At the same time it was just as evidently a necessity, and I resigned myself to it in advance, since by definition an analysis cannot follow or encompass the changing and diverse complexity of reality. If [on the other hand] one attempts to stick to [that reality], one inevitably becomes as confused and obscure as the sources themselves, and runs the risk of producing only a useless compilation. The reader should be on his guard, however, against the excessive rigidity and exaggerated simplicity from which this study seems to suffer. The work of the religious in New Spain is complex, but it is indivisible. The founding and stabilization of the Church, which the requirements of my account have obliged me to treat separately in the interest of clarity, are not in fact two successive activities, or even parallel, but simply two aspects of the same thing. Languages were studied and schools were built; baptisms were performed and hospitals were founded; the catechism was taught and plays were put on; marriages were blessed, confessions were heard, communion was administered, and aqueducts and fountains were built; and all of this was done at the same time and by the same men. Indians were gathered into organized villages to facilitate elementary instruction in the Christian doctrine, and few measures contributed as much to the stabilization of the new Church. Now that I have completed my analysis, it will be well for me to arrange my facts, bring together the scattered elements, distinguish the general characteristics of the work of the Mexican missionaries, and make at least a rapid examination of the influence that the primitive evangelization of New Spain had on the destinies of the Church in Mexico and the evolution of the Mexican nation.

It seems possible, roughly speaking, to distinguish two principal missionary attitudes toward pagan civilizations and religions, or, if one prefers, two systems: that of the *tabula rasa,* or an absolute rupture, and the system one may call "an opportunistic preparation." In the first, the missionary considers everything he finds upon his arrival completely corrupt: religious, political, and social institutions, as well as souls and spirits. He condemns native traditions *en bloc.* Hence, everything that existed before the coming of the missionaries must be wiped out, and a completely new edifice built upon new foundations with new materials. The neophyte must make a clean break with his former environment and life; conversion for him will not be an achievement or a perfecting, in the original sense of the word, but a total renewal. Broadly speaking, with obvious exceptions, this is the system that prevailed in the old missions of the sixteenth, seventeenth, and eighteenth centuries.

The second system is more recent. It had antecedents, not so rare as has at times been thought, but it spread everywhere after the middle of the nineteenth century. It is not my purpose to determine why it occurred then and then only, nor why the Holy See, while naturally allowing the missionary orders great freedom within the bounds of orthodoxy, seems today to look upon [this system] with an especially favorable eye. Its fundamental principle is that any people, however decadent its beliefs and institutions, is not totally in error and sin, for hidden among the most backward is at least a modicum of truth and an obscure aspiration toward light and perfection. The problem is to discover this modicum and to make this aspiration conscious (an exceedingly difficult task, to be sure), and to use them as a base and point of departure for the evangelization. Thus the neophyte will not be obliged to break entirely with his former life, and will be allowed to retain that part of his traditions which is naturally good and true. He is trusted. According to the formula of a missionary in Africa, Father Gautier: "The missionary invents nothing, but takes what he finds in pagan customs and brings it into the Christian plan." [1]

The Mexican mission used both systems. Its eclectic character is evident from the presence of three different Orders, Franciscan, Dominican, and Augustinian. One might think *a priori* that each of the Orders had its own methods and policies, quite distinct from the others. The Franciscans, indeed, seem to me to have been especially interested in ethnographic and linguistic studies, and more concerned [than the others] with training a native clergy; the Dominicans, more scrupulously attached to orthodoxy and less optimistic about the Indians' religious capacities; the Augustinians, more competent in organizing native communities, more given to building vast monasteries, and more interested in giving their neophytes a higher and more advanced spiritual training. These, however, are only nuances, not openly displayed. The three Orders did not in fact go their separate ways. After 1541, on the initiative of Zumárraga, they voluntarily and methodically pooled their procedures and experiments. The authorities, theologians, and specialists of the three Orders periodically met in one of the convents of Mexico City to examine and reach agreement on the problems and difficulties that arose in the *doctrinas,* and to assure a uniformity in presenting the catechism.[2] So they shared their procedures and experiments; the errors and disappointments of some were of profit to the others, and a kind of common store of methods came into being, which explains the eclecticism of the Mexican mission. To this must be added the individual tendencies, often divergent, sometimes hostile, within the Orders. I have mentioned the two currents among the Franciscans which at certain moments collided violently. One was represented by Sahagún and the religious who favored a scientific and sympathetic study of the native civilization; the other was represented by Escalona and the religious who were inclined to a somewhat lazy empiricism, who were less curious about Indian matters, and who were tempted to give themselves up to a peaceful convent life in that mission country. All these different tendencies and concepts, which have been studied in detail [above], become fused and neutralized when one judges things with a little perspective and tries to take a broad view of them, and then they are seen to be nothing more than the unity lying beneath the surface of a common task.

The Mexican missionaries adopted the concept of the *tabula rasa* because of their insistence upon not only destroying idolatry, but whatever might suggest a memory of it. They destroyed temples, suppressed all pagan feasts, banished idols, and trained children to search them out and to track down all pagan ceremonies which the Indians still practiced in secret. At least in the field of religion, therefore, a complete rupture occurred. The very superficial analogies that might be observed between Mexican paganism and Christianity were not used. The missionaries thought that baptism, confession, and communion among the ancient Mexicans had nothing in common with the sacraments of the Church, as was indeed evident, but were only a satanic parody of them and an invention of the devil to keep the Indians in error and prevent their accepting the true religion. The missionaries, even those with the boldest ideas, like Acosta, recoiled from them in horror. The remarks of Sahagún on the subject of [the native] confession lead one to believe [that he thought] these analogies were more harmful than useful, because of the confusions they bred among the Indians and the errors they led the missionaries to commit. I have detected only a feeble effort to adapt them in the presentation of dogma. The missionaries came from a nation that has always been extremely hostile to heterodoxy. Their activity coincided with the spread of Protestant heresies, and they were particularly haunted, so to speak, by the fear of a pagan-Christian syncretism. This terror was especially evident in Montúfar, who was a former judge in the Holy Office, and, one may say, it was general in New Spain.

This obsession was manifested in the suppression of the works of Motolinía and the *Chronicle of Michoacán,* and in the hostility encountered by religious suspected of studying, with too passionate a curiosity, the native languages and civilizations, religious such as Gilberti and especially Sahagún, despite the fact that Sahagún now seems to have been mistrustful and overcautious. Does he not denounce syncretism at every step? Nothing is more revealing of the fact than that he was judged to be too complacent! This same obsession was particularly marked in the field of language. We have seen how in Mexico, as in every mission country, there was the delicate problem of translating Christian terms in the various native tongues, terms representing things or concepts radically new to the converts. In this regard we have also seen that two approaches were possible. The first was always to translate, even if one had to make more or less complicated paraphrases in the native language. The second, on the other hand, was forcibly to insert European words in the native texts, either in their Latin form, or in the form they had in the national language of the missionary. The religious of Mexico adopted this second approach, not only because it was evidently simpler, but also because it was perhaps much the safer from a strictly orthodox point of view. Besides, would it not have been imprudent, in fact, to use for baptism, confession, and communion, native terms which were superficially analogous, but which were entirely different in meaning and scope? The precaution of Zumárraga is understandable, when he prohibited the use of the word *Papa* to designate the Sovereign Pontiff, and the warning of the Crown against the use of any term that might cause confusion in the minds of the Indians, and it is understandable why religious texts in native languages are sprinkled with Spanish and Latin words, such as *Dios, Apóstoles, Yglesia, Misa, Sanctus Spiritus,* and so on.

The Mexican mission adopted the first approach for another reason, namely, the very low opinion that most religious seem to have formed of the spiritual capacities of the Indians. They showed this especially in their reluctance to dispense certain sacraments. By and large, they administered only baptism and marriage, without which the new society would not have deserved the name of Christian. Doubtless, and contrary to what has been too often lightly affirmed, a large number of Indians were admitted to confession and communion in a more or less regular fashion. But do not these sacraments, especially communion, appear as a reward for exceptional virtue and piety, rather than as the means of arriving at that virtue and piety? And with what scruples and infinite precautions the administration of penitence and the Eucharist was surrounded! I am well aware that one should bear in mind the time, and that in the sixteenth

287

century most laymen and even lay brothers took communion only a few times a year. One should also bear in mind that Spain, even before Jansen, was the least Jansenist of countries, as it still is, and that the barriers erected around the Eucharist by the Spanish religious of Mexico reflected their fears. We may except the Augustinians, whose efforts to raise the spiritual life of their neophytes I have described, and who seem to have developed to some extent the practice of regular communion. But—and this is the essential omission that has weighed heavily upon the destinies of the Church in Mexico—they, like the Dominicans and Franciscans, did not admit the natives into the monastic life or sacrament of the Order. Here again, assuredly, and even in this hasty attempt at a synthesis, one must make distinctions, and remember the experiment of the College of Tlatelolco, which does honor to the apostolic far-sightedness of the Franciscans and Viceroy Mendoza. But, although the College of Tlatelolco had perhaps an unexpected but very real success, and performed a most precious service as the center of higher Mexican studies, it was virtually stillborn. Surrounded by the suspicion and hostility of the other Orders, the secular clergy, and lay elements, it was foredoomed to failure. Even the Franciscans themselves, who had founded it, still had not enough confidence in the Indians to persevere in the struggle against the tempest that raged on all sides. They were too soon discouraged because they did not obtain from the beginning the results they had hoped for, which would have silenced its adversaries.

There is a paradox here, because the religious of New Spain loved their Indians deeply and passionately. This is why their work bore the mark of the second system, which scrupulously and systematically respected the native personality and soul. They would not countenance any attempt to Hispanicize or Europeanize the natives.[3] It was held that for the Mexican to become a true Christian he had to break entirely with his past, except, and this is an important fact, in his language, because it was clearly understood that to become a true Christian he did not at all have to become a Spaniard, that it was perfectly allowable, and even recommended, that he remain a Mexican. The Church is above nationalities and places the spiritual needs of humanity above the individual interests of the

288

various countries; she does not ask her children to betray their country or disown their race.

The missionaries' respect for the natives appears in several ways, bodily protection, for example. Forced by the necessities of religious instruction to gather the Indians into villages, by that very act they found themselves responsible for their lives. It was not enough to catechize the Indians; they must also make it possible for them to subsist. Hence, the teaching and development of agriculture, the introduction of new crops and industries, like silk, which was fomented by Zumárraga, the opening of roads to facilitate the transport of food, the building of aqueducts like that of Zempoala, the founding of hospitals [and hospices] to care for the sick and give shelter to travelers, this to spare the Indians the burdens of hospitality. The organization of primary schools, technical schools, and schools of music obeyed the same impulse. It was not a matter of imprudently submerging the country in a flood of more or less spoiled "intellectuals," but of training good workmen useful to the community and providing them with a sure and honest way to earn a living.

Respect for the soul of the natives was apparent in the very short duration of the catechumenate and the readiness with which they were admitted to baptism. It is true that for the bulk of the population the problem did not come up until a little later. The system of mass conversion as practiced by the missionaries showed in this all its advantages. Within a relatively brief period the Indians were baptized at birth, so the question of a catechumenate disappeared automatically. On the other hand it is evident that mass conversion, which solved these difficulties so quickly, was only made possible by the speed and liberality with which the pagans were admitted to baptism in the early days of the mission. In this there is a striking contrast with the precautions and delays with which the other sacraments were surrounded. This is doubtless another example of eclecticism, explainable by other reasons, which I shall examine below. The same respect was evident in the frequency and splendor of religious ceremonies, for the missionaries thought it would be cruel as well as imprudent to deprive the natives of the magnificent ceremonies that long heredity had made a necessity for them. It should be remarked above all that, although the spectacular pantomimes and edifying plays, which were closely connected with the service, and which were produced on feast days, and inevitably of Christian inspiration, were entirely and uniquely native in the actors and language.

Finally, and especially, this respect is evident in the jealous solicitude of the religious to protect the Indians from contact with the Europeans. The villages in which the missionaries had gathered them were purely native villages, from which Europeans were excluded, and with them their abuses and the deplorable examples which they too frequently afforded. The priests were practically the masters of these villages, and this gave them a formidable power, a situation that gave rise to repeated difficulties with the civil administration, which was bothered by the temporal power of the religious Orders, as well as with the bishops, who saw that the Indians were escaping them, and who complained of being relegated to an inferior rank. The missionaries strove to erect, or, more exactly, to maintain another barrier between the Christian Indians and the European menace, the barrier of language. Never, despite the formal orders of the Crown, did they consent to teach Castilian, except to an elite. The primary instruction given to the masses remained a purely native instruction, and, to remedy the multiplicity of tongues, the religious limited themselves to the use of Nahuatl, the principal Indian language. The consequence of this method was that every missionary was obliged to have a solid linguistic training. So most of the religious learned Nahuatl, and frequently also the less important languages spoken in the provinces under the charge of their Orders. Thus there came into being a whole native literature: dictionaries, grammars, catechisms, collections of sermons, *confesionarios,* and so on, only a minute part of which has survived The great names [among the authors] are Fray Alonso de Molina, Fray Andrés de Olmos, Fray Maturino Gilberti, and Fray Bernardino de Sahagún.

It is no less evident that Christianity could hardly help being a novelty. This, indeed, was the first thing that seems to have swept it along. Assuredly, there was no desire at all to turn the Indians into Spaniards. It seems, nevertheless, that the main purpose of the missionaries was not to institute a new formalism, but to create a new environment, in which to allow a new spirit to unfold. Before the arrival of the Spaniards, paganism had permeated the whole life of the Indians, from birth to death, from the temple to the hearth, in war and in peace. Such was the life that had to be imbued with Christianity. The Indian once saw his pagan dieties on every hand; he was obsessed by them and could not get them out of his mind. From that point on, it would be Christ who obsessed him; he would see Him or His priests on every hand; from birth to death he would be a member of the Church of Christ. He would find Christ in the hearts of His servants, who had abandoned everything to come and work for his physical well-being and his eternal health. He would find Him in the monasteries, where he was taught the catechism, reading, and writing; in the churches, where magnificent ceremonies were staged; in the work-shops, where he was taught a trade; in the hospitals, where he would be cared for when sick. He would find Him in the streets and square of his village. Here stood the church; there the processions marched past; and there was the stage for the next *auto sacramental*. Christ would pursue him even within his family, which he could establish only according to His law, even in his own house, where he would hear the bells ringing for services, or where the catechist would come to summon him to Mass or school. Christ would pursue him even in his pleasures, for all his pagan diversions had been replaced by Christian diversions, just as brilliant, just as animated, just as seductive. He was born, lived, and died, in Christ.[4] The missionaries of Mexico transmitted to their Indians a whole Christianity, for Christianity really deserves its name only when it informs and penetrates, when it becomes all the life of a man, even in his slightest act and most fleeting thoughts.

It would be a strange mistake to ascribe to me the intention of denigrating this [Christian] work, admirable in so many ways. But I am obliged to say that it had its hidden weaknesses, rather, in a single but capital one, which is implied by the constant presence of *foreign* missionaries. I said a while back that the missionaries of Mexico passionately loved their Indians; but they loved them as children, or as some parents love their children, never resigning themselves to seeing them grow up. The Indians could not entitle themselves *gente de razón,* a term reserved for whites and mestizos.[5] This feeling is a partial explanation of why the religious did not teach them Castilian and why they did not give them priests of their own race. Ignorance of Castilian had the immediate advantage of shielding the Indians from the dangerous contact of the European; but it created a gulf between the two elements which kept the Indian mass outside the general evolution of the country.[6] The religious served as guides for the administration and as intermediaries [between it and the Indians]; but when they disappeared, or when their zeal was extinguished, the bridge was broken. The Indian communities, disoriented, and incapable of getting along without the direction [of the missionaries], found themselves abruptly face to face with the Europeans, with whom they collided. The Indians were once more isolated, morally above all, and retreated within themselves, and the result is that today one of the essential problems of Mexico is to incorporate the Indian into civil and civilized life.[7]

Children were baptized very young, because their godparents were there to look after them. For a similar reason the missionaries liberally granted baptism to [adult] Indians, for they counted on being always at their side to see that they fulfilled their engagements. But they hardly even dreamed of admitting them to the priesthood, for it would have implied an emancipation that they were not planning. A native clergy seemed useless to them, and the mere thought of a native episcopate would have been regarded as nonsensical, running counter to the system of tutelage. Nevertheless, there was a grave danger here. Lacking a complete native clergy, the Church of New Spain could never attain a sufficiently national character, and this fact, perhaps, explains in large part the history of Catholicism in Mexico and the hostility with which governments have persecuted it for more than a century.

As always, however, the problem looks much simpler on paper than it was in reality, for the evolution of New Spain seems to have been shaped by forces beyond the will of man. Indeed, one runs up against an almost insurmountable obstacle, namely, the ethnic complexity of the country.[8] The problem of forming a native clergy has not been easy to solve even in China, which has a relatively strong racial unity, where the whites are all foreign subjects, and where yellow bishops could be nominated, directing a yellow clergy and yellow Christians. Such was not the case in Mexico. Side by side with the Indian mass were the mestizos, whose numbers increased from day to day, and a white minority, very important in civil offices, social position, and wealth. In such conditions would it have been possible to create a native clergy? It is self-evident that such a solution would have been exceedingly dangerous. Even if the Spaniards had been without color prejudice, can one believe that the viceroy would have admitted as an equal a purely Indian archbishop of Mexico? Would the white population, especially the white clergy, have submitted to the orders of Indian bishops? Moreover, it would have been virtually impossible to separate geographically the Indians from the rest of the population, give them an Indian clergy all their own, and Indian bishops.[9] And then what could have been done with the innumerable mestizos? [The creation of an Indian clergy] might have split the population into two distinct societies, distrusting and hating each other, and if later the Indian clergy should be swept away in some tempest, the situation of the Indians would be worse than it was when the missionaries disappeared. When Independence proclaimed the political equality of Indians, whites, and mestizos, all of whom were now Mexican citizens, the situation became more complicated. A while back I mentioned the example of China, where the formation of a native clergy was possible because the whites there are, from a legal point of view, foreigners. Now, foreigners who profit by the hospitality of a country, any country, cannot claim the right of having their own clergy, and, normally, when they have no priests of their own they go to the national clergy. But in Mexico the whites are no more foreigners than the Indians, and there is no reason to sacrifice either group.[10]

A comparison will bring the problem closer and show its complexity more clearly. However odd it may seem at first glance, the difficulties of Mexico bring to my mind the situation in Algeria. Despite their obvious and considerable differences, which it would be unnecessary to point out, in one respect the two countries present a striking analogy. In both there is a strong minority of Europeans in the face of a native multitude. Indeed, outside their own continent, Europeans are either a crushing majority or a tiny minority. In the first case one may say that the native problem never arises; in the second, it is more easily solved, because the life of the country has not been disturbed by the massive introduction of new elements. The Europeans do not establish themselves permanently, do not own the soil, and the agrarian question can arise only among the natives, not between natives and Europeans.[11] In Algeria, the ethnic complexity of the population has brought about problems like those of Mexico. The analogy does not carry over into the religious terrain, because the Europeans in Algeria are Christians, at least nominally, while the natives are Moslems. But it is evident that if the Moslems of Algeria should suddenly be converted *en masse,* the same difficulties would arise as those of Mexico, equally great, in the formation of a native clergy. Whoever knows Algeria, even superficially, cannot imagine that the European colonists would consent to live under the authority of a *bicot* bishop. The unjust contempt that they have for the Kabyle Christians is sufficiently revealing in this regard.

For all these reasons it seems that the organization of a complete native clergy in Mexico would not have been practicable. Even such open proponents of a native clergy as Ribadeneyra do not seem to have envisaged the possibility of a native episcopate.[12] But, by the force of circumstances, because there were no longer enough foreign priests, little by little the Indians were admitted to holy orders, save that it was done haphazardly, without method and without a general policy on the part of the episcopate.[13] The Indian priests were relegated to small country parishes, given subordinate posts, and the matter ended in the existence of two clergies, who did not know each other, who loved each other not at all, and whose mutual antagonism may be symbolized by the rivalry of the two Virgins, the Indian *Virgen de Guadalupe* and the Spanish *Virgen de los Remedios* ("La Gachupina")[14]: a poor Indian clergy for the Indians, and a white clergy, to which the great dignitaries belonged, for the whites.[15]

If one wished to point out the extreme consequences of this lack of cohesion and equilibrium, one would be led to examine, not only the religious history of Mexico in the nineteenth century, but even more recent events [the Cristero revolt] which have violently disturbed

Mexican opinion, and which would be difficult to appraise here. It will be understood why I have refrained from undertaking a statement which would be manifestly premature. It is not indispensable, however, to know in detail the evolution of Mexico in order to grasp the significance of the early evangelization and divine the influence it had on the destiny of the country. I hope, at least, that these last observations of mine will allow the reader to understand that, in the religious domain as in the others, the sixteenth century was the important period, the period in which Mexico was created, and of which the rest of her history has been only the almost inevitable development.

Appendix I

PREFACE TO THE SPANISH EDITION OF 1947

THE book here offered in translation to the Spanish-speaking public is the result of investigations undertaken between 1922 and 1932, edited in the summer of the latter year, and printed in the winter of 1932–1933. On the whole, therefore, the work reflects the knowledge and thought of the author in 1932, and the additions and corrections he was able to make in the proofs turned out to be of little importance, in quality as well as in number. What I have just said will suffice to convince the Spanish or Spanish American reader that my essay would require, not perhaps a total revision, but at least copious additions and rectifications. Indeed, since 1932 a great deal of work has been done everywhere, especially in Mexico, on the facts and the men that constitute the body of my study: historical and archaeological monographs on regions and monuments, particularly religious ones; biographies of conquistadors, bishops, friars, and priests; editions or new editions of documents and chronicles; essays and articles of all kinds—all of which have been published in such abundance that, although I thought I might list them here, I had to give it up for fear of making unjust or regrettable omissions. Moreover, I should have had to take into account all the work that has been done in the very wide field of missions and mission methodology. It will be enough to mention, for example, all the material, historical or methodological, accumulated in France by the *Revue d'Histoire des Missions,* and in Belgium by the

Semaines de Missiologie of Louvain. I myself have published an article on the methods of the Jesuit missionaries in Brazil, which may yield useful points of comparison.[1] Circumstances, however, have not permitted me to gather up the results of this great effort. Here in this African capital, which is so populous, vibrant, and active, but which is also naturally more preoccupied with the problems of its own continent than with those of America, I lack the time and the means to undertake the work of revision which would have been the only proper way to acknowledge the honor accorded me in translating my work into the language of the missionaries of New Spain. Since, however, this task is denied me, and since I must resign myself to having this translation published as the original was published, and since also, to make a long story short, we cannot spend our lives redoing our work in a chimerical and sterile quest for perfection, I should like at least, in a few brief pages, to point out several things that seem to me to be of special interest, to examine certain questions or objections made by friendly and benevolent critics, and, finally, to make some observations of a very general nature on the meaning of my essay.

It will be readily understood that the two chapters of my book that perhaps stand in need of the most important revisions are those that treat of the chronology of the founding of the convents and the monastic architecture of New Spain in the sixteenth century. Indeed, chronology and architecture are the fields in which documentation, either in texts or monuments, has a decisive importance, and in which the publication of a few lines or the photographs of a previously unknown building is enough to demolish the most attractive theory, or at least to modify profoundly the most well-founded (or apparently well-founded) statements. I do not mean by this that these two chapters require a complete rewriting. I still think they are accurate in the main, but only in the main. In their details there would be a considerable amount of correcting and amplifying to do, on the basis of the studies published since 1932 and the investigations pursued during recent years. To cite a single example: The matter of "open air chapels" has been studied in detail, and perhaps definitively, by García Granados, in a work published by the *Archivo Español de Arte y Arqueología* in 1935.[2] Something similar, but of smaller dimensions, occurs in the pages devoted to feasts and plays. Even after my book was published, I have kept up my interest in the plays (*fiestas*) of Moors and

Christians,[3] and Rojas Garcidueñas has published studies of the Mexican theater [4] which, if they had appeared a few years earlier, would have been truly useful to me.

When I presented my book at the Sorbonne as my principal thesis for the doctorate, on May 13, 1933, Professor Henri Hauser, after making a number of very interesting observations on the evangelization of Mexico by the Spanish missionaries, expressed regret that to my pages on catechism, sacraments, liturgy, religious plays, and a native clergy, I had not added a chapter devoted especially to the study of Mexican spiritual life in the sixteenth century. And Professor Martinenche, alluding to the work of Sor Juana [Inés de la Cruz], added that this famous woman of letters of the seventeenth century could hardly have been a sudden and unexpected phenomenon, but must have had precursors that would explain her appearance. I do not know up to what point one can explain the appearance of figures so far out of the main stream, like Sor Juana, and I should say the same, for example, of a mystic like Santa Teresa. Nevertheless, I still believe that a study of Mexican spiritual life in the sixteenth century would have fallen outside the scope of my work. That, however, does not mean that the subject itself does not have the greatest interest for me, and I was so convinced of it that I immediately began to collect materials on mystic problems and increase my knowledge of them in general, especially of Spanish mysticism, with the intention of writing an article or perhaps a small volume on the subject. But several circumstances, such as lack of time and especially of materials, induced me little by little to give up my project, which I have just placed in the hands of a young Spanish Capuchin now residing in France, Father Benito de Ros, brother of Father Fidèle de Ros, the author of an excellent book on Francisco de Osuna.[5] I should not like to spoil the work that he has undertaken; but, leaving to one side the general aspect of the problem, I think it will be proper for me to make a few marginal notes here on the spiritual life of New Spain in the sixteenth century.

Naturally, the Spaniards brought to America the Catholic tradition that prevailed in the mother country, together with the corpus of ideas, sentiments, and customs that it encompassed. In the spiritual life of Mexico, therefore, are to be found all the basic and common elements of Catholic spiritual life. So one should not give great importance to the fact that the Franciscan Fray Juan de Goana translated into Nahuatl certain homilies of St. John Crisostom, or that the Augustinians taught their Indians certain prayers of St. Thomas Aquinas, or that the first book printed in Mexico was a translation of *La Escala Espiritual* of St. John Climacus, an author whose popularity in the Spanish world is well attested by the Toledo translation of 1504, and by that of Fray Luis de Granada.[6] Nevertheless, one must underline a few influences that seem to have operated with greater force upon the religious tendencies of New Spain and perhaps contributed to impose upon them certain specific traits. It is true that in some cases it was a matter of the [proper] subjects of interrogation rather than anything else. Did Fray Pedro de Gante bring with him from Germany and Flanders anything from that school of mystics best known under the name of Ruysbroeck, which had such a wide influence at the end of the Middle ages? Did Fray Alonso de la Vera Cruz bring something of the spirit and thought of his illustrious friend, Fray Luis de León? Was there, as in Spain, some influence of the Jews who swarmed into Mexico during the colonial period?[7] These questions can be answered only after long investigation. In other cases, however, we are on firmer ground. The recent studies by Bataillon and Silvio Zavala[8] have demonstrated that there was an influence of Erasmus and St. Thomas More, who, because of their well-known friendship, influenced each other. And perhaps we may see in that humanistic current one of the possible sources of the genius of Sor Juana.

Another influence that I insist upon even more strongly, for I do not believe it has been pointed out as it deserves, is that of St. Antoninus of Florence. We know that [Francisco de] Vitoria translated the *Summa Aurea* of this Dominican theologian,[9] and that Francisco de Osuna read his works.[10] We know, moreover, that his great confession entitled *Defecerunt* was printed several times in Spain in the fifteenth and sixteenth centuries. Hence it seems that in the Peninsula (I say Peninsula because there are indications that what can be said of Spain can be said equally of Portugal), St. Antoninus of Florence was widely read. It seems, furthermore, that he was read just as widely in Mexico. The archbishop of Florence [Antoninus] appears among the authors cited by Vasco de Quiroga;[11] the *Summa Antonina* is mentioned twice in the volume of documents entitled *Libros y Libreros en el Siglo XVI;*[12] Fray Juan Bautista, in the first part of his *Advertencias para los confesores de los naturales,* frequently cites St. Antoninus;[13] and, finally, during my stay in Mexico I myself had in my hands a copy of the *Defecerunt,* lent to me by the frustrated Luis González Obregón from his marvelous personal library. It was printed in Alcalá in 1526, and bears the following inscription: "De San Antonio de Tetzcoco." According to what González Obregón told me, in Alfredo Chavero's opinion the *Defecerunt* was widely circulated among the religious of New Spain.

I have mentioned the volume entitled *Libros y Libreros en el Siglo XVI*. Irving A. Leonard's *Romances of Chivalry in the Spanish Indies* is a work of the same character and scope.[14] A close study of these two volumes would probably lead to important conclusions about the reading habits of the cultured people of Mexico in the sixteenth century. I already hinted at some of this in my reference to Antonio de Guevara and Bernardino de Laredo.[15] Finally, it has been justly said that a study of the rules and programs of the seminaries in any country would yield information of positive value about the character of the spiritual life of the time. I do not think that one can gather much from the rules of the College of Tlatelolco, except the hint that the students did not take communion during the daily Mass. Indeed, the contrary is implied from the library catalogues studied by Father Francis B. Steck.[16] For example, it is interesting to learn that they listed letters of Erasmus and the chronicle of St. Antoninus, the presence of which confirms what I said above.

Besides all this, there are a few points which I only touched upon in passing, but which could bear closer scrutiny. [For example], abstention from conjugal relations the night before taking communion, which was imposed upon the Indians, or advised, was tied in with the whole tendency of spiritual life, but is today in large part abandoned. Its complicated and exaggerated expression in France took the form of Jansenism. This pessimistic severity—which unconsciously includes the false notion that matrimony is only a pious concession on God's part to the low instincts of sinful humanity, merely a remedy for concupiscence, while [in fact] it has higher purpose[17]—tends to disappear for two principal reasons: first, because a more exact comprehension of the sacrament [of communion] has been attained, I believe, by which sexual relations—which are not of themselves a shameful act, but a natural one, which is evil [only] outside of matrimony, but good within it—acquire, so to speak, a supernatural dignity and character, laudable or obligatory; second, by the urging of Pope Pius X in particular, the Eucharist is no longer considered to be a reward, but, on the contrary, a remedy and an encouragement, and the practice of frequent and even daily communion has become widespread, a practice entirely incompatible with abstention the night before, unless one admits the absurd hypothesis that Christians get married in order to live in perpetual chastity, without any desire to beget children. The historic problem of frequent communion in Spain has been studied by Father Zarco Cuevas, who was killed during the Spanish Civil War, in a little book which I did not know when I wrote my essay on the evangelization of Mexico, but which I was able to use in my article on the evangelization of Brazil.[18] This little book is very useful and interesting, although somewhat out of date—it was published in 1912—and could be amplified, not only by the studies I point out in my article just cited, but also by several others. For example, there are interesting items in the book of Father Gerardo de San Juan de la Cruz, C. D., on Julián de Avila, in which one will find cases of secular priests who, well along in the sixteenth century, took communion three times a week and even daily.[19] An examination of the opinions of Father Zarco and the data supplied by other writers, as well as a comparison with the Jesuit missions in Brazil, lead to a certain conclusion: that, in propagating the practice of the Eucharist, the majority of the friars of New Spain, with the notable exception of Fray Nicolás de Agreda, Fray Pedro de Agurto, and Fray Juan Bautista, were much more hesitant than the Spanish clergy, who were operating in a very different environment, and more hesitant than the Portuguese Jesuits of Brazil, who carried on their missionary task among people less civilized and less endowed than the Mexicans. In this matter, as in many others, an objective study makes one believe that the Jesuits distinguished themselves principally by the reasoned and intelligent boldness of their procedures.

Two other points remain which I wish to bring out in these brief comments. I said that the Indian children educated in the convents were taught to practice silent prayer. I said later that the Augustinians strove to initiate the Indians into the contemplative life. It would be worth our while to carry these comments deeper, to determine, if possible, what this contemplative life consisted of, and what kind of silent prayer was taught to the Indian children. Moreover, I also mentioned the existence of confraternities of the Immaculate Conception in the Franciscan hospitals. It would be of interest to attempt to establish the place that this kind of prayer had in Mexican communities. It was definitely Franciscan, for

301

the religious of that Order admitted and venerated the Immaculate Conception of the Virgin many centuries before it was officially proclaimed as dogma by Pope Pius IX in 1854.

The very meaty and favorable review of my book by Dr. Angel María Garibay K., in the *Gaceta Oficial del Arzobispado de México*,[20] poses the problem of another cult, that of the Virgin of Guadalupe. Dr. Garibay does not explain "the minor place [I give to] the tradition of Guadalupe in its historicity and its influence on the evangelization." It is true that in my book Our Lady of Guadalupe is given only four pages, and I can understand why it seems too little. As I stated in the subtitle of my study and repeated in my Introduction, I have preferably limited myself to the activity of the friars, and I thought I had demonstrated that the cult of Guadalupe was not their invention. It was born, and it matured and triumphed, under the active influence of the episcopate (Zumárraga and Montúfar), in the midst of Dominican and Augustinian indifference, and despite the hostile anxiety of the Franciscans. But, in a more general article on the spiritual life of Mexico, these considerations would be no hindrance to giving a more important place to the cult of Guadalupe.[21] As for the historicity of her appearances, which is an obscure problem in itself, and which has been obscured even more by the passionate arguments of those who have discussed it publicly, I thought it had no relevance to the topic of my book, for which reason I took it up in a special article.[22]

There is another criticism that I wish to answer here, to put things in their proper perspective. It was published in *El Debate* of Madrid, November 4, 1934, and was, to be sure, flattering enough. It was not signed, but there is reason to believe that its author was Angel Herrera himself, the former editor of the paper, who at the time held the high position of president of the Junta Central de Acción Católica in Spain. It runs as follows: "We are astonished that the eminent author, speaking of the difficulty of introducing Christian marriage among the Indians, should say that natural marriage is no less indissoluble than sacramental marriage. Ricard knows very well that, although natural marriage is indissoluble in itself, legal marriage is even more so. A natural marriage may sometimes be dissolved; a legal one, never." I suppose that the author is alluding to the so-called Pauline privilege, and it does not annoy me to admit he is right. What happened was that I thought it necessary to insist

302

upon the existence of natural marriage, its recognition by the Church, and the impossibility of dissolving it in the majority of cases, for my book is not addressed solely to theologians and professors of canon law, and it deals with a matter beyond the knowledge of many people, except such specialists. This preoccupation made me put the business of the Pauline privilege far back in my mind, to the point of silencing it altogether, with the extenuating circumstance that it seems to have been seldom invoked in Mexico because of the total and almost immediate conversion of the Indians.

Finally, in a long and equally flattering article published in the French review *Etudes,*[23] Father Brou, S. J., hints at a difficulty which, in his eyes, occurs in a passage of Clavijero, concerning the problem of [forming] a native clergy. Clavijero speaks of thousands of "American" priests, adding that many of them were parish priests, canons, and doctors. And [Brou] wonders whether there is not a contradiction between the statement of the Mexican Jesuit [Clavijero] and mine, [for I said] that in colonial Mexico the native priests who did appear little by little were restricted to small parishes and subordinate posts. Actually, there is no contradiction between the two statements. Father Brou realizes that it all hinges upon the meaning of the word "American," as used by Clavijero. One does not have to know Spanish American literature very thoroughly to assert that the word means Criollo, and that Clavijero was referring only to Spanish priests born in America.

Furthermore, it seems to me that in Father Brou's article, as well as in the final statement of another critic, who also speaks of my essay with evident sympathy, that is, Father Lino Gómez Canedo, O. F. M., present editor of the *Archivo Americano* of Madrid,[24] there is some misunderstanding. I tried to show that certain aspects of the activity of the Spanish missionaries, especially their attitude of "tutelage" toward the Indians, and their decision to keep them out of the priesthood and the religious Orders, had unfavorable consequences for the history of the Church and perhaps for the Mexican nation itself. This, however, was a statement of fact, not a censure. For the rest, I said that it was easy for us, after four centuries and in view of later events, to understand these consequences, but that in the sixteenth century one would have had to be endowed with the gift of prophecy to foresee them. On the other hand, I did not pass over the enormous difficulties of all kinds which the Spanish missionaries had to struggle with. Nevertheless, I probably did not express myself with sufficient clarity, since not only Father Brou and Father Gómez Canedo, but also the reviewer of *El Debate*—all three of whom are very kind to me —gathered the impression that I was censuring the missionaries. Perhaps out of friendliness for me they did not pursue this impression to its end, but I think it is behind several of their criticisms. For example, Father Gómez Canedo says:

It very infrequently happens, certainly, that one meets with an author with the preparation and equilibrium that Ricard shows in his work. He knows and recognizes the weak points and advances his conclusions with the greatest restraint. But, since we have to do with an essay in the interpretation and evaluation of facts, divergencies in shades of meaning are inevitable. Take, for example, those pointed out by Father Brou, S. J., in his stimulating commentary on Ricard's book. I should like to call attention to the testimony of Father Jiménez, in his *Vida de Fray Martín de Valencia* (AIA, Vol. 26, p. 211), which seems to demonstrate that from very early times the missionaires foresaw the trouble that might arise from their excessive tutelage of the Indians. When did they change it? Was a different procedure possible and preferable at the time? I confess that I am troubled by the same doubts with respect to the other facts analyzed by Robert Ricard.

Well, I should like to say that the questions Father Gómez Canedo brings up are the very ones I asked myself, and the same doubts that trouble him troubled me also. But, although the interpretation of facts is always open to discussion, the facts are still there. "Was a different procedure possible and preferable at the time?" I don't know, but what I do know is that the missionaries did practice the system of tutelage, because that is a fact. And what I also know is that in the long run the system put great obstacles in the way of establishing the Church and developing the Mexican nation, because that is another fact. And that is all. I neither approve nor condemn; I report. Save that I do not merely report, but strive to understand.

For his part the writer in *El Debate* says:

The conclusions [of Ricard] have not entirely convinced us. In our judgment the missionaries did well to break with the whole Mexican religious tradition, which in fact was abominable. They also did well not to force [the natives] to learn Castilian. Hispanization would occur, and did occur, more gently. With respect to the formation of a native clergy, Ricard himself recognizes that in practice it met with insuperable difficulties. And the author himself proves that something, possibly enough, was done in this direction when he gives us the portrait of the twelfth bishop of Oaxaca, Nicolás del Puerto (1679–1681), the first native priest elevated to the episcopate. Would any other nation of the time have done as much?

I am afraid that in his last question my colleague of *El Debate* has confused apologetic with historical writing. I think that in my essay I did the Spanish missionaries all the justice they deserve—and they deserve a full and generous portion, for their work on the whole was admirable— but it is possible that my critic, consciously or unconsciously, was wounded in his legitimate patriotism by the fact that my book was not from nose to tail, so to speak, an absolute and unconditional eulogy of the evangelization of Mexico.[25] If this is the case, I confess that we see things with different eyes, because I never believe in pronouncing absolute and unconditional eulogies, even when I am, by excessive courtesy, the object of them. Not only do I not believe in them, but they fill me with instant distrust. As Manuel Toussaint said very well a few months ago: "Unconditional eulogy is a censure rather than a eulogy."[26] The truth is that I have in the bottom of my heart, along with the conviction of my own limitations and gaps in my knowledge, a feeling that every human activity in one way or another is imperfect. Not even the saints are perfect, in the sense that sainthood is not the equivalent of infallibility, and that heroism in virtue may very well be accompanied by some defect or other of temperament, natural gifts, or intelligence. A saint can be a bad preacher, can have an exceedingly bad artistic taste, or a bad memory. For this reason I have always found it impossible to write praises [of them] without shades or reservations, and this state of mind has led me to point out the inevitable flaws in the work of the missionaries in Mexico. In this there is not the remotest intent of malevolent censure, and, as far as my book is concerned, it would not be necessary to set oneself up as an advocate of the Spanish missionaries, since they are not on trial. Outside the cases in which crime is evident and horrifying, the historian is an interpreter, not a judge, which, especially in this field, only God can be.

I have thought it necessary to insist upon these points, so that the misunderstanding about the final reflections that I am about to make will not be repeated, and their meaning will be more clearly seen. I insist that they are what I have just said they are, reflections, suggestions, and even questions that I put to myself and the friendly reader, and not at all a hostile and systematic censure. In these lines I shall be able more precisely to define my purpose in writing my book, and to put in relief a few conclusions that perhaps have not been as clear as they should have been.

I shall begin by reminding [the reader] that one of the most noteworthy phenomena of Hispano-Portuguese colonization is the Christianization, profound or superficial, but indisputable, of the immense territories, or, more exactly, the numerous native groups that were subjugated by the two Peninsular powers. Even today the Philippine Islands are still the great Christian block of the Far East. In this grandiose mission structure of the Iberian world, the historian who is interested in the origins of all these new Churches has only the embarrassment of choice. The Philippines themselves, which I have just mentioned, the activity of the Jesuits in Brazil or Portuguese India, San Luis Beltrán, and New Granada, the conversion of Peru, the [Jesuit] reductions in Paraguay, are so many other matters among which one may be permitted to hesitate.

My reasons for choosing New Spain are various. The first is that it is the region, with Peru, in which the Spaniards found the most flourishing native civilization. Equally, without doubt, also as in Peru, it is the country in which the colonizing and evangelizing effort was most efficacious and intelligent. Finally, it is the country in which a great mass of the native population lived and still lives. Besides, there were technical advantages that did not exist in the same degree elsewhere: easily determined geographical divisions, a sharply marked chronological framework, and a sufficient amount of preparatory work, some of it excellent.

I shall mention in second place an idea that is daily gaining greater acceptance among the theologians concerned with mission problems, the idea that the essential purpose of a mission among the pagans is not the conversion of individuals, but above all the establishment of a visible Church, with all the functions and institutions that the expression "visible Church" implies. I should not like to put myself forward as a theologian —which I am not—, but let me say that this concept, which is partially new, fits perfectly within the logic of Catholic doctrine. If divine grace is what converts a man (and I use the word "converts" in its wide as well as in its narrow sense), and if the Church, by means of its sacraments, is the normal agent of spreading divine grace, since it is the intermediary between God and His creatures, it is logical to suppose that the principal task of the missionary consists in placing the normal means of conversion at the disposition of the pagans. It is because of this fundamental trait that the Catholic mission, I do not say contrasts, for the word would be too strong, with the Protestant missions of certain denominations, but at least is different from them. In many Protestant missions individual conversion occupies first place, and I think that this concept also fits within the logic of the spirit of the Reformation. This has strongly attracted my attention in the book of Raoul Allier,[27] which I have cited many times, and in which, to be sure, this characteristic of certain Protestant missions stands out even more prominently, because his is a psychological study. I emphasize this point because I think it would not be possible to complete a monograph on the Protestant mission precisely like a monograph on the Catholic mission, and because all these reasons have induced me to put the Church in first place and to consider the missionaries, in this methodological study, doubtless as converters, but even more as founders of the Church.

What were the characteristics of the foundation of the Mexican Church? What appears at first glance is that this Church was founded by religious; it was, to adopt the words of Ramírez Cabañas, a Church of friars. It will be said that this is what generally happens in mission territories, and that, although the secular clergy [also] works in them, it is commonly done in the form of more or less recent societies, like the Society of Foreign Missions of Paris, or that of the African Mission of Lyon, but whose rules, in spite of certain canonical difference, practically make them organizations similar to the regular Orders. Also, moreover, in modern missions the general rule is that in one apostolic vicarate there is only one society, and that the apostolic vicar himself is a member of it, so that the actions of the society and those of the bishop are mixed and fused together. In the American missions of the sixteenth century, established before the Propaganda [Fidei], that unity did not exist. On one side were the bishops and the secular clergy, few in number and mediocre in quality; on the other, the friars, who remained completely outside the episcopal authority, even when they served as parish priests, and, far from being restricted to this or that diocese, depending on their Order, they were scattered all over the country. As a result, therefore, their activity was outside the episcopate and parallel to it at the same time. And, since in Mexico the religious were much more numerous than the clergy subjected to the bishops, and since they had a better discipline and

307

organization, and, finally, since they were on a higher moral and intellectual plane, there is nothing surprising in the fact that, taking things as a whole, their activity surpassed that of the bishops, and even obscured it in many cases. It is natural, therefore, that a history of the foundation of the Mexican Church should be limited essentially to a study of the methods of the Mendicant Orders.

These very methods, it seems to me, are characterized by eclecticism, an eclecticism that I believe to have been spontaneous and instinctive, perhaps because the systematic spirit is one of the things most alien to the Spanish temperament. Moreover, Europe in the sixteenth century had had a very brief experience in missionizing. This was an undeniable handicap for the evangelization of Mexico, although, because of her long contact with the Moslem world, Spain was perhaps the one European nation best prepared for a great missionary enterprise. But this handicap had at least one advantage, that of protecting the friars from preconceived ideas and too theoretical views, and allowed them to look upon the problems with fresh eyes. In these psychological and historical reasons I see the explanation of the mixed character of their methods, which I emphasized in the Conclusions of my book.

In them I also tried to show that the main weakness of the evangelizing work accomplished by the Spaniards can be attributed to the failure of the College of Tlatelolco and to the vast gap made by the absence of a complete native clergy. This conclusion, as we have seen, is what has occasioned the severest criticism of my book. Nevertheless, I am still convinced of the truth of my statement, at least in its general lines. The Mexican Church, like that of Peru, which I have also had the opportunity of studying, although not so closely, was an incomplete foundation.[28] Rather, a Mexican Church was not founded [at all], and a Creole Church was barely founded. What was founded, before and above all, was a Spanish Church, organized along Spanish lines, governed by Spaniards, in which the native Christians played the minor part of second-class Christians. The rule of the [Royal] Patronato, to which I did not give in my book the importance it deserves even from a methodological point of view, accentuated still further this aspect of the Church in America. It is true that the king was not the head of this Church, and that he never aspired, even remotely, to shake off the authority of the Holy See. But it sufficed, practically, for the monarch to have the disposal of bishops, clergy, and friars, to make its national character, that is, Spanish, even stronger and more evident. In short, a Spanish Church was imposed upon a native Christian society, and the Mexican Church appeared finally, not as an emanation of Mexico itself, but of the mother country, something brought in from without, a foreign framework applied to the native community. It was not a national Church, but a colonial Church, for Mexico was a colony, not a nation.

These last remarks show that if a mistake was made, it was an inevitable mistake. As I said in my book, only if one had the gift of prophecy could one foresee that some day Mexico would cease being a colony and become an independent nation. So it was everyone's mistake, not just the missionaries', and the few who tried to avoid it, or who pointed it out, were precisely the missionaries themselves. The fact remains, however, that it weighed heavily upon the history of Catholicism and the destiny of the Church in Mexico. This final statement underlines the interest of the study of the Spiritual Conquest of New Spain. Such a study allows one not only to explain how a new Church comes into being, but also allows one to see, more clearly than in many other cases, the decisive influence that such a beginning can have on the whole life of a nation.

ROBERT RICARD.

University of Algiers. [1940].

Appendix II

ESSAY ON SOURCES

THE present study is based upon published and unpublished archival documents, and upon chronicles and the like, either in late editions or in more or less rare old ones. It is particularly necessary to examine these chronicles and documents, determine their interrelationship or points of agreement, and appraise their historical value. Before undertaking such critical study, however, I must list the principal collections of [published] archival documents I have used. Four such collections are singularly precious for the student of the religious history of Mexico in the sixteenth century:

1. The documentary appendix (270 pages) of the biography of Zumárraga by the Mexican historian and bibliographer, Joaquín García Icazbalceta.[1] This appendix includes a series of documents of the first importance for the history of the Church in Mexico from 1529 to 1548. A few others, which Icazbalceta was able to consult only in the extracts made by Muñoz, have [since] been published in full by Father Mariano Cuevas.

2. The *Nueva Colección de documentos para la historia de México* published in 1886–1892, also by Icazbalceta. This collection (called *nueva* to distinguish it from an earlier one which he published in 1858–1870), fills five volumes, of which the first two (1886 and 1889) are especially useful. They contain numerous letters and reports written by religious, and a large part of the second volume is a collection of documents concerning the Franciscans, known as the *Códice Franciscano,* in which

one may find a multitude of informative items about the evangelizing procedures employed by them.[2]

3. Volume 15 of the *Documentos inéditos o muy raros para la historia de México,* published by Genaro García in 1907. It is entitled *El Clero de México durante la dominación española según el archivo inédito archiepiscopal metropolitano.* The editor is hostile to the missionaires, but this volume of documents is very important from all points of view, and, despite some carelessness in the printing of dates, will be of great value to the historian who wishes to determine the chronology of the religious history of Mexico in the sixteenth century.

4. The *Documentos inéditos del siglo XVI para la historia de México,* collected and annotated by Mariano Cuevas. S. J., and published under the direction of Genaro García, Mexico, 1914. These documents are from the Archivo General de Indias and are almost all of the greatest interest. They are introduced by biographical notes, full and generally accurate, as is the index. Several letters of Zumárraga [included among them] had already been published by Fabié, but that does not diminish the merit of this excellent volume. Father Cuevas, in his *Historia de la Iglesia en México,* also cited or reproduced a number of unpublished documents from the Archivo General de Indias (AGI).

Along with these great collections limited to Mexico there are also two collections of useful documents having to do with Spanish America as a whole and the history of Spanish colonization. The first of these collections is the *Cartas de Indias* (Madrid, 1877), which is too heavy and unwieldy; the second, the *Colección de documentos inéditos relativos al descubrimiento, conquista y colonización de las posesiones españolas en América y Oceanía, sacados en su mayor parte del Real Archivo de Indias* (Madrid, 1864–1889), 42 vols., generally cited as *Colección de documentos inéditos del Archivo de Indias,* here as CDIAI. Both collections are well known. The second has been severely criticized, not without reason. Nevertheless, a large number of important documents can be found in it, the originals of which could seldom be examined except with difficulty and a waste of time.

Several partial collections of published documents should also be mentioned: the first volume of the *Colección de documentos históricos . . . referentes al Arzobispado de Guadalajara,*[3] and the letters of Zumárraga published by Jiménez de la Espada, Fabié, and Serrano y Sanz.[4] I have myself published a number of documents concerning the history of the religious Orders in Mexico, in the *Revue d'Histoire Franciscaine* (RHF) and the *Journal de la Société des Américanistes* (JSA),[5] also the *Lettres de Fr. Alonso de Montúfar, second archevêque de México,* in my *Études et documents pour l'histoire missionnaire de l'Espagne et du Portugal.*[6]

Some of the documents I published in the course of my researches are in the National Library of Madrid; others are in the Archivo General de Indias. I am listing below the unpublished documents from the AGI which I have used in my study:

Real Patronato, 1–2–9/29 *(Ramo 7°)*

"Ynformación de la vida, costumbres y naturaleza de Don Frai Bernardo de Alburquerque, electo obispo de Oajaca, dominicano y natural de Alburquerque, México, 14 de agosto de 1559".

Audiencia de México

58–3–8. Viceroy Luis de Velasco to Philip II, Mexico, September 30, 1558.

59–4–3. The *Regidores* of Huejotzingo to the King (n. d.).

60–2–16. Various Dominicans to the Council of the Indies, Mexico, September 18, 1553.

The provincials of the Franciscans, Dominicans, and Augustinians to Charles V, Mexico, September 15, 1555.

Fray Francisco de Toral to Philip II, Mexico, January 23, 1558.

Anon. to Philip II, Mexico, September 1, 1559.

Fray Francisco de Toral to Philip II, March 13, 1560.

Fray Pedro de la Peña to Philip II, July 25, 1561.

Various Dominicans to the Council of the Indies, January 22, 1564.

Audiencia de Guadalajara, 67–1–18

No. 4. The *oficiales* of New Galicia to Charles V, Compostela, December 20, 1549.

No. 7. Lic. Hernando Martínez de la Marcha to Charles V, Compostela, February 8, 1551.

No. 10. Lic. Lebrón de Quiñones to Prince Philip, Mexualan, September 10, 1554.

No. 86. Lic. Oseguera to Philip II, Guadalajara, January 29, 1563.

No. 104. Fray Pedro de Ayala, Bishop of New Galicia, to the Council of the Indies, 1563 (?).

Nos. 105 and 106. Fray Pedro de Ayala to Philip II, Guadalajara, February 6, 1565 (with duplicate).

No. 110. Same to same, Mexico, November 10, 1565.

No. 118. Same to same, New Galicia, February 29, 1566.

No. 127. Same to same, Tlazazalca, March 16, 1567.

No. 144. Same to same, Mexico, March 18, 1569.[7]

Unnumbered item. *Cédula* on the founding of the convent of Zacatecas, El Escorial, November 9, 1569.

No. 153. The Audiencia of New Galicia to Philip II, Guadalajara, March 20, 1570.

No 157. The Cathedral Chapter of Guadalajara to Philip II, Guadalajara, April 1, 1570.

Justicia de Indias

47-5-55/11. "Fr. Marcos de Alburquerque, Procurador de los Regiosos del Orden de S. Agustín que residen en la Nueva España con el Obispo, Clero de Mechoacán, sobre los malos tratamientos y vejaciones que hicieron a los Religiosos doctrineros de aquellas provincias y año de 1560 . . ."

51-6-10/27, No. 2. *Ramo 5°*. "El Arzobispo de México Don Fray Alonso de Montúfar, y Don Vasco de Quiroga, Obispo de Mechoacán, con los religiosos de Sn. Francisco, Sn. Agustín y Sto. Domingo, sobre haber adquirido cierta jurisdicción de territorio y dar malos tratos a los Indios." 1561.

Indiferente general, 146-1-8

Fray Diego de Olarte, Fray Toribio de Motolinía and Fray Alonso de Escalona to Charles V, Mexico, January 28, 1552.

Along with the unpublished documents, the official records of the Dominican chapters, the chronicle of Méndez, and the Sicardo MS should be listed. I shall speak of them later.

The bibliography of Franciscan studies on their missions in New Spain is extremely rich.[8] As general works we have three fundamental chronicles: the *Historia de los Indios de la Nueva España,* of Fray Toribio Motolinía; the *Historia Eclesiástica Indiana* (HEI), of Fray Jerónimo de Mendieta; and the *Teatro Mexicano,* of Fray Agustín de Vetancurt.[9] We do not know the exact date when Motolinía's *Historia* was completed; we only know that the *Epístola Proemial* addressed to the Conde de Benavente is dated 1541.[10] In any event, we know quite well that Motolinía was in the first Franciscan mission, the famous one of the Twelve, which is why his account, even though it is not the most complete, is perhaps the most precious, for here we have a witness who records faithfully and naïvely, but not uncritically, what he has done and what he has seen.[11] Besides, he has saved for us the substance of the biography of Martín de Valencia by Fray Francisco Jiménez, the text of which was considered lost until these very last years.[12] Unfortunately, the *Historia de los Indios* was not definitely put in final form by the author, as is proved by various passages and by the slovenliness of the composition. It is not impossible that this *Historia* and another of Motolinía's books, known by the title of *Memoriales*,[13] are two fragments of a large work on Mexico, since lost, which Mendieta may have used.[14]

This last-named did not arrive in Mexico until 1554.[15] Even so, if, among the facts relating to the primitive period that he records, he had only Motolonía to guide him, he himself saw a great deal more up to a very late date, for he began his work in 1571 and completed it in 1596.[16] Moreover, he had known a number of eye witnesses, even some of the Twelve.[17] In addition to the writings of Motolinía, to which he frequently refers,[18] he drew from those of Fray Andrés de Olmos and Fray Bernardino de Sahagún,[19] and the archives of the convent of San Francisco in Mexico City.[20] For the rest, according to the prologue of Father Domayquia, Mendieta, "in this history says nothing that he has not seen with his own eyes, and the things he has not seen he learned from trustworthy persons who had seen them, from accounts and depositions certified by notaries, and from the documents that he found in the archives of convents." [21] And then Mendieta has very remarkable gifts as a historian, such as one does not encounter in Motolinía in the same degree. Nevertheless, he can be reproached for certain regrettable lacunae. He says not a word, for example, about the seculars, whose relations with the regular clergy were seldom good; not a word about the councils by which the episcopate tried to limit the independence of the religious.[22]

Fray Agustín de Vetancurt (c. 1620–c. 1700[23]) did not have the same authority as his precursors. He leaned heavily on Mendieta, *via* Torquemada.[24] Nevertheless, he furnishes details which one looks for in vain in previous works. We do not know his source, but we have no reason not to accept them.

The reader will perhaps be astonished at my not including the *Monarquía Indiana* of Fray Juan de Torquemada among the fundamental works;[25] but up to the publication of Mendieta's *Historia* by Icazbalceta the value of his book as a source for the history of the evangelization of Mexico, and especially that of the Franciscan missions, was, it seems, greatly mistaken. Icazbalceta, in the introduction to his edition of Mendieta, clearly shows that Torquemada borrowed from his predecessor almost all his account of the Franciscan apostolate in New Spain, and makes a definite list of these borrowings.[26] The author, moreover, does not hide the fact that he was reproducing Mendieta's text, merely rearranging it, for Fray Juan Bautista, writing in 1606 on the subject of [Mendieta's] *Historia Eclesiástica Indiana,* says publicly: "It profited by falling into the hands of Fray Juan de Torquemada, guardian of the convent of Santiago Tlatelolco, my pupil and particular friend, who will give it no less life and force [than he gave to] the life and miracles of the blessed Fray Sebastián de Aparicio which he has had printed these past years." [27] Mendieta himself had bequeathed his manuscript to Fray Juan Bautista for publication, and the latter had sent it to Torquemada.

Besides these general chronicles, we have some regional chronicles that are not without importance. The oldest document of this type is the *Memorial* of Fray Diego Muñoz about the province of Michoacán, which goes back to 1583,[28] and which Mendieta and Vetancurt certainly used, summarizing and expanding it, for everything relating to that province.[29] Still, this *Memorial* of Muñoz is not a formal chronicle. One must wait until almost the middle of the seventeenth century to find an official and methodical chronicle of Michoacán. La Rea's work was not completed until 1639, and did not appear until 1643, in Mexico City.[30] La Rea's chronicle contains many details of the history of the province, but the author borrowed enormously from Torquemada, that is to say, from Mendieta, and he neglects chronology in a truly excessive way.[31] Almost contemporaneous with the work of La Rea is the chronicle of the spiritual and temporal conquest of Jalisco that Fray Antonio Tello, himself a Franciscan, composed about 1650, if one may believe Mota Padilla.[32] Icazbalceta thinks that he was twenty-five at the time, and that the interest of his documentation lies in his use of the evidence supplied by the conquerors themselves, whom he could have known, for otherwise he had recourse only to printed and well-known works.[33] Unfortunately, we have only the second book of this chronicle, of which the last twenty-four chapters were edited by Fray Jaime de Rieza Gutiérrez, and it is still incomplete. The first book is lost; the third, not by Tello, contained the biographies of the Franciscans "who evangelized the Tzacatecas, Cascanes, Tecuexes, and Huicholes of this part of the province." José López-

315

Portillo thought it would be useless to publish it, and since then it also has disappeared.[34] This is all the more regrettable in that, if Tello's chronicle was used by Mota Padilla and Frejes,[35] these last naturally did not reproduce everything that Tello says in the part that we can read, and it is probable that, if they used the rest, they left out a good many things.[36] Fray Pablo Beaumont, the second chronicler of Michoacán, who wrote at the end of the eighteenth century, does not seem to have used the *Memorial* of Muñoz, but he did know Tello and refers to Gonzaga, Torquemada, La Rea, and Vetancurt constantly. In his preface he severely criticizes La Rea's chronicle, which he thinks is too summary. He himself, he says, had recourse to the archives of the Order and to manuscript works, such as the chronicle of Espinosa. Beaumont's work, although annoyingly thrown out of balance by an interminable preamble, is therefore original in a certain sense and may be consulted with profit for the history of Michoacán and the northern missions.[37] For the history of these missions one must also read the *Crónica de la Provincia de N. S. P. S. Francisco de Zacatecas* by Fray José Arlegui, published in Mexico in 1737.[38] Father Arlegui claims to have used the archives of his Order. In any case, he is superior to most of the religious chroniclers, for he includes many chronological data. Unfortunately, this chronology is only apparently exact and is often contradictory.

Works relative to the general history of the Order, or to the history of the Order in Spain, are naturally of less interest for us. Among the authors there is hardly one that was not used by Motolinía or Mendieta, and frequently by both, who added nothing much of their own. Father Atanasio López has even demonstrated that Gonzaga (whose *De Origine Seraphicae Religionis Franciscanae,* to be sure, was published in Rome in 1587, nine years before the completion of the *Historia Eclesiástica Indiana* in 1596) drew on Mendieta for everthing regarding Mexico,[39] and at the same time used the *Memorial* of Muñoz. The very rare *Memorial* of Father Moles [40] seems to have been based on Gonzaga's work, to which the author frequently refers; but in reality, although Moles published his book five years after Gonzaga, they worked at the same time.[41] The authors who followed borrowed almost everything they said about Mexico from the essential works of Motolinía and Mendieta, either directly, or almost always by way of Gonzaga, Moles, and Torquemada. This is the case with Fray Antonio Daza, Fray Pedro de Salazar, Fray Juan de la Trinidad, and Fray Andrés de Guadalupe.[42] Although Daza leaned

heavily on Gonzaga, Moles, the *Life of Martin de Valencia* by Fray
Francisco Jiménez, the Dominican chronicle of Dávila Padilla, the *Mesa
Franca* of Fray Antonio de San Román,[43] and the *De moribus Indorum*
of Fray Toribio Motolinía,[44] he states in his "Prólogo al Letor" that he has
had in his hands many unpublished documents. Since he is a conscientious historian his evidence is not negligible.[45] It should be added that
each of the authors following Daza has ransacked his work or that of his
predecessors. Fray Manuel Barbado de la Torre, who published the first
volume of his mediocre work in 1745 in Madrid, used the works of
Vetancurt besides.[46]

The Dominican chronicles are not numerous. The principal one for this
study is that of Dávila Padilla, published in Madrid in 1596.[47] Dávila
Padilla, as he states in his preface, dated January 15, 1596, had access to
good sources of information. "This book," he says, "was written in the
Indies, which is why one speaks as if one were there. It was begun by
Fray Andrés de Moguer about forty years ago; it was continued by Fray
Vicente de las Casas and Fray Domingo de la Anunciación;[48] it was
translated into Latin by Fray Tomás Castelar, until, in the year 1589, the
general chapter of Mexico ordered me to collect all the papers and write
this history in the vulgar tongue; and it was necessary to verify the greater
part of it with living witnesses, because of the brevity with which things
had been related in the papers."[49] At the end of his chronicle he adds:
"Fray Tomás Castelar, who had come from the Province of Aragón,
wrote in Latin the lives of the saints of our Province. And his papers came
to my hands along with all those in the Province, when the chapter
ordered me to write this history, in the year 1589. And we owe to this
Father many things that he learned while he was reader in the College of
San Luis de Predicadores."[50] The chronicle of Dávila Padilla is therefore
a fundamental source, which would be even more valuable if the author
had been less miserly with chronological data and less prodigal with
edifying sentences and anecdotes, and if, being excessively concerned with
singing the personal virtues of his confreres, he had not too often put the
main task in the background.
    All the following chroniclers of the Order, whether they wrote general
chronicles or works especially dedicated to the Mexican missions, have
heavily relied on the text of Dávila Padilla. Remesal,[51] who, to be sure, is
concerned almost exclusively with Central America, shows some inde-

pendence when he treats questions already touched upon by Dávila Padilla, and he attempts to rectify some of Dávila Padilla's errors.[52] But the religious who continued the history of the Preaching Friars after Dávila Padilla, that is to say, Ojea and Franco,[53] added almost nothing new to the so-called primitive period, which, to be sure, was not the essential purpose of their work. Most facts they record happened after 1572, and most of the personages they studied lived after that date.

But we must leave a place for Fray Juan Bautista, whose *Crónica de la Provincia de Santiago de México del Orden de Predicadores* has not yet, unfortunately, been published. I was lucky enough to be able to consult a copy in Mexico, doubtless an autograph, thanks to the kindness of its owner, Federico Gómez de Orozco, to whom I am indebted for so many valuable services.[54] Father Méndez assuredly documented himself fully with Dávila Padilla, Remesal, and Burgoa; but he adds to this study that of the *actas capitulares,* which have been lost, except for a few fragments. Again thanks to the amiability of Gómez de Orozco I was able to have in my hands these fragments,[55] which made it possible to verify the conscientious exactness of Father Méndez in several points.

Fray Francisco de Burgoa, in his *Palestra Historial* and his *Geográfica Descripción,*[56] which were finished, it seems, the first in 1667, the other at the end of 1670 or the beginning of 1671, limited himself to the region of Oaxaca, but we shall see the primordial interest this region had for the history of the Preaching Friars in Mexico. Few writers are more diffuse and confused than Burgoa; few works are more boring and undigested than his. Precise and positive information is submerged in recollections and Biblical citations, and drowned in a morass which was meant to edify and succeeds only in fatiguing. Nevertheless, they abound in information, so it is indispensable to resign oneself to digest these two heavy books.

The histories of the convent of San Esteban de Salamanca published by Father Cuervo[57] seem at first glance to be of great richness. We know that this celebrated convent furnished a large number of men for the American missions. But one perceives very quickly that the principal one of these historians, Fray Alonso Fernández,[58] contributes nothing of importance that is not already in Dávila Padilla, who himself was largely used by the later chroniclers of the community, Fray Juan de Araya and Fray Jerónimo de Quintana.[59] The *Memorial* and the *Insinuación* that Father Cuervo includes at the end of his book[60] furnish nothing original either—it all comes from Dávila Padilla, Remesal, and Fernández principally. One could say the same of the unpublished history of Fray Esteban de Mora, which was noticed by Father Cuervo and which has been preserved in the convent of San Esteban, where I was able to examine it.[61] It is a compilation of slight value. With respect to chronicles, the principal sources are the works of Dávila Padilla, Méndez, and Burgoa, which, despite their weaknesses, are the most reliable.[62]

Although it is not comparable to the Franciscan literature, the Augustinian literature I studied is appreciably more considerable than the Dominican literature. Here also one must distinguish carefully between the works especially dedicated to Mexico and those concerning the history of the whole Order, or the history of the Order in Spain.

The fundamental work is the chronicle of Grijalva,[63] which in a way is for the history of the Augustinians in Mexico what the chronicle of Dávila Padilla is for the history of the Dominicans. Grijalva's chronicle is also based upon an abundant first-hand documentation. "The Fathers of my Order," he says to the reader, "noticing that this history lacks many things that we all know, were annoyed and unhappy. I am familiar with all these things, for I have had access to very copious accounts, not all of which, nevertheless, are worthy of the history, either because they repeat each other, or because they had no importance, so I decided that to write everything would be to mix the grain with the straw." [64] Grijalva was able to use works that are no longer extant, such as the biography of Fray Juan Bautista de Moya by Fray Agustín de la Coruña.[65] Moreover, he certainly had in his hands the chronicle begun by Fray Alonso de Buica and finished by Fray Francisco Muñoz—he had only to put it into shape.[66] And Father Buica had himself drawn upon the most reliable sources.[67]

Grijalva's study was to be completed by three other works, the chronicles of Michoacán by Fray González de la Puente and Fray Diego Basalenque, and the *Americana Thebaida* of Fray Matías de Escobar.[68] The chronicle of González de la Puente, who worked at the same time as Grijalva, and who moreover studied a much less vast domain,[69] has original value. Basalenque, who wrote his chronicle in 1644,[70] knew and used Grijalva. His work, on the other hand, is only a recasting of that of González de la Puente, whom he does not even mention. Still, he has his own significance. In fact, in his prologue to the reader, he says:

I deserve no less credit for the first Book, in which is related what happened during the sixty years that this Province was part of that of Mexico, for, since

319

my profession at the age of sixteen, I was a companion of Fray Diego de Soria, who was Prior of Mexico, then almost eighty, and who was among the young men who came from Spain and one of the first to take the habit here. Later I was also for four years a companion of Fray Luis Marín, rector of San Pablo, one of the first religious born in this country and taking the habit here. Most of the information I got from all these men concerned the founding of the Mexican Province and what happened at that time. I was also in touch with the Lord Bishop Don Fray Pedro de Agurto, who admitted me to the Order, and with Father Fray Juan de Santa Catalina, the first novices born here, whom I heard relate at length the events that happened at that time. So the water has not flowed through many canals, but has come to me from the said Fathers, all of whom are worthy of credit. So one can trust the first Book with all confidence, for the things related in it are as if I had seen them myself.[71]

On the subject of Father Moya he adds: "Father Juan Bautista . . . I knew and saw, and I was in touch with him and associated with him for more than twenty-five years."[72] He also knew Fray Melchor de los Reyes.[73] With respect to Escobar, although he used all previous chronicles,[74] he added many things and is particularly rich in bibliographical detail. But, as happens in this kind of work with such annoying frequency, his chronology is extremely poor. To the study of these four chronicles it will be well to add that of the manuscript additions made by Father Sicardo to Grijalva's chronicle, now in the National Library of Madrid, where I was able to inspect them.[75]

General works, or those relating to the history of the Order in Spain, are mostly of a very inferior quality. In chronological order here is the list of those I have consulted: the chronicle of Fray Jerónimo Román, that of Pamphile, the *Monasticum* of Crusenius (Kruesen), the *Alphabetum Augustinianum* and the *Historia . . . del Convento de Salamanca* by Herrera, the chronicle of Portillo, the general history of the Discalced Augustinians by Fray Andrés de San Nicolás, and that of the Augustinians of Salamanca by Vidal.[76] The data supplied by Fray Jerónimo Román are very thin, for he hardly gives more than the dates of the chapter [meetings] and the succession of the provincials. Pamphile also, conscientiously and precisely, following the archives of the Order, gives the dates of the chapters and foundations. He limits himself to this entirely external history, but from that point of view his chronicle has value. The other works have the defects that we know and have already pointed out with respect to some Franciscan and Dominican chronicles.

The authors, who were moralists rather than historians, always strive to edify the reader and arouse in him a pious admiration. This is the case, in particular, with the very mediocre compilation of Portillo, who, for the rest, like all the others except Román, Pamphile, and the summary and boring Crusenius, has recourse to Grijalva's chronicle whenever he has to talk about Mexico. It should be added that these authors copied each other. Except for Román, Pamphile, and Crusenius again, they use Grijalva for a common source, but Herrera used Román, Andrés de San Nicolás and Portillo used Herrera, Vidal utilized Portillo and Herrera, while the chronicle of Vidal is nothing more than a very inferior development of the history of Herrera. Andrés de San Nicolás, in his biographies of the first Augustinian missionaries of New Spain,[77] proposed only to study the origins of the Recollets.[78] The most serious of all these works are those of Herrera, particularly his *Historia . . . del Convento de Salamanca*.[79] In this work he doubtless used Grijalva and Calancha, and repeated many things that he had written in the *Alphabetum;* but his information about Mexico is less dispersed and his documentation much greater and more precise, for the subject was more limited. One finds in it, among other things, some facts that do not appear in Grijalva, allowing one several times to correct the latter's statements.[80]

Finally, after the chronicles of each Order, it will be necessary to consider briefly what credit they deserve and the characteristics of certain very general works from the pens of ecclesiastical authors, relating either to the religious history of Spain and the Indies, or to the history of Mexico. In 1577, Fray Esteban de Salazar, an Augustinian turned Chartreux, who had lived in New Spain and known the first evangelizers of the country, in his *Discursos sobre el Credo,* gave a very rapid sketch of the whole conversion of Mexico to Christianity, and told several edifying anecdotes about some of the missionairies.[81] In 1583, an Augustinian, Fray Antonio de San Román, author of the *Consuelo de Penitentes,* also in the edifying genre, gave the biographies of the "nueve varones de la fama."[82] These two works, which are especially interesting because of their dates and because they show the immediate popularity of the Mexican missionaries in the Spanish religious world, have, however, only slight historical value. The *Consuelo,* meanwhile, was used by Herrera, and also by Fernández in his *Historia eclesiástica de Nuestros tiempos.*[83] For the history of the Franciscans in Mexico Fernández had recourse to Gonzaga, and to Dávila Padilla for the history of the Dominicans. Nevertheless, he is not entirely a second-hand historian, for he devoted himself to personal researches.[84] As for the *Teatro* of Gil González Dávila,[85] this conscientious and sometimes useful compilation cannot be considered a source of real importance.

Aside from these, it is necessary to mention a very curious work of a very special character, which cannot be included in any preceding category, the *Rhetorica Christiana* published in 1579 by the Franciscan Fray Diego Valadés.[86] It is before all else a treatise on rhetoric, the evangelization of Mexico, and is especially cited by way of illustration; but the author, who had labored in New Spain on the conversion of the Indians, gives some very interesting bits of information on the method that the religious, especially the Franciscans,[87] used for instructing the natives in the Catholic faith, and he inserted in his book some pictures they used for teaching the catechism in a lively and concrete fashion. Still, it should be observed that the résumé of the evangelization of Mexico which fills four chapters (XXII to XXV) of the fourth part, decorated besides with picturesque and amusing illustrations, add virtually nothing to what is learned elsewhere. Nevertheless, we owe to Valadés the publication of a posthumous work of the famous French Franciscan established in Mexico, Fray Juan Focher, the *Itinerarium Catholicum proficiscentium ad infideles convertendos* (Seville, 1574). This is a theoretical work rather than a historical exposition, as one can divine merely by the title. In it one finds a series of precepts and counsels for the evangelization of infidels in general. There is nothing definite on the evangelization of Mexico. Focher, who was a canonist and an eminent theologian, looks especially into problems of theology, law, and liturgy which come up in missions among the non-Christians.[88]

Abbreviations Used In Notes

AG1	Archivo General de Indias (Seville)
AGN	Archivo General de la Nación (Mexico)
AHHA	Archivo Histórico Hispano-Agustiniano
AIA	Archivo Ibero-Americano
BAE	Biblioteca de Autores Españoles
CDIAI	Colección de Documentos inéditos relativos al descubrimiento, conquista y colonizaciónde las posesiones españolas en América y Oceanía, sacados en su mayor parte del Real Archivo de Indias
DIHE	Documentos inéditos para la Historia de España
E&D	Etudes et documents (R. Ricard)
HEI	Historia Eclesiástica Indiana (Jerónimo de Mendieta)
JSA	Journal de la Société des Americanistes
NBAE	Nueva Biblioteca de Autores Españoles
RHF	Revue d'Histoire Franciscaine
RLI	Recopilación de Leyes de los Reynos de las Indias (2d ed., 1756)

NOTES TO INTRODUCTION
(Pages 1–11)

[1] For all these geographical divisions in the colonial period see Juan López de Velasco. Tabasco, which at first was attached to the government of Chiapas, was later attached to Yucatan.

[2] Parras, vol. 2, pp. 295–296; J. Ramírez Cabañas, pp. 34–35; Miguel O. de Mendizábal, "La conquista," p. 160.

[3] Cuevas, *Historia,* vols. 1 and 2; Dudon, "L'Evangélisation," pp. 161–194.

[4] *Bulletin Hispanique,* Jan.–March, 1931, p. 81.

[5] A. Léon, pp. 253–254.

[6] *Revue de l'Amérique Latine,* August, 1931, pp. 164–166.

[7] See pp. 137–153, 169–180, 207–209, for the Mexican ecclesiastical bibliography.

[8] Pp. 330–349. This chapter was published previously as *"Die Christianisierung Mexikos,"* in *Zeitschrift für Missionswissenschaft,* vol. 14, pp. 145-160.

[9] Lemmens, pp. 199–226.

[10] H. Holzapfel, pp. 452–455; Maarschalkerweerd, pp. 904–907.

[11] D. Pérez Arrilucea, pp. 298–310; 420–428; and "Los Agustinos en Méjico en el siglo XVI," *ibid.,* vol. 94, pp. 335–343; vol. 95, pp. 5–16; vol. 96, pp. 111–119; vol. 97, pp. 115–126; vol. 98, pp. 265–276, 363–372; vol. 99, pp. 253–261.

[12] It is only just to add that since then the National Library of Madrid has been almost completely reorganized, and one is able today to work under the best conditions.

NOTES TO CHAPTER 1
(Pages 15–38)

[1] Díaz del Castillo, vol. 2, pp. 505 ff.; Motolinía to Charles V, pp. 275–277; Cuevas, *Historia,* vol. 1, pp. 109–112; R. Ricard, "Sur la politique des alliances dans la conquête du Mexique," p. 249 and No. 4; C. Bayle, *Santa María en Indias,* pp. 98 ff., and pp. 253–254; Jean Babelon; Carlos Pereyra, *Hernán Cortés.*

[2] Alamán, vol. 1, pp. 408–414.

[3] H. Cortés, vol. 1, p. 31; Cuevas, *Historia,* vol. 1, p. 111.

[4] Cuevas, *Historia,* vol. 1, pp. 106–107.

[5] Bernal Díaz, vol. 2, p. 266.

[6] CDIAI, vol. 23, pp. 353 ff.

[7] Bernal Díaz, vol. 2, pp. 535–536.

[8] Cervantes de Salazar, p. 398.

[9] Cuevas, *Historia,* vol. 1, p. 139.

[10] G. Dufonteny, "La Méthode," p. 366.

[11] Cuevas, *Historia,* vol. 1, pp. 101–117, 130–156.

[12] Bernal Díaz, vol. 1, pp. 116–128.

[13] Cervantes de Salazar, pp. 184–185; Alamán, vol. 1, pp. 249–250.

[14] Bernal Díaz, vol. 1, pp. 158 ff.; Cuevas, *Historia,* vol. 1, p. 137.

[15] Bernal Díaz, vol. 1, p. 193.

[16] *Ibid.,* p. 279; Michel Chevalier, p. 174.

[17] Motezuma, p. 370; Bernal Díaz, vol. 1, pp. 226 ff.

[18] Díaz, vol. 1, p. 197, and pp. 289–299.

[19] *Ibid.,* pp. 391–392, 413–418.

[20] *Ibid.,* p. 356, and pp. 391–392.

[21] Motezuma, p. 489.

[22] Bernal Díaz, vol. 1, p. 325.

[23] *Ibid.,* pp. 327–328.

[24] *Ibid.,* p. 333.

[25] *Ibid.,* pp. 392–394; Cervantes de Salazar, pp. 30–33, 341–354; Cuevas, *Historia,* vol. 1, pp. 140–144.

[26] Bernal Díaz, vol. 1, p. 464.

[27] *Ibid.,* pp. 535–536, 545.

[28] Cuevas, *Historia,* vol. 1, p. 104.

[29] *Ibid.,* p. 116; H. Cortés, pp. 112 and 119; Alamán, vol. 1, p. 196; Icazbalceta, *Biografías,* vol. 2, pp. 204–206; Pedro Nolasco Pérez, 1st Part, pp. 21–30.

[30] Cuevas, *Historia,* vol. 1, p. 117.

[31] A. López, "Los primeros franciscanos," pp. 21–28; Ricard, *Bulletin Hispanique,* July–Sept., 1923, pp. 253–265, and Jan.–March, 1924, pp. 68–69; E&D, pp. 25–30.

[32] *Cartas de Indias,* pp. 52 and 92; Icazbalceta, *Nueva Colección,* vol. 2, pp. 221 and 229; HEI, Book 3, chap. 4; Book 6, chaps. 17–18; Muñoz Camargo, pp. 162–163; Alamán, vol. 2, p. 202; Lemmons, pp. 199–200, 215; Andrade, "Disquisición histórica," pp. 214–220.

[33] H. Cortés, vol. 1, pp. 121–124; López de Gómara, pp. 404–405.

[34] Cuevas, *Historia,* vol. 1, pp. 157–178; *Cartas de Indias,* p. 55; Valadés, 4th Part, p. 171; HEI, Book 4, chap. 11; Alva Ixtlilxóchitl, p. 398; Muñoz Camargo, pp. 241–242; A. Herrera, Book 2, chap. 19; A. López, "Los doce primeros apóstoles."

[35] Dirks, pp. 41–42.

[36] Icazbalceta, *Zumárraga,* pp. 111–112; Angel, pp. 157 ff.; Cuevas *Historia,* vol. 1, pp. 163–165; Holzapfel, pp. 272–273, 453; HEI, Book 3, chap. 4 ff.; Streit, vol. 2, pp. 47–48; Gonzaga, pp. 1123–1126; Grijalva, Book 2, pp. 276–282; Ripoll, pp. 407–408; Matritensis, vol. 1, pp. 108–114; Hernaez, vol. 1, pp. 377–381, 383–385; Levillier, pp. 41–44.

[37] Cuevas, *Historia,* vol. 1, pp. 213–225; Icazbalceta, *Opúsculos,* vol. 2, pp. 369–380.

[38] That is to say, vicar general.

[39] This is the list given by Dávila Padilla and Remesal; that of Mendieta is a little different (V. Riva Palacio, *México a través de los siglos,* vol. 2, p. 285, note 1).

[40] Icazbalceta, *Opúsculos,* p. 374, note 3; CDIAI, vol. 5, pp. 45–451; Dávila Padilla, Book, 1, prelim. chap., p. 5.

[41] Icazbalceta, *Opúsculos,* pp. 375–377; Cuevas, *Historia,* vol. 1, pp. 215–217; DII, vol. 27, p. 448.

[42] L. González Obregón, *Los precursores,* pp. 124–125.

[43] Dávila Padilla, Book 1, p. 60*b*.

[44] Morel-Fatio, p. 374.

[45] Grijalva, Book 1, ff. 10–11; Escobar, p. 59; Sicardo, f. 4 v^0; Pamphile, f. 112 v^0; T. Herrera, *Salamanca,* pp. 263–264, 275 ff.; Icazbalceta, *Opúsculos,* vol. 2, pp. 415–419.

[46] *Cartas de Indias,* pp. 141–142; Cuevas, *Documentos,* p. 187.

[47] Sahagún, *Historia,* p. 48, note 1, and p. 673; Staub, p. 284; Diguet, *Le Mixtécapan,* pp. 15–43; Beuchat, pp. 277 ff.; Joyce, chaps. 1–8; Cuevas, *Historia,* vol. 1, first chapters; Spinden, pp. 201 ff.; Moreno.

[48] Moreno, pp. 48–49; Schmieder, pp. 16–19; Joyce, p. 119.

[49] Diguet, "Contribution a l'ethnographie," pp. 1–8.

[50] Diguet, *Le Mixtécapan,* p. 40.

[51] See p. 47, n. 33.

[52] N. León, "Los popolacas."

[53] Rivet, *Les langues du monde,* pp. 622–626; 630–637.

[54] These four phratries, Moyotlán, Teopan, Aztacalco, and Cuepopan, survived into the colonial period as the *barrios* of San Juan, San Pablo, San Sebastián, and Santa María la Redonda.

[55] Capitan and Lorin, pp. 40 ff.

[56] J. Vasconcelos, pp. 32 ff.; Crokaert, p. 76.

[57] Noguera, pp. 249–310.

[58] Joyce, pp. 95–101.

[59] Spinden, pp. 165–169.

[60] Seler, "Die alten Bewohner," pp. 33–156; Spinden, pp. 244–245.

[61] Spinden, pp. 156–165.

[62] Sahagún, *Historia,* p. 634.

[63] Ibid., pp. xlvii–xlviii; Diguet, *Le Mixtécapan,* p. 21.

[64] Sahagún, *Historia,* pp. 221 ff., pp. xl, xlix; Joyce, pp. 101–103; L. Lévy-Bruhl, *L'âme primitive,* pp. 251–252, 291, 380; Mendizábal, *Ensayos,* pp. 79–81.

[65] Gregorio García, chaps. 5–10; Sahagún, *Historia,* p. 791, and p. lxxvii; Michel Chevalier, pp. 90–93; Chavero, Appendix to Duran's *Historia,* vol. 2, pp. 78 ff.; A. Réville, pp. 91–93, 106–108, 139 ff.; Lumholtz, vol. 1, pp. 170–174.

[66] G. Raynaud, "Les noms sacrés," pp. 235–261; Spinden, pp. 158, 164.

[67] Raynaud, "Le dieu aztec," p. 279; Beuchat, p. 316.

[68] Spinden, p. 231.

[69] Robelo, pp. 251–286.

[70] Raynaud, "Le dieu aztec," p. 43.

[71] J. G. Frazer, *Le rameau d'or,* vol. 2, pp. 99–104; Sahagún, *Historia,* p. 33; Cuevas, *Historia,* vol. 1, p. 87.

[72] Sahagún, *Historia,* pp. 82, 277–281, 454–458; pp. xli–xlii; Höltker, pp. 465–526, 491–493.

[73] Pettazzoni, "La confessione," pp. 191–237; Sahagún, *Historia,* pp. 24–27, 339–343.

[74] Acosta, Book, 5, chaps., 15, 16, 17, 23, 24, 28; Pettazzoni, "La confessione," pp. 303–304; HEI, Book 2.

[75] Allier, *La psychologie,* vol. 1, pp. 180 ff.; vol. 2, pp. 16, 79–84.

[76] Sahagún, *Historia,* p. 635.

[77] De la Motte Lambert et Pallu, *Instructions,* p. 81.

[78] Marcel Bataillon, "Honneur et Inquisition," pp. 5–17.

[79] See p. 163.

[80] Sahagún, *Historia,* p. 635.

[81] Icazbalceta, *Zumárraga,* chap. 22.

[82] J. Vasconcelos, pp. 144–145.

[83] RLI, vol. 1, f. 2 v⁰.

[84] L. Baudin, p. 130.

[85] Sahagún, *Historia,* p. 635.

[86] *Ibid.,* p. 48, note 1; Rea, Book 1, chap. 21.

[87] Burgoa, *Geografica Descripcion,* chap. 28, ff. 156–157.

[88] Icazbalceta, *Zumárraga, Appendix,* p. 102.

[89] Pereyra, *Cortés,* pp. 292–293.

[90] Sahagún, *Historia,* 640.

NOTES TO CHAPTER 2

(Pages 39–60)

[1] Acosta, vol. 2, p. 137.

[2] Chavero, *Obras*, vol. 1, pp. 79–140; Icazbalceta, *Bibliografía*, pp. 253–308; Alfonso Toro, vol. 2, pp. 263–267; Streit, vol. 2, pp. 216–221; José María Póu y Marti, vol. 3, pp. 281–333 (see my reviews in RHF, July, 1925, pp. 435–439, and in E&D, pp. 179–183); Zelia Nuttall, ed., *El libro perdido*, vol. 1, Appendix, pp. 101–154; E. Díaz Molleda, pp. 169 ff.

[3] Bibliographical notes will be found in the works of Chavero, Toro, Póu y Marti, Díaz Molleda, and especially Streit.

[4] I have preferred to use the French translation of D. Jourdanet and Rémi Siméon.

[5] Prologue to Book 1, pp. 5–6.

[6] Sahagún, *Historia*, pp. 593–594, and p. 597, note 1.

[7] *Ibid.*, pp. 633–642.

[8] Baptized Indians very frequently took a Spanish name, generally that of their godfather.

[9] Sahagún, *Historia*, pp. 1–3; Chavero, *Sahagún*, pp. 49 ff.; Icazbalceta, *Bibliografía*, pp. 274–282; Streit, vol. 2, pp. 217–218.

[10] Sahagún, *Historia*, p. 765, gives a list of their names.

[11] *Ibid.*, p. 5.

[12] *Ibid.*, p. 1. Fray Francisco Toral was provincial from 1557 to 1560.

[13] Chavero, *Sahagún*, p. 43; Toro, p. 7; Streit, vol. 2, p. 217.

[14] Streit, vol. 2, p. 197.

[15] Toro, p. 10.

[16] Cuevas, *Historia*, vol. 2, pp. 177–178. Father Rivera was named commissary general in 1569 (HEI, Book 2, chap. 42).

[17] Icazbalceta, *Códice Franciscano*, p. 267; Póu, p. 293; Streit, vol. 2, p. 218; Nuttall, *Ex libro perdido*, p. 103.

[18] This manuscript is in the library of the Royal Academy of History in Madrid. Another copy is in the Laurentienne of Florence. Both are bilingual. See note by Luis González Obregón on Paso y Troncoso, in *Boletín de la Biblioteca Nacional de México*, vol. 12, pp. 172–173.

[19] Published in DIHE, vol. 53, pp. 7–293. See A. López, AIA, vol. 13, pp. 262–271, and vol. 14, pp. 105–111; N. León, *Revista Mexicana de Estudios Históricos*, Sept.–Oct., 1927, pp. 191–213. A. López, in *Los doce primeros apóstoles de Méjico*, pp. 210–211, has rejected the authorship of Fray Martín de Jesús, but is convinced that it was written by one of the Twelve.

[20] See Appendix II, p. 313. The *Memoriales* were published by Luis García Pimentel.

[21] A. López, in *Illuminaire*, Jan.–Feb., 1931.
[22] HEI, *Prólogo al cristiano lector*, pp. 75–76.
[23] Toro, p. 2, note 4.
[24] Allier, *La psychologie*, vol. 1, pp. 55 ff.
[25] Cuevas, *Documentos*, p. 196.
[26] Muñoz Camargo, pp. 162–165.
[27] Dávila Padilla, Book 2, chap. 76; Franco, Book 3, p. 16.
[28] Icazbalceta, *Nueva Colección*, vol. 4, p. 8; Cuevas, *Documentos*, p. 336.
[29] Dávila Padilla, p. 209; A. Fernández, *San Esteban*, Book 1, chap. 27 (Cuervo, p. 80) and *Concertatio*, pp. 292b–293a.
[30] AGI, *Real Patronato*, 1-2-9/29, Ramo 7°, *Ynformación de la vida, costumbres y naturaleza de Don Frai Bernardo de Alburquerque, electo obispo de Oajaca, dominicano y natural de Alburquerque, México*, August 14, 1559. Dávila Padilla, p. 367; Fernández, *San Esteban*, vol. 1, p. 45 (Cuervo, vol. 3, p. 226).
[31] Dávila Padilla, p. 79; DIAI, vol. 5, pp. 452–453.
[32] Francisco de los Ríos Arce, vol. 2, p. 37.
[33] Auguste Génin, p. 2; Carreño, *Fray Miguel de Guevara*, p. 166, note 1, and p. 259, note 3; Grijalva, pp. 111–112; Basalenque, f. 67; González de la Puente, p. 322.
[34] Grijalva, chap. 8; Ricard, "Un document inédit," pp. 21–49, and E&D, pp. 119–154.
[35] Paso y Troncoso, *Papeles*, vol. 5, p. 281; Ricard, "Un document inédit," p. 46, and E&D, p. 150.
[36] Cuevas, *Historia*, vol. 1, p. 167.
[37] Icazbalceta, *Biografías*, vol. 1, p. 167.
[38] Muñoz, pp. 398–399.
[39] Salinas, "Datos para la historia de Toluca"; Schuller, pp. 175–194.
[40] Muñoz, p. 415, note 4; AIA, March–April, 1923, p. 262.
[41] HEI, p. 249; San Román, ff. 449 v°–450 r°.
[42] Motolinía, *Historia*, vol. 3, p. 165.
[43] See Motolinía's letter to Philip II, Mexico, January 23, 1558, AGI, *Audiencia de México*, 60-2-16; Fernández, *Historia eclesiástica*, Book 1, chap. 17; Rea, Book 1, chap. 36.
[44] Rivet, "Langues américaines," pp. 625, 630, 634–637.
[45] See p. 47, n. 34.
[46] Viñaza, Nos. 45 and 46.
[47] J. T. Medina, *La Imprenta*, vol. 1, pp. 169, 298, 374; Viñaza, pp. 22–23.
[48] Staub, p. 284; Diguet, in JSA, 1906, pp. 15–43.
[49] Cuevas, *Documentos*, p. 159.
[50] Luis de Velaso to Philip II, September 30, 1558, AGI, *Audiencia de México*, 58-3-8.

[51] Icazbalceta, *Códice Franciscano,* p. 168.

[52] Grijalva, Book 2, chap. 8.

[53] Cuevas, *Historia,* vol. 1, p. 36.

[54] *Ibid.,* vol. 2, p. 313.

[55] *Ibid.*

[56] Madrid, July 14, 1536, in CDIAI, vol. 23, pp. 456–457.

[57] Puga, vol. 2, pp. 87–88; García, pp. 106–108; Sicardo, f. 50 r°; RLI, vol. 2, f. 190 r°.

[58] According to Arlegui, p. 31, the young *donado* Lucas had taught the children of the region of Nombre de Dios to pray in Spanish; but this is an exception that confirms the rule, in the sense that Lucas was himself a native.

[59] Vera y Zuria, p. 587.

[60] Suárez de Peralta, p. 31; Viceroy the Conde de Monterrey to Philip III, June 11, 1599, in Cuevas, *Documentos,* p. 473.

[61] Cuevas, *Documentos,* p. 473.

[62] J. M. A. Aubin, p. 25, note 2.

[63] E&D, pp. 72–76.

[64] Motolinía, *Historia,* vol. 3, p. 157; Moles, f. 36 v°.

[65] HEI, Book 4, chap. 42, and Book 5, chap. 42; Vetancourt, Book 4, p. 269; Beuchat, p. 352.

[66] HEI, Book 4, p. 365.

[67] Luis de Velasco to Philip II, February 7, 1554, in Cuevas, *Documentos,* pp. 196–197.

[68] Cuevas, *Historia,* vol. 1, p. 184; Ponce, vol. 2, p. 17.

[69] Rivet, *Les langues du monde,* pp. 630, 634–637; Cuevas, *Historia,* vol. 1, pp. 31 ff.

[70] Diguet, "Le Mixtécapan," p. 40.

[71] HEI, Book 3, pp. 219–220.

[72] Letter of January 29, 1552, No. 100 of the Thibaut translation, vol. 3, p. 96; Alexandre Brou, *Saint François Xavier,* 2d ed., vol. 2, pp. 188 and 217.

[73] Allier, *La psychologie,* vol. 1, p. 435.

[74] Métraux, pp. 52–56; Allier, *La psychologie,* vol. 1, pp. 58–59, 64–65.

[75] Sahagún, *Historia,* p. 786; *Libros y Libreros,* p. 84.

[76] E&D, pp. 220–228.

[77] Icazbalceta, "Noticia de una obra en tarasco," pp. 62–64.

[78] Acosta, vol. 2, p. 8; Cuevas, *Historia,* vol. 1, p. 38, note 4; Marcou, "Le symbolisme"; J. F. Ramírez' biography of Motolinía, in Icazbalceta, *Colección de documentos,* vol. 1.

[79] Las Casas, chap. 138.

[80] Muñoz Camargo, pp. 144–145; Georg Friederici, p. 75.

[81] Sahagún, *Evangelarium.*

[82] *Ibid.,* pp. 1–4.

[83] *Ibid.,* p. 61.

[84] Fortino H. Vera, *Colección de documentos eclesiásticos de México,* vol. 1, p. 222.

[85] Lorenzana, pp. 143–144.

[86] *Ibid.,* pp. 201–202.

[87] Cuevas, *Historia,* vol. 2, pp. 257 ff.

[88] Ricard, RHF, April, 1924, pp. 217–218, 228; E&D, pp. 112–113.

[89] Icazbalceta, *Nueva Colección,* vol. 1, p. 4; Viñaza, No. 59: Gilberti, *Thesoro spiritual de pobres* (1575), dedication.

[90] Sahagún, *Historia,* p. 635.

[91] Nuttall, "El libro perdido," pp. 102–103.

[92] *Libros y libreros,* p. 570; Chavero, *Sahagún,* pp. 87 ff.; J. T. Medina, *La Imprenta,* vol. 1, No. 98.

[93] Viñaza, No. 723, p. 245.

[94] *Libros y libreros,* p. 82; Fernández del Castillo, "Aclaraciones históricas," pp. 344–352; *Libros y libreros,* pp. 514 and 516; Icazbalceta, *Zumárraga,* pp. 276–277.

[95] *Libros y libreros,* pp. 482 ff., especially p. 503.

[96] Icazbalceta, *Bibliografía,* pp. 207–208; N. León, "Fray Maturino Gilberti y sus escritos inéditos," pp. 129–138; Streit, vol. 2, pp. 300–303.

[97] RHF, April, 1924, p. 225, note 1; E&D, p. 53, note 27; A. M. Carreño, "La imprenta y la Inquisición," pp. 91–114.

[98] E&D, pp. 66 ff.

[99] Lemmens, p. 222, note 146.

[100] *Libros y libreros,* pp. 4–37, 454–455, 545–550.

[101] Dahlmann, pp. 143–181.

NOTES TO CHAPTER 3

(Pages 61–80)

[1] Méndez, Book 2, f. 34 v°.

[2] *Ibid.,* Book 3, f. 50 v°; Burgoa, *Palestra,* ff. 25 v°–26 r°.

[3] Mena and Rangel, pp. 7, 17–18; Motolinía, *Historia,* Book 2, p. 99; Paso y Troncoso, *Papeles,* vol. 6, p. 176; HEI, Book 5, p. 654; R. García Granados, "Calpan," p. 370.

[4] Motolinía, *Historia,* Book 2, p. 100; HEI, Book 3, p. 259; R. Heliodoro Valle, pp. 9–10.

[5] HEI, Book 3, pp. 248, 285; Motolinía, *Historia,* Book 2, p. 116; Paso y Troncoso, *Papeles,* vol. 6, pp. 302–303.

[6] HEI, Book 3, pp. 48, 262; Paso y Troncoso, *Papeles,* vol. 5, p. 42, and vol. 3, p. 32; Salinas, *Datos,* pp. 50–51, 77–78; 61–62.

[7] HEI, Book 3, p. 222.

[8] Cuevas, *Historia,* vol. 3, pp. 409–410.

[9] HEI, Book 3, p. 248.

[10] *Ibid.,* Book 4, p. 376; Rea, Book 1, chap. 17; N. León, *Historia, geografía,* p. 29.

[11] Mendizábal, "El lienzo," p. 26; N. León, "La Relación de Michuacán," p. 204.

[12] Beaumont, Book 1, vol. 3, p. 305.

[13] *Ibid.,* Book 2, vol. 4, pp. 22–23.

[14] *Ibid.,* vol. 4, p. 22; Mendizábal, "El lienzo" p. 26; Rea, Book 1, chap. 38.

[15] Tello, p. 137, and pp. 144–145; Beaumont, Book 1, vol. 3, pp. 361, 424–425, 431; J. G. Montes de Oca, "La villa de Ocotlán," p. 10; Miguel Galindo, pp. 241–242.

[16] Paso y Troncoso, *Papeles,* vol. 5, pp. 42–43.

[17] N. León, *Los popolocas,* pp. 7–8.

[18] Salinas, *Datos,* p. 53.

[19] R. García Granados, *Calpan,* p. 373.

[20] HEI, Book 3, pp. 333–334, and chap. 58.

[21] Paso y Troncoso, *Papeles,* vol. 5, p. 42.

[22] HEI, Book 3, p. 352; Paso y Troncoso, *Papeles,* vol. 6, p. 226.

[23] N. León, *Los Popolocas,* p. 5.

[24] Paso y Troncoso, *Papeles,* vol. 6, p. 182.

[25] *Ibid.,* p. 303.

[26] Tello, pp. 201–202; Beaumont, vol. 3, p. 503.

[27] Tello, p. 224; Beaumont, vol. 3, pp. 558–559; HEI, Book 5, p. 736.

[28] HEI, Book 4, p. 377; D. Muñoz, p. 384; Tello, p. 226.

[29] A. S. Aiton, p. 120, note 7; E. de Gandía, p. 62, note 7; M. O. Mendizábal, *La evolución del Noroeste de México,* p. 31.

[30] Aiton, pp. 120–121; Gandía, pp. 64–67; Mendizábal, *La evolución,* p. 32. [C. O. Sauer (*The Road to Cíbola,* 1932) makes it quite clear that Fray Marcos de Niza did not discover the "Seven fantastic Cities"; that, in fact, he did not come within several hundred miles of them—*Trans.*]

[31] Tello, pp. 473–477; Beaumont, vol. 4, pp. 467–468; A. López, in *AIA,* March–April, 1923, pp. 261–262.

[32] Arlegui, 1st Part, pp. 11–12; Mecham, p. 72.

[33] Arlegui, 1st Part, pp. 20–21.

[34] Mecham, pp. 72–84.

[35] E&D, pp. 41–53.

[36] Tello, pp. 341–342; Beaumont, vol. 4, pp. 239–240.

[37] Tello, pp. 479–480.

[38] *Ibid.*, pp. 479–480; Beaumont, vol. 4, pp. 465–467, 470.

[39] Tello, p. 536; Beaumont, vol. 5, pp. 87–88; A. López, in *AIA,* March–April, 1923, p. 239.

[40] Tello, p. 536; A. López, p. 239.

[41] Beaumont, vol. 5, pp. 103 ff.

[42] Tello, pp. 545–547; Beaumont, vol. 5, pp. 130–132; A. López, pp. 239, 251.

[43] Tello, p. 549.

[44] *Ibid.*, pp. 621, 609.

[45] Arlegui, 1st Part, p. 33.

[46] *Ibid.*, p. 34; 2d Part, p. 59.

[47] *Ibid.*, 1st Part, pp. 34–35; Mecham, pp. 189, 235.

[48] Arlegui, 1st Part, pp. 35–36, 39; 2d Part, p. 66.

[49] *Ibid.*, 2d Part p. 60; Mecham, pp. 153–154.

[50] D. Muñoz, p. 384; HEI, Book 4, p. 377; Rea, Book 1, chap. 19; Tello, pp. 600–601.

[51] Arlegui, 1st Part, p. 39.

[52] Arlegui, 1st Part, p. 58; Mecham, p. 90.

[53] Arlegui, 1st Part, chap. 4; Ricard, E&D, pp. 56–59.

[54] Tello, pp. 610–611.

[55] Icazbalceta, *Opúsculos,* vol. 2, pp. 373–379.

[56] Méndez, Book, 1, f. 7 r^0; Dávila Padilla, Book 1, p. 62*a*; F. H. Vera, *Itinerario parroquial,* pp. 35, 14, 16.

[57] HEI, Book 4, 1, p. 365.

[58] Dávila Padilla, Book 1, chap. 14; Book 2, chap. 25.

[59] Méndez, Book 2, f. 33 v^0; f. 37 r^0.

[60] Veytia, *Historia de . . . Puebla,* vol. 2, pp. 178–179.

[61] Méndez, Book 2, f. 34 v^0.

[62] *Ibid.*, Book 3, f. 75 v^0.

[63] *Ibid.*, Book 3, f. 81 r^0.

[64] Vera, *Itinerario,* p. 7; Méndez, Book 4, f. 90 r^0; Paso y Troncoso, *Papeles,* vol. 6, p. 250.

[65] Méndez, Book 4, ff. 115 r^0; 139 r^0; Vera, *Itinerario,* p. 9.

[66] See p. 70, n. 6. Méndez, Book 4, ff. 139 r^0 and 90 r^0 and v^0.

[67] Méndez, Book 4, f. 139 r^0; Paso y Troncoso, *Papeles,* vol. 6, p. 79.

[68] Méndez, Book 4, f. 106 v^0.

[69] *Ibid.*, ff. 90 r^0, 139 r^0; Dávila Padilla, Book 1, chap. 21.

[70] Paso y Troncoso, *Papeles,* vol. 6, p. 289; Méndez, Book 4, f. 106 v^0; López de Velasco, pp. 204–205.

[71] López de Velasco, p. 224.

[72] *Ibid.*, p. 224.

[73] Burgoa, *Geografica Descripcion,* f. 143; Méndez, Book 3, f. 88 r⁰.

[74] The nomination of the Dominican Fray Bernardo de Alburquerque to the see of Oaxaca in 1559 is probably owing to the preponderance of his Order in the diocese.

[75] Burgoa, *Palestra,* ff. 3 r⁰–4 r⁰; Méndez, Book 1, f. 8 r⁰.

[76] Burgoa, *Palestra,* f. 6 r⁰.

[77] *Ibid.*, ff. 29 v⁰–30 v⁰; Burgoa, *Geografica Descripcion,* ff. 131 r⁰–132 r⁰; Méndez, Book 2, ff. 33 v⁰– 34 r⁰.

[78] Méndez, Book 2, f. 34 v⁰.

[79] Burgoa, *Geografica Descripcion,* chaps. 25 ff.

[80] Méndez, Book 3, f. 81 r⁰.

[81] *Ibid.*, Book 4, ff. 90 r⁰–91 r⁰.

[82] *Ibid.*, Book 4, f. 139 r⁰.

[83] *Ibid.*, Book 3, f. 75 v⁰; f. 81 r⁰.

[84] *Ibid.*, Book 4, f. 90 r⁰.

[85] *Ibid.*, Book 4, f. 139 r⁰.

[86] *Ibid.*, Book 4, f. 91 r⁰.

[87] Burgoa, *Palestra,* f. 36 v⁰; Méndez, Book 3, f. 88 r⁰.

[88] *Cartas de Indias,* No. 24, p. 130.

[89] Cuevas, *Historia,* vol. 1, pp. 217–220; Reichert, vol. 4, p. 249; Ripoll, vol. 4, pp. 512–513.

[90] F. Gómez de Orozco, "Monasterios," pp. 40–54.

[91] Grijalva, Book 1, chaps. 7–8; Sicardo, ff. 5 r⁰–6 r⁰.

[92] Gómez de Orozco, "Monasterios"; Paso y Troncoso, *Papeles,* vol. 6, p. 11; see above, p. 51, n. 59.

[93] Grijalva, Book 1, chaps. 18, 19, 20; Sicardo, ff. 16 r⁰–18 r⁰.

[94] Grijalva, Book 1, chap. 21; Basalenque, Book 1, chaps. 1, 3, 7; Sicardo, ff. 18 r⁰–20 r⁰.

[95] R. Redfield, *Tepoztlán,* p. 27.

[96] N. León, *El Ylmo. Señor Don Vasco de Quiroga,* p. 24; Beaumont, 20, vol. 3, pp. 323 ff.

[97] Arlegui, 2d Part, p. 59.

[98] Gómez de Orozco, "Monasterios," p. 49.

[99] *Après la conversion,* p. 25.

[100] HEI, Book 3, pp. 333–347.

[101] *Ibid.*, Book 3, pp. 347–358; Icazbalceta, *Zumárraga,* p. 34, note 3.

[102] P. Charles, *Les Dossiers,* No. 1.

[103] Mendizábal, "El lienzo," p. 26.

[104] Gómez de Orozco, "Monasterios," p. 46.

[105] Motolinía, Historia, Book 2, pp. 134–136; HEI, Book 3, pp. 323–327.

335

[106] HEI, Book 3, pp. 353–354.

[107] *Ibid.,* Book 3, last chap.

[108] E&D, p. 96, 105.

[109] Puga, vol. 2, pp. 162–163.

[110] *Ibid.,* vol. 2, pp. 210–211.

[111] *Ibid.,* vol. 1, pp. 291–292.

[112] Genaro García, pp. 143–144; E & D, p. 105.

[113] Letter to Charles V, Guadalajara, May 5, 1552, in *Cartas de Indias,* No. 19, pp. 104–105.

[114] Orozco y Jiménez, p. 268.

[115] Letter to Philip II, Guadalajara, January 29, 1563, AGI, *Audiencia de Guadalajara,* 67–1–18, 86.

[116] To same, Guadalajara, January 31, 1563, in Orozco y Jiménez, p. 268.

[117] To same, Guadalajara, February 6, 1565, AGI, *Audiencia de Guadalajara,* 67–1–18, p. 106; Orozco y Jiménez, pp. 280 ff.; RLI, vol. 1, ff. 62 v°–63 r°.

[118] AGI, 154–1–18.

[119] Burgoa, *Palestra,* ff. 35 v°–37 r° and *Geografica Description,* ff. 36 v°–37 r°; also ff. 43r°–44 r°.

[120] Grijalva, Book 1, pp. 54–55.

NOTES TO CHAPTER 4
(Pages 83–95)

[1] P. Charles, *Les Dossiers,* No. 126; *Les Conversions,* pp. 176–184.

[2] A. Brou, *Saint François Xavier* (Bruges), pp. 36–39.

[3] Brou, *Saint François Xavier* (Paris), vol. 1, pp. 135, 132 ff.; vol. 2, pp. 256–257, and *Conditions et Méthodes,* pp. 36–39.

[4] Lorenzana, pp. 42–43; Icazbalceta, *Zumárraga,* p. 99.

[5] Icazbalceta, *Zumárraga,* p. 208.

[6] Grijalva, Book 1, ff. 44 r°, 43 v° (pp. 139–141).

[7] HEI, Book 3, pp. 256–257; Icazbalceta, *Zumárraga,* p. 95.

[8] Tello, p. 566.

[9] Pedro de Gante, Letter of June 27, 1929.

[10] Alva Ixlilxochitl, vol. 1, p. 399.

[11] Motolinía, *Historia,* vol. 1, p. 27.

[12] CDIAI, vol. 3, pp. 369–377; L. Pérez Verdía, pp. 168–173.

[13] Basalenque, Book 1, f. 7 r°; Dávila Padilla, Book 1, p. 80a.

[14] Motolinía, *Historia,* vol. 2, p. 112.

[15] Allier, *La psychologie,* vol. 1, p. 517.

[16] HEI, Book 3, p. 257.

[17] See above, p. 39, n. 2.

[18] See above, p. 59.

[19] Póu y Marti, pp. 23–24.

[20] *Ibid.*, p. 25.

[21] In the sixteenth century the primitive custom of giving communion immediately after baptism had been abandoned, but has been restored today and recommended by the Ritual.

[22] RHF, July, 1925, pp. 437–439; E & D, pp. 181–183.

[23] Tello, p. 104, Nos. 4 and 5.

[24] Hernaez, vol. 2, pp. 382–384; Cuevas, *Historia,* vol. 1, p. 171.

[25] Icazbalceta, *Códice Franciscano,* pp. 92–93; Basalenque, Book 1, f. 8 v⁰b.

[26] Icazbalceta, *Códice Franciscano,* pp. 91–92; Dávila Padilla, Book 1, pp. 144b–145a.

[27] Cuevas, *Historia,* vol. 1, pp. 226–237.

[28] HEI, Book 4, p. 367.

[29] F. Rousseau, pp. 52–53; F. J. Montalbán, pp. 23–24.

[30] Dávila Padilla, Book 1 pp. 160b–180b; Lorenzana, pp. 16–29; Hernaez, vol. 1, pp. 56–65; Streit, vol. 1, p. 14.

[31] Dávila Padilla, Book 1, chap. 30.

[32] *Ibid.,* Book 1, pp. 111b–113a; Matritensis, vol. 1, p. 138; Streit, vol. 1, p. 15, vol. 2, pp. 272, 281; Hernaez, vol. 1, pp. 102–103; Vera, *Colección,* vol. 2, pp. 237–238; Lorenzana, pp. 33–34; Levillier, vol. 2, pp. 53–54; Cuevas, *Documentos,* pp. 84–86, 88, and *Historia,* vol. 1, pp. 232, 235–237; P. Hernández, vol. 1, pp. 43–49, 58–63; Levillier, vol. 2, pp. 47–48.

[33] Icazbalceta, *Zumárraga,* p. 355, note; *Opúsculos,* vol. 2, p. 83, note; Harrisse, No. 119, pp. 179–183; Leclerc, No. 26, pp. 8–9; Icazbalceta, *Zumárraga,* pp. 354–355 (Appendix, pp. 57–62), and *Opúsculos,* vol. 2, pp. 80–83; C. Pérez Pastor, pp. 29–31; J. T. Medina, *Biblioteca Hispano-Americana,* No. 119; H. de Castries, 1st ser., vol. 1, pp. 8–14; Streit, vol. 1, pp. 9–12, 290–293; vol. 2, pp. 76, 78.

[34] *Cartas de Indias,* No. 9, p. 55; Icazbalceta, *Nueva Colección,* vol. 2, pp. 177–186.

[35] Daza, Book 2, pp. 91–92; Icazbalceta, *Bibliografía,* pp. 394–400; Cuevas, *Historia,* vol. 1, pp. 159–161, Harrisse, No. 186, pp. 308–310; J. T. Medina, *Biblioteca,* No. 93.

[36] Motolinía, *Historia,* vol. 2, pp. 107–108, 113, 127; vol. 3, p. 164.

[37] *Ibid.* vol. 2, pp. 99–100.

[38] Motolinía, *Historia,* vol. 2, p. 113, explains that exorcism is a function of baptism, but the text is still obscure, for the rite of the *flato,* which is taken up later on, is also considered an exorcism.

[39] Motolinía, *Historia,* vol. 2, pp. 110–111; Torquemada, Book 16, p. 155.

[40] Holy oil was unknown in Mexico at the time.

⁴¹ Zumárraga to Suero del Aguila, February 13, 1537, in *Revista de Archivos,* 1901, p. 491.

⁴² N. León, *El Ylmo. Señor Don Vasco de Quiroga,* p. 34.

⁴³ Zumárraga to the Council of the Indies, February 8, 1537, in Cuevas, *Documentos,* pp. 73–74; Icazbalceta, *Zumárraga,* Appendix, pp. 95–96.

⁴⁴ Grijalva, Book 1, ff. 44 v⁰–45 r⁰, pp. 141–142.

⁴⁵ HEI, Book 3, pp. 269–271; Ripoll, vol. 7, p. 137; Matritensis, vol. 1, pp. 135–138; Lorenzana, pp. 29–33; Hernaez, vol. 1, pp. 65–67; Vera, *Colección,* vol. 2, pp. 220–224; Icazbalceta, *Zumárraga,* pp. 98–99; Levillier, vol. 2, pp. 49–52.

⁴⁶ HEI, Book 3, pp. 267–279; Grijalva, Book 1, chap. 26; see also the biography of Motolinía by J. F. Ramírez, in Icazbalceta, *Colección,* vol. 1, pp. liv–lv, lxii–lxiii.

⁴⁷ Juan Bautista, *Advertencias,* 1st Part; Icazbalceta, *Zumárraga,* pp. 99–100; Appendix, pp. 117–136; Vera, vol. 2, pp. 384–407; Cuevas, *Historia,* vol. 1, pp. 429–431; Streit, vol. 2, pp. 107–108.

⁴⁸ Biblioteco Nacional de Madrid, B. U. 3148; Icazbalceta, *Zumárraga,* pp. 243–248 and *Bibliografía,* pp. 2–6; N. León, *Vasco de Quiroga,* pp. 34–39; Streit, vol. 2, p. 108; Focher, ff. 94 ff.; Icazbalceta, *Códice Franciscano,* pp. 87–91.

⁴⁹ HEI, Book 3, p. 375.

⁵⁰ Motolinía, *Historia,* vol. 2, p. 113.

⁵¹ *Bulletin des Missions,* Nov.–Dec., 1929, p. 512.

⁵² P. Charles, *Les Dossiers,* No. 66.

⁵³ Dufonteny, in *Les conversions,* pp. 30–32; E. Laveille, *L'Evangile au centre de l'Afrique,* pp. 182–183, 312–313.

NOTES TO CHAPTER 5

(Pages 96–108)

¹ Cuevas, *Documentos,* p. 54.

² Icazbalceta, *Zumárraga,* Appendix, p. 122; Vera, *Colección,* vol. 2, pp. 390–391.

³ Icazbalceta, *Códice Franciscano,* p. 66.

⁴ Cuevas, *Documentos,* pp. 68, 489.

⁵ Alamán, vol. 2, p. 236.

⁶ Valadés, 4th Part, p. 212.

⁷ CDIAI, vol. 4, p. 498.

⁸ Icazbalceta, *Códice Franciscano,* pp. 66–67; HEI, Book 3, pp. 245–247; Vetancurt, vol. 3, p. 22.

[9] Icazbalceta, *Códice Franciscano,* pp. 79–84; Cuevas, *Documentos,* p. 285; Valadés, p. 212.

[10] Cuevas, *Documentos,* p. 159.

[11] Tello, pp. 567 and 475.

[12] Brou, *Saint François Xavier,* vol. 1, p. 227; *Conditions et Méthodes,* pp. 56–57; B. Arens, pp. 213–215; H. Dubois, pp. 75–86.

[13] C. Noriega Hope and Fortuno López R., vol. 2, pp. 225, 245; Vera y Zuria, pp. 109, 279–280.

[14] Icazbalceta, *Códice Franciscano,* pp. 63–64; Motolinía, *Historia,* vol. 2, p. 138.

[15] Motolinía, *Historia,* vol. 1, p. 24.

[16] Sahagún, *Historia,* pp. 226 ff., 458 ff., 636; Höltker, pp. 515–517.

[17] Icazbalceta, *Códice Franciscano,* pp. 64–65; Sahagún, *Historia,* pp. 636–637; Martín de Valencia . . . to Charles V, November 17, 1532, in *Cartas de Indias,* No. 9, p. 56 (also in Icazbalceta, *Nueva Colección,* vol. 2, pp. 177 ff.); Pedro de Gante to Philip II, Mexico, June 23, 1558, in Icazbalceta, *Nueva Colección,* vol. 2, pp. 222–223, 230–231; CDIAI, vol. 40, pp. 472–473, 495, 508–509.

[18] Motolinía, *Historia,* vol. 3, p. 218.

[19] Icazbalceta, *Códice Franciscano,* pp. 62–63.

[20] Daza, Book 2, p. 30.

[21] HEI, Book 3, p. 318; Icazbalceta, *Opúsculos,* vol. 2, p. 427.

[22] Motolinía, *Historia,* vol. 1, pp. 20, 28.

[23] Motolinía, *ibid.;* Sahagún, *Historia,* pp. 638–639.

[24] Cuevas, *Historia,* vol. 1, p. 184.

[25] Motolinía, *Historia,* vol. 2, p. 128.

[26] Muñoz, pp. 403–404.

[27] Motolinía, *Historia,* vol. 3, pp. 218–228; Muñoz Camargo, Book 2, pp. 245–248; HEI, Book 3, chaps. 25–27; Dávila Padilla, Book 1, chaps. 22–23; Lemmens, pp. 215–216.

[28] Motolinía, *Historia,* vol. 3, pp. 218–221; HEI, Book 3, chap. 24; Schmidlin, p. 336.

[29] CDIAI, vol. 40, pp. 474–475, 596–497, 522; Cuevas, *Documentos,* pp. 186, 493.

[30] Salmerón to Charles V, January 22, 1531, in CDIAI, vol. 13, p. 190; Audiencia of Mexico to same, August 14, 1531, *ibid.,* vol. 41, p. 84.

[31] Luis de Velasco to Philip II, September 30, 1558, in AGI, *Audiencia de México,* 58–3–8.

[32] Sahagún, *Historia,* pp. 636–637.

[33] Motolinía, *Historia,* vol. 3, p. 229; HEI, Book 3, p. 221; Muñoz Camargo, p. 242; Daza, Book 2, p. 81*b;* Vetancurt, vol. 3, pp. 11 ff.

[34] AIA, March–April, 1929, p. 261.

[35] *Descripción del Arzobispado de México,* pp. 86, 132–133, 259.

[36] Icazbalceta, *Zumárraga,* pp. 188–189, 266–268; Vera, *Apuntamientos históricos,* p. 8.

[37] Icazbalceta, *Códice Franciscano,* pp. 33 ff. See also Appendix 1, below, No. 6.

[38] Bayle, *Santa María en Indias,* pp. 24, 54–57, 63.

[39] A distinction was made between the seven corporal works of mercy and the seven spiritual works. They were normally taught at this time as part of the catechism.

[40] Probst, pp. 176–189.

[41] Ricard, "Morisques et Indiens," pp. 35–357 and "Remarques," pp. 229–236, and in E&D, pp. 209–228.

[42] Levillier, vol. 1, pp. 186–189.

[43] *Cartilla para enseñar a leer a los niños. Con la doctrina que se canta.*

[44] Bataillon, "Erasme au Mexique," pp. 31–44.

[45] *Libros y libreros,* p. 11.

[46] *Ibid.,* p. 21.

[47] *Ibid.,* p. 35.

[47] *Ibid.,*p. 35.

[48] *Información que el arzobispo de México D. Fray Alonso de Montúfar mandó practicar,* pp. 1–54. The second edition (Mexico, 1891) is more complete. Ricard, in *Revue d'Histoire des Missions,* June, 1931, p. 254. See also p. 191.

[49] Motolinía, *Historia,* vol. 1, p. 21; *Descriptio Codicum franciscalium,* in AIA July–Dec., 1919, pp. 402–403; Lorenzana, p. 45.

[50] Icazbalceta, *Códice Franciscano,* p. 67; HEI, Book 3, pp. 249–250; Valadés, 2d Part, pp. 212, 221, especially the engraving on p. 211.

[51] Sahagún, *Historia,* p. lxiii; Aubin, p. 24; Vetancurt, vol. 4, p. 147.

[52] N. Sentenach, 1900, pp. 599–609; Pérez Bustamante, pp. 96, 97; Aubin, pp. 22–30; Boban, vol. 2, pp. 171–182.

[53] See above, p. 53.

[54] Muñoz, p. 417.

[55] Motolinía, *Historia,* vol. 3, pp. 164–165.

[56] Icazbalceta, *Nueva Colección,* vol. 2, pp. 223–224, 231–232.

[57] See below, Appendix 2.

[58] *Ibid.;* Icazbalceta, *Zumárraga,* pp. 262–265, 302; *Descripción del Arzobispado,* pp. 49, 132, 170.

[59] Sahagún, *Historia,* p. 636; Lumholtz, p. 326.

[60] Cuevas, *Historia,* vol. 1, pp. 216–217 (reproduction of a *doctrina* in ideograms used by the Dominicans).

[61] Wilberforce, p. 331.

[62] Dávila Padilla, Book 1, pp. 320*b*–324*a;* Burgoa, *Geografica Descripcion,* ff. 12 v⁰–13 r⁰, and *Palestra,* f. 34 v⁰.

[63] Grijalva, Book 2, f. 72; Escobar, pp. 96–97.

[64] Escobar, pp. 660–661 and 95.

[65] Icazbalceta, *Zumárraga,* p. 243; Harrisse, pp. 365–377, No. 232; Dávila Padilla, Book 2, p. 670; Franco, Book 3, p. 565; González Dávila, f. 23; Baltasar de Medina, No. 815, f. 233 r⁰; Quétif et Echard, vol. 2, p. 252*b;* Martínez Vigil, p. 278; Icazbalceta, *Opúsculos,* vol. 1, pp. 17–22; J. T. Medina, *La Imprenta en México,* vol. 1, pp. xlvii ff.; L. González Obregón, *México viejo,* p. 593.

NOTES TO CHAPTER 6

(Pages 109–127)

[1] Icazbalceta, *Zumárraga,* pp. 111–112, and *Códice Franciscano,* pp. 111 ff.; Grijalva, Book 2, chap. 16; Biblioteca Nacional de Madrid, MS No. 10,081, ff. 401 ff.

[2] Grijalva, Book 3, pp. 459–462; Tello, pp. 604–608; Hernaez vol. 1, pp. 397–399; Levillier, vol. 2, pp. 114–117; Cuevas, *Documentos,* p. 332, and *Historia,* vol. 1, p. 502; J. T. Medina, *Imprenta,* vol. 1, No. 59.

[3] Hernández, vol. 1, pp. 324–325, 281–282, 557–559; Parras, vol. 2, pp. 298–307; Beaumont, Book 2, vol. 5, pp. 376 ff.

[4] Allier, *La psychologie,* vol. 1, pp. 576 ff.; vol. 2, pp. 84 ff.

[5] Tello, pp. 143–144.

[6] Icazbalceta, *Zumárraga,* Appendix, p. 91.

[7] Tello, pp. 201–202, 353–354.

[8] Motolinía, *Historia,* vol. 2, pp. 126, 165; Rea, Book 1, pp. 106–107.

[9] Grijalva, Book 1, chap. 7, *in fine.*

[10] Sicardo, f. 8.

[11] Dufonteny, "La Méthode d'évangelisation," pp. 520–531.

[12] Motolinía, *Historia,* vol. 2, pp. 126, 165; Cuevas, *Documentos,* p. 493; Höltker, p. 504.

[13] Cuevas, *Documentos,* p. 158; HEI, Book 4, chaps. 32–35.

[14] Genaro García, vol. 19, pp. 37–38; Icazbalceta, *Zumárraga,* App. p. 91.

[15] Motolinía, *Historia,* Vol. 2, p. 126.

[16] Grijalva, Book 1, pp. 139–140, Basalenque, Book 1, ff. 7 v⁰*b*–8 r⁰.

[17] Motolinía, *Historia,* vol. 2, p. 126 and p. 128.

[18] Cuevas, *Documentos,* p. 493; E&D, p. 44–45.

[19] Bautista, *Advertencias* ff. 7 r⁰–9 r⁰.

[20] López de Gómara, p. 405; Alva Ixtlilxochitl, vol. 1, pp. 401–402; Moles,

chap. 8, f. 31; Alamán, vol. 2, p. 221; Vera, *Colección de documentos,* vol. 2, pp. 382–384.

[21] Höltker, pp. 476–477, 503–504; Moreno, p. 74.

[22] Icazbalceta, *Bibliograía,* pp. 67–68, 82; J. T. Medina, *Imprenta,* vol. 1, No. 31; Streit, vol. 1, p. 30; Santiago Vela, *Ensayo,* pp. 155–174; Viñaza, No. 6.

[23] Motolinía, *Memoriales,* Book 2, chaps. 7–9; HEI, Book 2, chap. 25; Höltker, pp. 476–477, 503–504, 507.

[24] Bautista, *Advertencias;* Grijalva, Book 1, p. 140; Sicardo, f. 28 v⁰.

[25] HEI, Book 3, p. 303; Icazbalceta, *Zumárraga,* pp. 104–107.

[26] Allier, *La psychologie,* vol. 2, p. 34.

[27] Sahagún, *Historia,* p. 638.

[28] Motolinía, *Historia,* vol. 2, pp. 127–128.

[29] Cuevas, *Documentos,* pp. 253–254.

[30] See above, p. 59.

[31] Puga, vol. 2, pp. 202–204.

[32] *Procesos de indios idólatras y hechiceros,* pp. 79 ff.

[33] Icazbalceta, *Códice Franciscano,* pp. 61, 105–109.

[34] Motolinía, *Historia,* vol. 2, p. 125; HEI, Book 3, pp. 296–298; López de Gómara, p. 450.

[35] Motolinía, *Historia,* vol. 2, p. 116; *Cartas de Indias,* Nos. 9, p. 56, and 10, pp. 62–66.

[36] Icazbalceta, *Códice Franciscano,* pp. 61, 97–102.

[37] Escobar, p. 100; Grijalva, Book 1 pp. 147–150; Basalenque, Book 1, ff. 8 v⁰b–9v⁰b.

[38] Paso y Troncoso, *Papeles,* vol. 3, pp. 82, 93.

[39] *Ibid.,* pp. 93–94.

[40] Pettazzoni, *La confessione,* pp. 236–237; see above, p. 32, n. 73.

[41] Sahagún, *Historia,* pp. 46–47.

[42] *Ibid.,* p. 26; Pettazzoni, *La confessione,* p. 227.

[43] Escobar, pp. 87–89, and pp. 466–467; Grijalva, Book 3, pp. 410–411.

[44] Bautista, *Advertencias,* ff. 1 r⁰–4 r⁰.

[45] Levy-Bruhl, *Les fonctions mentales,* pp. 116 ff; Leroy, pp. 81 ff.

[46] Allier, *La psychologie,* vol. 1, p. 156, and *Le non-civilisé,* pp. 87–91; Lumholtz, vol. 2, p. 465.

[47] Aviat, p. 363.

[48] Lévy-Bruhl, *Les fonctions mentales,* p. 206–207; Allier, *Le non-civilisé,* pp. 254–255.

[49] L. Brunschvicg, pp. 176–180.

[50] Parras, vol. 2, pp. 429–432; Allier, *La psychologic,* vol. 1, pp. 421 ff; Lévy-Bruhl, *Le surnaturel,* pp. 56–57.

[51] Grijalva, Book 3, pp. 410–411.

[52] Motolinía, *Historia*, vol. 2, p. 116.

[53] *Ibid.*, vol. 2, p. 122; Valadés, 2d Part, chap. 27, pp. 95–96; Cuevas, *Historia*, vol. 1, p. 186.

[54] Valadés, 4th Part, pp. 213–214.

[55] Grijalva, Book 1, pp. 147–148.

[56] Motolinía, *Historia*, vol. 2, p. 116, and vol. 3, p. 165.

[57] *Ibid.*, p. 165.

[58] CDIAI, vol. 4, p. 497.

[59] *Cartas de Indias*, No. 22, p. 123–124.

[60] Brou, *Conditions et méthodes*, p. 41.

[61] Dávila Padilla, Book 2, p. 755; Franco, Book 1, pp. 17–18.

[62] CDIAI, vol. 4, p. 501.

[63] Allier, *La psychologie*, vol. 2, pp. 134 ff.

[64] Motolinía, *Historia*, vol. 2, pp. 119, 121; Zorita, vol. 1, pp. 210–211.

[65] Morel-Fatio, 4th ser, p. 339.

[66] BAE, vol. 22, p. 450; Brou, *Saint François Xavier*, vol. 2, p. 24; Suau, p. 385.

[67] J. L. Cossío, pp. 297–307; *Mexican Folkways*, June–July, 1925, pp. 24–25, 28.

[68] Motolinía, *Historia*, vol. 2, pp. 119–121.

[69] *Ibid.*, pp. 116–117; HEI, Book 3, pp. 293–296.

[70] Motolinía, *Historia*, vol. 2, p. 124.

[71] HEI, Book 4, pp. 377–378; Rea, Book 1, chap. 31.

[72] Cuevas, *Documentos*, p. xiii; Streit, vol. 1, p. 104; Hernández, vol. 1, pp. 47–49; Santiago Vela, *Ensayos*, vol. 1, pp. 34 ff.

[73] Icazbalceta, *Zumárraga*, App., p. 131; Motolinía, *Historia*, vol. 2, pp. 123–124.

[74] HEI, Book 3, p. 295; Vera, *Concilios* p. 8.

[75] Agurto, *Tractado;* Grijalva, Book 1, chap. 28; Icazbalceta, *Bibliografía*, pp. 187–188; J. T. Medina, *Imprenta*, vol. 1, No. 66; Santiago Vela, *Ensayos*, vol. 1, pp. 63 ff; Streit, vol. 1, pp. 50–51; Ricard, "Un document inédit," in JSA, 1926, pp. 45–46; E&D, pp. 149–150; Bautista, *Advertencias*, ff. 54 v°ff.

[76] HEI, Book 3, p. 295.

[77] *Libros y libreros*, p. 28.

[78] Icazbalceta, *Códice Franciscano*, pp. 102–105; A. López and L. Núñez, pp. 390 ff.

[79] Dávila Padilla, Book 1, p. 102.

[80] Grijalva, Book 1, chap. 28, and Book 2, pp. 232–233; Basalenque, Book 1, ff. 9 v°b– 10 v°a; Escobar, pp. 90–91.

[81] Paso y Troncoso, *Papeles*, vol. 3, p. 82.

[82] *Ibid.*, vol. 3, p. 93.

[83] *Ibid.,* vol. 5, p. 283.

[84] *Ibid.,* vol. 3, p. 108.

[85] *Ibid.,* vol. 3, p. 135.

[86] Huonder, *Der einheimische Klerus in den Heidenländern,* pp. 18–20; Schmidlin, p. 338.

[87] Icazbalceta, *Códice Franciscano,* p. 97; HEI, Book 3, p. 280; Lorenzana, p. 2; Icazbalceta, *Zumárraga,* p. 192.

[88] Icazbalceta, *Zumárraga,* Appendix, p. 169 and *Revista de Archivos,* 1901, p. 491.

[89] Lorenzana, p. 6.

[90] Icazbalceta, *Códice Franciscano,* pp. 109–110; HEI, Book 3, p. 307; see p. 157.

[91] Grijalva, Book 1, pp. 155–156; Basalenque, Book 1, f. 10v⁰; Paso y Troncoso, *Papeles* vol. 3, pp. 82, 93, 94, 135; vol. 5, p. 283.

[92] See p. 123.

NOTES TO CHAPTER 7
(Pages 128–131)

[1] HEI, Book 3, p. 250.

[2] Moles, chap. 14, f. 36 v⁰; Cuevas, *Historia,* vol. 1, pp. 165 ff.

[3] Daza, Book 2, p. 30; Francisco Jiménez, in A. López, AIA, July–August, 1926, p. 67; Motolinía, *Historia,* vol. 3, pp. 157, 159; J. Trinidad, Book 2, pp. 219*b*–220*a*.

[4] Trinidad, Book 2, p. 282*b*.

[5] Muñoz, p. 401.

[6] Dávila Padilla, Book 1, pp. 80*b*–81*a*; A. Fernández, "San Esteban," in Cuervo, *Historiadores,* vol. 1, p. 72, and *Historia eclesiástica,* p. 76*a*.

[7] Dávila Padilla, Book 1, p. 44.

[8] E&D, pp. 72 ff.

[9] Cuevas, *Documentos,* p. 245.

[10] Fray Agustín de la Coruña to Philip II, July 10, 1561, in *Cartas de Indias,* No. 31, pp. 153–154.

[11] Cuevas, *Documentos,* p. 141; Cervantes de Salazar, Book 4, p. 319.

[12] Cuevas, *Historia,* vol. 1, pp. 167–168.

[13] Mota Padilla, p. 29.

[14] Cuevas, *Documentos,* p. 160.

[15] Zumárraga to Juan de Sámano, December 20, 1537, in *Cartas de Indias,* pp. 174–175.

[16] Cuevas, *Documentos,* p. 187.

[17] Dávila Padilla, Book 1, pp. 209–210; Book 2, p. 788*a*; Franco, Book 1, pp. 16–18, 38–42, 57.

[18] Sahagún, *Historia,* p. 20; Friederici, p. 90.

[19] Sahagún, *Historia,* pp. 519, 736; Friederici, p. 17.

[20] Herrera, *Salamanca,* p. 333*a.*

[21] San Román, ff. 430 r⁰ ff.; Fernández, *Historia eclesiástica,* Book, 2, chap. 33; Grijalva, Book 2, chaps. 20 ff.

[22] Suárez de Peralta, p. 65.

[23] Motolinía, *Historia,* vol 3, p. 168.

NOTES TO CHAPTER 8

(Pages 135–153)

[1] Schmieder, pp. 12–13, 16, 23–24, Plate 33*a.*

[2] Redfield, p. 54; see also M. Gamio *La Población del Valle de Teotihuacán,* vol. 2, pp. 381–382.

[3] Francisco de Guzmán to Charles V, Toluca, May 10, 1551, in Cuevas, *Documentos,* pp. 167–168; also, p. 187 for Viceroy Velasco's observations on Tlaxcala and Oaxaca.

[4] Motolinía, *Historia,* vol. 3, pp. 202–203; Lotar, "Le déchet dans les conversion," p. 16, in *Après la conversion.*

[5] Motolinía to Charles V, Mexico, May 15, 1550, in Cuevas, *Documentos,* p. 166; Pedro de Gante to Charles V, Mexico, February 15, 1552, in *Cartas de Indias,* No. 18, p. 101.

[6] Fray Bernardo de Alburquerque, *et al.,* to the Council of the Indies, Mexico, September 18, 1553, in AGI, *Audiencia de México,* 60–2–16.

[7] Cuevas, *Documentos,* p. 240.

[8] Pedro de Ayala to the Council of the Indies, *c.* 1563–1564, in AGI, *Audiencia de Guadalajara,* 67–1–18, 104.

[9] Viñas y Mey, *El estatuto del obrero en la colonización española,* p. 143.

[10] Cuevas, *Historia,* vol. 1, p. 169, note.

[11] *Disposiciones complementarias de las leyes de Indias,* vol. 1, No. 7, p. 15.

[12] RLI, vol. 2, f. 190.

[13] *Cédulas* of March 21, 1551, Oct. 3, 1558 (two), Feb. 19, 1560, Sept. 13, 1565, Nov. 10, 1568, Feb. 19, 1570, in Puga, vol. 2, pp. 318–320, 338–339; RLI, vol. 2, ff. 198 r⁰–199 r⁰.

[14] Icazbalceta, *Zumárraga,* Appendix, p. 52; Cuevas, *Documentos,* p. 490.

[15] Icazbalceta, *Zumárraga,* Appendix, pp. 88, 166–167; RLI, vol. 2, f. 198 r⁰; Vera, *Concilios provinciales,* p. 7; Lorenzana, pp. 147–148.

[16] Viceroy Velasco to Philip II, Mexico, Februaury 7, 1554, in Cuevas, *Documentos,* p. 204.

[17] Anon. to Philip II, Mexico, September 1, 1559, in AGI, *Audiencia de México*, 60–2–16.

[18] *Parecer cerca de la necesidad de juntar los indios* (1570?), in Icazbalceta, *Nueva Colección*, vol. 4, pp. 136–141.

[19] Dávila Padilla, Book 1, p. 303*b*.

[20] Rea, Book 1, chaps. 24 and 25; Muñoz, p. 399; Ponce, vol. 2, pp. 144–145.

[21] Beaumont, Book 1, vol. 3, p. 266.

[22] Audiencia de México to Charles V, August 14, 1531, in CDIAI, vol. 4, pp. 84–86.

[23] HEI, Book 6, p. 654; Cuevas, *Historia*, vol. 3, p. 38, note 2; Ricard, in JSA, 1931, p. 252.

[24] Grijalva, Book 2, p. 222.

[25] Escobar, p. 564.

[26] *Ibid.*, p. 672.

[27] Basalenque, Book 1, f. 16 v°*a*; González de la Puente, Book 2, pp. 126–127.

[28] Basalenque, Book 1, f. 20 r°; Escobar, pp. 146, 736.

[29] Grijalva, Book 1, chap. 20; "Relación de la provincia de Meztitlán," p. 109.

[30] Grijalva, Book 1, chap 8; Book 3, chap. 19.

[31] Basalenque, Book 1, chap. 15; Escobar, pp. 772, 820.

[32] Grijalva, Book 1, chap. 9.

[33] *Ibid.*, Book 2, p. 223; *Relación de los obispados*, pp. 122–124.

[34] Rodrigo de la Cruz to Charles V, May 4, 1550, in Cuevas, *Documentos*, p. 160.

[35] See above, p. 29.

[36] Valadés, 4th Part, pp. 209–210; Paso y Troncoso, *Papeles*, vol. 4, pp. 27, 53; vol. 5, pp. 46, 146; vol. 6, pp. 48, 69, 86, 183; Latorre, pp. 13, 21, 25, 33; Pérez Bustamante, pp. 28, 50, 62.

[37] Beaumont, Book 2, vol. 4, pp. 27–43.

[38] Montúfar to the Council of the Indies, May 15, 1556, in CDIAI, vol. 4, p. 494.

[39] See above, p. 81, n. 112.

[40] HEI, Book 4, pp. 496–498.

[41] Paso y Troncoso, *Papeles*, vol. 3, p. 135.

[42] See above, p. 81.

[43] See above, p. 98.

[44] *Descripción Geográfica de los Reynos de Galicia, Vizcaya, y León*, p. 36.

[45] RLI, vol. 2, f. 189 v°; Puga, vol. 1, pp. 460–464.

[46] Cuevas, *Documentos*, p. 204, and *Historia*, vol. 4, pp. 99–100.

[47] Paso y Troncoso, *Papeles* vol. 3, pp. 92–93.

[48] *Ibid.*, vol. 3, pp. 108–109, 135.

[49] G. Goyau, pp. 189–190.

[50] Cervantes de Salazar, Book 3, p. 242; Book 4, pp. 318–319; Puga, vol. 2, pp. 241–242; Paso y Troncoso, *Papeles* vol. 6, pp. 218–219; Dávila Padilla, Book 1, p. 51*b*.

[51] Motolinía, *Memoriales,* p. 159.

[52] Cuevas, *Historia,* vol. 1, p. 418.

[53] Dávila Padilla, Book 1, p. 210*a;* Burgoa, *Geografica Descripcion,* f. 130 v⁰; Schmieder, p. 19.

[54] Grijalva, Book 2, p. 222.

[55] Rea, Book 1, p. 110.

[56] Pedro de la Peña to Philip II, July 25, 1561, in AGI, *Audiencia de México,* 60–2–16; Cuevas, *Historia,* vol. 2. p. 487.

[57] Burgoa, *Geografica Descripcion,* ff. 130 v⁰, 151 v⁰.

[58] Icazbalceta, *Opúsculos,* vol. 1 pp. 125–261, esp. pp. 138–140.

[59] Dávila Padilla, Book 1, pp. 209*b*–210*a*, 303*b*.

[60] Icazbalceta, *Zumárraga,* pp. 237–238, and *Opúsculos,* vol. 1, pp. 141–143.

[61] Icazbalceta, *Zumárraga,* Appendix, p. 236.

[62] "Relación descriptiva del Valle de Oaxaca," in Cuevas, *Cartas y otros documentos de Hernán Cortés,* p. 256.

[63] Motolinía, *Historia,* vol. 1, pp. 7–8, ed. Sánchez Garcia; Motolinía, *Historia,* vol. 3, p. 195.

[64] Burgoa, *Geografica Descripcion,* f. 151 v⁰.

[65] Pérez Bustamante, p. 130, note 4.

[66] *"Relación de la provincia de Meztitlán,"* p. 116; Ricard, JSA, 1926, p. 45; E&D, p. 149.

[67] Pereyra, *L'oeuvre de l'Espagne en Amérique,* p. 100. [The definitive study of silk in Mexico is Woodrow Borah's *Silk Raising in Colonial Mexico* (Berkeley and Los Angeles, 1943).—*Trans.*]

[68] Rea, Book 1, p. 111; Lumholtz, vol. 2, pp. 429 ff.

[69] Dávila Padilla, Book 1, p. 304*a;* Sorre, pp. 62–63.

[70] Pamphile, f. 115 v⁰.

[71] Grijalva, Book 2, p. 222.

[72] Basalenque, Book 1, f. 20 v⁰a; Escobar, p. 145.

[73] Sicardo, ff. 43 r⁰, 44 r⁰; Escobar, p. 772.

[74] Paso y Troncoso, *Papeles,* vol. 5. p. 18.

[75] [M. Ricard originally gave 1550 as the date of completion. A commission appointed by the Mexican government in 1878 to study the famous *Arcos de Tembleque* and the reason for their abandonment, gives 1553–1571 as the period of their construction. The aqueduct flowed for about 123 years. Its

failure was not caused by any structural defect, but probably by the sinking of the source. ("Informe del Ingeniero Salazar al ministerio de Fomento," in *Anales del ministerio de Fomento,* vol. 3, p. 146; summarized in *México a Través de los Siglos,* vol. 2, pp. 531–533).—*Trans.*]

[76] Ponce, vol. 1, pp. 112, 213; Mme. Calderón de la Barca, vol. 1, pp. 243–244; M. Romero de Terreros, "Los acueductos de México," pp. 131–142; Vetancurt, vol. 3, pp. 379–380; Alamán, vol. 2, pp. 244–245.

[77] Ponce, vol. 2, pp. 514–516.

[78] Redfield, pp. 60–63; McBride, pp. 123–124.

[79] Viñas y Mey, "El Régimen de la tierra en la colonización española," in *Humanidades,* vol. 10, pp. 71 ff., and *España y los orígenes de la política social,* pp. 99–107, and, especially, his *El estatuto del obrero indígena,* pp. 95–140; Focher, f. 89 v°; Váldez de la Torre, pp. 109–115; Baudin, pp. 105 ff.

[80] Dávila Padilla, Book 1, p. 303*b*.

[81] *Cédula* of February 1, 1561, in *Disposiciones complementarias,* No. 119, pp. 155–156; RLI, vol. 2, ff. 203 v°–204 r°.

[82] *Relación del Arzobispado de Méjico,* in CDIAI, vol. 4, pp. 491–530; also published at the end of the *Descripción del Arzobispado de México,* pp. 421 ff.

[83] *Pintura del Gobernador, Alcaldes, y Regidores,* pp. 9–10.

[84] AGI, *Audiencia de México,* 60–2–16.

[85] Motolinía, *Historia,* vol. 3, p. 175; Franco, Book 1, p. 19.

[86] Pedro Juárez de Escobar to Philip II, April 1, 1579, in Cuevas, *Documentos,* p. 311.

[87] Allier, *La psychologie,* vol. 1, p. 52.

[88] *Les conversions,* p. 124.

[89] Simão de Vasconcelos, Book 1, p. 55; Book 2, chaps. 9–10; Book 1, pp. 120–122.

[90] Allier, *La psychologie,* vol. 2, pp. 20–23; chap. 1, 3d Part, pp. 9–29; vol. 2, p. 368.

[91] Lumholtz, vol. 1, p. 135.

[92] *L'Ame des peuples à evangéliser,* pp. 18–20; *Les conversions,* pp. 151–159; *Revue missionnaire des Jésuites belges,* March, 1930, pp. 131–133.

[93] Allier, *La psychologie,* chap. 1, 3d Part; *l'Ame des peuples à evangéliser,* p. 21.

[94] Burgoa, *Geografica Descripcion,* ff. 17 v°–18 r°.

[95] Pedro de Ayala to Philip II, March 16, 1567, in AGI, *Audiencia de Guadalajara,* 67–1–18, 127; Orozco y Jiménez, pp. 343–344.

[96] RLI, vol. 2, f. 201 r°.

[97] *Ibid.,* f. 200 v°.

[98] M. Gamio, *La Población del Valle de Teotihuacán,* vol. 1, p. 400.

NOTES TO CHAPTER 9

(Pages 155–161)

[1] Franco, Book 1, p. 19; Tello, p. 549.

[2] Esteban García, Book 5, pp. 25–27; N. León, *Los precursores de la literatura médica mexicana,* pp. 3–94; Icazbalceta, "Los médicos," in *Opúsculos,* vol. 1, pp. 65–124.

[3] Streit, vol. 1, p. 57.

[4] Icazbalceta, "Los médicos," pp. 89–90, 104–105.

[5] Sahagún, *Historia,* pp. 787–790, 641, 825; HEI, Book 4, pp. 514–515; Grijalva, Book 2, chaps. 3 and 4; Méndez, Book 2, f. 42 r°; Viceroy Enríquez to Philip II, October 31, 1576, in *Cartas de Indias,* No. 58, p. 331; Humboldt, vol. 1, p. 333; vol. 4, pp. 161–162.

[6] E&D, p. 85.

[7] Lorenzana, pp. 144–145; Cuevas, *Historia,* vol. 2, pp. 93–94.

[8] Cuevas, *Documentos,* p. 328.

[9] Dávila Padilla, Book 1, p. 155*a;* Méndez, chap. 10, f. 38 r°; Paso y Troncoso, *Papeles,* f. 1 r°, MS No. 3048 of the Biblioteca Nacional de Madrid; Zumárraga to the Council of the Indies, November 24, 1536, in Cuevas, *Documentos,* p. 56; *Descripción del Arzobispado de México,* p. 452.

[10] Beaumont, Book 2, chap. 20, *passim.*

[11] Arlegui, vol. 2, pp. 58–59.

[12] Tello, p. 574.

[13] Tello, p. 475; Frejes, *Historia breve,* p. 159.

[14] "Descripción de Querétaro," in *Colección de documentos para la historia de San Luis Potosí,* vol. 1, p. 48.

[15] Paso y Troncoso, *Papeles,* vol. 5, pp. 43, 105; vol. 6, p. 303.

[16] *Descripción del Arzobispado,* p. 287.

[17] Flores, vol. 2, pp. 235–236.

[18] Motolinía, *Historia,* vol. 2, pp. 131–132; Cervantes de Salazar, Book 3, p. 242; A. Ortega, pp. 266–277.

[19] Muñoz, p. 399; Rea, Book 1, chap. 27; Daza, Book 2, p. 121*a.*

[20] Muñoz, pp. 399–400; Rea, Book 1, chap. 27; Tello, pp. 525–526.

[21] Cuevas, *Historia,* vol. 1, p. 413, and 404 ff.

[22] Escobar, pp. 672, 705, 792.

[23] Escobar, p. 159; Basalenque, Book 1, f. 21; Sicardo, f. 20 r°.

[24] Escobar, pp. 98, 162, 792.

[25] Escobar, p. 161.

[26] Grijalva, Book 1, pp. 54–58; Zumárraga to the Council of the Indies, February 8, 1537, in Cuevas, *Documentos,* p. 77; deposition of same in the

residencia of the second Audiencia, in Icazbalceta, *Zumárraga,* Appendix, pp. 84–86; Report of Archbishop Moya de Contreras, April 4, 1583, in Cuevas, *Documentos,* p. 328; Zorita, vol. 1, p. 275; "Privilegio" of April 12, 1711, published by N. León in *Anales del Museo Michoacano,* 2d year, pp. 179–182; N. León, *Don Vasco de Quiroga,* pp. 11–19.

[27] Cuevas, *Historia,* vol. 1, pp. 414–417.

[28] Pedro de Gante to Charles V, October 21, 1532, in *Cartas de Indias,* No. 8, p. 52.

[29] Icazbalceta, *Códice Franciscano,* p. 73.

NOTES TO CHAPTER 10

(Pages 162–175)

[1] Montes de Oca, "Tlaxcala, la ciudad muerta," pp. 161–205, especially p. 196.

[2] Romero de Terreros, *La Iglesia y Monasterio de S. Agustín Acolman,* p. 8; Toussaint, *Iglesias,* vol. 6, p. 21.

[3] Toussaint, *Oaxaca,* p. 10; A. Cortés and Genaro García, *Album.* The present convent of Santo Domingo de Oaxaca was begun about 1570 (*Iglesias,* vol. 6, p. 49).

[4] Michel, *Histoire de l'Art,* vol. 17, 3d Part, p. 1026; Vera y Zuria, *Cartas a mis seminaristas,* p. 556.

[5] Tello, pp. 308–309.

[6] Mier, p. 154.

[7] Toussaint, *Iglesias,* vol. 6, pp. 7–54; Diez Barroso, pp. 57–60.

[8] Toussaint, *Iglesias,* vol. 6, p. 23.

[9] *Instrucciones que los Vireyes de Nueva España dejaron a sus sucesores,* vol. 1, p. 48; Toussaint, *Iglesias,* vol. 6, pp. 49–50, 63–64.

[10] Gamio, *La Población del Valle de Teotihuacán,* vol. 2, p. 223.

[11] R. García Granados, in *Universidad de México,* March, 1931, pp. 370–374; Toussaint, *Iglesias,* vol. 6, p. 33 and pp. 119–120.

[12] *Ibid.,* vol. 6, pp. 23, 37.

[13] *Ibid.,* vol. 6, p. 25.

[14] Ibid., vol. 6, pp. 47, 49; Toussaint, *"Paseos coloniales, Coixtlahuaca,"* pp. 184–189.

[15] Motolinía, *Memoriales,* pp. 92–93, and *Historia,* vol. 1, p. 67.

[16] Toussaint, *Iglesias,* vol. 6, pp. 16, 22, 24; Ponce, vol. 1, pp. 162–163; R. García Granados, "Sobre las huellas pretéritas"; Toussaint, in *Revista Mexicana de Estudios Históricos,* July–August, 1927, pp. 173–180.

[17] Toussaint, *Iglesias,* vol. 6, pp. 16, 24, 25.

[18] *Ibid.,* pp. 16, 48–49, 50–52, figs. 41–45.

[19] Burgoa, *Geografica Descripcion,* f. 191.

[20] Toussaint, *Iglesias,* vol. 6, p. 16.

[21] Levillier, vol. 2, p. 232.

[22] Zumárraga to Charles V, April 17, 1540, in Cuevas, *Documentos,* No. 23, p. 99.

[23] Icazbalceta, *Códice Franciscano,* p. 66.

[24] Cuevas, *Documentos,* pp. 59–60.

[25] Icazbalceta, *Códice Franciscano,* p. 66; Escobar, p. 102; Lumholtz, vol. 1, p. 137; vol. 2, p. 6.

[26] Cuevas, *Documentos,* p. 77 and p. 245.

[27] CDIAI, vol. 4, pp. 519–521; Cuevas, *Documentos,* pp. 261–262; Montúfar and Vasco de Quiroga *vs.* the Mendicant Orders, 1561, in AGI, 51–6–10/27, No. 2.

[28] Lebrón de Quiñones to Prince Philip, September 10, 1554, in AGI, *Audiencia de Guadalajara,* 67–1–18, No. 10.

[29] Cervantes de Salazar, Book 3, p. 242; Motolinía, *Historia,* vol. 3, p. 235.

[30] Icazbalceta, *Opúsculos,* vol. 2, pp. 410–411, note.

[31] Icazbalceta, *Zumárraga,* p. 35, note, and Appendix, p. 254 (Second Audiencia to the Empress, March 30, 1531); Toussaint, *Iglesias,* vol. 6, p. 44.

[32] Toussaint, *Oaxaca,* p. 32.

[33] Pedro Juárez de Escobar to Philip II, April 1, 1579, in Cuevas, *Documentos,* p. 310.

[34] González de la Puente, Book 2, pp. 253–256.

[35] Pamphile, f. 116 v⁰.

[36] Basalenque, Book 1, chap. 16; Toussaint, *Iglesias,* vol. 6, p. 41.

[37] "Relación de la provincia de Meztitlán," pp. 109–110; *Relación de los obispados,* pp. 141–151.

[38] Cervantes de Salazar, Book 4, p. 317; Pamphile, f. 113 r⁰; Zorita, vol. 1, p. 184; *Cédula* of February 22, 1549, in *Disposiciones complementarias de las Leyes de Indias,* vol. 1, p. 95.

[39] Genaro García, No. 43, p. 83.

[40] *Pintura del Gobernador,* pp. 8–9.

[41] HEI, Book 3, pp. 340–341; Icazbalceta, *Zumárraga,* p. 34, note 3.

[42] Genaro García, No. 43, p. 84.

[43] Officials of New Galicia to Charles V, December 20, 1549, in AGI, *Audiencia de Guadalajara,* 67–1–18, No. 4.

[44] AGI, *Audiencia de Guadalajara,* 67–1–18, No. 157.

[45] *Cédula* of December 19, 1531, in Puga, vol. 1, pp. 247–248.

[46] *Cédula* of May 12, 1552, in Puga, vol. 2, pp. 156–157; Zumárraga, *Opúsculos,* vol. 2, pp. 378–379.

[47] Cuevas, *Documentos,* p. 262; Icazbalceta, *Opúsculos,* vol. 2, p. 417.

⁴⁸ Icazbalceta, *Opúsculos,* vol. 2, pp. 410–411, note; Toussaint, *Iglesias,* vol. 6, p. 24.

⁴⁹ *Ibid.,* vol. 6, p. 17.

⁵⁰ Genaro García, No. 44, pp. 128–130.

⁵¹ Pedro de Ayala to the Council of the Indies, no date, in AGI, *Audiencia de Guadalajara,* 60–4–39; Cuevas, *Historia,* vol. 2, p. 170.

⁵² Oseguera to Philip II, January 29, 1563, in AGI, *Audiencia de Guadalajara,* 67–1–18, No. 86.

⁵³ M. Gamio, *La población del Valle de Teotihuacán,* vol. 1, p. 479; Vera y Zuria, pp. 112, 121, 326, 373.

⁵⁴ See above, p. 129.

⁵⁵ Paso y Troncoso, *Papeles,* vol. 5, pp. 280–281.

⁵⁶ *Cartas de Indias,* No. 19, p. 106.

⁵⁷ HEI, Book 3, p. 255.

⁵⁸ Motolinía, *Historia,* vol. 3, p. 235.

⁵⁹ AGI, *Audiencia de México,* 60–2–16; *Cédula* of August 16, 1563, in *Recopilación,* vol. 1, f. 11 r⁰.

⁶⁰ Ricard, "L'incorporation' de l'Indien," p. 64.

⁶¹ Jean-Marie de Sacré-Coeur, pp. 34–35.

⁶² Icazbalceta, *Opúsculos,* vol. 2, pp. 409–410; Cervantes de Salazar, Book 4, p. 319.

⁶³ Brou, *Saint François Xavier,* vol. 2, pp. 252–253; Suau, p. 443; St. Theresa, *Camino de Perfección,* chap. 2 *in fine.*

NOTES TO CHAPTER 11

(Pages 176–193)

¹ Motolinía, *Historia,* vol. 1, p. 67.

² *Ibid.,* pp. 68–69.

³ *Ibid.,* vol. 3, p. 214; Icazbalceta, *Códice Franciscano,* pp. 65–66; Valadés, 4th Part, p. 188; chap. 25, pp. 226–227; Dávila Padilla, Book 1, pp. 97*a*–99*b;* A. Fernández, *San Esteban,* pp. 328–329; Grijalva, Book 2, pp. 226–227; Escobar, p. 100.

⁴ Motolinía, *Historia,* vol. 1, pp. 81, 214–215; Genaro García, pp. 141–142; Ríos Arce, vol. 2, doc. no. 17. For the *chirimía* and the *vihuela de arco,* see the passages in Covarrubias cited by Barry in his classical edition of Alarcón's *La Verdad Sospechosa,* verses 706–707; León Diguet, "Le Chimalhuacán," p. 12. For the *sacabuche,* see Simonet, *Glosario,* p. 504. For the *atabal,* see Sahagún, *Historia,* p. 868; Motolinía, *Memoriales,* pp. 340–341.

⁵ Cuevas, *Documentos,* p. 99.

⁶ Lumholtz, vol. 2, pp. 377 ff.

[7] N. León, *Los Tarascos,* p. 478.

[8] Motolinía, *Historia,* vol. 3, p. 214; HEI, Book 4, pp. 412–413; Muñoz Camargo, Book 1, p. 214; Alamán, vol. 2, p. 240; Ponce, vol. 1, p. 211.

[9] Motolinía, *Historia,* vol. 3, p. 215.

[10] *Ibid.,* p. 215.

[11] Rea, Book 1, p. 105.

[12] Tello, p. 204; Beaumont, Book 1, p. 504.

[13] Basalenque, Book 1, ff. 21 v^0–22 r^0; Escobar, pp. 97–98.

[14] Basalenque, Book 1, ff. 67 v^0–68 r^0; Escobar, p. 791.

[15] Motolinía, *Historia,* vol. 3, p. 214.

[16] Alonso de la Mota, p. 37.

[17] Grijalva, Book 2, p. 227.

[18] Basalenque, Book 1, f. 22 r^{0}a; Escobar, p. 168.

[19] Lorenzana, pp. 140–141.

[20] See above, p. 177.

[21] Cuevas, *Documentos,* p. 265.

[22] *Pintura del Gobernador,* p. 8.

[23] Motolinía, *Historia,* vol. 1, pp. 67–70; HEI, Book 4, pp. 429–434.

[24] Vetancurt, vol. 3, pp. 128–131; HEI, Book 4, pp. 436–437; Escobar, pp. 100–102.

[25] Motolinía, *Historia,* vol. 1, pp. 69–70; Zorita, vol. 1, pp. 191, 210–211, 512.

[26] RHF, April, 1924, p. 231; E&D, p. 113, note 3, and p. 117.

[27] Escobar, pp. 97–98.

[28] Grijalva, Book 2, pp. 227–228.

[29] Méndez, Book 1, f. 8; Alamán, vol. 2, p. 278; L. González Obregón, *México viejo,* pp. 440–444.

[30] Vetancurt, vol. 3, p. 128; vol. 4, p. 214; A. Fernández, *Historia eclesiástica,* Book 1, p. 53*b;* Daza, Book 2, p. 89*b.*

[31] Zorita, vol. 1, pp. 191, 211; HEI, Book 4, pp. 420–421; Rea, Book 2, chap. 7; Vetancurt, vol. 3, pp. 128 ff.

[32] Dávila Padilla, Book 2, chaps. 5 ff.; Méndez, Book 4, f. 123 v^0; Paso y Troncoso, *Papeles,* vol. 6, p. 64.

[33] Grijalva, Book 2, pp. 227–228.

[34] *Pintura del Gobernador,* p. 8.

[35] Icazbalceta, *Códice Franciscano,* pp. 76–77.

[36] Acosta, vol. 2, p. 224.

[37] *Ibid.,* pp. 227–228.

[38] *Ibid.,* pp. 225–226; Motolinía, *Historia,* vol. 1, p. 67.

[39] See above, p. 58, note; Viñaza, p. 41.

[40] A. Peñafiel, R. Campos, p. 15.

[41] Genaro Estrada, ed., *Ordenanzas de Gremios de la Nueva España*, p. 273; Icazbalceta, *Opúsculos*, vol. 2, pp. 443–451; L. González Obregón, *México viejo*, chap. 4.

[42] Mendizábal, "La poesía indígena y las canciones populares," pp. 79–84.

[43] Nuñez y Domínguez, pp. 12–22; Cuevas, *Historia*, vol. 3, p. 483.

[44] Motolinía, *Historia*, vol. 1, p. 67.

[45] Diez de Sollano, pp. 213–227.

[46] Redfield, p. 227.

[47] Toor, "Fiesta de la Santa Vera Cruz en Taxco," in *Mexican Folkways*, April–June, 1930, pp. 89–91.

[48] Ricard, "Contribution a l'étude des fêtes de 'moros y cristianos' au Mexique," pp. 51–84.

[49] Icazbalceta, *Zumárraga*, Appendix, pp. 120–121; Vera, *Colección*, vol. 2, pp. 387–388.

[50] Lorenzana, pp. 146–147.

[51] Sahagún, *Historia*, p. 867.

[52] Lorenzana, pp. 141–142; R. García Granados, "Simulacros de misas."

[53] Lorenzana, p. 194.

[54] P. Charles, "Les pèlerinages," in *Dossiers*, No. 136, and *Après la conversion*, pp. 74–82.

[55] Cuevas, *Historia*, vol. 1, pp. 147–148.

[56] Grijalva, Book 2, chap. 14.

[57] Ricard, "Les apparitions de Notre-Dame," pp. 247–262; Velázquez, *La aparición*; Ricard, review of preceding, in *Revue Historique*, May–June, 1932, pp. 612–613; Fernández del Castillo, García Granados, MacGregor, and Rosell, "México y la Guadalupana," in JSA, 1931, p. 466.

[58] Velázquez, *La aparición*, p. 108.

[59] *Ibid.*, p. 340 and p. 5.

[60] Ricard, "Les apparitions de Notre-Dame," pp. 254, 258–260; Velázquez, *La aparición*, pp. 24–27, 397 ff.

[61] Montúfar, *Información*, p. 52; Ricard, "Les apparitions de Notre-Dame," p. 254, note 2.

[62] Montúfar, *Información*, pp. 32–35, 39–41, 38–40.

[63] *Ibid.*, pp. 46–50.

[64] *Descripción del Arzobispado de México*, p. 390; Velázquez, *La aparición*, pp. 7–8.

[65] Cuevas, *Historia*, vol. 4, p. 22.

[66] Velázquez, *La aparición*, pp. 6–9, 41; López de Velasco, p. 190.

[67] Velázquez, *La aparición*, pp. 44–45; Montúfar, *Información*, pp. 14–18, 31–35.

[68] Cuevas, *Historia*, vol. 4, p. 24; Icazbalceta, *Opúsculos*, vol. 2, pp. 435–441.

[69] Velázquez, *La aparición,* pp. 24–28.

[70] See above, p. 103.

[71] See above, p. 56; Velázquez, *La aparición,* pp. 352–353, 388.

[72] Montúfar, *Información, passim.*

[73] Vera, *Santuario del Sacromonte.*

[74] *Ibid.,* pp. 22–36.

[75] Vera y Zuria, pp. 437–438; M. Loayzaga.

[76] Tello, p. 139.

[77] *Ibid.,* pp. 855–856.

[78] F. Florencia; J. Sardo; Mendizábal, "El santuario de Chalma," pp. 93–103.

[79] Vázquez Santana, p. 227.

NOTES TO CHAPTER 12

(Pages 194–206)

[1] F. Pimentel, pp. 86–135; Menéndez y Pelayo, *Antología de Poetas Hispano-Americanos,* vol. 1, pp. xlvi–xlix; Icazbalceta, "Representaciones reliogiosas de México en el siglo XVI," in *Opúsculos,* vol. 2, pp. 307–368; Icaza, vol. 2, 56–76; Huonder, *Zur Geschichte des Missionstheaters,* pp. 6–22; Cuevas, *Historia,* vol. 1, pp. 383–385; González Peña, pp. 108–113; P. Charles, in *Dossiers,* No. 40, and "Le théatre missionnaire," in *Après la conversion,* pp. 181–191.

[2] R. and M. d'Harcourt, pp. 112–113.

[3] The *autos* translated and studied by Paso y Troncoso are: *Sacrificio de Isaac, Auto en lengua mexicana* (anonymous) *escrito en el año 1678,* (Florence, 1899); *Adoración de los Reyes, Auto en lengua mexicana* (anonymous), (Florence, 1900); "Comédies en langue nauatl," in *Congrès international des Américanistes, Xii° Session, Paris, 1900,* pp. 309–316; *Comedia de los Reyes escrita en mexicano a principios del siglo XVII (por Agustín de la Fuente),* (Florence, 1902); *Destrucción de Jerusalén, Auto en lengua mexicana* (anonymous), *escrita con letra de fines del siglo XVII* (Florence, 1907). *Cf.* Icaza, p. 57, note 1. Only Icaza and Huonder have listed these texts.

[4] As, for example, the *Invención de la Santa Cruz por Santa Elena,* also translated by Paso y Troncoso. *Cf.* Icaza, p. 57, note 1, and p. 59.

[5] This is the opinion of Paso y Troncoso with respect to the *Sacrificio de Isaac,* pp. 4–5.

[6] See Native-language Works in Bibliography, below, No. 62.

[7] According to Pimentel, pp. 86–87, a certain Father Las Casas dedicated a *Cancionero Espiritual* (1546) to Zumárraga which contained, among other

things, a "farce" entitled *El Juicio Final*. This Father Las Casas was probably Father Vicente de las Casas, a novice in the first Dominican mission [1526].

[8] Las Casas, *Apologética historia de las Indias,* p. 165; Icazbalceta, *Opúsculos,* vol. 2, p. 338; see Native-language Works, No. 26.

[9] Motolinía, *Historia,* vol. 1, pp. 79 ff.

[10] We do not know that these *autos* were among the dialogues of Father Fuensalida.

[11] Icazbalceta, *Opúsculos,* vol. 2, p. 325; Ricard, "Contribution," pp. 62–63.

[12] Ricard, "Contribution," p. 63.

[13] We do not know that this *auto* is the same as that published by Paso y Troncoso; Las Casas, *Apologética historia,* pp. 164–165; Icazbalceta, *Opúsculos,* vol. 2, p. 313, note 1.

[14] The manuscript has the date of 1678, but Paso y Troncoso thinks that the play, in its general lines, is much older (pp. 4–5).

[15] Gómez de Orozco, "Dos escritores indígenas del siglo XVI," pp. 128–130.

[16] Ponce, vol. 2, pp. 39–43, 115.

[17] According to Ponce, the crèche was outside; according to Paso y Troncoso, it was inside the church, where the Magi came to offer their presents. This second version is closely tied to the service.

[18] Ricard, "Contribution," pp. 67–69.

[19] Icazbalceta, *Opúsculos,* vol. 2, p. 312; Paso y Troncoso, in *Congrès international des Américanistes, XII° session,* p. 313; *Cf.* Lumholtz, vol. 1, pp. 347–348.

[20] Icazbalceta, *Opúsculos,* vol. 2, pp. 311–312.

[21] Allier, *La psychologie,* vol. 1, p. 514.

[22] Icaza, pp. 58–59, 60 note 1; Ricard, "Contribution," p. 77; "Les fêtes de 'moros y cristianos' au Mexique," J. G. Frazer, *Le Bouc Emissaire,* p. 265; Sahagún, *Historia, passim.*

[23] Granada, *Obras,* p. 440.

[24] Pimentel, p. 126.

[25] Motolinía, *Historia,* vol. 1, p. 84.

[26] *Ibid.,* p. 93.

[27] *Ibid.,* p. 95.

[28] *Ibid.,* p. 27.

[29] *Ibid.,* pp. 28–29.

[30] Ponce, vol. 2, p. 42.

[31] Motolinía, *Historia,* vol. 1, p. 68; Icazbalceta, *Opúsculos,* vol. 2, p. 312; Pimentel, p. 134.

[32] Ponce, vol. 2, p. 43.

³³ *Autour du problème de l'adaptation,* p. 116.
³⁴ Pimentel, p. 127; Viñaza, p. 50.
³⁵ "Los Pastores. A Mexican Play of the Nativity," in *Memoirs of the American Folklore Society,* vol. 9, 1907. *Cf.* Huonder, pp. 19–21; Hirshfield, pp. 156–161.
³⁶ N. León, *Los Tarascos,* pp. 435–452.
³⁷ *Mexican Folkways,* June–July, 1925, pp. 21–28; Aug.–Sept., 1925, pp. 27–29; Feb.–March, 1927, pp. 53–61; R. and M. d'Harcourt, pp. 115–116.
³⁸ Icazbalceta, *Opúsculos,* vol. 2, p. 339.
³⁹ Merimée, p. 5; Valbuena, pp. 14–15.
⁴⁰ Mâle, pp. 35 ff.
⁴¹ Ricard, "Contribution," p. 79.
⁴² Bataillon, "Chanson pieuse et poésie de dévotion," pp. 228–238, 233–234, 236.

NOTES TO CHAPTER 13

(Pages 207–216)

¹ V. Roelens, in *Bulletin des Missions,* June, 1930, p. 97.
² Icazbalceta, "La instrucción pública," in *Opúsculos,* vol. 1, pp. 163–270.
³ Alamán, vol. 2, pp. 219–220; Muñoz Camargo, p. 162, note 1 (by Chavero); *Boletín de la Real Academia de la Historia,* vol. 40, 1902, p. 525.
⁴ González Dávila, f. 74; HEI, Book 6, chaps. 43–44.
⁵ Icazbalceta, *Opúsculos,* vol. 2, pp. 422–424.
⁶ Tello, p. 547.
⁷ Icazbalceta, "La instrucción pública," p. 176.
⁸ *Cartas de Indias,* No. 18, p. 101.
⁹ Ricard, in RHF, April, 1924, p. 228, note 2; E&D, p. 112, note 2; Daza, Book 2, chap. 23; Vetancurt, vol. 4, pp. 213–216; Ricard in *Bulletin Hispanique,* July–Sept., 1925, pp. 245–246.
¹⁰ HEI, Book 4, pp. 418–419.
¹¹ Beuchat, pp. 353–354.
¹² Valadés, 2d Part, pp. 99–100.
¹³ Icazbalceta, "La instrucción pública," p. 173; Boban, vol. 2, pp. 171, 175.
¹⁴ Franco, Book 1, p. 57.
¹⁵ Grijalva, Book 1, f. 17 r°; Book 2, f. 72 r°; *Relación de los obispados,* pp. 122–124.
¹⁶ Basalenque, Book 1, f. 21 v°; Sicardo, f. 20 r°; Escobar, p. 167; N. León, *Los Tarascos,* p. 369.
¹⁷ A. Ortega, "Las primeras maestras"; González Dávila, f. 23 r°; Icazbalceta, "El colegio de niñas," in *Opúsculos,* vol. 2, pp. 427–343.

[18] Icazbalceta, *Zumárraga,* p. 88, 210.

[19] *Ibid.,* Appendix, p. 94; Ortega, "Las primeras maestras," pp. 372–374.

[20] Höltker, p. 517.

[21] Icazbalceta, *Zumárraga,* pp. 121–122, and Appendix, pp. 93–94, 99.

[22] Basalenque, Book 1, f. 20 r⁰–b.

[23] Allier, *La psychologie,* vol. 2, pp. 58–59.

[24] N. León, *Valadés,* p. 3.

[25] HEI, Book 4, chap. 13; RHF, April, 1924, p. 231; E&D, p. 116; Daza, Book 2, pp. 88b–89a; Vetancurt, vol. 4, p. 213; Icazbalceta, "La instrucción pública," p. 177.

[26] N. León, *Valadés,* p. 4; Romero de Terreros, *Historia sintética del arte colonial de México,* p. 50.

[27] HEI, Book 4, p. 409; Torquemada, Book 20, p. 531a; Vetancurt, vol. 4, pp. 78–79; Romero de Terreros, *Las artes industriales,* p. 186; Muñoz, pp. 412–414.

[28] Rea, Book 1, chap. 24.

[29] *Ibid.,* chap. 9.

[30] HEI, Book 4, p. 410; Zorita, vol. 1, p. 296; Baudin, p. 155; Beuchat, p. 734.

[31] Romero, *Las artes industriales,* p. 154.

[32] Grijalva, Book 2, p. 223.

[33] Basalenque, Book 1, f. 20; Escobar, pp. 146–149.

[34] Las Casas, pp. 161–162.

[35] Motolinía, *Historia,* vol. 3, pp. 213–214, 216–217.

[36] Romero de Terreros, *Historia sintética,* pp. 52–53; Bernal Díaz, chap. 91; Cuevas, *Historia,* vol. 4, pp. 43–44; Velázquez, *La aparición,* pp. 52 ff.

[37] *Boletín del Museo Nacional,* Jan.–March, 1924, p. 121.

[38] Lumholtz, vol. 2, p. 212.

[39] Toussaint, *Iglesias,* vol. 6, pp. 35, 25.

[40] Cuevas, *Historia,* vol. 3, pp. 86–87.

[41] Toussaint, *Iglesias,* vol. 6, p. 47; *Universidad de México,* Jan., 1931, p. 187.

[42] Toussaint, *Iglesias,* vol. 6, p. 33.

[43] R. García Granados, "Calpan," p. 373.

[44] Toussaint, *Iglesias,* vol. 6, pp. 40, 45, fig. 34.

NOTES TO CHAPTER 14

(Pages 217–235)

[1] Bayle, "España."

[2] N. León, *Los Tarascos,* p. 369; and see above, p. 210.

[3] CDIAI, vol. 41, pp. 145–148; Cuevas, *Documentos,* pp. 86–88.

[4] Bayle, "España," pp. 214–215.

[5] Icazbalceta, *Códice Franciscano,* pp. 62–65; and see above, p. 98.

[6] Chavero, *Sahagún;* Icazbalceta, *Zumárraga,* pp. 211–224; Chavero, "Colegio de Tlatelolco"; Zepeda R., pp. 29 ff.; Ricard, "Le collège indigène de Santiago Tlatelolco," in E&D, pp. 155–160; *Les élites en pays de mission,* pp. 83–89.

[7] Icazbalceta, *Zumárraga,* Appendix, p. 93; Cuevas, *Documentos,* p. 56; Ortega, p. 383.

[8] Motolinía, *Historia,* vol. 3, p. 215.

[9] Icazbalceta, *Zumárraga,* Appendix, p. 99.

[10] Icazbalceta, *Códice Franciscano,* pp. 70–73; HEI, Book 4, chap. 15.

[11] HEI, Book 4, chap. 15; Cervantes de Salazar, Book 4, p. 320; Beaumont, Book 2, chap. 3; Book 4, pp. 91–95.

[12] J. T. Medina, *La Imprenta,* vol. 1, No. 38, pp. 124–126.

[13] HEI, Book 4, chap. 15; Moles, f. 70 v°; Daza, Book 2, pp. 81*b*–82*a*; Ventacurt, vol. 3, pp. 209–211; Trinidad, Book 2, pp. 259*b*–260*a;* Icazbalceta, *Zumárraga,* p. 218.

[14] Zorita, vol. 1, pp. 186–187.

[15] Cuevas, *Historia,* vol. 1, p. 386; and see p. 222.

[16] Sahagún, *Historia,* pp. 2, 640; HEI, Book 4, p. 415.

[17] Icazbalceta, *Zumárraga,* Appendix, p. 93; Ortega, "Las primeras maestras," p. 384.

[18] Motolinía, vol. 3, p. 215.

[19] HEI, Book 4, p. 447.

[20] Cuevas, *Documentos,* p. 56; Ortega, p. 383.

[21] Francisco de Toral to Philip II, March 13, 1560, AGI, *Audiencia de México,* 60–2–16.

[22] Sahagún, *Historia,* pp. 641–642. Jourdanet-Siméon's translation is spoiled here by a bad contradiction: "Nos moines en *ordonnèrent* quelquesuns," "faire d'autres *ordinations"* (p. 641). The passage does not concern ordinations, but regulations (*ordenanzas*).

[23] The date is impossible to determine. Sahagún is the only one to give chronological data, and they do not agree. It was more than ten years after the founding of the college, he says, when its administration was given over to the students—which would put it at about 1547–1548, since the college was opened at the beginning of 1536. This regime, he adds, lasted twenty years, which brings us to 1567–1568, when he noticed that the college was going to ruin. But he immediately adds that it was forty years after the founding of the college (hence in 1576) when the situation was investigated.

[24] Cuevas, *Historia,* vol. 2, p. 285; Bayle, "España," p. 216.

[25] Cuevas, *Documentos*, p. 3.

[26] HEI, Book 4, p. 414; Vetancurt, vol. 3, p. 95.

[27] HEI, Book 4, p. 414; Aiton, p. 95, note 2; pp. 105–106.

[28] Icazbalceta, *Zumárraga*, p. 212.

[29] Cuevas, *Historia*, vol. 1, p. 386; Zepeda, p. 30; Bayle, "España," p. 216, note 6.

[30] Cuevas, *Documentos*, p. 56.

[31] Charles V to the bishops of Mexico, Guatemala, and Antequera, August 23, 1538, in Genaro García, vol. 23, pp. 49, 52–53; vol. 24, pp. 54–55; vol. 30, pp. 61–62.

[32] Icazbalceta, *Zumárraga*, pp. 220–221; Cuevas, *Historia*, vol. 1, pp. 388–389; Zepeda, p. 36.

[33] Motolinía, vol. 3, p. 215.

[34] HEI, Book 4, p. 447; RHF, July, 1925, p. 438, note 1.

[35] Viñaza, pp. 59–60.

[36] Sahagún, *Historia*, p. 641.

[37] Póu, p. 23; RHF, July, 1925, pp. 437–438; E&D, pp. 181–182.

[38] Bayle, "España," p. 219.

[39] Cuevas, *Historia*, vol. 1, p. 201, note 8.

[40] Icazbalceta, *Zumárraga*, p. 219.

[41] Cuevas, *Historia*, vol. 1, p. 386.

[42] Icazbalceta, *Zumárraga*, Appendix, p. 137; Cuevas, *Documentos*, p. 107.

[43] Icazbalceta, *Zumárraga*, pp. 215–217.

[44] This trial will be discussed in chapter 16.

[45] Cuevas, *Historia*, vol. 1, pp. 388–389; Zepeda, pp. 36–37.

[46] Pérez Bustamante, doc. 19, pp. 190–192; Cuevas, *Historia*, vol. 2, p. 252.

[47] Sahagún, *Historia*, p. 640.

[48] Cuevas, *Historia*, vol. 1, pp. 389–390; Bayle, "España," pp. 221–222.

[49] Icazbalceta, *Códice Franciscano*, p. 71; Zepeda, p. 38.

[50] Pérez Bustamante, p. 136; Cuevas, *Historia*, vol. 1, pp. 390–391.

[51] Sahagún, *Historia*, pp. 640–641; Acosta, vol. 2, p. 223.

[52] Ponce, vol. 1, pp. 22–23.

[53] N. León, *Los Tarascos*, p. 369.

[54] A. López, "Cuestionario histórico"; Cervantes de Salazar, *Crónica*, Book 4, p. 320.

[55] See above, p. 122.

[56] Icazbalceta, *Zumárraga*, p. 124; Lemmens, p. 222; Muñoz, pp. 395–397; Streit, vol. 1, pp. 107–109.

[57] HEI, Book 4, p. 450.

[58] Aiton, p. 95, note 35.

[59] Pérez Bustamante, p. 136.

[60] HEI, Book 4, p. 448.

[61] Sahagún, *Historia*, p. 635.

[62] Lorenzana, pp. 105–107.

[63] Icazbalceta, *Códice Franciscano*, p. 110.

[64] Icazbalceta, *Zumárraga*, Appendix, p. 119; Cuevas, *Historia*, vol. 1, pp. 430–431.

[65] Icazbalceta, *Zumárraga*, p. 124; Cuevas, *Historia*, vol. 2, p. 165; Lemmens, pp. 220–221.

[66] *Actas capitulares.*

[67] Muñoz, p. 404.

[68] Sahagún, *Historia*, pp. 635–636; HEI, Book 4, p. 450.

[69] Sahagún, *Historia*, p. 637; Ponce, vol. 1, pp. 170–171.

[70] Motolinía, *Historia*, vol. 2, p. 132.

[71] *Libros y libreros*, p. 26; Ricard, E&D, p. 101, note 10; Icazbalceta, *Zumárraga*, p. 124, note 3; Cuevas, *Historia*, vol. 2, p. 77.

[72] Motolinía, *Historia*, vol. 3, p. 230.

[73] Zumárraga to Charles V, August 27, 1529, in CDIAI, vol. 13, pp. 133–134.

[74] Ponce, vol. 1, p. 171.

[75] HEI, Book 4, pp. 442–443.

[76] Motolinía, *Historia*, vol. 2, pp. 132–133; Muñoz, pp. 403–404; HEI, Book 4, p. 445.

[77] HEI, Book 4, chaps. 22–23; Cuevas, *Historia*, vol. 2, pp. 453–457; vol. 3, pp. 499–509, 537, 542–544.

[78] Ribadeneyra, p. 273.

[79] Huonder, *Der einheimische Klerus*, pp. 20 ff.; Schmidlin, p. 338; Cuevas, *Historia*, vol. 4, p. 189.

[80] Cuevas, *Historia*, vol. 3, p. 174.

[81] Cuevas, *Historia*, vol. 3, p. 110.

NOTES TO CHAPTER 15

(Pages 239–263)

[1] Levillier, vol. 2, pp. 148–149.

[2] He had arrived November 26, 1562, at the moment when several Augustinians were writing to the Council of the Indies. See p. 251.

[3] Ricard, "Un document inédit," and E&D, pp. 123–131.

[4] CDIAI, vol. 23, p. 458.

[5] Icazbalceta, *Zumárraga*, pp. 34–35, and Appendix, p. 255.

[6] HEI, Book 3, chaps. 57–60; and above, p. 80.

[7] See p. 121, n. 60; Motolinía to Charles V against Las Casas, January

2, 1535, in CDIAI, vol. 7, pp. 254 ff.; Icazbalceta, *Nueva colección,* vol. 1, pp. 251; Motolinía, *Historia,* pp. 257 ff.

[8] Genaro García, p. 85.

[9] E&D, p. 93; Puga, vol. 2, pp. 268–271.

[10] E&D, pp. 96–97.

[11] RLI, vol. 1, f. 82 r⁰.

[12] Cuevas, *Documentos,* pp. 256, 260.

[13] CDIAI, vol. 4, pp. 494–495, 497.

[14] E&D, p. 101.

[15] Cuevas, *Documentos,* pp. 264–265.

[16] AGI, *Justicia,* 51–6–10; Icazbalceta, *Zumárraga,* Appendix, p. 95; Genaro García, p. 84; Cuevas, *Documentos,* pp. 252–253.

[17] AGI, *Justicia,* 51–6–10, f. 2 r⁰.

[18] *Ibid.,* ff. 9, 12 v⁰–13 r⁰; Puga, vol. 2, pp. 348–349.

[19] See above, p. 109.

[20] Suárez de Peralta, pp. 65, 33.

[21] CDIAI, vol. 13, p. 211.

[22] Icazbalceta, *Zumárraga,* pp. 89–91, Appendix, pp. 94–95.

[23] *Ibid.,* p. 129; Vera, *Colección,* vol. 2, p. 398.

[24] Icazbalceta, *Zumárraga,* Appendix, p. 120; Vera, vol. 2, p. 388.

[25] Cuevas, *Documentos,* pp. 252–254; *Pintura del Gobernador,* pp. 7–8.

[26] CDIAI, vol. 4, p. 496; *Pintura del Gobernador,* p. 9.

[27] Francisco del Toral to Philip II, February 20, 1559, in *Cartas de Indias,* No. 27, p. 139.

[28] RLI, vol. 1, f. 39 r⁰.

[29] E&D, pp. 78 ff.

[30] AGI, *Justicia,* 51–6–10, f. 2 r⁰.

[31] Cuevas, *Historia,* vol. 2, p. 55.

[32] *Ibid.,* pp. 92–96.

[33] Cuevas, *Documentos,* pp. 254–255.

[34] *Ibid.,* p. 243.

[35] *Cartas de Indias,* No. 27, p. 140.

[36] Cuevas, *Documentos,* p. 334.

[37] *Ibid.,* pp. 264–265; see above, p. 244; Puga, vol. 2, pp. 340–341.

[38] *Disposiciones complementarias,* No. 298, pp. 370–374; Puga, vol. 2, pp. 287–289; RLI, vol. 1, f. 55 r⁰.

[39] N. León, *Vasco de Quiroga,* pp. 56–58.

[40] RHF, April, 1924, pp. 225–226; E&D, pp. 53–56.

[41] AGI, *Justicia,* 47–5–55/11; N. León, *Quiroga,* p. 61.

[42] *Libros y libreros,* pp. 25–27.

[43] Cuevas, *Documentos,* pp. 255, 263–264.

[44] *Ibid.,* p. 260.

[45] These dispositions had not yet been corrected by the Holy See.

[46] Pedro de Ayala to Philip II, November 10, 1565, in AGI, *Audiencia de Guadalajara,* 67–1–18, ff. 110, 118, 157; Mota Padilla, chap. 45, p. 227.

[47] N. León, *Quiroga,* pp. 63–69, 221–222, 227, 235; Velázquez, *La aparición,* chap. 2, *passim;* Beaumont, Book 2, chap. 29.

[48] Cuevas, *Documentos,* pp. 335, 492.

[49] *Ibid.,* pp. 336–338, 342; Zorita, Appendix; Cuevas, *Historia,* vol. 2, pp. 490–491.

[50] RHF, April, 1924, p. 226; E&D, p. 55; *Cartas de Indias,* No. 19, pp. 107–108.

[51] *Libros y libreros,* p. 26.

[52] *Ibid.,* pp. 14, 16–17.

[53] *Procesos de indios idólatras,* pp. 221 ff.

[54] CDIHE, vol. 26, p. 286; *Instrucciones que los virreyes,* vol. 1, p. 11; *Descripción del Arzobispado,* p. 9.

[55] Cuevas, *Historia,* vol. 2, p. 169.

[56] Genaro García, *Clero,* vol. 43, pp. 83–86.

[57] Cuevas, *Documentos,* pp. 260–261; RHF, April, 1924, p. 235, note 2; E&D, p. 61, note 40.

[58] *Libros y libreros,* pp. 27, 36.

[59] Pedro Gómez Maraver to Charles V, December 12, 1550, in Orozco y Jiménez, p. 213.

[60] Francisco Morales to Las Casas, September 1, 1559, in *Colección de documentos inéditos para la historia de Ibero-América,* p. 231.

[61] *Libros y libreros,* p. 27.

[62] RHF, April, 1924, pp. 231–232; Cuevas, *Documentos,* p. 343; E&D, pp. 117–118.

[63] Cuevas, *Documentos,* p. 261; see above, p. 247.

[64] Puga, vol. 1, pp. 309–327, 326–377, 459–460.

[65] Icazbalceta, *Nueva Colección,* vol. 1, p. xxi.

[66] CDIAI, vol. 7, pp. 526–542.

[67] Cuevas, *Documentos,* pp. 161–167.

[68] AGI, *Audiencia de México,* 60–2–16.

[69] Icazbalceta, *Nueva Colección,* vol. 4, pp. 1–18; *Cartas de Indias,* No. 30, pp. 147–151.

[70] Cuevas, *Documentos,* pp. 242–244.

[71] *Ibid.,* pp. 289–290; Velázquez, *La aparición,* pp. 22–23.

[72] Cuevas, *Documentos,* p. 335.

[73] Paso y Troncoso, *Papeles,* vol. 6, p. 289; Latorre, p. 35.

[74] Cuevas, *Documentos,* p. 259.

[75] See above, p. 225.

[76] Cuevas, *Documentos,* p. 68; *Cartas de Indias,* No 19, pp. 105–106.

[77] Cuevas, *Documentos,* pp. 489, 492–493.

[78] RLI, vol. 1, ff. 3 v^0–4 r^0.

[79] Cuevas, *Documentos,* p. 335.

[80] Burgoa, *Geografica Descripcion,* chap. 10, f. 44 v^0.

[81] N. León, *Quiroga,* p. 24; Beaumont, vol. 3, pp. 323 ff., 410; Burgoa, *Geografica Descripcion,* chap. 10, f. 44 r^0.

[82] Orozco y Jiménez, pp. 209, 218.

[83] See above, p. 303.

[84] Puga, vol. 1, pp. 227–229, 229–231.

[85] Motolinía, *Historia,* vol. 2, pp. 136–137; Icazbalceta, *Zumárraga,* pp. 16–80, and Appendix, Docs. 1, 2, 5, 7, 10, 51, 52, 53, 54, 55, 56, 57; Cuevas, *Documentos,* pp. 17–46, 8–10; Cuevas, *Historia,* vol. 1, pp. 252–270; Simpson, pp. 97–111; Santana; Lois K. Dyer, p. 433.

[86] CDIHE, vol. 26, p. 285; *Instrucciones que los vireyes,* vol. 1, p. 10.

[87] Luis de Velasco to Philip II, February 1, 1558, in Cuevas, *Documentos,* pp. 244–245.

[88] AGI, *Indiferente General,* 146–1–8; RHF, April, 1924, p. 226, note 1; E&D, p. 54, note 28.

[89] E&D, p. 96; see above, p. 245.

[90] Cuevas, *Documentos,* pp. 255–256, 264.

[91] Cuevas, *Historia,* vol. 2, pp. 55–57.

NOTES TO CHAPTER 16

(Pages 264–282)

[1] Motolinía, *Historia,* vol. 2, p. 99.

[2] Burgoa, *Geografica Descripcion,* chap. 28, f. 156 r^0.

[3] Saravia, pp. 6 ff.; Arlegui, 4th Part; see above, pp. 67, 141.

[4] Pedro Gómez Maraver to the King, December 12, 1550, in Orozco y Jiménez, p. 208.

[5] Pérez Bustamante, pp. 154–155; Appendix, Doc. 9, pp. 152–168; Aiton, p. 140, note 6.

[6] Pérez Bustamante, p. 156.

[7] *Ibid.,* p. 157.

[8] *Ibid.,* p. 161; Mota Padilla, chap. 26; Lévy-Bruhl, *Le surnaturel et la nature,* pp. 74–76.

[9] Aiton, pp. 137–156; Pérez Bustamante, chap. 7, pp. 73–85; Appendix, Doc. 32, p. 206; Baltasar de Obregón, Book 1, pp. 31–38; Mota Padilla, chaps. 23 ff.

[10] Cuevas, *Documentos,* p. 493; Allier, *La psychologie,* vol. 1, pp. 136–139; Brou, *Saint François Xavier,* vol. 1, p. 239.

[11] Póu, pp. 310 ff.

[12] *Ibid.,* p. 301.

[13] Grijalva, Book 1, pp. 49–51, 109–110.

[14] Genaro García, vol. 35, pp. 69–70; Motolinía, *Historia,* vol. 3, p. 218; *Bulletin catholique international,* Feb. 1929, pp. 81–82; E&D, pp. 170–171; HEI, Book 4, p. 217.

[15] Icazbalceta, *Zumárraga,* App., pp. 106–107; Cuevas, *Documentos,* p. 61; Höltker, p. 507.

[16] Cuevas, *Documentos,* p. 57.

[17] *Procesos de Indios idolátras, passim; Libros y libreros,* p. 465.

[18] Cuevas, *Documentos,* p. 204; see above, p. 141.

[19] Pedro de Ayala to Philip II, February 6, 1565, AGI, *Audiencia de Guadalajara,* 67–1–18, 105; Orozco y Jiménez, pp. 299–300.

[20] Sahagún, *Historia,* p. 639.

[21] Vera, *Colección,* vol. 2, pp. 389–390.

[22] Icazbalceta, *Zumárraga,* Appendix p. 91; Cuevas, *Documentos,* pp. 492–493.

[23] Cuevas, *Documentos,* p. 258; Burgoa, *Geografica Descripcion,* chap. 11, f. 46 v°.

[24] Mendizábal, "El santuario de Chalma," pp. 97–98.

[25] Motolinía, *Historia,* vol. 1, p. 32; *Memoriales,* p. 30; Román y Zamora, *Repúblicas de Indias,* vol. 1, pp. 82–83.

[26] HEI, Book 3, pp. 309–310.

[27] Dávila Padilla, Book 2, chap. 38.

[28] HEI, Book 3, p. 234.

[29] Motolinía, *Memoriales,* p. 33.

[30] *Cartas de Indias,* No. 9, p. 56; Motolinía, *Historia,* vol. 3, chap. 20; *Memoriales,* p. 30; Dávila Padilla, Book 1, p. 81*b;* Sahagún, pp. 5, 792; Suárez de Peralta, pp. 277–278.

[31] See above, p. 268.

[32] *Procesos de indios idólatras,* pp. 3–5, 177 ff., 185 ff., 141 ff., 221 ff.

[33] *Ibid.,* pp. 3, 7, 8, 87 ff., 201–203.

[34] *Ibid.,* 109 ff.; *Libros y libreros,* p. 465.

[35] *Procesos de indios idólatras,* pp. 205 ff.

[36] Beuchat, pp. 331–332; Joyce, pp. 95–101.

[37] Dávila Padilla, Book 2, p. 788*a.*

[38] Muñoz Camargo, Book 1, pp. 164–165.

[39] *Relación de . . . Michoacán,* pp. 108–110.

[40] Grijalva, Book 1, p. 155.

[41] *Procesos de indios idólatras,* pp. 17 ff., HEI, Book 2, p. 109; Icazbalceta, *Zumárraga,* p. 9.

[42] Pérez Bustamante, p. 74, note 2.

[43] Méndez, Book 3, ff. 49 v^0–50 r^0; Aiton, pp. 174–175; Pérez Bustamante, p. 113.

[44] L. González Obregón, *Proceso,* vol. 1; Icazbalceta, *Zumárraga,* pp. 149–150; *Obras,* vol. 10, p. 308; Cuevas, *Historia,* vol. 1, pp. 369–379.

[45] L. González Obregón, *Proceso,* pp. 6, 37, 41–42, 52.

[46] See above, p. 320.

[47] Suárez de Peralta, p. 279.

[48] Iguíniz, "Calendario Mexicano."

[49] Humboldt, vol. 2, p. 206.

[50] Burgoa, *Geografica Descripcion,* ff. 168 v^0–169 r^0.

[51] Nuttall, "L'évêque Zumárraga"; *Procesos de Indios idólatras,* pp. 115 ff.

[52] Motolinía, *Historia,* vol. 2, p. 135.

[53] Valadés, 4th Part, pp. 183–190.

[54] M. Gamio, *Forjando patria,* pp. 149 ff., and *Teotihuacán,* vol. 1, pp. xxxi, xliv, lxxix, and *Mexican Immigration,* pp. 108–127; R. Rivera, pp. 92–97; E. Gruening.

[55] N. León, *Los popolacas,* pp. 13–16.

[56] M. Gamio, *Forjando patria,* pp. 159–160, and *Mexican Immigration,* p. 110.

[57] Lombardo Toledano.

[58] N. León, *Los Tarascos,* pp. 476–477.

[59] Domínguez Assiayn, pp. 209 ff.

[60] Andrade, "Idolatrías y supersticiones."

[61] A. Rivera, p. 10, note; Noriega Hope, in *Teotihuacán,* vol. 2, p. 209.

[62] Noriega Hope, pp. 208–230.

[63] Vera y Zuria, pp. 113, 140.

[64] Bergson, pp. 107; et ff.; Brouillard, pp. 192–206.

[65] M. Gamio, *Forjando patria,* p. 161; R. Rivera, p. 93.

[66] Lecanuet, pp. 156–159.

[67] Vera y Zuria, p. 218.

[68] Bautista, *Advertencias,* ff. 51 v^0–53 v^0.

[69] M. Gamio, *Forjando patria,* p. 161; R. Rivera, p. 95.

[70] See above, p. 183; Solórzano Pereyra, Book 2, vol. 1, p. 191.

[71] Ricard, in *Revue de l'Amérique Latine,* August, 1931, p. 165; Pinard de la Boullaye, vol. 1, pp. 70–71, 89–90, 166–168, 206–207.

[72] I reached these conclusions before I had seen M. Gamio's *Mexican Immigration.* His remarks, on pp. 115–116, in spite of our different points of

view, agree with mine and confirm the description of the spiritual geography of Mexico that I have just outlined.

NOTES TO CHAPTER 17

(Pages 283–295)

[1] *Après la conversion*, p. 80.
[2] Grijalva, Book 30, *in fine*.
[3] Kenny, p. 9.
[4] P. Rivet, "Le christianisme."
[5] Humboldt, vol. 2, p. 281.
[6] *Ibid.*, vol. 1, p. 398; Ricard, "L'incorporation de l'Indien.
[7] Rabasa, pp. 236, 262, 308; Sorre, p. 73.
[8] T. Esquivel Obregón, p. 49; Ricard, bibliography in "L'incorporation," above, p. 455–457, especially Nos. 2, 4, 5, 7, 8, 29.
[9] Rabasa, pp. 240–241, 257.
[10] *Ibid.*
[11] Bernard, pp. 22, 23.
[12] Ribadeneyra, chap. 13, p. 273.
[13] Cuevas, *Historia,* vol. 3, p. 110.
[14] Humboldt, vol. 3, p. 115, note.
[15] Humboldt, vol. 1, pp. 439–442; *La lucha de los católicos mejicanos,* pp. 63–70 (Anon.). It should be noted that this attempt followed others, in 1859, 1866, and one under President Carranza; also, that the "Patriarch of the Mexican Church," created by General Calles, was a Mixtec Indian, José Joaquín Pérez. See also H. Blanco Fombona, pp. 72–73.

NOTES TO APPENDIX I

(Pages 296–309)

[1] Ricard, "Les Jésuites au Brésil.
[2] R. García Granados, "Capillas de indios."
[3] JSA, vol. 29, pp. 220–227, and vol. 30, pp. 375–376; *Bulletin hispanique,* vol. 40, pp. 311–312.
[4] J. J. Rojas Garcidueñas, *El teatro de Nueva España en el siglo XVI.*
[5] Ros, *Le Père François d'Osune.*
[6] The prayers of St. Thomas Aquinas are in the pamphlet of Fray Hernando de Talavera, "En qué manera se deve haver la persona que ha de comulgar," in NBAE, vol. 16, pp. 40–41.
[7] Ricard, "Fray Hernando de Ojea."

[8] Bataillon, *Erasme en Espagne,* pp. 580–590; S. Zavala, *La Utopía de Tomás Moro.*

[9] Getino, *El Maestro Fray Francisco de Vitoria,* pp. 308–311; Villoslada, *La Universidad de París,* pp. 12 (note), 120–121, 272, 361.

[10] Ros, pp. 249, 261, 271.

[11] Zavala, pp. 18, 42.

[12] *Libros y libreros,* pp. 269–270.

[13] J. Bautista, *Advertencias.*

[14] Leonard, *Romances of Chivalry.*

[15] Ros, "Antonio de Guevara," and "La Première *Josephina."*

[16] Steck, "The first college in America."

[17] Gilson, *Héloise et Abélard,* pp. 37–112.

[18] Zarco, *España y la comunión.*

[19] G. San Juan de la Cruz, *Vida del Maestro Julián de Avila,* pp. 195–196, 208, 210.

[20] Garibay K, Angel Maria, "Un Libro Rico."

[21] It is apparent that my point of view here is not as different from that of Dr. Garibay as it might seem, but I confess that I do not understand so well his criticism of me in the following lines: "I think the credit [Ricard] gives to certain really famous writers and books is mistaken, although perhaps not censurable, for in the light of a more serene and better informed judgment they do not deserve the confidence he shows in them, at least as a whole. Gamio may be a writer and may even be a master of his materials, but his judgment is strictly one-sided and very far from a serene and scientific objectivity" (p. 35).

It is surprising that Dr. Garibay did not notice pages 000 of my book, where I do nothing but criticize the ideas of Dr. Gamio, which I think are exact only in certain aspects. It is hard to believe that [Dr. Garibay] was led astray by my moderation in my difference with Dr. Gamio—a moderation which, of course, I think necessary in every scientific discussion.

[22] Ricard, "Les apparitions," in *Revue d'histoire des missions,* 1931, pp. 247–262.

[23] *Ibid.,* Dec., 1938, pp. 588–607.

[24] AIA, vol 38, 1938, pp. 459–467.

[25] In the lines I have quoted it seems to me an historical error to state that Hispanization occurred more slowly. It was only partially effected. It is enough to read, for example, the pastoral letter of Lorenzana of October 6, 1769, in which the archbishop of Mexico complains that many Indians are ignorant of Spanish, after two and a half centuries since the conquest. See my article, "L'incorporation de l'Indien par l'école au Mexique."

[26] *Letras de México,* p. 7, March 15, 1940.

[27] Allier, *La psychologie.*

[28] Ricard, "Les origines de l'Eglise sud-américaine."

NOTES TO APPENDIX II

(Pages 310–322)

[1] Mexico, 1881.

[2] Lejeal, Nos. 27 and 28. Icazbalceta published the texts of Motolinía and Mendieta in his first collection. They will be discussed below. At the end of Icazbalceta's *Códice Franciscano* (pp. 268 ff.), is a series of additions and corrections to *Zumárraga,* reproduced in Icabalceta's *Obras,* vol. 10, pp. 299–321.

[3] Orozco y Jiménez, vol. 1.

[4] See Bibliography.

[5] RHF, April, 1924, pp. 216–235; RHF, January, 1926, pp. 119–121; JSA, 1926, pp. 21–49; JSA, 1927, pp. 390–392.

[6] Louvain, 1931, pp. 66–118. My publications in the RHF and the JSA are also collected in this volume.

[7] Letters No. 105–106, 110, 118, 127, and 144 are in Orozco y Jiménez, pp. 280–301, 302–309, 314–320, 329–345, and 364–368.

[8] García Méndez y Desgardin.

[9] There are four editions of Motolinía: London, 1848 (in Kingsborough, *Antiquities of Mexico,* vol. 9); Mexico, 1858 (in Icazbalceta, *Colección de documentos,* vol. 1, pp. 1–249); Madrid, 1869 (in *Colección de documentos inéditos para la historia de España,* vol. 53, pp. 297–474); Barcelona, 1914, ed. Daniel Sánchez García. This last is the best, along with that of Icazbalceta, and also the most manageable and easiest to find. See Ricard, "Notes sur les éditions et le manuscrit de la *Historia de los Indios de la Nueva España* de Fray Toribio de Motolinía," in RHF, Oct. 1924, pp. 493–500; E&D, pp. 31–39; Streit, vol. 2, pp. 112–115. The manuscript of Motolinía's *Historia* is in the Library of the Escorial. Mendieta's history was published by Icazbalceta until 1870. Vetancurt's *Teatro* was published for the first time in 1698. I have used the four volume edition printed in Mexico, 1870–1871.

[10] It ends with these words: "día del glorioso apóstol San Matías, año de la Redención humana 1541." The feast of St. Matthias falls on February 24.

[11] For Motolinía, see the essay by Ramírez at the beginning of Icazbalceta's edition, the note by C. Fernández Duro in *Colección bibliográfico-biográfica de las noticias referentes a la Provincia de Zamora,* pp. 465–467, No. 705 (Madrid, 1891), and the articles by A. López, in *El Eco Franciscano,* vol. 32, pp.

713–717; vol. 33, pp. 14–18; vol. 34, pp. 65–68 (Santiago de Compostela, 1915–1917).

[12] This biography was published by A. López in AIA, July–August, 1926, pp. 48–83; rather, Father López published the incomplete copy in the Provincial Library of Toledo.

[13] Ed. Luis García Pimentel (Paris, 1903).

[14] A. López, *Fray Toribio.*

[15] For Mendieta, see Icazbalceta, *Nueva Colección,* vol. 1, pp. xxi–xxxix, Larínaga, *Fr. Jerónimo de Mendieta,* and Viñaza, *Bibliografía española de lenguas indígenas,* p. 63.

[16] Larrínaga, "Fray Jerónimo de Mendieta," p. 354.

[17] Book V[1], p. 617. Mendieta certified that he knew Fray Juan de Ribas, one of the Twelve, and knew Motolinía. He also certified that he knew Fray Diego de Olarte and Archbishop Montúfar.

[18] Among other things, Mendieta borrowed chapter 14 of the *Tratado Tercero* from Motolinía's *Historia* and incorporated it in chapters 24–27 of his third Book, which Torquemada in his turn copied in Book 15, chaps. 24, 30–35, of his *Monarquía Indiana.* (A. López, *"Cuestionario Histórico"* and especially his article in *Illuminaire.*)

[19] Icazbalceta, HEI, p. xxvii; A. López, AIA, in his important article, "Misiones o doctrinas de Michoacán," pp. 341–425.

[20] HEI, Book V[1], p. 617.

[21] Icazbalceta's edition, p. 7. Cf. Larrínaga, AIA, vol. 4, 1915, p. 372.

[22] Cf. remarks of Primo Feliciano Velázquez, in *La aparición,* pp. 377–378.

[23] For the biography of Vetancurt, see editors' note at the beginning of vol. 1 of his *Teatro Mexicano,* pp. iii–vii. See A. López, in AIA Nov.–Dec., 1922, pp. 377–380. The most interesting parts for this study are the *Crónica de la Provincia del Santo Evangelio,* which forms vol. 3 of the 1870–1871 edition, and the *Menologio franciscano,* in the series of biographies of the religious, which forms vol. 4.

[24] Icazbalceta, HEI, p. xxix.

[25] The *Monarquía Indiana* was approved in 1613, published in Seville in 1615, and reprinted in 3 volumes in Madrid, 1723. The second edition is the only one available. I shall discuss it later. The 3d Part (vol. 3), dedicated to the evangelization of Mexico, is the only one that interests us directly.

[26] HEI, "Introduction," pp. xxx–xlv. The only chapters of the 3d Part of the *Monarquía Indiana* that seem to present some originality are the following: Book 15, chaps. 3, 6, 21, 22, 27, 45, 46, 47; Book 16, chaps. 8, 13, 14, 25; Book 17, chap. 9; Book 19, chaps. 1, 10, 11, 15, 16, 18, 19, 20, 24, 25, 29, 30; Book 20, chaps. 12, 53, 54, 55, 57, 62, 68, 69, 70, 73, 76, 78–85; Book 21, chaps. 10, 11, 12.

²⁷ Viñaza, *Bibliografía*, p. 63. A. López, in his article on Motolinía in *Illuminaire* (cited above) is inclined to think that Mendieta and Torquemada had a common source. which may have been the great hypothetical work of Motolinía, which is known today only in a fragmentary fashion through his *Historia* and *Memoriales*. This seductive conjecture will necessarily remain undemonstrable until we have the full text of that work. Besides, it clashes with the passage of Fray Juan Bautista, who, although he does not contradict it absolutely, seems to anticipate Icazbalceta's opinion.

²⁸ This *Memorial* was published by A. López, in AIA, Nov.–Dec., 1922, pp. 383–425. For Fray Diego Muñoz see Rea's chronicle, below.

²⁹ A. López, AIA, Nov.–Dec., 1922, pp. 344–346, 382.

³⁰ Rea's *Chronica* is divided into three books, of which the first is especially important here. The original edition is very rare. There is a copy in the National Library of Madrid, R-4019. An edition was published by *La Voz de México* in 1882. I shall discuss the two texts below.

³¹ Granados y Gálvez, pp. 300, 312.

³² Fray Antonio Tello. For the date of composition, see the introduction to Tello's *Crónica* by José López-Portillo y Rojas, page v.

³³ For Tello's chronicle, see Juan B. Iguíniz' article in *Boletín de la Biblioteca Nacional* (Mexico), vol. 12, No. 2, August–Oct., 1917, pp. 57–65. For its sources, see A. López, AIA, Nov.–Dec., 1922, pp. 365–367, and, in AIA, March–April, 1923, pp. 235–270, the article by the same author entitled "Misiones o doctrinas." Tello, it seems, did not know the *Memorial* of Muñoz.

³⁴ López-Portillo, p. viii; Iguíniz, *Boletín*, p. 57.

³⁵ Icazbalceta, *Biografías*, vol. 2. Frejes' *Historia breve* was first published in Zacatecas in 1839. His *Memoria histórica* was published in Guadalajara in 1833, under the initials F. F. F. and was reprinted in 1879, also in Guadalajara. It is less important.

³⁶ Fray Baltasar de Medina's *Chronica* is of slight value. The author borrowed heavily from Gonzaga, that is to say, from Mendieta, for the period in which we are interested. He goes especially into events after 1580, and proposes to edify the reader rather than satisfy his curiosity.

³⁷ Beaumont's *Chronica* fills vols. 7–11 of the *Colección de Memorias de Nueva España, que en virtud de órdenes de Su Magestad, del Exmo. Sr. Conde de Revilla Gigedo, y del M. R. P. Provincial Fr. Francisco García Figueroa, colectó, extractó, y dispuso en XXXII Tomos un religioso del Santo Evangelio de México por el año de 1792 (el P. Fr. Manuel de la Vega de la Observancia de San Francisco)*. This collection is in manuscript in the library of the Royal Academy of History in Madrid (12–23-5ª, 122, ff.). The collection numbered 10–9–2 is incomplete. For Beaumont's chronicle and the Vega collection, see

Civezza, *Saggio*, Nos. 68 and 750; Alfredo Chavero, *Obras*, vol. 1, pp. 217–230; A López, AIA, Nov.–Dec., 1922, pp. 354–364. I shall refer to the *Iberia* edition, which is more accessible. (*Biblioteca Histórica de la Iberia*, vols. 15–19, Mexico, 1873–1874). For the sources of the *Chronica*, see the *Aviso al benévolo lector y plan de esta obra*, in vol. 1, pp. 17–33.

[38] For Arlegui's *Crónica* I shall refer to the Mexican edition of 1851. See also, Juan Ruiz de Larrínaga, O. F. M., "P. José Arlegui: rasgos bio-bibliográficos," in AIA, May–June, 1928, pp. 289–307.

[39] A. López, AIA, Nov.–Dec., 122, pp. 346–348. Father López leans especially on the evidence of Fray Juan de Domayquia in his *Advertencias preámbulas* to the HEI, pp. 9–10. But Mendieta himself speaks of the *Memorial* that he had sent to Gonzaga (Book V[1], chap. 20, p. 616). Cf. Larrínaga, AIA, vol. 4, 1915, p. 266, note 2.

[40] Moles, *Memorial*. His notes on Mexico are scattered. The chapters of most interest here are chaps. 7 and 8, and 12 to 24.

[41] For Moles, see Streit, vol. 1, p. 86, and A. López, AIA Nov.–Dec., 1922, p. 376. Moles did not know the *Memorial* of Muñoz. He made a first draft of his work in 1583, and was obliged to do it all over again. In his *Epístola* to the Duque de Feria he says: "The *Memorial de la Prouincia de San Gabriel* was written and arranged in 1583, by order of Father Fray Francisco Gonzaga, General of the Order of our Seraphic Father Saint Francis, and . . . the writing of it fell to me. Since, at the insistence of the Father General, I had written it hastily, and since meanwhile several writings and accounts of noteworthy things had been discovered, I was obliged to repeat it, more slowly, in the style and form that it has now" (f. 1). This *Epístola* is not dated, but Father Moles says the same thing in his *Epístola* to Fray Juan de Avila, provincial of San Gabriel, dated at the convent of San Gabriel de Badajoz, December 25, 1584 (f. 6). The *Memorial* of Moles, therefore, was finished several years before its publication, and, since he has seen the notes sent by Mendieta to Gonzaga, there is reason to think that these notes were sent to Gonzaga before December, 1584, very probably during that year. Mendieta's notes must have been among the "writings" of which Moles speaks. Fray Juan de Domayquia says also that Gonzaga and Moles worked at the same time. Cf. A. López, AIA, Nov.–Dec., 1922, p. 347.

[42] Daza, *Cuarta parte de la Chronica General*. This work is divided into four books, Book 2 being especially concerned with the West Indies. Salazar, *Cronica y Historia*. J. Trinidad, *Chronica* (a posthumous work; see especially Book 2). Guadalupe, *Historia*. Scattered bits will be found in Books 5, 6, and 8. Cf. Streit, vol. 1, p. 246.

[43] For Dávila Padilla and San Román, see below.

[44] See, for example, Book 2, chaps. 13 and 14, especially pp. 49 and 53. The

story of the martyrdom of the boys Diego, Antonio, and Juan, and that of the little Cristóbal, is borrowed from Motolinía and Dávila Padilla. The latter's account is in chaps. 22 and 23 of his first Book. The story of the three child martyrs of Tlaxcala is in Motolinía's *Historia,* "Tratado 3," chap. 14, pp. 218–228. See note by Ramírez to chap. 8, Book 2, of Muñoz Camargo's *Historia de Tlaxcala;* also, Viñaza, *Bibliografía,* No. 878. For the *De moribus Indorum* see A. López, AIA, March–April, 1925, p. 222.

[45] For Daza's chronicle, see A. López, AIA, Nov.–Dec., 1922, pp. 376–377. For Daza in general, see notes of A. López, AIA, Sept.–Oct., 1921, pp. 243–247; July–August, 1922, pp. 123–126.

[46] Barbado de la Torre, vol. 1.

[47] Dávila Padilla, *Historia.* Cf. Streit, vol. 2, pp. 271–272. For the biography of Dávila Padilla, see Fernández del Castillo.

[48] Martínez Vigil, in his *La Orden de Predicadores* (p. 236) distinguishes Fray Domingo de la Anunciación, to whom he attributes the *Relaciones de algunos religiosos antiguos, desde la fundación de la provincia de México hasta el año 80* and the *Conquistas espirituales de los religiosos de la Orden de Predicadores en la provincia de Méjico* (Mexico, 1550), from Fray Domingo de la Anunciación Elcía, author of a *Historia de los primeros fundadores de la provincia de Méjico, y de los primeros Predicadores* (p. 275). I do not know on what evidence he bases this distinction, for in the chronicles one finds only a single Fray Domingo de la Anunciación.

[49] Fray Andrés de Moguer had written a biography of Fray Domingo de Betanzos. Cf. Fernández, *San Esteban,* Book 1, chap. 41, in Cuervo, *Historiadores,* vol. 1, p. 119.

[50] Dávila Padilla, Book 2, p. 815. In CDIAI, vol. 5, pp. 447–478, I found a *Relación de la fundación, capítulos y elecciones, que se han tenido en esta provincia de Santiago de esta Nueva España,* taken from vol. 89 of the Muñoz Collection. According to Muñoz (p. 478, note 1), this *Relación* was sent to the General of the Dominicans. It is superfluous to wonder whether Dávila Padilla, who wrote his chronicle in America, was able to consult a copy of this relation there. It is evident that he must have found the same data in the papers he speaks of and uses.

[51] Remesal, *Historia general.* Cf. Fernández del Castillo, "Fray Antonio de Remesal."

[52] As, for example, on the subject of the date of arrival of the first Dominican mission in Mexico.

[53] Ojea, *Libro Tercero de la Historia Religiosa.* Book 3, which continues the two books of Dávila Padilla, was composed, at least partially, in 1607, but was not printed [then]. See Agreda's introduction, p. vi. Fray Alonso Franco, *Segunda Parte de la Historia.* According to Agreda (Introduction, p. 2), this

work was composed between 1637 and 1645, but was not published. See especially the first 14 chapters of Book 1 and chapters 26–28 of Book 3.

[54] The manuscript begins with three unnumbered folios. On the verso of the third is the *protesta* concerning the decree of Urban VIII, written and signed by J. B. Méndez. The chronicle, in the same hand, fills the next 141 numbered folios. The text is incomplete, ending abruptly at the bottom of the verso of folio 141, a little after the beginning of chapter 52 of the Book 4, and goes only to 1564. For the chronicle of Méndez, see Cuevas, *Historia,* vol. 1, p. 10, and vol. 2, p. 79; also the *Album Histórico,* pp. 157–158.

[55] *Convento de Santo Domingo de la Ciudad de México. Actas Capitulares.* This collection includes only the acts of five chapters: Sept., 14, 1559, Jan. 5, 1561, Sept. 25, 1568, Sept. 27, 1576, April 22, 1581. Méndez also had access to the *relación* sent in 1569 to the General [of the Order], of which I have already spoken. See ff. 19 v[0] and 138 v[0] of his chronicle.

[56] *Palestra Historial* and *Geografica Descripcion.* These two works are exceedingly rare. [They have since been published by the AGN, 1934.—*Trans.*] The oldest approbation of the *Palestra* is May 20, 1667, and the prologue of the *Geografica Descripcion* is dated January 20, 1671.

[57] Justo Cuervo, *Historiadores.*

[58] Alonso Fernández, *Historia.* Also in Cuervo, *Historiadores,* vol. 1, pp. 1–344. This history was written between 1616 and 1625 (*Prólogo,* p. vi). See especially chapters 19–34 of Book 1. The *Concertatio Predicatoria* by the same author rests entirely, for Mexico, on the chronicle of Dávila Padilla. See Streit, vol. 1, pp. 164–165.

[59] Juan de Araya, *Historia* 2d Part. Also in Cuervo, *Historiadores,* vol. 2, pp. 5–444. This history was written toward the end of the eighteenth century. Book 1, pp. 5–152, concerns Mexico. Jerónimo de Quintana, *Segunda Parte de Historia.* Also in Cuervo, *Historiadores,* vol. 3, pp. 5–500. Quintana drafted his work between October, 1705, and the end of 1706. Cf. vol. 1, pp. vii–viii. See especially Book 1.

[60] *Memorial Histórico de los Servicios del Convento de S. Esteban de Salamanca a la Iglesia y la Patria en el Nuevo Mundo.* In Cuervo, vol. 3, pp. 501–528. This undated document is addressed to the King by the prior of San Esteban, in the name of the convent. The *Memorial* was completed in 1778 by the *Insinuación de lo que algunos religiosos dominicos hijos del Convento de San Esteban de Salamanca han servido a la Iglesia y al Rey de España en las Indias y en la Europa,* by Fray Juan Cenjor. Cuervo, vol. 3, pp. 529–625. It contains several summary biographies of Dominicans.

[61] Esteban de Mora, *Historia Analística del Convento de San Esteban. Orden de Predicadores.* The manuscript is in the library of the convent of San Esteban; vol. 2, which contains Books 3 and 4, with notes and supporting

1564–1600. Vol. 3 is missing, but this loss does not seem very regrettable to judge by the volumes that were saved. See Cuervo, *Historiadores,* vol. 1, pp. vii–viii.

[62] The *Coronica* of Fray Juan de la Cruz yields virtually nothing about Mexico proper.

[63] Juan de Grijalva, *Cronica.* It has four books, but the author evidently intended to write a fifth, for he says (f. 71 v^0, p. 225: "In the fifth book of this history I shall give a brief account of all the convents of the Province, and the notable things there are in them.") Grijalva's chronicle was reprinted in Mexico by the Augustinian Fathers, under the direction of Nicolás León and Federico Gómez de Orozco.

[64] Grijalva, p. 10.

[65] Book 3, f. 127 v^0, p. 401. Cf. Santiago Vela, *Ensayo,* vol. 2, p. 157. The text of Fray Juan de Medina Rincón is given in Herrera, *Salamanca,* pp. 326–335, and Vidal, *Agustinos,* vol. 1, Book 3, chap. 7, pp. 237–247.

[66] For Buica, see Santiago Vela, *Ensayo,* vol. 1, pp. 463–464. For Buica and Muñoz, *ibid.,* vol. 3, pp. 305–306; also, the AHHA, April, 1918, pp. 243–248.

[67] He had probably used the following works, all now lost: *Relación de los progresos de la Cristiandad espiritual en el Nuevo Mundo,* by Fray Juan Estacio (Santiago Vela, *Ensayo,* vol. 2, p. 354); *Descripción de la Provincia de México,* by Fray Luis Hurtado de Peñalosa (*Ensayo,* vol. 3, p. 662); *Relación de la Conquista espiritual de Tlapa y Chilapa,* by Fray Agustín de la Coruña (*Ensayo,* vol. 2, p. 157); *De Rebus ac viris clarissimis Provinciae Mexicanae Fratrum Augustiniensium,* by Fray Diego de Salamanca; *Monumentos y memoriales históricos de los conventos y curatos de la Provincia del Smo. Nombre de Jesús de Agustinos calzados de la Nueva España,* by Fray Juan Núñez (*Ensayo,* vol. 4, p. 44); and the precious notes of Fray Alonso de la Veracruz.

[68] González de la Puente, *Primera Parte de la Choronica.* The original is almost unobtainable. I used the reprint in the first volume of the *Colección de documentos inéditos y raros para la historia eclesiástica mexicana publicados por el Ilmo. Sr. Obispo de Cuernavaca D. Francisco Plancarte y Navarrete* (Cuernavaca, 1907). According to a note by Nicolás León (pp. 1–2), the second part of the chronicle, which was presented in manuscript to the intervening chapter of Tiripitío (1630), is lost. For González de la Puente, see Santiago Vela, *Ensayo,* vol. 3, pp. 239–240, and AHHA, March–April, 1923, pp. 128–132.

Basalenque's *Historia* was reprinted in Mexico in 1886, 3 vols. (*La Voz de México*). For Basalenque, see Santiago Vela, *Ensayo,* vol. 1, pp. 331–334, and AHHA, June, 1928, pp. 408–418. The work is divided into three books, of which the first (1533–1602) is the only one of interest here.

The work of Escobar, *Americana Thebaida,* has been published twice, the first time at Morelia, in 1890, by Nicolás León, incomplete; the second time in Mexico, in 1924, at the expense of the Augustinian Fathers of Michoacán and under the direction of León. The first edition, however meritorious it may have been, was justly criticized by Father Gregorio de Santiago Vela, who had the original manuscript in his hands and gave a complete table of contents of it. See his article, "La Provincia augustiniana de Michoacán y su historia," in *Archivo Histórico Hispano-Agustiniano,* March–April, 1923, pp. 129–144, especially pp. 134–143. See also his *Ensayo,* vol. 2, pp. 332–333. The edition of 1924 is superior to that of 1890; it has especially the advantage of supplying us with the complete text. But it is not without defects. The text of chapter 17 of Book 1 in this edition is not established with as much care as the text published the year before by Santiago Vela.

For Grijalva and the last three authors, see Santiago Vela, *Ensayo,* vol. 1, pp. xiv–xv.

[69] Cf. G. de la Puente, Book 1, p. 73: "And since Father Maestro Fr. Juan de Grijalva, Prior of the Convent of our Father St. Augustine of Mexico, will soon publish its Chronicle, with great learning and erudition, he will fulfill the two obligations of his office, filling out the material, and making his History enjoyable, as he did with that of San Guillermo. I shall speak only of the apostolic men of our Order who are buried in this Provincia of San Nicolás de Michoacán."

[70] Cf. I. Monasterio, p. 410, note 1.

[71] Basalenque, "Prólogo al lector" in *Historia.*

[72] Basalenque, Book 1, f. 47 v⁰. Basalenque, who was born in 1577, entered the Augustinian Order at the age of sixteen, or toward 1593.

[73] Cf. Santiago Vela, *Ensayo,* vol. 1, p. 331.

[74] He says so himself in his introduction. Cf. Santiago Vela, in AHHA, March–April, 1923, pp. 135. See alos Santiago Vela, *Ensayo,* vol. 2, pp. 332–333. In some passages Escobar slavishly copies Basalenque.

[75] Manuscript Section, 4349. This manuscript has been described and the additions studied at length by Santiago Vela in *Ensayo,* vol. 3, pp. 63–65, and in *Archivo Histórico,* April, 1918, pp. 250–254. See my notes in JSA, 1926, pp. 21–24, and in E&D, pp. 119–123. There is a biography of Fray Juan Estacio in the *Coronica moralizada* by Fray Antonio de la Calancha (Book 1, pp. 168 ff.); also a biography of Fray Jerónimo Meléndez (Book 1, pp. 219 ff.), a biography of Fray Juan de la Magdalena (Book 1, pp. 230–231), and a biography of Fray Agustín de la Coruña (Book 3, pp. 690 ff.). But everything concerning the life of these religious in the Mexican period comes from Grijalva.

One may say almost the same of the work of Fray Gaspar de San Agustín,

Conquistas de las Islas Filipinas, 1st Part, in which one finds many biographies of religious who have lived in the Philippines and Mexico: Fray Jerónimo Jiménez de San Esteban, Fray Nicolás de Perea, Fray Sebastián de Trassierra, Fray Alonso de Alvarado). Gaspar de San Agustín also used González de la Puente, Basalenque, and Sicardo.

[76] Jerónimo Román y Zamora, *Chronica.* Extracts of this chronicle were published at the end of the second volume of the *Repúblicas de Indias,* by the same author (Madrid, 1897). See Santiago Vela, *Ensayo,* vol. 6, pp. 661–663.

Chronica Ordinis Fratrum Eremitarum Sancti Augustini Fratre Ioseph Pamphilo Episcopo Signino Auctore (Rome, 1581). I owe my acquaintance with this chronicle to the kindness of Federico Gómez de Orozco.

Fray Nicolas Crusenius, *Monasticon Augustinianum* (Munich, 1623).

Fray Tomás de Herrera, *Alphabetum Augustinianum.* 2 vols. (Madrid, 1644), and *Historia del Convento de San Augustin de Salamanca* (Madrid, 1652).

Fray Sebastián de Portillo, *Chronica Espiritual Augustiniana,* 4 vols. (Madrid, 1731–1732). Written in 1651 and published by Fray Francisco de Avilés.

Fray Andrés de San Nicolás, *Historia General de los Religiosos Descalzos.* Vol. 1 (Madrid, 1664), containing an introduction and the three decades from 1588–1620, is the only one of interest here. Vol. 2 (Madrid, 1681) is by Fray Luis de Jesús.

Fray Manuel Vidal, *Augustinos de Salamanca,* 2 vols. (Salamanca, 1751).

For all these works, except that of Pamphile, see Santiago Vela, *Ensayo,* vol. 1, pp. vii ff., and vol. 8, pp. 188–192; also Streit, vol. 1, pp. 177, 210, 225, and 251. For Román, Pamphile, Crusenius, Herrera, and Andrés de San Nicolás, see Pedro M. Vélez, O. S. A., *Leyendo nuestras crónicas. Notas sobre nuestros cronistas y otros historiadores,* Tome 1 (Madrid, 1932); vol. 1, pp. 43–126, 140–144, and 293 ff; vol. 2, pp. 909 ff., and pp. 1026 ff.

[77] The biographies are in chapter 7 of the *Introducción a las Decadas.* The author studies in turn: Fray Jerónimo de San Esteban (pp. 71–72), Fray Alonso de la Veracruz (pp. 76–77), Fray Agustín de la Coruña (pp. 77–84), Fray Juan Bautista de Moya (pp. 84–88), Fray Antonio de Roa (pp. 88–91), Fray Juan Estacio (pp. 92–93), Fray Nicolás Perea (pp. 93–94), Fray Nicolás Witte (pp. 94–95), Fray Juan Cruzate (p. 95), Fray Juan Pérez (pp. 95–96), Fray Juan de Medina Rincón (pp. 96–97), Fray Pedro Suárez de Escobar (pp. 97–98), Fray Juan de Alvarado (p. 98), and Fray Pedro de Agurto (pp. 99–101).

[78] Chapter 7 of the *Introducción* (pp. 65–101) is entitled "Motivos y Exemplares, que en la Orden precedieron a la ereccion y principio desta Reforma, y Descalcez postrera." And the author adds: "It is beside our purpose

here to do anything but write a proper account of some of these Fathers, for they were the ones who, with their austere Habit and Barefootedness (which all uniformly observed until the year 1574, as Grijalva himself says), persuaded the Most Prudent Monarch to solicit and demand that convents be established in Spain which would observe the primitive rule followed by the true Preachers. This was effected, as we shall see, in the houses of the Recollets which were erected later, and which continue today under the name of *Congregación de Descalzos.* (p. 70; see also p. 68).

[79] For the *Alphabetum,* see Santiago Vela, *Ensayo,* vol. 3, pp. 594 ff. Herrera did not know the chronicle of González de la Puente until he was composing vol. 2 of the *Alphabetum.* Cf. vol. 1, p. 489, and Santiago Vela, *Ensayo,* vol. 3, p. 240. For the *Historia,* see the *Ensayo,* vol. 3, pp. 606–608.

[80] This is also true to some extent for the *Alphabetum.* For example, the biography of Fray Esteban de Salazar (*Alphabetum,* vol. 2, pp. 402–403) contains much information not found in Grijalva.

[81] Fray Esteban de Salazar, *Veynte Discursos: Discurso Quarto,* chap. 2, f. 33 v°; *Discurso Octavo,* ff. 57 v°°; *Discurso Diez y Seis,* ff. 193 r°–194 r°. For this work, see Mendieta, Book 4, p. 369, and Icazbalceta's note. The *Discursos* were also published in Lyon, 1584, Alcalá, 1591, Barcelona, 1591, and Alcalá, 1595. For Salazar himself, see my article, "Un document inédit sur les Augustins du Mexique en 1563," in JSA, 1926, p. 39 (E&D, pp. 141–142). According to Zorita, *Historia de la Nueva España,* ed. Serrano y Sanz, pp. 15–16 (Madrid, 1909), Esteban de Salazar may have written in Latin a history of the conquest of New Spain, of which the MS must be lost.

[82] The "Nueve varones de la fama" were the Augustinians Fray Juan Bautista de Moya, Fray Antonio de Roa, Fray Francisco de la Cruz; the Franciscans Fray Martín de Valencia, Fray Andrés de Olmos, Fray Juan de San Francisco; the Dominicans Fray Cristóbal de la Cruz, Fray Domingo de Betanzos, Fray Tomás del Rosario. The expression "los nueve de la fama" is borrowed. It was originally applied to three Jews: Josuah, Daniel, Judas Maccabeus; three gentiles: Alexander, Hector, Julius Ceasar; three Christians: King Arthur, Charlemagne, Godfroy de Bouillon. See Lope de Vega's play *El Nuevo mundo descubierto,* verse 2813 (ed. Barry, p. 163, note 1). Fray Antonio de San Román should not be confused with Fray Jerónimo Román y Zamora.

[83] Fray Alonso Fernández, *Historia eclesiástica.* The biographies of Fray Antonio de Roa and Fray Juan Bautista de Moya (Book 1, chaps. 33–34) are copied from San Román. For his life of Martín de Valencia he borrowed a great deal (Book 1, chap. 12) from Gonzaga and San Román. See Streit, vol. 1, p. 142.

[84] Cf. J. T. Medina, *La imprenta en México,* p. xxviii.

[85] Gil González Dávila, *Teatro Eclesiástico,* fills the first 70 folios of vol. 1.

[86] For Valadés, see Icazbalceta, *Opúsculos,* vol. 2, p. 447, note 1. Nicolás León wrote a thin volume on Valadés, which has no date or place of publication. He kindly wrote to me on the subject of this religious and his book: "On the back of the title page of this work there is a Latin verse that gives the true nationality of Valadés, who was a Spaniard (*iberus*) and not a Mexican, as I had guessed in the short biography of him that I wrote." For the *Rhetorica Christiana,* see Streit, vol. 1, pp. 58–59.

[87] "Opportune autem," he says in his preface to the reader, "rerum Indicarum, quibus, ipsi non modo interfuimus, sed et praefuimus, aliqua adhibuimus exempla: certissimo credentes, eam rem non modo ob lectamento sed et magno bono, commodoque futuram, utpote unde Rhetoricae ipsius initia, progressus, et usus; liquidissime cernuntur (vel ipso Cicerone iudice) dum inquit, fuit quoddam tempus, cum in agris, bestiarum more, homines vagabantur, et victu ferino vitam sibi propagabant: nec ratione animi quidquam, sed pleraque viribus corporis administrabant. Nemo legitimas viderat nuptias, nemo certos inspexerat liberos. Quo tempore quidam magnus videlicet vir dispersos homines in agris, et locis sylvestribus abditos, ratione quadam compulit in unum locum et congregavit, et eos ex feris et immanibus, mites reddidit, et mansuetos. Huius, inquam, rei admirandi effectus, multo clarius, quan unquam in novi Indiarum Maris Oceani orbis hominum mansuefactione apparent." [And so, he says in his preface to the reader, we did not interfere in matters of concern only to the Indians, but we did take the lead in teaching them a few examples, assuredly trusting them to put them into practice, not indeed for their pleasure, but for their great and proper edification, thereby giving them a start in learning, as well as in progress and manners. In this way they would see the light most clearly (and this is the opinion of Cicero himself), for, he says, once upon a time men wandered in the fields like beasts and lived on wild food, not only for their minds but for their bodies. No man was legitimately married, no man looked after his children. So at times one of our leaders would gather up the men who were scattered about the countryside or hidden in the woods, and would bring them together and congregate them in one place, thereby changing them from frightful wild beasts into mild and gentle creatures. Such a man, I say, who brought to pass these amazing things, is the most illustrious of all those who took part in the pacification of the men of the New World of the Indies of the Ocean sea.]

[88] See Icazbalceta, *Biografías,* vol. 2, pp. 251 and 254 ff. (in his note repeated from the *Códice Franciscano,* pp. xxvi–1.)

Bibliography

Acosta, José de, S. J. *Historia natural y moral de las Indias*. 2 vols. (Madrid, 1894).

Agurto, Pedro, O. S. A. *Tractado de que se deven administrar los Sacramentos de la Sancta Eucharistia y Extrema uncion a los indios de esta nueva España*. (Mexico, 1573).

Aiton, A. S. *Antonio de Mendoza, First Viceroy of New Spain*. (Durham, N.C., 1927).

Alamán, Lucas. *Disertaciones sobre la historia de Méjico*, vols. 1–2. (Mexico, 1899–1900).

Allier, Raoul. *La psychologie de la conversion chez les peuples noncivilisés*. 2 vols. (Paris, 1925).

————. *Le non-civilisé et nous*. (Paris, 1927).

Alva Ixtlilxochitl, Fernando de. *Obras históricas*. Ed. A. Chavero. 2 vols. (Mexico, 1891–1892).

L'âme des peuples à évangeliser. Compte rendu de la sixième Semaine de Missiologie. (Louvain, 1928).

Andrade, Vicente de P. *Primer estudio sobre los conquistadores espirituales de la Nueva Esapña (1519–1531)*. (Mexico, 1896).

————. "Disquisición histórica sobre la muerte de los frailes Juan de Tecto y Juan de Aora." In *Congreso Internacional de Americanistas. Actas de la Undécima Reunión. México, 1895*, pp. 214–220. (Mexico, 1897).

————. "Idolatrías y supersticiones de los Indios." In *Reseña de la Segunda Sesión del XVII Congreso Internacional de Americanistas*, pp. 287–294. (Mexico, 1912).

381

Angel, Miguel, O. M. Cap. "La vie franciscaine en Espagne entre les deux couronnements de Charles-Quint." In *Revista de Archivos, Bibliotecas y Museos,* vol. 26, pp. 131–133. (Madrid, 1912). *Après la conversion. Compte rendu de la neuvième Semaine de Missiologie.* (Louvain, 1931).

Araya, Juan de, O. P. *Historia del Convento de San Esteban de Salamanca, Segunda Parte.* Vol. 2 of Justo Cuervo, *Historiadores.*

Arens, Bernard, S. J. *Manuel des Missions Catholiques.* (Louvain, 1925).

Arlegui, José, O. F. M. *Crónica de la Provincia de N. S. P. S. Francisco de Zacatecas.* (Mexico, 1737, 1851).

Aubin, J. M. A. *Mémoires sur la peinture didactique et l'écriture figurative des anciens Mexicains.* (Paris, 1885).

Autour du problème de l'adaptation. Compte rendu de la quatrième Semaine de Missiologie. (Louvain, 1926).

Aviat, Paul. "Primitifs et civilisés." In *Bulletin des Missions* (Saint-André de Bruges), March–April, 1929, pp. 359–368.

Ayres, Atlee B. *Mexican Architecture.* (New York, 1926).

Azevedo, João Lúcio de. *Os Jesuitas no Grão Pará.* 2d ed. (Coimbra, 1930).

Babelon, Jean. *La Vie de Fernand Cortès.* 4th ed. (Paris, 1928).

Barbado de la Torre, Manuel, O. F. M. *Compendio histórico Lego seraphico, Fundacion de la Orden de Menores,* vol. 1. (Madrid, 1745).

Basalenque, Diego, O. S. A. *Historia de la Provincia de San Nicolas de Tolentino de Michoacan, del Orden de N. P. S. Augustin.* (Mexico, 1673); 2d ed., 3 vols., *La Voz de México* (Mexico, 1886).

Bataillon, Marcel. "Honneur et Inquisition, Michel Servet poursuivi par l'Inquisition espagnole." In *Bulletin Hispanique,* January–March, 1925, pp. 5–17.

———. "Chanson pieuse et poésie de Dévotion, Fr. Ambrosio Montesino." In *Bulletin Hispanique,* July–September, 1925, pp. 228–238.

———. "Erasme au Mexique." In *Deuxième Congrès National des Sciences Historiques,* April 14–16, 1930, pp. 31–44. (Algiers, 1932).

———. *Erasme en Espagne.* (Paris, 1937).

Baudin, Louis. *L'empire socialiste des Inka.* (Paris, 1928).

Bautista, Juan, O. F. M. *Confessionario en lengua mexicana y castellana.* (Mexico, 1599).

———. *Advertencias para los Confessores de las Naturales . . . Primera Parte.* (Mexico, 1600).

Bayle, Constantino, S. J. *Santa María en Indias* (Madrid, 1928).

———. "España y el clero indígena de América." In *Razón y Fe,* February 10, 1931, pp. 213–225; March 25, 1931, pp. 521–535. (Madrid).

Beaumont, Pablo de la Purísima Concepción, O. F. M. *Cronica de la Provincia de los Santos Apostoles S. Pedro y S. Pablo de la Regular Observancia de N.*

de los Santos Apostoles S. Pedro y S. Pablo de la Regular Observancia de N. P. S. Francisco. Biblioteca Histórica de la Iberia, vols. 15–19. 5 vols. (Mexico, 1873–1874). Also in *Publicaciones del Archivo General de la Nación,* vols. 17–19. (Mexico, 1932).

Belausteguigoitia, R. de. *México de cerca.* (Madrid, 1930).

Benavente, Toribio de. (See Motolinía).

Bergson, Henri. *Les deux sources de la morale et de la religion.* 6th ed. (Paris, 1932).

Bernard, Augustin. "L'Algérie et la Tunisie." In *L'Afrique du Nord,* pp. 5–23. (Paris, 1913).

Beuchat, Henri. *Manuel d'Archéologie Américaine.* (Paris, 1912).

Blanco Fombona, Horacio. *Panoramas mejicanos.* (Madrid, 1929).

Boban, Eugène. *Documents pour servir à l'histoire du Mexique,* vol. 2. (Paris, 1891).

Bontemps, Father, S. J. "La réhabilitation du noir." In *L'âme des peuples à evangeliser,* pp. 18–23.

Bosque, Carlos. *Compendio de historia americana y argentina.* (Buenos Aires, 1925).

Braden, Charles S. *Religious aspects of the Conquest of Mexico.* (Durham, N.C., 1930).

Brou, Alexandre, S. J. *Saint François Xavier.* 2d ed. 2 vols. (Paris, 1922).

———. *Saint François Xavier, Conditions et méthodes de son apostolat.* (Bruges, 1925).

———. "Les statistiques dans les anciennes missions." In *Revue d'Histoire des Missions,* September 1, 1929, pp. 361–384. (Paris, 1929).

Brouillard, René. "Piété catholique et superstition." In *Etudes,* October 20, 1932, pp. 192–206. (Paris, 1932).

Brunschvicg, León. "Nouvelles études sur l'âme primitive." In *Revue des Deux Mondes,* July 1, 1932, pp. 172–202. (Paris, 1932).

Burgoa, Francisco de, O. P. *Palestra Historial de virtudes y exemplares apostolicos, Fundada del zelo de insignes Heroes de la Sagrada Orden de Predicadores en este Nuevo Mvndo de la America de las Indias Occidentales.* (Mexico, 1670).

———. *Geographica Descripcion de la Parte Septentrional, del Polo Artico de la America, y Nueva Iglesia de la America de las Indias Occidentales, y sitio astronomico de esta Provincia de Predicadores de Antequera Valle de Oaxaca . . .* (Mexico, 1674).

Calancha, Antonio de la, O. S. A. *Coronica moralizada de San Avgvstin en el Perv.* (Barcelona, 1638).

Calderón de la Barca, Marquesa de. *La vida en Méjico.* Trans. Enrique Martínez Sobral, vol. 1. (Mexico, 1920).

Campos, Rubén M. *El folklore y la música mejicana.* (Mexico, 1928).

Capitan, Dr., and Lorin, Henri. *Le travail en Amérique avant et après Colomb.* (Paris, 1914).

"Calendario Mexicano atrubuido a Fray Bernardino de Sahagún." See Iguíniz.

Carreño, Alberto M. *Fr. Miguel de Guevara y el célebre soneto castellano "No me mueve, mi Dios, para quererte."* (Mexico, 1915).

————. "La imprenta y la Inquisición en el siglo XVI." In *Estudios eruditos in memoriam de Adolfo Bonilla y San Martín,* vol. 1, pp. 91–114. (Madrid, 1927).

Cartas de Indias. (Madrid, 1877).

Cartilla para enseñar a leer a los niños. Con la doctrina christiana que se canta. (Pamplona, 1606).

Castries, Henry de. *Les Sources Inédites de l'Histoire du Maroc.* 1st Series, Espagne, vol. 1. (Paris-Madrid, 1921).

Cervantes de Salazar, Francisco. *Crónica de la Nueva España.* (Madrid, 1914).

Charles, Pierre, S. J. *Les Dossiers de l'Action missionaire.* (Louvain, 1927 *et seq.*).

————. "Le théatre missionaire." In *Après la conversion,* pp. 181–191.

Chavero, Alfredo. *Sahagún.* (Mexico, 1877). Also in *Obras,* vol. 1, pp. 79–140. (Mexico, 1904).

————. "Vega." In *Obras,* vol. 1, pp. 217–230.

————. "Colegio de Tlatelolco." In *Boletín de la Real Academia de la Historia,* vol. 40, pp. 517–529. (Madrid, 1902). Also in *Obras,* vol. 1, pp. 286–308.

Chevalier, Michel. *Le Mexique ancien et moderne.* 2d ed. (Paris, 1864).

Civezza, Marcelino da, O. F. M. *Saggio di Bibliografia . . . Sanfrancescana.* (Prato, 1879).

Colección de documentos inéditos para la historia de Ibero-América, vol. 1. Ed. S. Montoto. (Madrid, 1927).

Colección de documentos inéditos relativos al descubrimiento, conquista y colonización de las posesiones españolas en América y Oceanía, sacados en su mayor parte del Real Archivo de Indias. 42 vols. (Madrid, 1864 *et seq.*).

Les conversions. Compte rendu de la huitième Semaine de Missiologie. (Louvain, 1930).

Cortés, Antonio, and Genaro García. *Album. Arquitectura en México. Iglesia de Santo Domingo en la ciudad de Oaxaca y Capilla del Santo Cristo en Tlacolula, E. de Oaxaca.* (Mexico, 1924).

Cortés, Hernán. *Cartas de relación.* Ed. Dantín Cereceda. 2 vols. (Madrid, 1922).

Cossío, José L. "Tzintzuntzan." In *Boletín de la Sociedad Mexicana de*

Geografía y Estadistica, vol. 42, No. 4, pp. 297–307. (Mexico, July, 1930).

Crokaert, Jacques. *La Méditerranée américaine.* (Paris, 1927).

Crusenius, Nicolas, O. S. A. *Monasticon Avgvstinianum.* (Munich, 1623).

Cruz, Juan de la, O. P. *Coronica de la Orden de Predicadores.* (Lisbon, 1567).

Cuervo, Justo, O. P. *Historiadores del Convento de San Esteban de Salamanca.* 3 vols. (Salamanca, 1914–1916).

Cuevas, Mariano, S. J. *Documentos inéditos del siglo XVI para la historia de México.* (Mexico, 1914).

———. *Cartas y otros documentos de Hernán Cortés.* (Seville, 1915).

———. *Historia de la Iglesia en México.* 5 vols. (Mexico, 1921–1928).

Dahlmann, J., S. J. *El estudio de las lenguas y las misiones.* Trans. Jerónimo Rojas, S. J. (Madrid, 1893).

Dávila Padilla, Agustín, O. P. *Historia de la Fundacion y discurso de la Provincia de Santiago de Mexico, de la Orden de Predicadores, por las vidas de sus varones insignes, y casos notables de Nueva España.* (Madrid, 1596).

Daza, Antonio, O. F. M. *Cuarta Parte de la Chronica General de Nro. Padre San Francisco y de su Apostolica Orden.* (Valladolid, 1611).

Descripción del Arzobispado de México hecha en 1570 y otros documentos. (Mexico, 1897).

Díaz del Castillo, Bernal. *Historia verdadera de la conquista de la Nueva España.* Ed. Carlos Pereyra. 2 vols. (Madrid, 1928).

Díaz Molleda, Eloy. *Escritores españoles del siglo X al XVI.* (Madrid, 1929).

Diez Barroso, Francisco. *El arte en Nueva España.* (Mexico, 1921).

Diez de Sollano, Carlos. "Las fiestas de San Miguel." In *Revista Mexicana de Estudios Históricos,* September–October, 1927, pp. 213–227. (Mexico, 1927).

Diguet, Léon. "Contribution a l'ethnographie précolombienne du Mexique, Le Chimalhuacán et ses populations avant la conquête espagnole." In JSA, 1903, pp. 1–8. (Paris, 1903).

———. "Contribution a l'étude géographique du Mexique précolombien, Le Mixtécapan." *Ibid.,* 1906, pp. 15–43.

Dirks, Servais, O. F. M. *Histoire littéraire et bibliographique des Frères Mineurs de Saint François en Belgique et dans les Pays-Bas.* (Antwerp, 1885?).

Disposiciones complementarias de las leyes de Indias, vol. 1. (Madrid, 1930).

Domínguez Assiayn, Salvador. "Filosofía de los antiguos mexicanos." In *Contemporáneos,* November–December, 1931, pp. 209–225. (Mexico, 1931).

Dubois, Henri, S. J. "Les catéchistes." In *Autour du problème de l'adaptation,* pp. 75–86.

Dudon, Paul, S. J. "L'Evangelisation du Mexique au XVI° siècle." In *Revue d'Histoire des Missions,* June 1, 1929, pp. 161–194.

Dufonteny, G., S. SS. R. "Les griefs des inidgènes au sujet de l'apostolat." In *Autour du problème de l'adaptation,* pp. 11–35.

———. "La Méthode d'Evangelisation chez les Non-Civilisés." In *Bulletin des Missions,* November–December, 1927, pp. 365–375, and November–December, 1929, pp. 518–532.

Durán, Diego, O. P. *Historia de las Indias de Nueva-España y Islas de Tierra Firme.* 2 vols. (Mexico, 1867, 1880).

Dyer, Lois K. "History of the Cabildo of Mexico City, 1524–1534." In *The Louisiana Historical Quarterly,* vol. 6, No. 3, July, 1923, pp. 395–477. (New Orleans, 1923).

Echard. (See Quétif et Echard).

Les élites en pays de mission. Compte rendu de la cinquième Semaine de Missiologie. (Louvain, 1927).

Escobar, Matías de, O. S. A. *Americana Thebaida, Vitae patrum de los religiosos hermitaños de N. P. San Agustín de la Provincia de S. Nicolás Tolentino de Michoacán.* (Morelia, 1890; Mexico, 1924).

Esquivel Obregón, Toribio. *Influencia de España y los Estados Unidos sobre México.* (Madrid, 1918).

Estella, Gumersindo de, O. M. Cap. "Situación canónica de las antiguas misiones de América." In *Semana de Misiología de Barcelona,* vol. 2 of *Bibliotheca Hispana Missionum,* pp. 103–114. (Barcelona, 1930).

Estrada, Genaro. See *Ordenanzas de Gremios* . . .

Fabié, A. M. "Nueva colección de documentos para la historia de México." In *Boletín de la Real Academia de la Historia,* vol. 17, pp. 5–84. (Madrid, 1890).

Félix, Father, O. M. Cap. "Les colonies agricoles et les conversions." In *Les conversions,* pp. 151–159.

Fernández, Alonso, O. P. *Historia eclesiástica de nuestros tiempos.* (Toledo, 1611).

———. *Concertatio Predicatoria.* (Salamanca, 1618).

———. *Historia del Insigne Convento de San Esteban de Salamanca.* Vol. 1 of Cuervo, *Historiadores,* pp. 1–344.

Fernández, Salvador D. "Los colegios y la cultura en Nueva España." In *Anales de la Sociedad de Geografía e Historia de Guatemala,* vol. 7, pp. 18–28.

Fernández del Castillo, Francisco. "Fray Antonio de Remesal." In *Boletín de la*

Biblioteca Nacional, vol. 12, No. 9, July–December, 1920, pp. 151–173. (Mexico, 1920).

Fernández del Castillo, Francisco. "Aclaraciones históricas, Fray Alonso de Molina." In *Anales del Museo Nacional de Arqueología, Historia y Etnografía,* vol. 3, pp. 344–352. (Mexico, 1925).

———."Fray Agustín Dávila Padilla, Arzobispo de Santo Domingo." *Ibid.,* pp. 448–453.

———, and Rafael García Granados, Luis MacGregor, and Lauro E. Rosell. *México y la Guadalupana.* (Mexico, 1931).

Fernández Duro, C. *Colección biográfico-bibliográfica de noticias referentes a la Provincia de Zamora.* (Madrid, 1891).

Florencia, Francisco de, S. J. *Descripción histórica, y moral del yermo de San Miguel, de las Cuevas en el Reyno de la Nueva-España* . . . (Cadiz, 1690).

Flores, Francisco. *Historia de la medicina en México,* vol. 2. (Mexico, 1886).

Focher, Juan, O. F. M. *Itinerarium Catholicum profiscicentium, ad infideles convertendos.* (Seville, 1574).

Franco, Alonso, O. P. *Segunda Parte de la Historia de la Provincia de Santiago de Mexico Orden de Predicadores en la Nueva España.* Ed. Fr. Secundino Martínez. (Mexico, 1900).

Frazer, J. G. *Le rameau d'or.* Trans. Stiebel et Toutain, vol. 2. (Paris, 1908).

———. *Le bouc émissaire.* Trans. Sayn. (Paris, 1925).

Frejes, Francisco, O. F. M. *Historia breve de la conquista de los Estados Independientes del Imperio Mexicano.* (Guadalajara, 1878).

———. *Memoria histórica de los sucesos más notables de la conquista particular de Jalisco por los Españoles,* 2d ed. (Guadalajara, 1879).

Friederici, Georg. *Hilfswörterbuch für den Amerikanisten.* (Halle, 1926).

Galindo, Miguel. "Colima en el espacio, en el tiempo y en la vida." In *Boletín de la Sociedad Mexicana de Geografía y Estadística,* vol. 41, pp. 225–276. (Mexico, 1929).

Gamio, Manuel. *Forjando patria (Pro-nacionalismo).* (Mexico, 1916).

———. *Mexican Immigration to the United States. A study of human migration and adjustment.* (University of Chicago, 1930).

———, et al. *La Población del Valle de Teotihuacán. El medio en que se ha desarrollado. Su evolución étinca y social* . . . 3 vols. (Mexico, 1922).

———, and José Vasconcelos. *Aspects of Mexican civilization.* (University of Chicago, 1926).

Gandía, Enrique de. *Historia crítica de los mitos de la conquista americana.* (Buenos Aires and Madrid, 1929).

García, Esteban, O. S. A. *Crónica de la Provincia Agustiniana del Santísimo Nombre de Jesús de México.* Book 5. Ed. Gregorio de Santiago. (Madrid, 1918).

García, Genaro. *El clero de México durante la dominación española según el archivo inédito archiepiscopal metropolitano,* vol. 15. (Mexico, 1907). (See also Cortés).

García, Gregorio, O. P. *Predicacion del Evangelio en el Nuevo Mundo, viviendo los Apostoles.* (Baeza, 1625).

García Granados, Rafael. "Calpan." In *Universidad de México,* March, 1931, pp. 370–374.

——. "Simulacros de misas." In *Excelsior,* December 8, 1931. (Mexico).

——. "Sobre las huellas pretéritas." *Ibid.,* January 15, 1932. (See also Fernández del Castillo).

——. "Capillas de indios en Nueva España." In *Archivo español de arte y arqueología,* No. 31, 1935, 35 pp.

García Icazbalceta, Joaquín. *Don Fray Juan de Zumárraga Primer Obispo y Arzobispo de México.* (Mexico, 1881).

——. *Bibliografía mexicana del siglo XVI.* (Mexico, 1886).

——. *Códice Franciscano.* Vol. 2 of *Nueva colección,* below.

——. *Colección de documentos para la historia de México.* 2 vols. (Mexico, 1858).

——. *Nueva colección de documentos para la historia de México.* 5 vols. (Mexico, 1886–1892).

——. "Noticia de una obra en tarasco." In *Anales del Museo Michoacano,* 1888, pp. 62–64. (Morelia, 1888).

——. "Introducción de la imprenta en México." In *Opúsculos varios,* vol. 1, pp. 1–64. (Mexico, 1896).

——. "Los médicos de México en el siglo XVI." *Ibid.,* vol. 1, pp. 65–124.

——. "La industria de la seda en México." *Ibid.,* vol. 1, pp. 125–161.

——. "La instrucción pública en México durante el siglo XVI." *Ibid.,* vol. 1, pp. 163–270.

——. "La destrucción de antigüedades mexicanas." *Ibid.,* vol. 2, pp. 5–117.

——. "Representaciones religiosas de México en el siglo XVI." *Ibid.,* vol. 2, pp. 307–368.

——. "La Orden de Predicadores en México." *Ibid.,* vol. 2, pp. 369–380.

——. "La Iglesia y Convento de San Francisco de México." *Ibid.,* vol. 2, pp. 381–414.

——. "Los Agustinos en México." *Ibid.,* vol. 2, pp. 415–419.

——. "El colegio de niñas de México." *Ibid.,* vol. 2, pp. 427–434.

——. "Un Creso del siglo XVI en México." *Ibid.,* vol. 2, pp. 435–441.

——. "La Fiesta del Pendón en México." *Ibid.,* vol. 2, pp. 443–451.

García Icazbalceta, Joaquín. "El Lic. D. Matías de la Mota Padilla." In *Biografías,* vol. 2, pp. 91–108. (Mexico, 1897).

——. "Fray Francisco Pareja." *Ibid.,* vol. 2, pp. 197–206.

——. "Fr. Juan Focher." *Ibid.,* vol. 2, pp. 247–285.

García Méndez y Desgardin, Raquel. *Los cronistas religiosos del siglo XVI.* (Mexico, 1930).

García Muiños, Ramón, O. F. M. *Primicias religiosas de América.* (Santiago de Compostela, 1894).

Garibay K, Angel Maria. "Un libro rico." In *Gaceta Oficial del Arzobispado de México,* July, 1933, pp. 34–36.

Génin, Auguste. "Notes d'archéologie mexicaine." In JSA, 1900, pp. 1–42.

Getino, Luis G. Alonso, O. P. *El Maestro Fr. Francisco de Vitoria.* (Madrid, 1930).

Gillet, Louis. "L'art dans l'Amérique latine." In André Michel, *Histoire de l'Art,* vol. 8, 3d Part, pp. 1019–1096. (Paris, 1929).

Gilson, Etienne. *Héloise et Abélard, Etudes sur le Moyen Age et l'humanisme.* (Paris, 1938).

Gómara. (See López de Gómara).

Gómez de Orozco, Federico. "Monasterios de la Orden de San Agustín en Nueva España en el siglo XVI." In *Revista Mexicana de Estudios Históricos,* January–February, 1927, pp. 40–54.

——. "Dos escritores indígenas del siglo XVI." In *Universidad de México,* December, 1930, pp. 126–130.

Gómez Zamora, Matías, O. P. *Regio Patronato español e indiano.* (Madrid, 1897).

Gonzaga, Francesco de, O. F. M. *De Origine Seraphicae Religionis Franciscanae.* (Rome, 1587).

González Dávila, Gil. *Teatro Eclesiástico de la Primitiva Iglesia de las Indias Occidentales,* vol. 1. (Madrid, 1649).

González Obregón, Luis. *México viejo.* (Paris-Mexico, 1900).

——. *Los precursores de la independencia mexicana en el siglo XVI.* (Paris-Mexico, 1906).

——. "Don Francisco del Paso y Troncoso, sabio arqueólogo y lingüista mexicano." In *Boletín de la Biblioteca Nacional,* vol. 12, No. 6, October, 1918–March, 1919, pp. 167–179. (Mexico, 1919).

González Peña, Carlos. *Historia de la literatura mexicana.* (Mexico, 1928).

González de la Puente, Juan, O. S. A. *Primera Parte de la Choronica Augustiniana de Mechoacan* (Mexico, 1624). (In *Colección de documentos inéditos y raros para la historia eclesiástica mexicana publicados por el Ilmo. Sr. Obispo de Cuernavaca D. Francisco Plancarte y Navarrete,* vol. 1. (Cuernavaca, 1907).

Goyau, Georges. *Orientations catholiques.* 2d Ed. (Paris, 1925).
Granada, Luis de. *Breve tratado en que se declara de la manera que se podrá proponer la Doctrina . . . a los nuevos fieles.* In *Obras de Fr. Luis de Granada.* Ed. Justo Cuervo. (Madrid, 1908).
Granados y Gálvez, Joseph Joaquín. *Tardes americanas.* (Mexico, 1778).
Grijalva, Juan de, O. S. A. *Cronica de la Orden de N. P. S. Augustin en las provincias de la nueva españa. En quatro edades desde el año de 1533 hasta el de 1592.* (Mexico, 1624, 1924–1930).
Gruening, Ernest. "Pagan-Catholic Mexico." In *The Nation,* January 28, 1931. (New York, 1931).
Guadalupe, Andrés de, O. F. M. *Historia de la santa provincia de los Angeles.* (Madrid, 1662).

d'Harcourt, R. and M. *La musique des Incas et ses survivances.* (Paris, 1925).
Harrisse, Henry. *Bibliotheca Americana Vetustissima.* (New York, 1866).
Hernaez, Francisco Xavier, S. J. *Colección de Bulas, Breves y otros Documentos relativos a la Iglesia de América y Filipinas.* 2 vols. (Brussels, 1879).
Hernández, Pablo, S. J. *Organización social de las doctrinas guaraníes de la Compañía de Jesús.* 2 vols. (Barcelona, 1913).
Herrera, Antonio de. *Historia general de los hechos de los Castellanos en las islas i tierra firme del mar Oceano.* 4 vols. (Madrid, 1726–1730).
Herrera, Tomás de, O. S. A. *Alphabetum Augustinianum.* 2 vols. (Madrid, 1644).
———. *Historia del Convento de San Avgvstin de Salamanca.* (Madrid, 1652).
Hirshfield, Dorothy. "Los Pastores." In *Universidad de México,* December, 1930, pp. 156–161. (Mexico, 1930).
Höltker, Georg., S. V. D. "Die Familie bei den Azteken in Altmexiko." In *Anthropos,* pp. 465–526. (Vienna, 1930).
Holzapfel, H., O. F. M. *Manuale historiae ordinis fratrum minorum.* (Fribourg-en-Brisgau, 1909).
Hope, C. Noriega. See López R., Fortuno.
Humboldt, Alexandre de. *Essai politique sur le royaume de la Nouvelle Espagne,* 2d ed. 4 vols. (Paris, 1825–1827).
Huonder, Anton, S. J. *Der einheimische Klerus in den Heidenländern.* (Fribourg-en-Brisgau, 1909).
———. *Zur Geschichte des Missionstheaters.* (Aix-la-Chapelle, 1918).

Icaza, Francisco A. de. "Orígenes del teatro en México." In *Boletín de la Real Academia Española,* vol. 2, pp. 56–76. (Madrid, 1915).
Icazbalceta. (See García Icazbalceta).

Iglesias de México, 1525–1925. 6 vols., ed. Manuel Toussaint. (Mexico, 1927).

Iguíniz, Juan B. "La Crónica Miscelánea de la Provincia de Santiago de Jalisco." In *Boletín de la Biblioteca Nacional,* vol. 12, No. 2, August–October, 1917, pp. 57–65. (Mexico, 1917).

————. "Calendario Mexicano atribuido a Fray Bernardino de Sahagún." *Ibid.,* vol. 12, No. 5, April–September, 1920, pp. 189–221.

Información que el arzobispo de México D. Fray Alonso de Montúfar mandó practicar con motivo de un sermón que en la fiesta de la Natividad de Nuestra Señora, 8 de Setiembre de 1556, predicó en la capilla de S. José de los Naturales del Convento de S. Francisco de Mejico, su Provincial Fray Francisco de Bustamante acerca de la devoción y culto de Nuestra Señora de Guadalupe. (Madrid, 1888, 1891).

Instrucciones que los vireyes de Nueva España dejaron a sus sucesores. 2 vols. (Mexico, 1873).

Instructions aux missionaires de la S. Congregation de la Propagande. Trans. by a missionary of Scheut. (Louvain, n. d.).

Izquierdo Croselles, Joaquín. *Geografía de México.* (Granada, n. d.).

Jiménez de la Espada, M. "Tres cartas familiares de Fr. Juan de Zumárraga, primer obispo y arzobispo de México, y contestación a otra que le dirige Fr. Marcos de Niza." In *Boletín de la Real Academia de la Historia,* vol. 6, pp. 239–252. (Madrid, 1885).

Joyce, Thomas A. *Mexican Archaeology.* (London, 1914).

Kenny, Michael, S. J. *La crise mexicaine.* Trans. Larsimont, in *Etudes religieuses,* February 25, 1928. (Liége, 1928).

Lambert, De la Motte, et Pallu. *Instructions aux missionaires de la S. Congregation de la Propagande.* (Louvain, 1928?).

Larrínaga, Juan de, O. F. M. "Fray Jerónimo de Mendieta, historiador de Nueva España (1525–1604.)" In *Archivo Ibero-Americano,* vol. 1, 1914, pp. 290–300, 488–499; vol. 2, 1914, pp. 188–201, 387–404; vol. 4, 1915, pp. 341–373.

Las Casas, Bartolomé, O. P. *Apologética historia de las Indias.* Ed. Serrano y Sanz. (Madrid, 1927).

Latorre, Germán. *Relaciones geográficas de Indias.* (Seville, 1920).

Laveille, E., S. J. *L'Evangile au centre de l'Afrique. Le P. Van Henoxhoven.* (Louvain, 1926).

Lecanuet, Father. *L'Eglise de France sous la troisième République. La vie de l'Eglise sous Léon XIII.* (Paris, 1930).

Leclerc, Ch. *Bibliotheca Americana.* (Paris, 1867).

391

Lejeal, Léon. *Les Antiquités Mexicaines.* (*Bibliothèque de bibliographies critiques publiée par la Société des Etudes Historiques*). (Paris, 1902).

Lemmens, Leonhard, O. F. M. *Geschichte der Franziskanermissionen.* (Münster i. W., 1929).

Léon, Achille, O. F. M. *Saint François d'Assise et son oeuvre.* (Paris, 1928).

León, Nicolás. *Historia, geografía y estadística de la municipalidad de Quiroga en 1884.* (Morelia, 1887).

————. "Fray Maturino Gilberti y sus escritos inéditos." In *Anales del Museo Michoacano,* 1889, pp. 129–138.

————. "Privilegio del pueblo-hospital de Santa Fé de la Laguna, en la provincia de Mechoacán." *Ibid.,* pp. 179–182.

————. *El Ylmo. Señor D. Vasco de Quiroga, Primer Obispo de Michoacán.* (Mexico, 1903).

————. *Los popolacas.* (Conferencias del Museo Nacional, Sección de Etnología, No. 1, Mexico, 1905).

————. *Los Tarascos.* Tercera Parte. Etnografía post-cortesiana y actual. In *Anales del Museo Nacional,* 2ª Epoca, vol. 3, p. 298–479. (Mexico, 1906).

————. "Los precursores de la literatura médica mexicana en los siglos XVI, XVII, XVIII y primer tercio del siglo XIX (hasta 1833)." In *Gaceta médica de México,* January–April, 1915, vol. 10, Nos. 1–4, pp. 3–94. (Mexico, 1915).

————. "La Relación de Michuacán." In *Revista Mexicana de Estudios Históricos,* September–October, 1927, pp. 191–213. (Mexico, 1927).

————. *Fr. Diego Valadés.* (N. d., n. p.).

Leonard, Irving A. *Romances of Chivalry in the Spanish Indies with some registros of Shipments of books to the Spanish colonies.* In *University of California Publications in Modern Philology,* vol. 16. (Berkeley, 1933).

Leroy, Olivier. *La maison primitive.* (Paris, 1927).

Levillier, Roberto. *Organización de la Iglesia y Ordenes reliogiosas en el Virreinato del Perú en el siglo XVI.* 2 vols. (Madrid, 1919).

Lévy-Bruhl, Lucien. *Les fonctions mentales dans les sociétés inférieures.* 5th ed. (Paris, 1922).

————. *L'âme primitive.* (Paris, 1927).

————. *Le surnaturel et la nature dans la mentalité primitive.* (Paris, 1931).

Libros y libreros en el siglo XVI. Publicaciones del Archivo General de la Nación, No. 6. (Mexico, 1914).

Loayzaga, Manuel. *Historia de la milagrosissima imagen de Nra. Sra. de Ocotlán.* (Mexico, 1750).

Lombardo Toledano, Vicente. "Geografía de las lenguas de la Sierra de Puebla." In *Universidad de México,* November, 1931, pp. 14–96.

López, Atanasio, O. F. M. "Fr. Toribio de Motolinía." In *El Eco Franciscano,* vol. 32, 1915, pp. 713–717; vol. 33, 1916, pp. 14–18; vol. 34, 1917, pp. 65–68. (Santiago de Compostela, 1915–1917).

López, Atanasio, O. F. M. "Fr. Pedro Melgarejo." *Ibid.,* vol. 33, 1916, pp. 41–42.

———. "Los primeros franciscanos en Méjico." In AIA, vol. 13, pp. 21–28. (Madrid, 1920).

———. "La 'Relación de las ceremonias y ritos de la provincia de Mechuacan' ¿háse publicado íntegramente y se sabe quién fué su autor?" *Ibid.,* vol. 13, pp. 262–271.

———. "Los primeros franciscanos en Méjico, Fr. Martín de la Coruña." *Ibid.,* vol. 14, pp. 105–111.

———. "Obras del P. Fr. Antonio Daza." *Ibid.,* September–October, 1921, pp. 243–247; July–August, 1922, pp. 123–126.

———. "Misiones o doctrinas de Michoacán y Jalisco (Méjico) en el siglo XVI (1525–1585)." *Ibid.,* November–December, 1922, pp. 341–425.

———. "Misiones o doctrinas de Jalisco en el siglo XVI (Adiciones)." *Ibid.,* March–April, 1923, pp. 235–279.

———. "Cuestionario histórico: ¿Escribió Fr. Toribio Motolinía una obra íntitulada 'Guerra de los indios de la Nueva España o Historia de la conquísta de México'?" *Ibid.,* March–April, 1925, pp. 221–247.

———. "Descripción de los manuscritos franciscanos existentes en la Biblioteca Provincial de Toledo." *Ibid.,* 1926.

———. "Vida de Fr. Martín de Valencia, escrita por su compañero Fr. Francisco Jiménez." *Ibid.,* July–August, 1926, pp. 48–83.

———. "Los doce primeros apóstoles de Méjico." In *Semana de Misiología de Barcelona,* vol. 2, pp. 201–226. (Barcelona, 1930).

———. "Fray Toribio Motolinía, misionero e historiador de Méjico en el siglo XVI." In *Illuminaire,* January–February, 1931.

——— and Lucio M. Núñez, O. F. M. "Descriptio codicum franciscalium Bibliothecae Ecclesiae Primitalis Toletanae." In AIA, 1919, pp. 390–409.

López R., Fortino. "Estudios sobre la vida de los indios, Los otomíes." In *El sistema de Escuelas Rurales en México,* pp. 89–99. (Mexico, 1927).

López de Gómara, Francisco. *Conquista de Méjico.* BAE, vol. 22, pp. 295–455. (Madrid, 1853, 1931).

López de Velasco, Juan. *Geografía y Descripción Universal de las Indias.* Ed. Justo Zaragoza. (Madrid, 1894).

Lorenzana, Francisco Antonio. *Concilios provinciales primero, y segundo, celebrados en la muy noble y muy leal ciudad de México, presidiendo el Illmo. y Rmo. Señor D. Fr. Alonso de Montúfar, en los años de 1555, y 1565.* (Mexico, 1769).

Lorin, Henri. (See Capitan).

Lotar, Father, O. P. "Le déchet dans les conversions." In *Après la conversion,* pp. 14–27.

La lucha de los católicos Mejicanos. Anon. (Tarragona, 1927).

Lumholtz, Carl. *El México desconocido.* Trans. Balbino Dávalos. 2 vols. (New York, 1904).

Maarschalkerweerd, Pancratius, O. F. M. "Über die Akkomodation der Franziskanermissionäre an einheimische Sprachen und Gebräuche im 16. Jahrhundert." In *Festschrift Schmidt,* pp. 904–907. (Vienna, 1928).

McBride, George M. *The Land Systems of Mexico.* (New York, 1923).

MacGregor, Luis. (See Fernández del Castillo).

Mâle, Emile. *L'art religieux de la fin du moyen âge en France.* 2d Ed. (Paris, 1922).

Marcou, Philippe. "Le symbolisme du siège à dossier chez les Nahua." In JSA, 1924, pp. 93–98.

Marín Negueruela, Nicolás. *La verdad sobre Méjico.* 2d Ed. (Barcelona, n. d.; Santiago, Chile, 1928).

Martínez Añíbarro y Rives, Manuel. *Intento de un Diccionario biográfico y bibliográfico de autores de la provincia de Burgos.* (Madrid, 1890).

Martínez Vigil, Ramón, O. P. *La Orden de Predicadores, sus glorias, . . . seguidas del ensayo de una biblioteca de Dominicos españoles.* (Madrid, 1884).

Matritensis, Franciscus. *Bullarium Fratrum Ordinis Minorum Sancti Francisci Strictioris Observantiae Discalceatorum,* vol. 1. (Madrid, 1744).

Maza, Francisco de la. *Código de colonización y terrenos baldíos.* (Mexico, 1893).

Mazé, Father, P. B. "Les catéchistes agents de conversion dans le Vicariat du Nyassa." In *Les conversions,* pp. 171–184.

Mecham, J. Lloyd. *Francisco de Ibarra and Nueva Vizcaya.* (Durham, N.C., 1927).

Medina, Baltasar de, O. F. M. *Chronica de la S. Provincia de S. Diego de México de Religiosos Descalços de N. S. P. S. Francisco en la Nueva España.* (Mexico, 1682).

Medina, José Toribio. *Biblioteca Hispano-Americana.* (Santiago, Chile, 1912).

———. *La Imprenta en México (1539–1821),* vol. 1. (Santiago, Chile, 1912).

Mena, Ramón, and Rangel, Nicolás. *Churubusco-Huitzilopochco.* (Mexico, 1921).

Méndez, Juan Bautista, O. P. "Cronica de la Provincia de Santiago de Mexico del Orden de Predicadores" (unpublished manuscript).

Mendieta, Jerónimo de, O. F. M. *Historia Eclesiástica Indiana.* Ed. Joaquín García Icazbalceta. (Mexico, 1870).

Mendizábal, Miguel O. de. "La poesía indígena y las canciones populares." In *Boletín del Museo Nacional,* vol. 2, 4ª Epoca, 1923–1924, pp. 79–84. (Mexico, 1924).

————. *Ensayos sobre las civilizaciones aborígenes americanas.* (Mexico, 1924).

————. "El santuario de Chalma." In *Anales del Museo Nacional,* vol. 3, 4ª Epoca, 1925, pp. 93–103. (Mexico, 1925).

————. *El lienzo de Jucutácato, su verdadera significación.* (Mexico, 1926).

————. "La conquista y la independencia religiosa de los indígenas." In *Contemporáneos,* July, 1928, pp. 149–199. (Mexico, 1928).

————. *La evolución del Noroeste de México.* (Mexico, 1930).

Menéndez y Pelayo, Marcelino. *Antología de poetas hispano-americanos,* vol. 1. (Madrid, 1893).

————. *Antología de poetas líricos castellanos,* vol. 7. (Madrid, n. d.).

Mérimée, Henri. *L'art dramatique à Valencia.* (Toulouse, 1913).

"La méthode des villages chrétiens." In *Revue missionaire des Jésuites belges,* March, 1930, pp. 131–133. (Louvain, 1930).

Métraux, Alfred. *La religion des Tupinambas.* (Paris, 1928).

Mier, Fr. Servando Teresa de. *Memorias. Biblioteca Ayacucho,* vol. 17. (Madrid, n. d.).

Michel, André. *Historie de l'Art.* (Paris, 1905–1929).

Moles, Juan Bautista, O. F. M. *Memorial de la Provincia de San Gabriel de la Orden de los frayles Menores de la Observancia.* (Madrid, 1592).

Monasterio, Ignacio, O. S. A. "El P. Mtro. Basalenque, O. A. S." In *Archivo Agustiniano,* June, 1928, pp. 408–418. (Madrid, 1928).

Montalbán, Francisco-Javier, S. J. *El Patronato español y la conquista de Filipinas.* (Burgos, 1930).

Montes de Oca, José G. "Tlaxcala, la ciudad muerta." In *Memorias y Revista de la Sociedad Científica 'Antonio Alzate,'* vol. 47, pp. 161–205. Mexico, 1927).

————. "San Agustín Acolman." *Ibid.,* vol. 49, pp. 139–190.

————. "La Villa de Ocotlán." In *Boletín de la Sociedad Mexicana de Geografía y Estadística,* vol. 41, pp. 5–32. (Mexico, 1928).

Montúfar, Alonso de. *Información.* (Madrid, 1888, 1891).

Morcillo, Casimiro. "Apuntes de historia de la misiología en España." In *Semana de Misiología de Barcelona,* vol. 2, pp. 23–47. (Barcelona, 1930).

Morel-Fatio, Alfred. *Études sur l'Espagne,* 4th Series. (Paris, 1925).

Moreno, Manuel M. *La organización política y social de los Aztecas.* (Mexico, 1931).

Mota y Escobar, Alonso de la. *Descripcion Geographica de los Reynos de Galicia, Vizcaya, y León.* Ed. Ramírez Cabañas. (Mexico, 1930).

Mota Padilla, Matías de la. *Historia de la Conquista de la Provincia de la Nueva Galicia*. (Mexico, 1870).

Motezuma, Diego Luis de, S. J. *Corona mexicana*. Ed. Lucas de Torre. (Madrid, 1914).

Motolinía (Toribio de Benavente), O. F. M. *Historia de los Indios de la Nueva España*. Ed. Kingsborough, *Antiquities of Mexico,* vol. 9 (London, 1948); ed. Joaquín García Icazbalceta, *Colección de documentos para la historia de México,* vol. 1, (Mexico, 1858); ed. *Colección de documentos para la historia de México,* vol. 1, (Mexico, 1858); ed. *Colección de documentos inéditos para la historia de España,* vol. 53 (Madrid, 1869); ed. Daniel Sánchez García, O. F. M. (Barcelona, 1914).

———. *Memoriales*. Ed. Luis Garcia Pimeutel. (Paris, 1903).

Muñoz, Diego, O. F. M. "Descripción de la Provincia de los Apóstoles San Pedro y San Pablo en las Indias de la Nueva España." In AIA, Nov.–Dec., 1922, pp. 383–425.

Muñoz Camargo, Diego. *Historia de Tlaxcala*. Ed. A. Chavero. (Mexico, 1892).

Noguera, Eduardo. "Algunas características de la cerámica de México." In JSA, 1930, pp. 249–310.

Núñez, Lucio Ma., O. F. M. (See López, Atanasio).

Núñez y Domínguez, José de J. "El Alabado y Las Alabanzas." In *Mexican Folkways,* December–January, 1927.

Nuttall, Zelia. "L'évêque Zumárraga et les idoles principales du grand temple de México." In JSA, 1911, pp. 153–171.

———. "El libro perdido de las Pláticas o Coloquios de los Doce Primeros Misioneros de México por Fr. Bernardino de Sahagún." In *Revista Mexicana de Estudios Históricos,* vol. 1, App. pp. 101–154. (Mexico, 1927).

Obregón, Baltasar de. *Historia de los descubrimientos antiguos y modernos de la Nueva España*. Ed. Mariano Cuevas. (Mexico, 1924).

Ojea, Hernando de, O. P. *Libro Tercero de la Historia Religiosa de la Provincia de México de la Orden de Sto. Domingo*. Ed. Agreda y Sánchez. (Mexico, 1897).

Ordenanzas de Gremios de la Nueva España. Ed. Genaro Estrada. (Mexico, 1921).

Orozco y Jiménez, Francisco. *Colección de documentos históricos inéditos o muy raros, referentes al Arzobispado de Guadalajara,* vol. 1. (Guadalajara, 1922).

Ortega, Angel, O. F. M. "Las primeras maestras y sus colegios-escuelas de niñas en Méjico." In AIA, March–April, 1929, pp. 259–276; May–June, 1929, pp. 365–387.

Ortega, Angel, O. F. M. "Fr. Juan de Paredes y la fundación de los hospitales de San Juan de Ulúa-Veracruz." *Ibid.*, April–June, 1931, pp. 266–277.

Pamphile, Joseph, O. S. A. *Chronica Ordinis Fratrum Eremitarum Sancti Avgvstini.* (Rome, 1581).

Pareja, Francisco de, Merc. *Coronica de la provincia de la Visitacion de Nra. Sra. de la Merced, Redencion de Cautivos de la Nueva España.* (Mexico, 1882).

Parras, Pedro Joseph. *Gobierno de los Regulares de la América.* 2 vols. (Madrid, 1783).

Paso y Troncoso, Francisco del. *Sacrificio de Isaac. Auto en lengua mexicana (anónimo) escrito en el año 1678.* (Florence, 1899).

————. *Adoración de los Reyes. Auto en lengua mexicana (anónimo).* (Florence, 1900).

————. "Comédies en langue nauatl." In *Congrès international des Américanistes, XII° Session (Paris, 1900)*, pp. 309–316. (Paris, 1902).

————. *Comedia de los Reyes escrita en mexicano a principios del siglo XVII (por Agustín de la Fuente).* (Florence, 1902).

————. *Papeles de Nueva España.* Segunda Serie. Geografía y Estadística, vol. 3 (Madrid, 1905), vol. 4 (Madrid, 1905), vol. 5 (Madrid, 1905), vol. 6 (Madrid, 1906).

————. *Destrucción de Jerusalén. Auto en lengua mexicana (anónimo) escrito con letra de fines del siglo XVII.* (Florence, 1907).

Los Pastores. A Mexican Play of the Nativity. Translation, introduction and notes by M. R. Cole. *Memoirs of the American Folklore Society,* vol. 9. (Boston and New York, 1907).

Peñafiel, Antonio. *Cantares en idoma mexicano.* (Mexico, 1904).

Pereyra, Carlos. *L'oeuvre de l'Espagne en Amérique.* Trans. Baelen and Ricard. (Paris, 1925).

————. *Hernán Cortés.* (Madrid, 1931).

Pérez, Pedro Nolasco, Merc. *Religiosos de la Merced que pasaron a la América española.* 1st Pt. (Seville, 1923).

Pérez Arrilucea, Diego, O. S. A. "Trabajos apostólicos de los Primeros Misioneros Agustinos de Méjico." In *La Ciudad de Dios,* vol. 92, pp. 298–310, 42–428. (Escorial, n. d.).

————. "Los Agustinos en Méjico en el siglo XVI." *Ibid.,* vol. 94, pp. 335–343; vol. 95, pp. 5–16, 241–251; vol. 96, pp. 111–119; vol. 97, pp. 115–126; vol. 98, pp. 265–276; vol. 99, pp. 253–261.

Pérez Bustamante, C. *Don Antonio de Mendoza, primer virrey de la Nueva España.* (Santiago de Compostela, 1928).

Pérez Pastor, Cristóbal. *La imprenta en Medina del Campo.* (Madrid, 1895).

Pérez Verdía, Luis. *Historia particular del Estado de Jalisco,* vol. 1. (Guadalajara, 1910).

Pettazzoni, Raffaele. "La confessione dei peccati nelle antiche religioni americane." In *Studi e materiali di storia delle religioni,* vol. 2, pp. 163–229. (Rome, 1926).

———. *La confessione dei peccati. Parte Prima.* Ed. R. Monnot (Bologna, n. d.). French trans. (Paris, 1931).

Pimentel, Francisco. *Historia crítica de la poesía en México.* (Mexico, 1892).

Pinard de la Boullaye, Henri, S. J. *L'étude comparée des religions,* vol. 1, 3d ed. (Paris, 1929).

Pintura del Gobernador, Alcaldes y Regidores de México. Códice en geroglíficos mexicanos ye en lenguas castellana y azteca, existente en la Biblioteca del Excmo. Señor Duque de Osuna. (Madrid, 1878).

Ponce, Alonso, O. F. M. *Relación breve y verdadera de algunas cosas de las muchas que sucedieron al Padre Fray Alonso Ponce.* 2 vols. *Colección de Documentos Inéditos para la Historia de España,* vols. 57–58. (Madrid, 1873).

Portillo, Sebastián de, O. S. A. *Chronica Espiritual Augustiniana.* 4 vols. (Madrid, 1731–1732).

Póu y Martí, José Ma., O. F. M. "El libro perdido de las Pláticas o Coloquios de los doce primeros misioneros de México." In *Miscellanea Francesco Ehrle,* vol. 3, pp. 281–333. (Rome, 1924).

Probst, J. H. *Caractère et origine des idées du Bienheureux Raymond Lulle.* (Toulouse, 1912).

Proceso inquisitorial del cacique de Tetzcoco. In *Publicaciones del Archivo de la Nación,* vol. 1. (Mexico, 1910).

Procesos de indios idólatras y hechiceros. Ibid., vol. 3. (Mexico, 1912).

Puga, Vasco de. *Cedulario (Provisiones, Cédulas, Instrucciones de Su Magestad, Ordenanzas de Difuntos y Audiencia para la buena expedición de los negocios y administracion de justicia y govierno de esta Nueva España, y para el buen tratamiento y conseruacion de los indios desde el año de 1525 hasta este presente de 63).* (Mexico, 1563; 2 vols., Mexico, 1878–1879).

Quétif et Echard, O. P. *Scriptores Ordinis Praedicatorum,* vol. 2. (Paris, 1721).

Quintana, Jerónimo de, O. P. *Segunda Parte de la Historia del Insigne Convento de San Esteban de Salamanca.* Vol. 3 of Cuervo, *Historiadores.*

Rabasa, Emilio. *L'évolution historique du Mexique.* Trans. Carlos Docteur. (Paris, 1924).

Ramírez Cabañas, Joaquín. *Las relaciones entre México y el Vaticano.* 2d ed. (Mexico, 1928).

Rangel, Nicolás. (See Mena, Ramón).

Raynaud, G. "Le dieu aztec de la guerre." In *Revue de l'Histoire des Religions,* vol. 38, pp. 275–294; vol. 39, pp. 18–59. (Paris, 1898–1899).

———. "Les nombres sacrés et les signes cruciformes dans la Moyenne Amérique Précolombienne." *Ibid.,* vol. 44, pp. 235–261. (Paris, 1901).

Rea, Alonso de la, O. F. M. *Chronica de la Orden de N. Seraphico P. S. Francisco, Provincia de S. Pedro y S. Pablo de Mechoacan en la Nueva España.* (Mexico, 1643; 2d ed. *La Voz de México,* Mexico, 1882).

Rebolledo, Luis de, O. F. M. *Primera parte de la Chronica General de N. Seraphico P. S. Francisco, y de su Apostolica Orden.* (Seville, 1598).

Recopilación de las Leyes de los Reynos de las Indias. 2d ed. 4 vols. (Madrid, 1756).

Redfield, Robert. *Tepoztlán, a Mexican village. A study of Folk Life.* (Chicago, 1930).

Reichert, B. M., O. P. *Acta capitulorum generalium Ordinis Praedicatorum,* vol. 4. (Rome, 1901).

"Relación de la provincia de Meztitlán." In *Boletín del Museo Nacional,* 1923–1924, pp. 109–120. (Mexico, 1924).

Relación de las ceremonias y ritos, población y gobierno de los indios de la provincia de Mechuacan. Ed. Florencio Janer. In *Colección de documentos inéditos para la historia de España,* vol. 53, pp. 7–293. (Madrid, 1869).

Relación de los obispados de Tlaxcala, Michoacán, Oaxaca y otros lugares en el siglo XVI. Ed. Luis García Pimentel. (Paris, 1904).

Remesal, Antonio de, O. P. *Historia general de las Indias Occidentales, y particular de la Governacion de Chiapa y Guatemala.* (Madrid, 1620).

Réville, Albert. *Les religions du Mexique, de l'Amérique centrale et du Pérou.* (Paris, 1885).

Ribadeneyra, Antonio Joachín de. *Manual Compendio de el Regio Patronato Indiano.* (Madrid, 1755).

Ricard, Robert. "Note sur Fr. Pedro Melgarejo, évangélisateur du Mexique." In *Bulletin Hispanique,* July–September, 1923, pp. 253–256.

———. "Fr. Pedro Melgarejo." *Ibid.,* January–March, 1924, pp. 68–69.

———. "Documents pour l'historie des Franciscains au Mexique." In *Revue d'Histoire Franciscaine,* April, 1924, pp. 216–235.

———. "Notes sur les éditions et le manuscrit de la *Historia de los Indios de la Nueva España* de Fr. Toribio de Motolinía." *Ibid.,* October, 1924, pp. 493–500.

———. "Sur la politique des alliances dans la conquête du Mexique par Cortés." In JSA, 1926, pp. 245–260.

———. "Notes sur la biographie de Fr. Alonso de Montúfar, second archevêque de México (1551–1572)." In *Bulletin Hispanique,* July–September, 1925, pp. 242–246.

399

Ricard, Robert. "Une lettre de Fr. Juan de Gaona à Charles-Quint." In *Revue d'Historie Franciscaine,* January, 1926, pp. 119–121.

———. "Un document inédit sur les Augustins du Mexique en 1563." In JSA, 1926, pp. 21–49.

———. "Morisques et Indiens." *Ibid.,* 1926, pp. 350–357.

———. "Le collège indigène de Santiago Tlatelolco au Mexique." In *Les élites en pays de mission,* pp. 83–89.

———. "Une procuration en faveur de Las Casas." In JSA, 1927, pp. 390–392.

———. "Remarques sur l'*Arte* et le *Vocabulista* de Fr. Pedro de Alcalá." In *Memorial Henri Basset,* vol. 2, pp. 229–236. (Paris, 1928).

———. "Martyrs mexicains (1527 et 1529)." In *Bulletin Catholique International,* February 1, 1929, pp. 80–88 (Paris, 1929).

———. *Etudes et documents pour l'historie missionaire de l'Espagne et du Portugal.* (Louvain, 1931).

———. "Ecoles Normales Rurales au Mexique." In *Bulletin de l'Enseignement Public au Maroc,* April, 1931.

———. "Les apparitions de Notre-Dame de Guadalupe. A propos d'un ouvrage récent." In *Revue d'Historie des Missions,* June 1, 1931, pp. 247–262.

———. "Quelques publications récentes sur le Mexique." In *Revue de l'Amérique latine,* August, 1931, pp. 163–168. (Paris, 1931).

———. "L'incorporation de l'Indien par l'école au Mexique." In JSA, 1931, pp. 47–70, 441–457.

———. "La fresque des 'Douze Apôtres' du Mexique au couvent de Huejotzingo (Puebla)." *Ibid.,* 1931, pp. 252–253.

———. "Contribution a l'étude des fêtes de 'Moros y Cristianos' au Mexique." *Ibid.,* 1932, pp. 51–84.

———. "La période coloniale de l'historie du Mexique, d'après les publications récentes." In *Revue Historique,* May–June, 1932, pp. 604–614. (Paris, 1932).

———. "Les Jésuites au Brésil pendant la seconde moitié du XVIᵉ siècle (1549–1574): Méthodes missionaires et conditions d'apostolat." In *Revue d'histoire des missions,* 1937, pp. 321–366, 435–470.

———. JSA, 1937, pp. 220 ff.; 1938, pp. 375–376; *Bulletin Hispanique,* 1938, pp. 311–312.

———. "Fray Hernando de Ojea, apóstol de los judíos mejicanos." In *Abside,* August, 1937, pp. 21–28.

———. "Pour une étude du judaisme portugais au Mexique pendant la période coloniale." In *Revue d'histoire moderne,* 1939, pp. 516–524.

———. "La influencia de San Antonio de Florencia en el mundo hispánico." In *AIA.*

Ricard, Robert. "Les apparitions de Notre-Dame de Guadalupe." In *Revue d'histoire des missions,* 1931, pp. 247–262.

———. "Les origines de l'Eglise sud-américaine." In *Revue d'histoire des missions,* 1932, pp. 449–474.

Ríos Arce, Francisco de los, O. P. *Puebla de los Angeles y la Orden Dominicana.* 2 vols. (Puebla, 1910).

Ripalda, Jerónimo de, S. J. *Doctrina Christiana.* Ed. Juan M. Sánchez. (Madrid, 1909).

Ripoll, O. P. *Bullarium Ordinis FF. Praedicatorum,* vol. 4. (Rome, 1732); vol. 7. (Rome, 1739).

Riva Palacio, Vicente. *México a través de los siglos,* vol. 2. (Barcelona, n. d.).

———. *Establecimiento y propagación del cristianismo en Nueva España.* (Mexico, 1892).

Rivera, Agustín. *Entretenimientos de un enfermo. Notas de Agustín Rivera al artículo de un ex-estudiante sobre la enseñanza de los idiomas indios.* (Lagos, 1891).

Rivera, Ricardo. *La heterogeneidad étnica y espiritual de México.* 2d ed. (Mexico, 1931).

Rivet, Paul. "Le christianisme et les Indiens de l'Equator." In *Anthropologie,* 1906, pp. 81–101. (Paris, 1906).

———. "Langues américaines." In A. Meillet and M. Cohen, *Les langues du monde,* pp. 597–712. (Paris, 1924).

———. "L'extension du kičua dans le bassin du haut Napo." In JSA, 1928, p. 392.

Robelo, Cecilio A. "Dios. ¿Qué idea tenían de El los antiguos mexicanos?" In *Reseña de la Segunda Sesión del XVII Congreso Internacional de Americanistas (México, 1910),* pp. 251–286. (Mexico, 1912).

Roelens, V., P. B. "Les catéchuménats." In *Bulletin des Missions,* November–December, 1929, pp. 511–517.

———. "Les catéchistes dans les missions." *Ibid.,* June, 1930, pp. 96–104.

Rojas Garcidueñas, José J. *El teatro de Nueva España en el siglo XVI.* (Mexico, 1935).

———. *Autos y coloquios del siglo XVI.* (Mexico, 1939).

Román y Zamora, Jerónimo, O. S. A. *Chronica de la Orden de los Ermitaños de Santo Augustin.* (Salamanca, 1569).

———. *Repúblicas de Indias.* 2 vols. *Colección de libros o curiosos que tratan de América,* vols. 14–15. (Madrid, 1897).

Romero de Terreros, Manuel. *La Iglesia y Monasterio de S. Agustín Acolman.* (Mexico, 1921).

———. *Historia sintética del arte colonial de México.* (Mexico, 1922).

———. *Las artes industriales en la Nueva España.* (Mexico, 1923).

Romero de Terreros, Manuel. "Los acueductos de México." In *Anales del Museo Nacional,* vol. 3, 4ª Epoca, 1925, pp. 131–142. (Mexico, 1925).

Ros, Fidèle de, O. M. Cap. *Le Père François d'Osune.* (Paris, 1936–1937).

———. "Antonio de Guevara, auteur ascétique." In *Etudes franciscaines,* 1938, pp. 306–322, and pp. 609–634.

———. "La Premiere *Josephina* en espagnol." In *Bulletin de littérature eclésiastique,* 1939, pp. 3–24. (Toulouse).

Rosell, Lauro E. (See Fernández del Castillo).

Rousseau, François. *L'idée missionaire au XVIᵉ et XVIIᵉ siècles.* (Paris, 1930).

Roze, M. A., O. P. *Les dominicains en Amérique.* (Paris, 1878).

Ruiz Blanco, Matías, O. F. M. *Conversión en Piritú (Colombia) de Indios cumanagotos y palenques. Colección de libros raros o curiosos que tratan de América,* vol. 7. (Madrid, 1892).

Sacré-Coeur, Jean-Marie du, O. C. D. "Comment on assure la persévérance des convertis au diocèse de Quilon." In *Après la conversion,* pp. 28–29.

Sahagún, Bernardino de, O. F. M. *Psalmodia Christiana, y Sermonario de los Sanctos del Año, en lengua Mexicana.* (Mexico, 1583).

———. *Historia general de las cosas de Nueva España.* Ed. Carlos María de Bustamante. 3 vols. (Mexico, 1829–1830).

———. *Histoire générale des choses de la Nouvelle-Espagne.* Trans. Jourdanet et Siméon. (Paris, 1880).

———. *Evangelarium, Epistolarium et Lectionarium aztecum.* Ed. Biondelli. (Milan, 1858). (See also J. B. Iguíniz and Eduard Seler).

Salazar, Esteban de, Chr. *Veynte Discursos sobre el Credo.* (Granada, 1577).

Salazar, Pedro de, O. F. M. *Coronica y Historia de la Fvndacion y Progresso de la Provincia de Castilla, de la Orden del bienaventurado padre San Francisco.* (Madrid, 1612).

Salinas, Miguel. "Datos para la historia de Toluca. Fr. Andrés de Castro." In *Memorias de la Sociedad Científica 'Antonio Alzate.'* (Mexico, 1921).

———. *Datos para la historia de Toluca,* 1st Part. (Mexico, 1927).

San Agustín, Gaspar de, O. S. A. *Conquistas de las Islas Filipinas.* 1st Part. (Madrid, 1698).

San Antonio, Juan de, P. F. M. *Bibliotheca universa franciscana,* vols. 1–2. (Madrid, 1732).

San Juan de la Cruz, Gerardo, C. D. *Vida del Maestro Julián de Avila.* (Toledo, 1915?).

San Nicolás, Andrés de, O. S. A. *Historia General de los Religiosos Descalzos del Orden de los Ermitaños del Gran Padre y Doctor de la Iglesia San Avgustin . . . ,* vol. 1. (Madrid, 1664).

San Román, Antonio de, O. S. A. *Consuelo de Penitentes o Mesa Franca de spirituales manjares,* 2d ed. (Seville, 1585).

Santana, José E. *Nuño Beltrán de Guzmán y su obra en la Nueva España.* (Mexico, 1930).

Santiago Vela, Gregorio de, O. S. A. *Ensayo de una Biblioteca Ibero-Americana de la Orden de San Agustín,* vol. 1 (Madrid, 1913); vol. 2 (Madrid, 1916); vol. 3 (Madrid, 1917); vol. 6 (Madrid, 1922); vol. 8 (El Escorial, 1931).

————. "Historiadores de la Provincia agustiniana de México en los siglos XVI y XVII." In AHHA, April, 1918, pp. 241–255. (Madrid, 1918).

————. "La Provincia agustiniana de Michoacán y su historia." *Ibid.,* March–April, 1923, pp. 129–144; May–June, 1923, pp. 266–279.

Saravia, Atanasio G. *Los misioneros muertos en el Norte de Neuva España.* (Durango, 1920).

Sardo, Joaquín, O. S. A. *Relación histórica y moral de la portentosa imagen de N. Sr. Jesucristo Crucificado aparecida en una de las cuevas de S. Miguel de Chalma . . .* (Mexico, 1810).

Schmidlin, Joseph. "Die Christianisierung Mexikos." In *Zeitschrift für Missionswissenschaft,* vol. 14, pp. 145–160. (Berlin, 1924).

Schmieder, Oscar. *The Settlements of the Tzapotec and Mije Indians, State of Oaxaca.* (Berkeley, California, 1930).

Schuller, Rudolf. "An Unknown Matlatsinka Manuscript Vocabulary of 1555–1557." In *Indian Notes,* April, 1930, pp. 175–194.

Seler, Eduard. "Die alten Bewohner der Landschaft Michuacan." In *Gesammelte Abhandlungen zur amerikanischen Sprach- und Alterthumskunde,* vol. 3, pp. 33–156. (Berlin, 1906).

————. *Fray Bernardino de Sahagun. Einige Kapitel aus seinem Geschichtswerke wortgetreu aus dem Aztekischen übertragen.* 2 vols. (Stuttgart, 1926–1927).

Sentenach, Narciso. "Catecismos de la doctrina cristiana en jeroglíficos para la enseñanza de los indios americanos." In *Revista de Archivos,* 1900, pp. 599–609.

Serrano y Sanz Manuel. "Cartas de Frai Juan de Çumárraga de la Orden de San Francisco, primero obispo de México, escritas a Suero del Aguila." *Ibid.,* 1901, pp. 162 ff.; pp. 251 ff.; pp. 491 ff.; pp. 654 ff.

Sicardo, Father, O. A. S. (Additions to the chronicle of Grijalva). Manuscript in the National Library of Madrid, Manuscript Section, 4349. Studied in detail by Santiago Vela, *Ensayo,* vol. 3, and in AHHA, April, 1918, pp. 250–254. See also E&D, pp. 119–123.

Simonet, J. F. *Glosario de voces ibéricas y latinas usadas entre los mozárabes.* (Madrid, 1888).

Simpson, Lesley Byrd. *The Encomienda in New Spain.* (Berkeley, California, 1929).

Smedt, Father, Scheut. "Sur quelques moyens de conversion employés dans la mission de Chine." In *Les conversions,* pp. 114–128.

Solórzano y Pereyra, Juan de. *Política Indiana.* 2 vols. (Madrid, 1776).

Sorre, Max. *Mexique. Amérique Centrale.* In *Géographie Universelle, sous la direction de P. Vidal de La Blache et L. Gallois,* vol. 14. (Paris, 1928).

Spinden, Herbert J. *Ancient civilizations of Mexico.* 3d ed. revised. (New York, 1928).

Staub, Walther. "Le nord-est du Mexique et les Indiens de la Huaxtèque." In JSA, 1926, pp. 279–296.

Steck, Francis B., O. F. M. "The first college in America: Santa Cruz de Tlatelolco." In *Catholic Educational Review,* Oct., 1936, pp. 449–462; Dec., 1936, pp. 603–617.

Streit, Robert, O. F. M. *Bibliotheca missionum,* vol. 1 (Münster, i. W., 1916); vol. 2 (Aix-la-Chapelle, 1924).

Suárez de Peralta, Juan. *Tratado del descubrimiento de las Yndias y su conquista.* Ed. Justo Zaragoza in *Noticias históricas de la Nueva España.* (Madrid, 1878).

Suau, Pierre, S. J. *Histoire de saint François de Borgia.* (Paris, 1910).

Tello, Antonio, O. F. M. *Libro Segundo de la Crónica Miscelánea en que se trata de la Conquista Espiritual y Temporal de la Santa Provincia de Xalisco.* (Guadalajara, 1891).

Teresa de Avila, Santa. *Camino de Perfección.* (Burgos, 1922).

Thibaut, Eugène, S. J. *Lettres de S. François Xavier.* 4 vols. (Bruges, 1922).

Thoonen, Fr., Mill-Hill. "Conversion of Parents through the Children." In *Les conversions,* pp. 160–170.

Toor, Frances. "El drama de la Pasión en Tzintzuntzan." In *Mexican Folkways,* June–July, 1925, pp. 21–28; August–September, 1925, pp. 27–29. (Mexico, 1925).

———. "Semana Santa." *Ibid.,* February–March, 1927, pp. 53–61.

———. "Fiesta de la Santa Vera Cruz en Taxco." *Ibid.,* April–June, 1930, pp. 84–94.

Toro, Alfonso. "Importancia etnográfica y lingüística de las obras del padre Fray Bernardino de Sahagún." In *Annaes do XX Congreso Internacional de Americanistas,* vol. 2, 2d Part, pp. 263–277 (Rio de Janeiro, 1928); *Anales del Museo Nacional,* vol. 2, 4ª Epoca, 1924, pp. 1–18. (Mexico, 1924).

Torquemada, Fr. Juan de, O. F. M. *Monarquía Indiana.* 3 vols. (Madrid, 1723).

Toussaint, Manuel. *Oaxaca.* (Mexico, 1926).

———. "Un templo cristiano sobre el palacio de Xicotencatl." In *Revista*

Mexicana de Estudios Históricos, July–August, 1927, pp. 173–180. (Mexico, 1927).

Toussaint, Manuel. "Paseos coloniales: Coixtlahuaca." In *Universidad de México,* January, 1931, pp. 183–196.

————. *Iglesias.* See there.

Trinidad, Juan de la, O. F. M. *Chronica de la Provincia de San Gabriel.* (Seville, 1652).

Valadés, Diego, O. F. M. *Rhetorica Christiana ad cancionandi, et orandi usum accomodata utriusqve facultatis exemplis suo loco insertis: quae quidem, ex indorum maxime de prompta sunt historiis, unde praeter doctrinam, summa quoque delectatio comparabitur.* (Pérouse, 1579).

Valbuena, Angel. *Literatura dramática española. Colección Labor.* (Barcelona, 1930).

Váldez de la Torre, Carlos. *Evolución de las comunidades de indígenas.* (Lima, 1921).

Valle, Rafael Heliodoro. *El convento de Tepotzotlán.* (Mexico, 1924).

Vasconcelos, José. *Indología.* (Paris, 1927). (See also Gamio).

Vasconcelos, Simão de, S. J. *Chronica da Companhia de Jesu no Estado do Brasil.* 2d ed. 2 vols. (Lisbon, 1865).

Vázquez Santana, Higinio. *Historia de la Canción Mexicana.* (Mexico, 1931).

Velázquez, Primo Feliciano. *Colección de Documentos para la Historia de San Luis Potosí,* vol. 1. (San Luis Potosí, 1897).

————. *La aparición de Santa María de Guadalupe.* (Mexico, 1931).

Vélez, Pedro M., O. S. A. *Leyendo nuestras crónicas. Notas sobre nuestros cronistas y otros historiadores,* vol. 1. (Madrid, 1932).

Vera, Fortino Hipólito. *Itinerario parroquial del Arzobispado de México y reseña histórica, geográfica y estadística de las parroquias del mismo Arzobispado.* (Amecameca, 1880).

————. *Colección de documentos eclesiásticos de México, o sea antigua y moderna legislación de la Iglesia Mexicana.* 3 vols. (Amecameca, 1887).

————. *Apuntamientos históricos de los Concilios Provinciales Mexicanos y privilegios de América.* (Mexico, 1893).

————. *Santuario del Sacromonte. Lo que se ha escrito acerca de él desde el siglo XVI hasta el presente.* 4th ed. (Mexico, 1930).

Vera y Zuria, Pedro. *Cartas a mis seminaristas en la primera visita pastoral de la arquidiócesis.* 2d ed. (Barcelona, 1929).

Vetancurt, Agustín de, O. F. M. *Teatro Mexicano.* (Mexico, 1698). 2d ed., 4 vols. (Mexico, 1870–1871).

Veytia, Mariano, *Historia de Puebla.* 2 vols. (Mexico, 1931).

Vidal, Manuel, O. S. A. *Augustinos de Salamanca.* 2 vols. (Salamanca, 1751).

Vieira, Antonio, S. J. *Vieira brasileiro*. 2 vols. (Paris and Lisbon, 1921).

Villoslada, Ricardo G., S. J. *La Universidad de París duerme durante los estudios de Francisco de Vitoria, O. P.* (Rome, 1938).

Viñas y Mey, Carmelo. "El régimen de la tierra en la colonización española." In *Humanidades,* vol. 10, pp. 71 ff. (La Plata, 1925).

————. *España y los orígenes de la política social.* (Madrid, 1929).

————. *El estatuto del obrero indígena en la colonización española.* (Madrid, 1929).

Viñaza, Conde de la. *Bibliografía española de lenguas indígenas de América.* (Madrid, 1892).

Vocht, Henri de. "François et Pierre Titelmans." In *Biographie Nationale . . . de Belgique,* vol. 25, cols. 341–359.

Weber, Friedrich. *Beiträge zur Charakreristik der älteren Geschichtsschreiber über Spanisch-Amerika.* (Leipzig, 1911).

Wilberforce, B., O. P. *Vie de saint Louis Bertrand.* Trans. Folghera. (Paris, 1904).

Xavier, Saint François. (See Eugène Thibaut).

Zarco, Julián. *España y la comunión frecuente y diaria en los siglos XVI y XVII.* (El Escorial, 1912).

Zavala, Silvio A. *La Utopía de Tomás Moro en la Nueva España.* (Mexico, 1937).

Zepeda R., Tomás. *La instrucción pública en México durante el siglo XVI.* (Mexico, 1930).

Zorita, Alonso de. *Historia de la Nueva España.* Ed. M. Serrano y Sanz. (Madrid, 1909).

NATIVE-LANGUAGE WORKS

The following is a list of works in native languages, or relative to native languages, written by the religious between 1524 and 1572. This list, it goes without saying, does not claim to be complete, nor does the bibliography that follows each entry. For the latter the reader is referred to the very detailed inventory compiled by Robert Streit, O. M. I., *Bibliotheca Missionum,* vol. 2, pp. 287 ff. I have listed only those works that concern the evangelization of the country. Since many of them have been lost and I know them only at second hand, most of their titles are conjectural. A question mark after an entry indicates that either the existence of a work or its attribution is not certain.

I. FRANCISCAN WORKS.

[Since most Franciscan writers are mentioned by Jerónimo de Mendieta, O. F. M. (HEI, Books 4 and 5), or by Juan de San Antonio, O. F. M. (*Bibliotheca universa franciscana,* vols. 1 and 2), or by both, I have omitted individual references to them. This course seemed preferable to repeating the same citations for each entry.—*Trans.*]

1. Fray Alonso de Escalona. *Sermones en lengua mexicana* (Viñza, No. 737; Streit, p. 203).
2. ———. *Comentario sobre los diez preceptos del Decálogo en lengua mexicana* (Viñaza, No. 738; Streit, p. 203).
3. Fray Alonso de Herrera. *Sermonario dominical* [in Nahuatl] (Streit, p. 304).
4. ———. *De sanctis* [in Nahuatl].
5. ———. *Arte de la lengua mexicana y castellana* (Mexico, Pedro Ocharte, 1571) (Viñaza, No. 48; J. T. Medina, *Imprenta,* vol. 1, No. 64; Cuevas, *Historia,* vol. 2, p. 403). Reprinted in 1575 (Icazbalceta, *Bibliografía,* No. 69).
6. Fray Alonso de Molina. *Doctrina cristiana breve* [in Castilian and Nahuatl] (Mexico, 1546, printed by order of Zumárraga) (Viñaza, No. 5; Medina, vol. 1, No. 11; Icazbalceta, *Zumárraga,* pp. 266–268; Cuevas, *Historia,* vol. 2, p. 406). This *doctrina* has been reprinted many times (Streit, pp. 314–315).
7. ———. *Vocabulario en la lengua castellana y mexicana* (Mexico, 1555) (Viñaza, No. 22; Medina, vol. 1, No. 24; Cuevas, *Historia,* vol. 2, p. 401). A corrected and enlarged edition was published in Mexico in 1571 (Viñaza, No. 49; Medina, vol. 1, No. 65; Cuevas, *Historia,* vol. 1, p. 39). The 1571 edition was reproduced in facsimile by Platzmann, Leipzig, 1880 (Lejeal, No. 171).
8. ———. *Confessionario breve, en lengua mexicana y castellana* (Mexico, Espinosa, 1565) (Viñaza, No. 42; Medina, vol. 1, No. 48; *Descripción del Arzobispado,* p. 169; Cuevas, *Historia,* vol. 2, p. 414). Reprinted in 1577 (Icazbalceta, *Bibliografía,* No. 75).
9. ———. *Confessionario mayor, en lengua mexicana y castellana* (Mexico, Espinosa, 1565) (Viñaza, No. 41; Medina, vol. 1, No. 49).
10. ———. *Oficio parvo de la Virgen María* [in Nahutal] (Viñaza, No. 762). "Mendieta says that [Molina] translated the Hours of Our Lady, but they were seized because their translation into the popular tongue was forbidden." (San Antonio, vol. 1, p. 48).
11. ——— (?). *Aparejo para recibir la Sagrada Comunión y Oraciones y*

Devociones varias para instrucción de los indios [in Nahutal] (Viñaza, No. 764).
(Viñaza, No. 763).

12. Fray Alonso de Molina (?). *Los Evangelios traducidos al mexicano*

13. —— (?). *Vida de San Francisco de Asís* [in Nahuatl] (Viñaza, No. 761; Motolinía, vol. 2, chap. 8, p. 132). If the life of St. Francis mentioned by Motolinía was written by Molina, as seems probable, it appeared before 1541. For Molina see Medina, vol. 1, pp. 380–384; Streit, pp. 314–318.

14. Fray Alonso Rangel. *Arte de la lengua mexicana* (Viñaza, No. 786; Streit, p. 319).

15. ——. *Sermones del año en lengua mexicana* (Viñaza, No. 785; Streit, p. 319).

16. ——. *Arte i Doctrina Christiana en lengua otomi* (Viñaza, No. 784; Medina, vol. 1, pp. 390–391; Streit, p. 319; *Descripción del Arzobispado,* p. 211). These three works of Fray Alonso Rangel appeared before 1548, the year of his death.

17. Fray Andrés de Castro. *Arte y diccionario de la lengua matlalzinca* [or Piranda] (Viñaza, No. 732; Streit, p. 296; Salinas, pp. 207–208).

18. ——. *Doctrina cristiana* [in Piranda] (Salinas, pp. 207–208; Streit, p. 296; Viñaza, No. 733).

19. ——. *Sermones en lengua matlalzinca* (Salinas, pp. 207–208; Streit, p. 296; Viñaza, Nos. 3, 733). This work cannot be dated 1542, as Viñaza has it, for that was the year in which Fray Andrés de Castro went to Mexico. For Fray Andrés de Castro see Añíbarro y Rives, *Intento,* pp. 131–132; see also above p. 47.

20. Fray Andrés de Olmos. *Arte para aprender la lengua mexicana* (1547) (Madrid, Biblioteca Nacional, MS 10081, ff. 20r⁰–102v⁰). (San Román, *Consuelo,* f. 449⁰; Viñaza, Nos. 6–9). This grammar was published in Paris in 1875 by Rémi Siméon, and in Mexico in 1889 (Lejeal, No. 157).

21. ——. *Vocabulario de la lengua mexicana* (1547) (Viñaza, No. 10).

22. ——. *Siete sermones en mexicano* (1552?) (Viñaza, No. 771).

23. ——. *Tratado de los Santos Sacramentos en mexicano* (Viñaza, No. 768).

24. ——. *Tratado de los pecados capitales en lengua mexicana* (Viñaza, No. 767).

25. ——. *Tratado de los Sacrilegios en lengua mexicana* (Viñaza, No. 769).

26. ——. *Libellus de Extremo Judicio, lingua indica conscriptus* [in Nahuatl]. This was most likely the *auto sacramental* played before Antonio de Mendoza and Zumárraga, hence between 1535 and 1548. (Pimentel, *Poesía en México,* p. 126; Menéndez y Pelayo, *Antología de Poetas Hispano-Americanos,* vol. 1, p. xlix).

27. Fray Andrés de Olmos. *Arte y vocabulario de la lengua totonaca* (Viñaza, No. 772). Probably two separate works.

28. ———. *Arte, Vocabulario, Catecismo, Confesionario i Sermones Huastecos* (Viñaza, No. 773). Almost certainly several different works.

29. ——— (?). *Evangelios en mexicano* (Biblioteca del Capítulo de Toledo, 11, Cod. 35-22) Atanasio López and Lucio M. Núñez describe this manuscript and tentatively attribute it to Fray Andrés de Olmos (AIA, July–Dec., 1919, pp. 402–403). For Fray Andrés de Olmos see Viñaza, pp. 61–62; Añíbarro y Rives, *Intento,* pp. 371–374; Streit, pp. 171–173.

30. Fray Arnaldo de Nasaccio. *Sermones* [in Nahuatl] Viñaza, p. 61; Streit, p. 293).

31. ———. *Evangelios y Epístolas de las misas de todo el año, traducidos a la lengua mexicana* (Viñaza, Nos. 696, 723; Streit, p. 293). For Basaccio see Ponce, *Relación,* vol. 1, pp. 210–211, in which he is mistakenly called Hernando.

32. Fray Bernardino de Sahagún. *Arte de la lengua mexicana* (Viñaza, No. 779) According to Icazbalceta (*Bibliografía,* p. 268), this was published in 1569 and revised in 1585. A *vocabulario* is included in its appendix.

33. ———. *Evangelarium . . . Aztecum* (1558?) (Viñaza, No. 798). Published by Biondelli in Milan, 1858 (Lejeal, No. 168).

34. ———. *Tratado de las Virtudes teologales en lengua mexicana* (Viñaza, No. 801; Icazbalceta. *Bibliografía,* p. 267).

35. ———. *Vida de San Bernardino de Sena en mexicano* (Viñaza, No. 802). Before 1551, according to Icazbalceta (*Bibliografía,* p. 266).

36. ——— (?). *Sermones en mexicano* (1540–1563) (Viñaza, No. 2; Icazbalceta, *Bibliografía,* pp. 263–264). For Sahagún see Icazbalceta, *Bibliografía,* pp. 262–308; Póu y Marti, *Miscellanea Fr. Ehrle,* vol. 3, pp. 284–294 (Rome, 1924); Streit, pp. 216–221.

37. Fray Diego de Béjar. *Doctrina en lengua otomí* (*Descripción del Arzobispado,* p. 259).

38. Fray Francisco Gómez. *Varios opúsculos sobre la inteligencia de la lengua mexicana* (Viñaza, No. 914). It is not certain that these pamphlets appeared before 1572.

39. Fray Francisco Jiménez. *Arte y vocabulario de la lengua mexicana* (Viñaza, No. 837; Granados y Gálvez, *Tardes americanas,* p. 328).

40. Fray Francisco Toral. *Arte, vocabulario, doctrina cristiana y sermones en lengua totonaca* (Viñaza, No. 816; Streit, p. 175). These are almost certainly separate works.

41. Fray García de Cisneros. *Sermones* [in Nahuatl] (Viñaza, No. 734; Streit, p. 297). Published before 1537.

42. Fray Jerónimo Bautista. *Sermones en matlalzinca* (1562) (Viñaza, No. 36; Streit, p. 293).

43. Fray Juan de Ayora. *Arte y diccionario de la lengua mexicana* (Viñaza, No. 720; Streit, p. 292).

44. ————. *Tratado del Santísimo Sacramento en lengua mexicana* (Viñaza, No. 719; Medina, vol. 1, No. 176; Streit, p. 292). Before 1577, when Father Ayora left for the Philippines.

45. ————. *Arte y diccionario de la lengua tarasca* (Viñaza, No. 721; Streit, p. 292). According to Rea, Ayora wrote nothing in Tarascan.

46. Fray Juan Focher. *Arte de la lengua mexicana* (Viñaza, No. 742). For Focher see Icazbalceta, *Biografías,* vol. 2, p. 280.

47. Fray Jaun de Gaona. *Sermones dominicales en lengua mexicana* (Viñaza, No. 746). For Gaona see also Viñaza, No. 702.

48. ————. *Tratado de la Pasión de Nuestro Señor Jesucristo en lengua mexicana* (Viñaza, No. 748; Granados y Gálvez, *Tardes americanas,* p. 400; Viñaza, No. 698).

49. ————. *Homilías varias de San Juan Chrisóstomo traducidas en mexicano* (Viñaza, No. 747).

50. ————. *Colloquios de la paz y tranquilidad cristiana en lengua mexicana* (Viñaza, No. 745). Reprinted in 1582 (Icazbalceta, *Bibliografía,* No. 88; Viñaza, No. 73). Translation into Otomí (anon.) published in Mexico in 1582 (Viñaza, No. 749; Streit, p. 329). For Fray Juan de Gaona see Añíbarro y Rives, *Intento,* pp. 257–259; Streit, pp. 154–155.

51. Fray Juan de Ribas. *Doctrina cristiana en lengua mexicana* (Viñaza, No. 788; Medina, vol. 1, pp. 391–393).

52. ————. *Sermones* [in Nahuatl] (Viñaza, No. 789).

53. ————. *Diálogo de las costumbres del buen cristiano en lengua mexicana* (Viñaza, No. 790).

54. ————(?). *Vies des Pères de l'Eglise* [in Nahuatl], (San Antonio, vol. 2, p. 209).

55. ————(?). *Vies des premiers apôtres du Mexique* [in Nahuatl] (San Antonio, vol. 2, p. 209).

56. Fray Juan de Romanones. *Sermones* [in Nahuatl] (Viñaza, No. 1174).

57. ————. *Fragmentos de la sagrada Escritura* [in Nahuatl?] (HEI, Book 4, chap. 44, p. 552; Book V', chap. 51, p. 696).

58. Fray Juan de San Francisco. *Sermones morales y panegíricos en lengua mexicana* (Viñaza, No. 806).

59. ————. *Conferencias espirituales con ejemplos y doctrinas de Santos en lengua mexicana* (Viñaza, No. 807). For Fray Juan de San Francisco see Streit, p. 155.

60. Fray Juan Bautista de Lagunas. *Doctrina cristiana en lengua tarasca* (Viñaza, No. 755). For the author and his works see Viñaza, Nos. 55 and 682.

61. Fray Luis de Fuensalida. *Sermones* [in Nahuatl] (Viñaza, No. 743).

62. Fray Luis de Fuensalida. *Diálogos o Coloquios en mexicano entre la Virgen María y el Arcángel San Gabriel* (Viñaza, No. 744; Pimentel, *Poesía en México*, p. 125; Menéndez y Pelayo, *Antología*, vol. 1, p. xlix). For Fray Luis de Fuensalida, see Streit, p. 74.

63. Fray Luis Rodríguez. *Proverbios de Salomón* [trans. and commentary in Nahuatl] (*Libros y libreros*, p. 81; Viñaza, No. 793; Streit, p. 321.). Before 1572.

64. Fray Maturino Gilberti. *Arte de la lengua de Michoacán* (1558) (Viñaza, No. 24; Medina, vol. 1, No. 34). See Muñoz, AIA, Nov.–Dec., 1922, pp. 401–402; Rea, Book 1, chap. 36; San Antonio, vol. 2, p. 356; Cuevas, *Historia*, vol. 2, p. 402. Reprinted in Mexico in 1898 by Nicolás León (Lejeal, No. 154).

65. ———. *Vocabulario en lengua de Michoacán* (1559) (Viñaza, No. 26; Medina, vol. 1, No. 37).

66. ———. *Diccionario tarasco-español* (Nicolás León, *Anales del Museo Michoacano*, vol. 2, 1889, p. 133).

67. ———. *Diálogo de Doctrina Cristiana en lengua de Michoacán* (Mexico, 1559) (Viñaza, No. 27; Medina, vol. 1, No. 36).[3]

68. ———. *Tesoro espiritual en lengua de Michoacán* (1558) (Viñaza, No. 25; Medina, vol. 1, No. 35).

69. ———. *Evangelios en tarasco* (1560) (MS) (Viñaza, No. 30; N. León, *Anales del Museo Michoacano*, vol. 2, 1889, pp. 137–138; Viñaza, No. 750).

70. ———. *Cartilla para los niños en lengua tarasca* (Mexico, 1559) (Viñaza, No. 28; Medina, vol. 1, No. 39).

71. ———(?). *Sermones en tarasco* (N. León, *Anales*, p. 134).

72. ———(?). *Textos de la Sagrada Escritura, Evangelios y sermones para los domingos y fiestas de los Santos* [in Tarascan] (N. León, *Anales*, pp. 134–135).

73. ———(?). *Pláticas sobre los Evangelios del año* [in Tarascan] (N. León, *Anales*, pp. 135–136, 138). For Gilberti see N. León, *Anales*, pp. 129–138; *Libros y libreros*, pp. 545 ff.; Streit, pp. 300–303.

74. Fray Pedro de Gante. *Doctrina cristiana* [in Nahuatl] (Mexico, Juan Pablos, 1553) (Viñaza, No. 18; Medina, vol. 1, No. 20). See HEI, Book 4, chap. 44, p. 550; Barbado de la Torre, vol. 1, pp. 57, 75; Sentenach, *Revista de Archivos*, 1900, pp. 599–609; Cuevas, *Historia*, vol. 2, p. 407.

75. ———(?). *Doctrina christiana en lengua mexicana* (1547) (Viñaza, No. 11; Medina, vol. 1, No. 198). Attributed to Pedro de Gante by Icazbalceta, *Bibliografía*, No. 14.

76. ———(?). *Cathécisme en hiéroglyphes* (Sentenach, *Revista de Archivos*, 1900, pp. 599–600). For Pedro de Gante see Streit, p. 62.

77. Fray Pedro de Palacios. *Arte de la lengua otomí* (HEI, Book 4, chap. 44, p. 552; Streit, p. 319).
78. ———. *Doctrina cristiana* [in Otomí](HEI; Streit, p. 319).
79. Fray Toribio Motolinía. *Doctrina cristiana* [in Nahuatl] (Viñaza, No. 765). See also Gonzaga, p. 1236; Moles, f. 69v⁰; HEI; Daza, Book 2, chap. 21, p. 80*b;* Ramírez, in Icazbalceta, *Colección de documentos para la historia de México,* vol. 1, pp. cxxv–cxxvi; Icazbalceta, *Bibliografía,* p. xiv; Medina, vol. 1, pp. xlvii, 384–386.
80. ———. *Tratados espirituales en lengua mexicana* (?) (Viñaza, No. 766). This is probably a series of separate works.

II. DOMINICAN WORKS.

81. *Declaracion, y exposicion de la Doctrina Christiana en Lengua Española e Mexicana, echa por los religiosos de la orden de Sancto Domingo. Año de 1548* (National Library of Madrid, R-4035). Published twice in 1550 (Icazbalceta, *Zumárraga,* pp. 296–297; *Bibliografía,* Nos. 15, 18; Viñaza, Nos. 13, 15, 16; Medina, vol. 1, Nos. 13, 17, 18; Streit, p. 68. [This *doctrina* was originally included in the Appendix to this work, but, since it has lately appeared in *Ediciones Cutlura Hispánica,* Madrid, 1944, it has been decided to omit it.—Author to *Trans.*]
82. Fray Benito Fernández. *Doctrina cristiana en lengua misteca* (Mexico, 1550) (Viñaza, No. 14; Medina, vol. 1, No. 19). See also Dávila Padilla, Book 2, chap. 37, p. 600*a,* and chap. 93, p. 814*a;* Fernández, *San Esteban,* Book 1, chap. 27, in Cuervo, *Historiadores,* vol. 1, p. 80. Reprinted in 1564 (?) (Viñaza, No. 39), in 1567 (Icazbalceta, *Bibliografía,* No. 52; Martínez Vigil, p. 282; Viñaza, No. 45; Medina, vol. 1, No. 53; Streit, p. 299); in 1568 (Icazbalceta, *Bibliografía,* No. 53; Viñaza, No. 46; Medina, vol. 1, No. 57; Streit, p. 299).
83. ———. *Los Evangelios y Epístolas de las misas, traducidos en lengua misteca* (Viñaza, No. 741; Streit, p. 299).
84. Fray Bernardino de Alburquerque. *Catecismo o Tratado de la Doctrina Christiana en Lengua Zapoteca* (Viñaza, No. 705; Streit, p. 288). See also Dávila Padilla, Book 1, chap. 94, p. 366*b;* Fernández, *San Esteban,* Book 1, chap 45, in Cuervo, *Historiadores,* vol. 1, p. 128).
85. Fray Domingo de la Anunciación. *Doctrina cristiana* [in Nahuatl and Castilian] (Mexico, Pedro Ocharte, 1565) (Viñaza, No. 40; Medina, vol. 1, No. 47). See also *Descripción del Arzobispado,* p. 211; Dávila Padilla, Book 2, chap. 76, p. 252*b;* Franco, Book 1, chap. 3, p. 16; Quétif, vol. 2, p. 302a; Cuevas, *Historia,* vol. 2, pp. 408–409. The edition of 1545 (Viñaza, No. 4; Martínez Vigil, pp. 236, 276) seems to be imaginary.
86. ———. *Sermones* [in Nahuatl] (1545) (Quétif, vol. 2, p. 302a; Martínez

Vigil, p. 275). See also Dávila Padilla, Book 2, chap. 76, p. 752*b;* Franco, Book 1, chap. 3, p. 16. For Fray Domingo de la Anunciación see Streit, pp. 163–164.

87. Fray Domingo de Santa María. *Arte de la lengua mixteca* (Viñaza, No. 808). See also Dávila Padilla, Book 1, chap. 51, p. 209*b;* Fernández, *Concertatio,* p. 292*b;* Martínez Vigil, p. 374.

88. ———. *Doctrina cristiana* [in Mixtec] (Viñaza, No. 809). See also Dávila Padilla, Book 1, chap. 51, p. 209; Book 2, chap. 93, p. 814*b;* Fernández, *Concertatio,* p. 292*b;* Martínez Vigil, p. 374.

89. ———. *Epístolas y Evangelios en lengua mixteca* (Viñaza, No. 809). See also Dávila Padilla, Book 2, chap. 93, p. 814*b;* Fernández, *Concertatio,* p. 293*a;* Martínez Vigil, p. 374. For Fray Domingo de Santa María see Medina, vol. 1, pp. 395–396; Streit, p. 145.

90. Fray Francisco de Cepeda. *Arte de la lengua zoque* (Viñaza, No. 33; Martínez Vigil, p. 262).

91. Fray Gregorio Beteta. *Doctrina cristiana* [in Zapotec] (Viñaza, No. 726; Streit, p. 111).

92. Fray Juan Ramírez. *Santa Doctrina* (or *Suma de*) [Latin-Castilian-Nahuatl] (1537?) (Viñaza, No. 783). See also González Dávila, *Teatro,* f. 7; Icazbalceta, *Bibliografía,* pp. xi–xiv; Martínez Vigil, p. 356; Medina, vol. 1, pp. xvi–xx; Cuevas, *Historia,* vol. 2, p. 405. Doubtless never printed.

93. Fray Pedro de Córdoba. *Doctrina cristiana* [in Nahuatl] (Mexico, 1544). (Icazbalceta, *Bibliografía,* p. xvii and No. 8; Medina, vol. 1, No. 5). See also San Antonio, vol. 2, p. 235; Martínez Vigil, p. 265; Cuevas, *Historia,* vol. 1, p. 221; Streit, pp. 51–52.

94. Fray Pedro de Feria. *Vocabulario de la lengua zapoteca* (Viñaza, No. 739). See also Cuevas, *Historia,* vol. 1, p. 47.

95. ———. *Doctrina christiana en lengua castellana y çapoteca* (Mexico, Pedro Ocharte, 1567) (Viñaza, No. 44, pp. 21–22; Medina, vol. 1, No. 52). See also Dávila Padilla, Book 2, chap. 35, p. 594*a;* Martínez Vigil, p. 281.

96. ———. *Confesionario en lengua zapoteca* (Viñaza, No. 740). See also Dávila Padilla, Book 2, chap. 93, p. 814*a;* Cuevas, *Historia,* vol. 1, p. 49. For Fray Pedro de Feria see Streit, pp. 227–228.

III. AUGUSTINIAN WORKS.

97. Fray Agustín de Coruña. *Doctrina cristiana* [in Nahuatl] (Santiago Vela, *Ensayo,* vol. 2, p. 157, No. 2).

98. ———. *Doctrina fácil para enseñar a los indios* (c. 1560 [doubtless in Nahuatl] (Santiago Vela, *Ensayo,* vol. 2, p. 157, No. 2).

99. ———. *Varios cantares piadosos para uso de los indios de Chilapa* (Santiago Vela, *Ensayo,* vol. 2, p. 157, No. 1). See also Pimentel, *Poesía en*

México, p. 126. For Fray Agustín de Coruña see Añíbarro y Rives, *Intento*, pp. 137–138; Streit, p. 181.

100. Fray Juan de la Cruz. *Arte de la lengua huaxteca* (Viñaza, p. 27; Santiago Vela, *Ensayo*, vol. 2, pp. 178–179).

101. ———. *Doctrina christiana en la lengua Guasteca con la lengua castellana* (Mexico, Pedro Ocharte, 1571) (Santiago Vela, *Ensayo*, vol. 2, pp. 176–178). See also Viñaza, No. 50; Medina, vol. 1, No. 63; Cuevas, *Historia*, vol. 2, p. 409; Streit, p. 311.

102. Fray Juan de Guevara. *Doctrina cristiana* [in Huaxtec] (1548) (Viñaza, Nos. 12, 753; Medina, vol. 1, No. 14; Streit, p. 304). See also Icazbalceta, *Bibliografía*, No. 17; Santiago Vela, *Ensayo*, vol. 3, p. 400; Cuevas, *Historia*, vol. 2, pp. 407, 409.

103. Fray Martín de Rada. *Arte de la lengua otomí* (Santiago Vela, *Ensayo*, vol. 6, p. 448, No. 2).

104. ———. *Sermones morales* [in Otomí] (Santiago Vela, *Ensayo*, vol. 6, p. 448).

ANONYMOUS WORKS.

105. *Arte y vocabulario de la lengua mexicana* (Viñaza, No. 695).

106. *Breve y más compendiosa doctrina en lengua mexicana y castellana* (Mexico, Cromberger, 1539) (Viñaza, No. 1; Cuevas, *Historia*, vol. 2, pp. 405–406). Printed by order of Zumárraga.

107. *Sermones* [in Nahuat] (followed by a *Confesionario* in Nahuatl and an incomplete explanation of the *Miserere*) (Viñaza, No. 701).

108. *Doctrina cristiana en lengua de Michoacán* (1537 or 1538) (Icazbalceta, *Anales del Museo Michoacano*, vol. 1, 1888, pp. 62–64).

109. *Sermones en lengua matlalzinca* (Viñaza, No. 700).

Index of Proper and Place Names

416

420